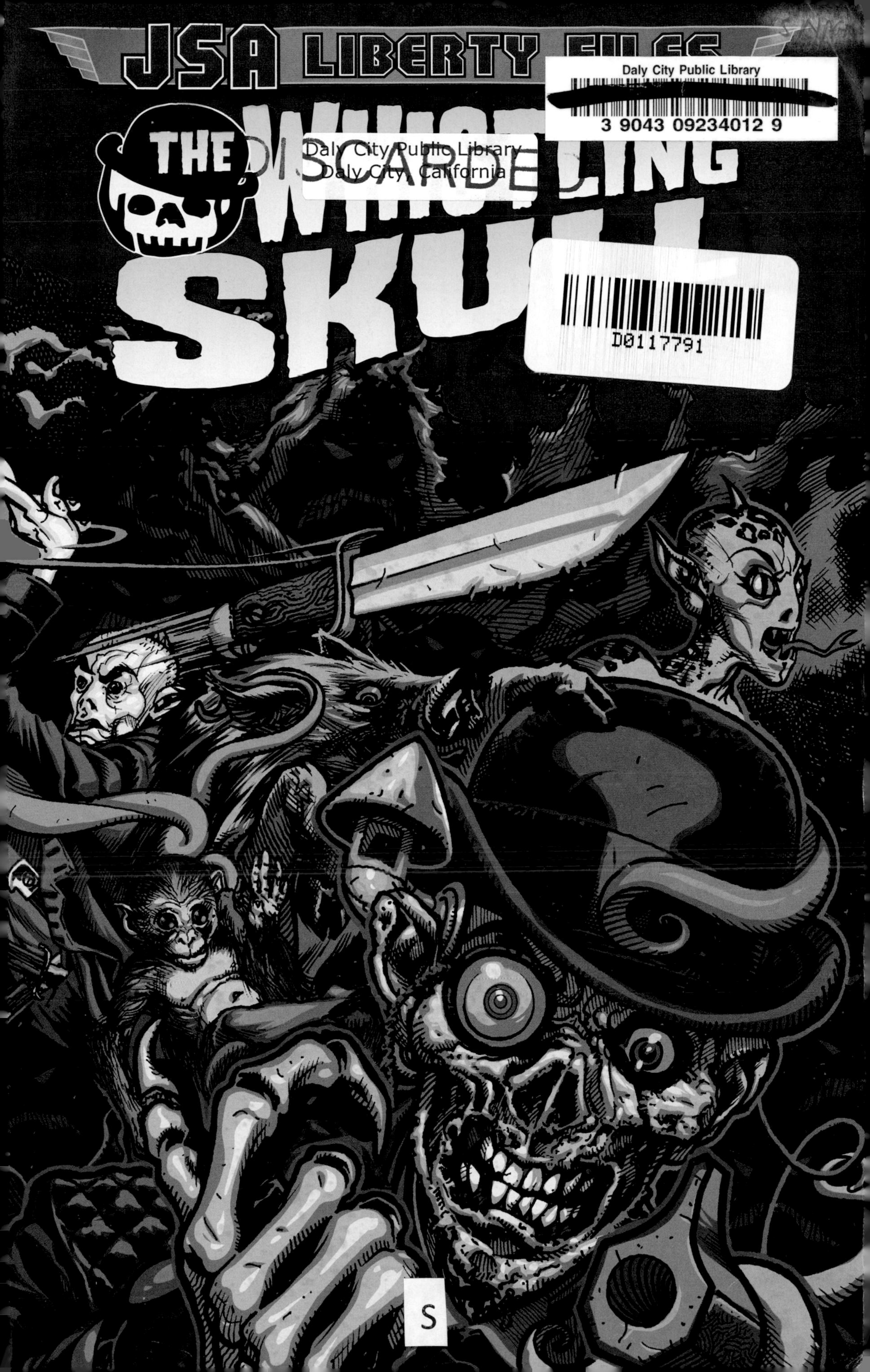
JSA LIBERTY
THE
SK

JSA LIBERTY FILES

THE WHISTLING SKULL

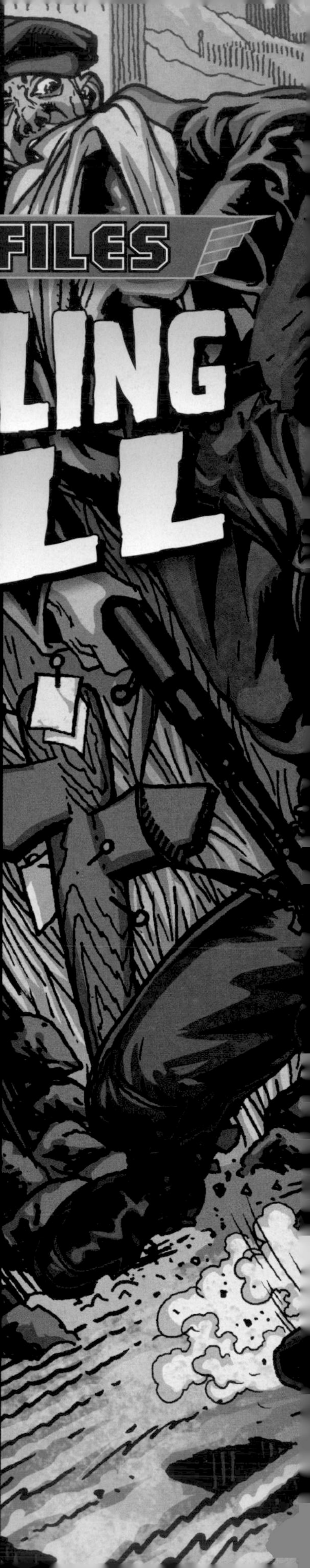

B. CLAY MOORE
WRITER

TONY HARRIS
ARTIST

DAVE McCAIG
COLORIST

WES ABBOTT
LETTERER

TONY HARRIS
COLLECTION and
ORIGINAL SERIES COVER ARTIST

THE WHISTLING SKULL created by
B. CLAY MOORE and **TONY HARRIS**

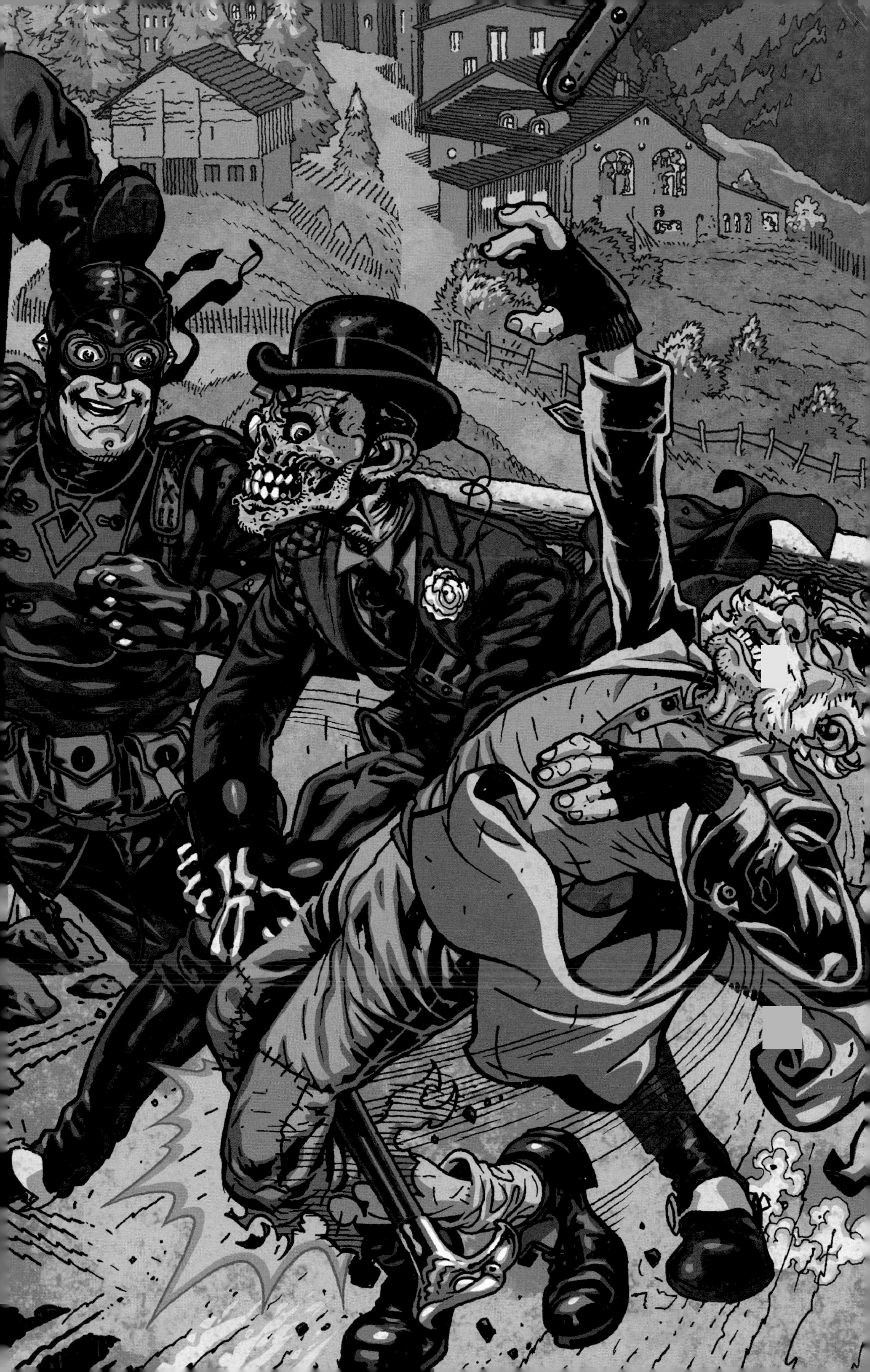

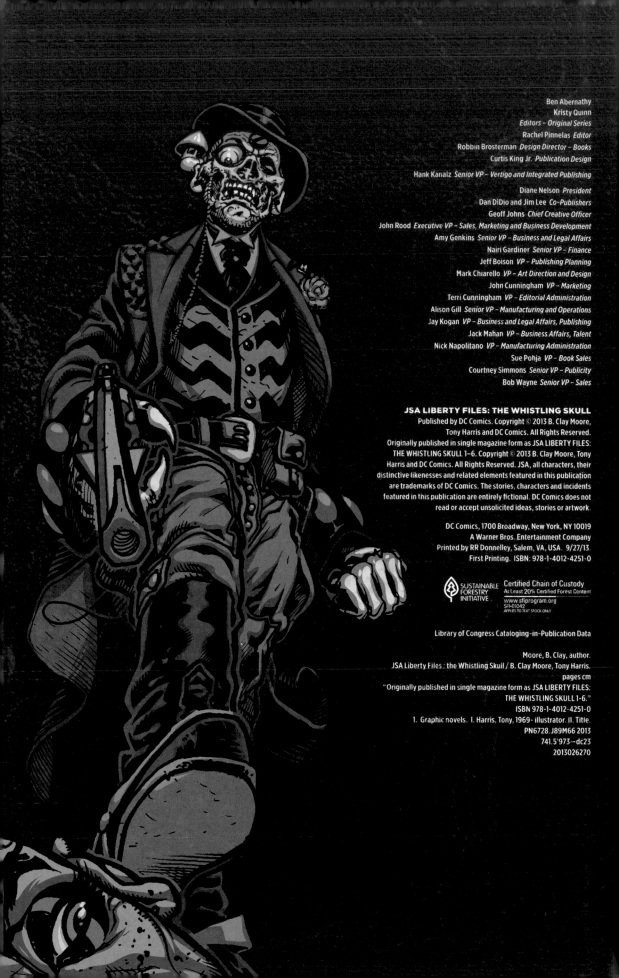

Ben Abernathy
Kristy Quinn
Editors – Original Series
Rachel Pinnelas *Editor*
Robbin Brosterman *Design Director – Books*
Curtis King Jr. *Publication Design*

Hank Kanalz *Senior VP – Vertigo and Integrated Publishing*

Diane Nelson *President*
Dan DiDio and Jim Lee *Co-Publishers*
Geoff Johns *Chief Creative Officer*
John Rood *Executive VP – Sales, Marketing and Business Development*
Amy Genkins *Senior VP – Business and Legal Affairs*
Nairi Gardiner *Senior VP – Finance*
Jeff Boison *VP – Publishing Planning*
Mark Chiarello *VP – Art Direction and Design*
John Cunningham *VP – Marketing*
Terri Cunningham *VP – Editorial Administration*
Alison Gill *Senior VP – Manufacturing and Operations*
Jay Kogan *VP – Business and Legal Affairs, Publishing*
Jack Mahan *VP – Business Affairs, Talent*
Nick Napolitano *VP – Manufacturing Administration*
Sue Pohja *VP – Book Sales*
Courtney Simmons *Senior VP – Publicity*
Bob Wayne *Senior VP – Sales*

JSA LIBERTY FILES: THE WHISTLING SKULL

DC Comics, 1700 Broadway, New York, NY 10019
A Warner Bros. Entertainment Company
Printed by RR Donnelley, Salem, VA, USA. 9/27/13.
First Printing. ISBN: 978-1-4012-4251-0

SUSTAINABLE FORESTRY INITIATIVE

Certified Chain of Custody
At Least 20% Certified Forest Content
www.sfiprogram.org
SFI-01042
APPLIES TO TEXT STOCK ONLY

Library of Congress Cataloging-in-Publication Data

Moore, B. Clay, author.
JSA Liberty Files : the Whistling Skull / B. Clay Moore, Tony Harris.
pages cm
"Originally published in single magazine form as JSA LIBERTY FILES:
THE WHISTLING SKULL 1-6."
ISBN 978-1-4012-4251-0
1. Graphic novels. I. Harris, Tony, 1969- illustrator. II. Title.
PN6728.J89M66 2013
741.5'973—dc23
2013026270

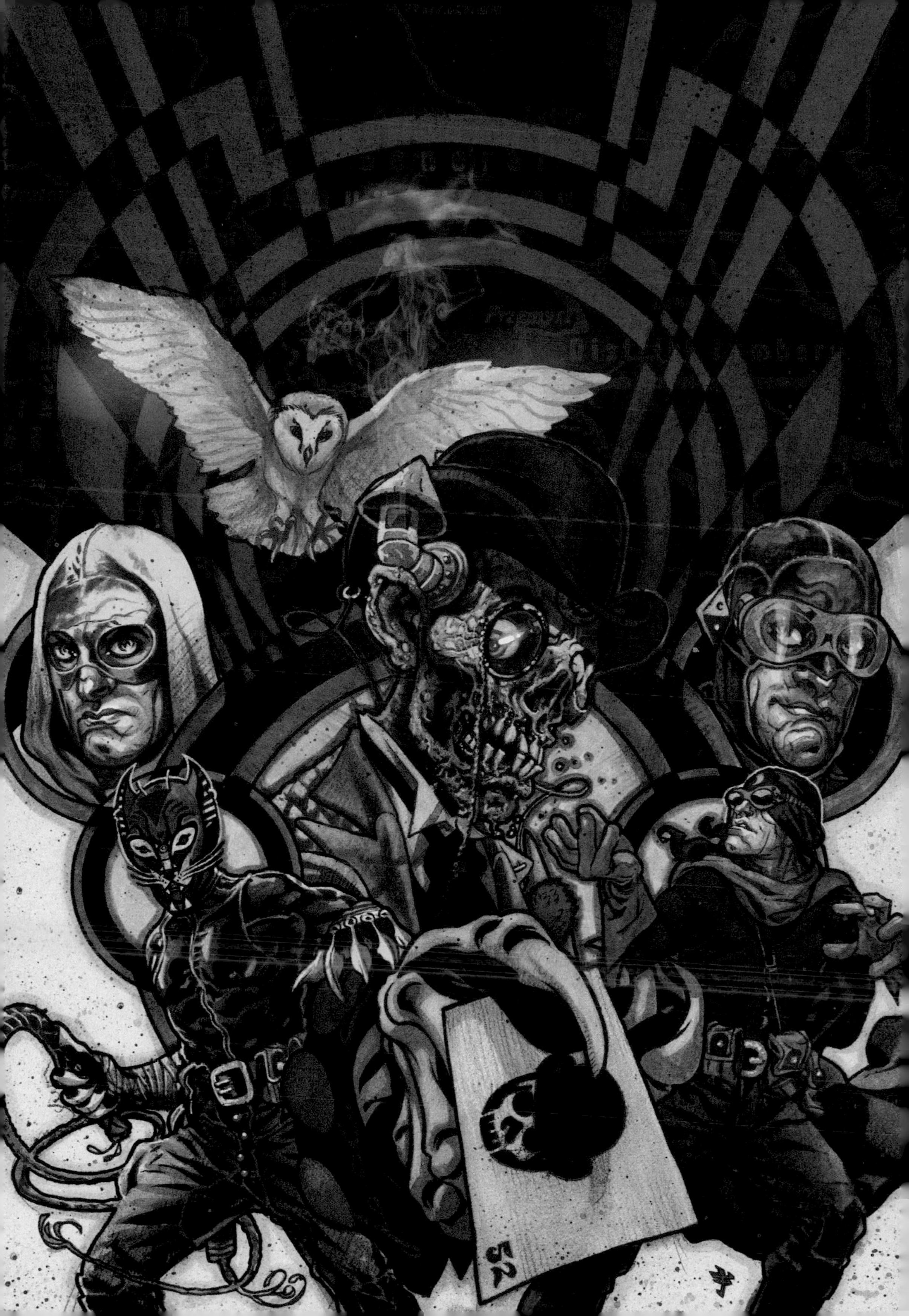
52

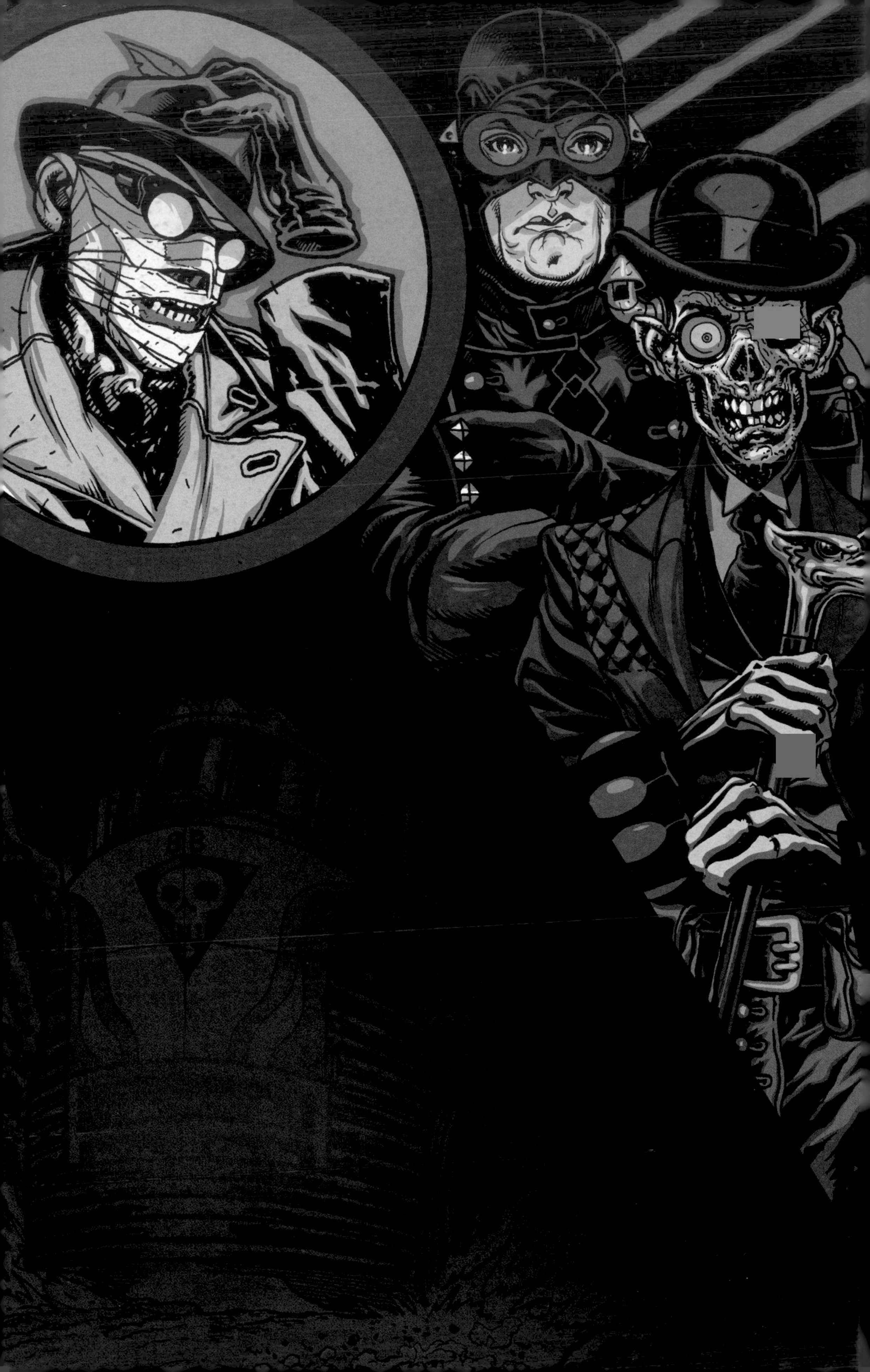

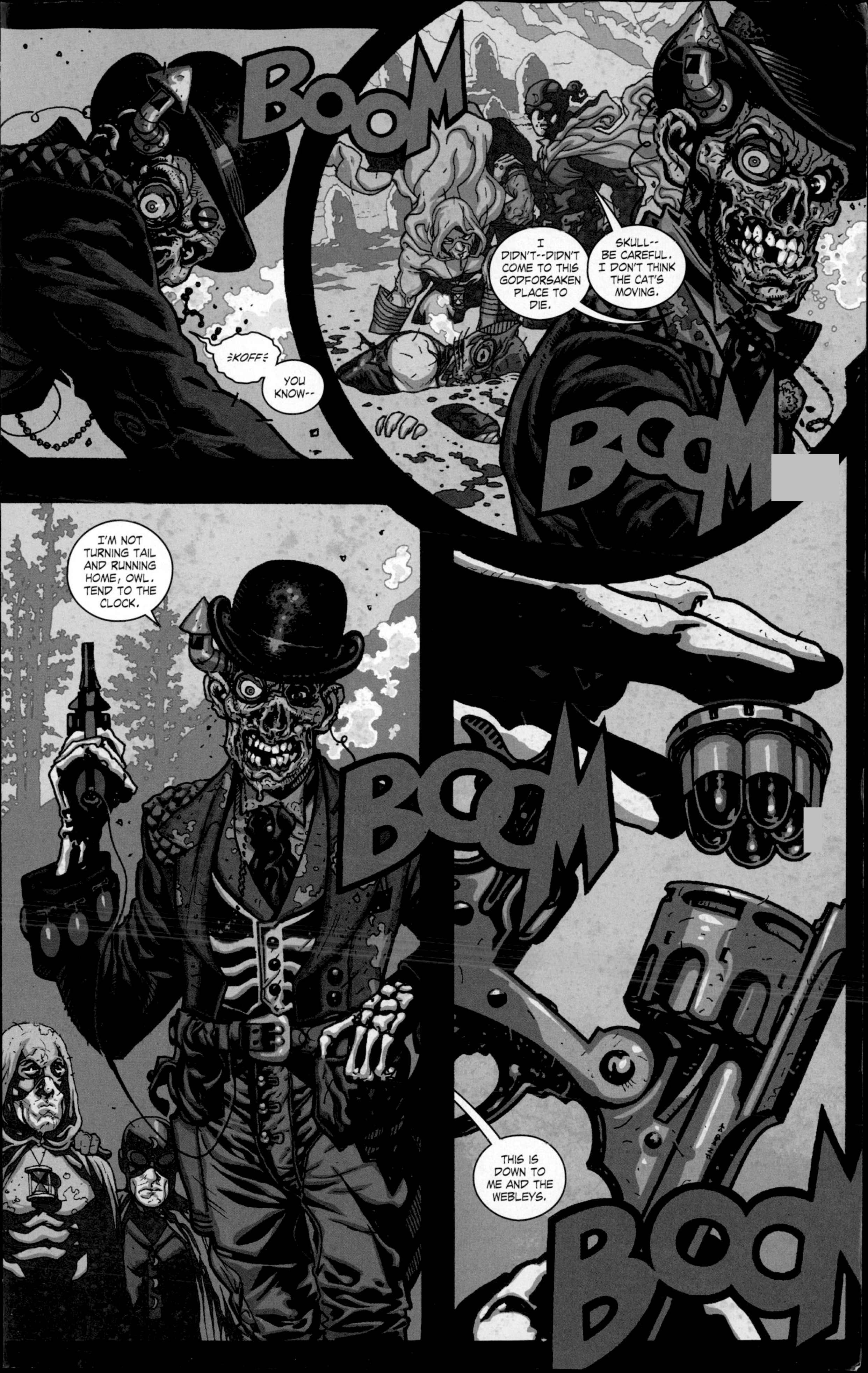
BOOM
ƎKOFFƐ
YOU KNOW--
I DIDN'T--DIDN'T COME TO THIS GODFORSAKEN PLACE TO DIE.
SKULL-- BE CAREFUL. I DON'T THINK THE CAT'S MOVING.
BOOM
I'M NOT TURNING TAIL AND RUNNING HOME, OWL. TEND TO THE CLOCK.
BOOM
THIS IS DOWN TO ME AND THE WEBLEYS.
BOOM

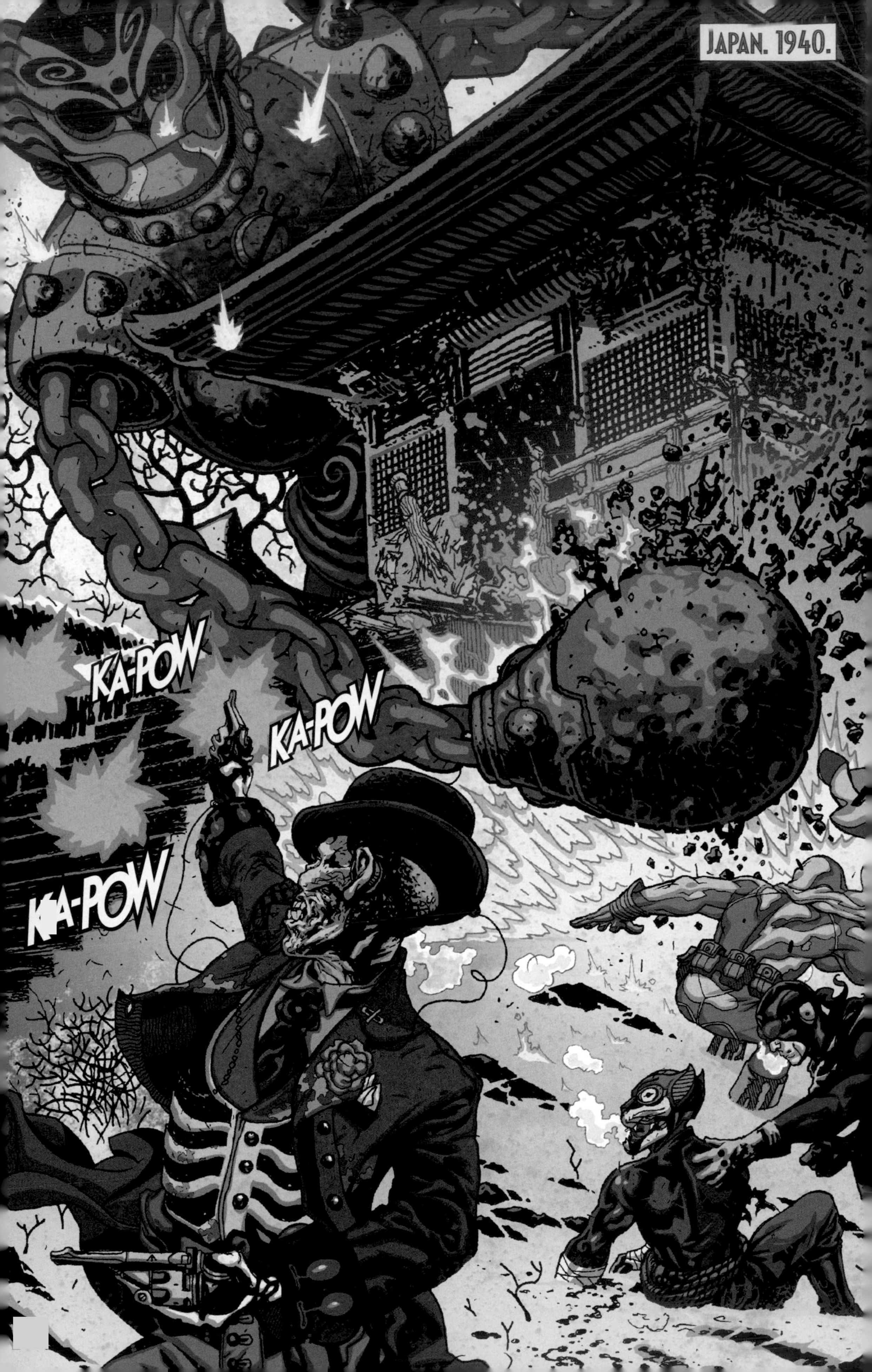
JAPAN. 1940.
KA-POW
KA-POW
KA-POW

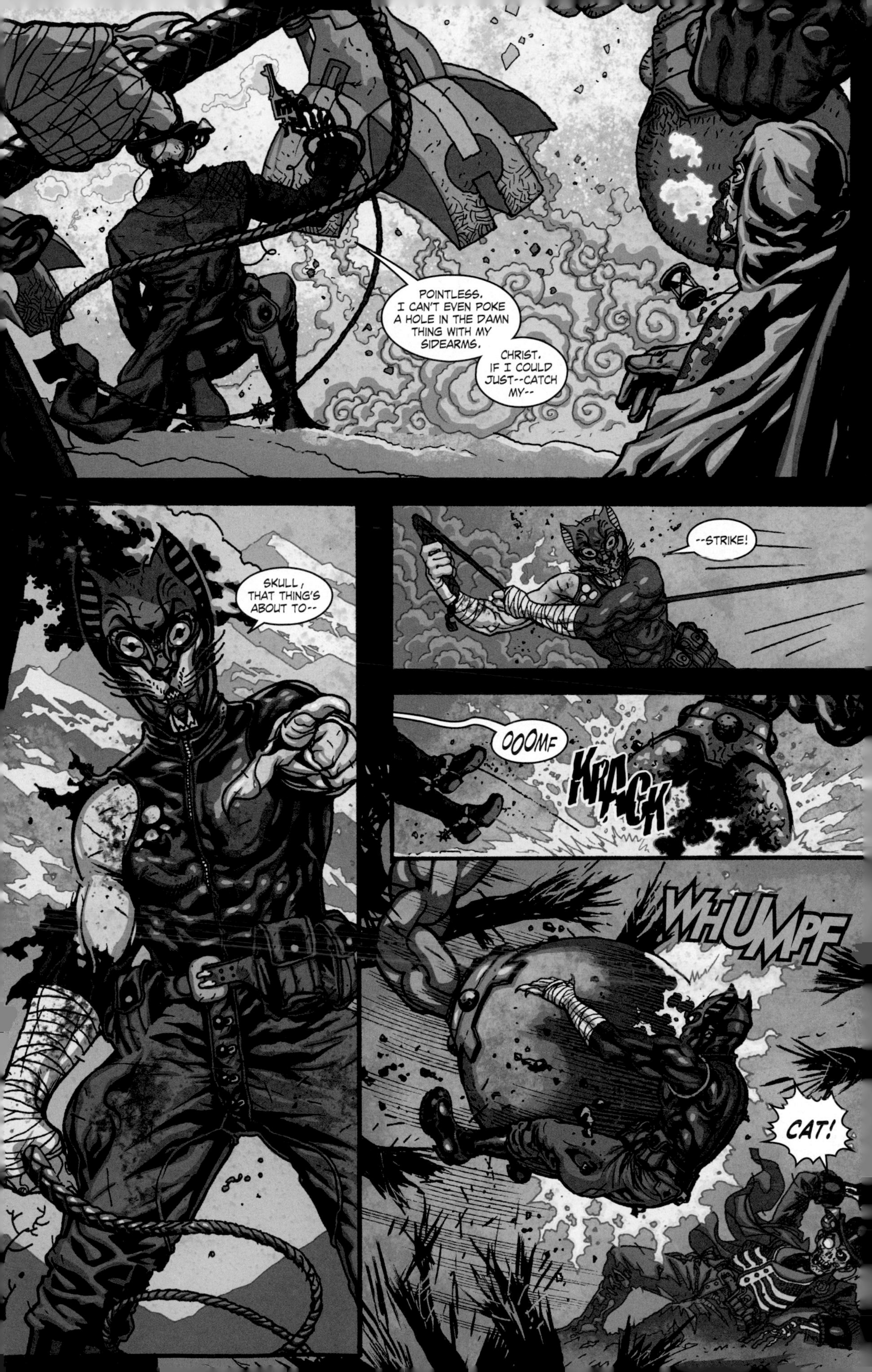
POINTLESS. I CAN'T EVEN POKE A HOLE IN THE DAMN THING WITH MY SIDEARMS.
CHRIST. IF I COULD JUST--CATCH MY--
SKULL, THAT THING'S ABOUT TO--
--STRIKE!
OOOMF
KRACK
WHUMPF
CAT!

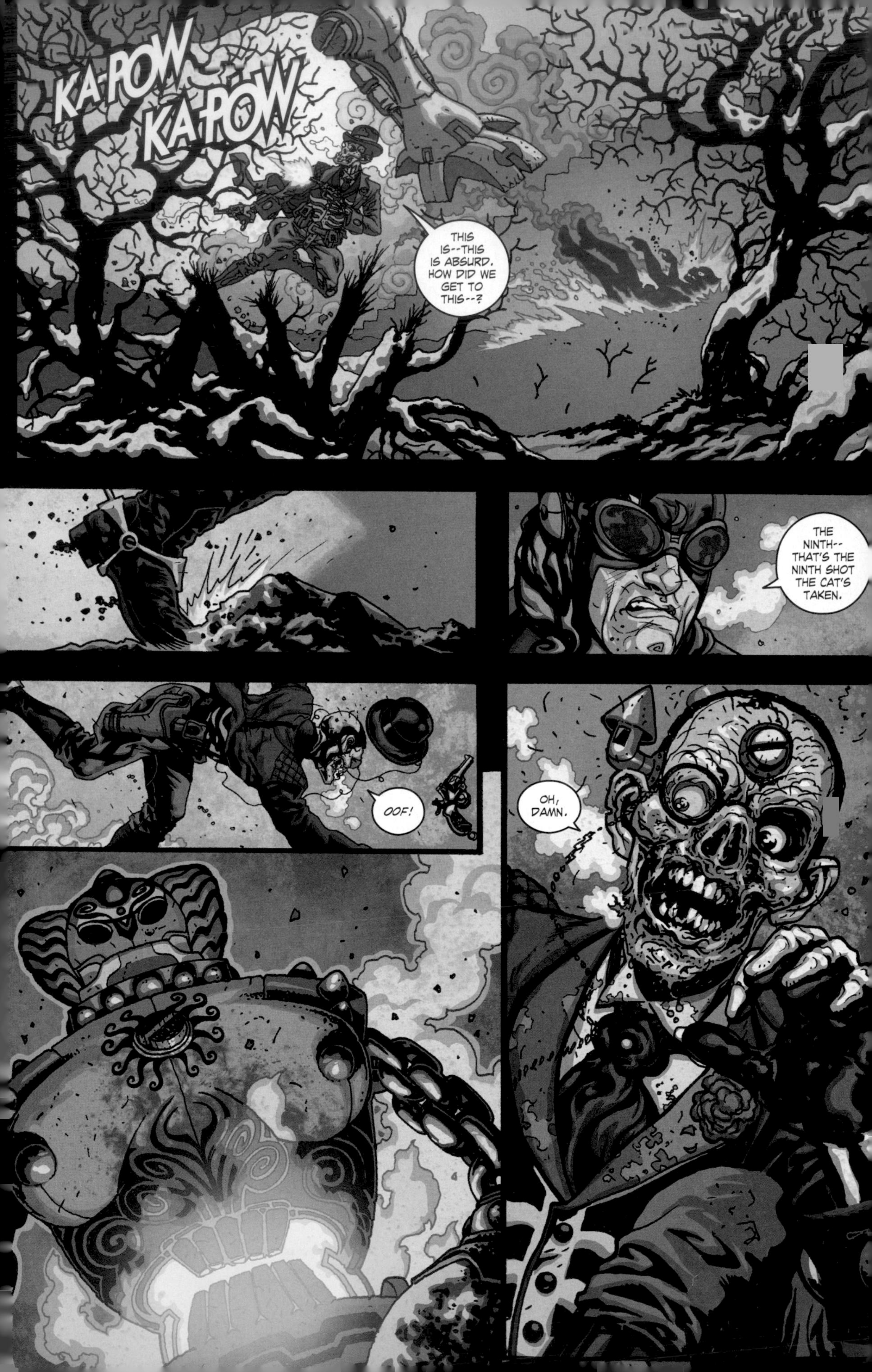
KA-POW
KA-POW
THIS IS--THIS IS ABSURD. HOW DID WE GET TO THIS--?
THE NINTH--THAT'S THE NINTH SHOT THE CAT'S TAKEN.
OOF!
OH, DAMN.

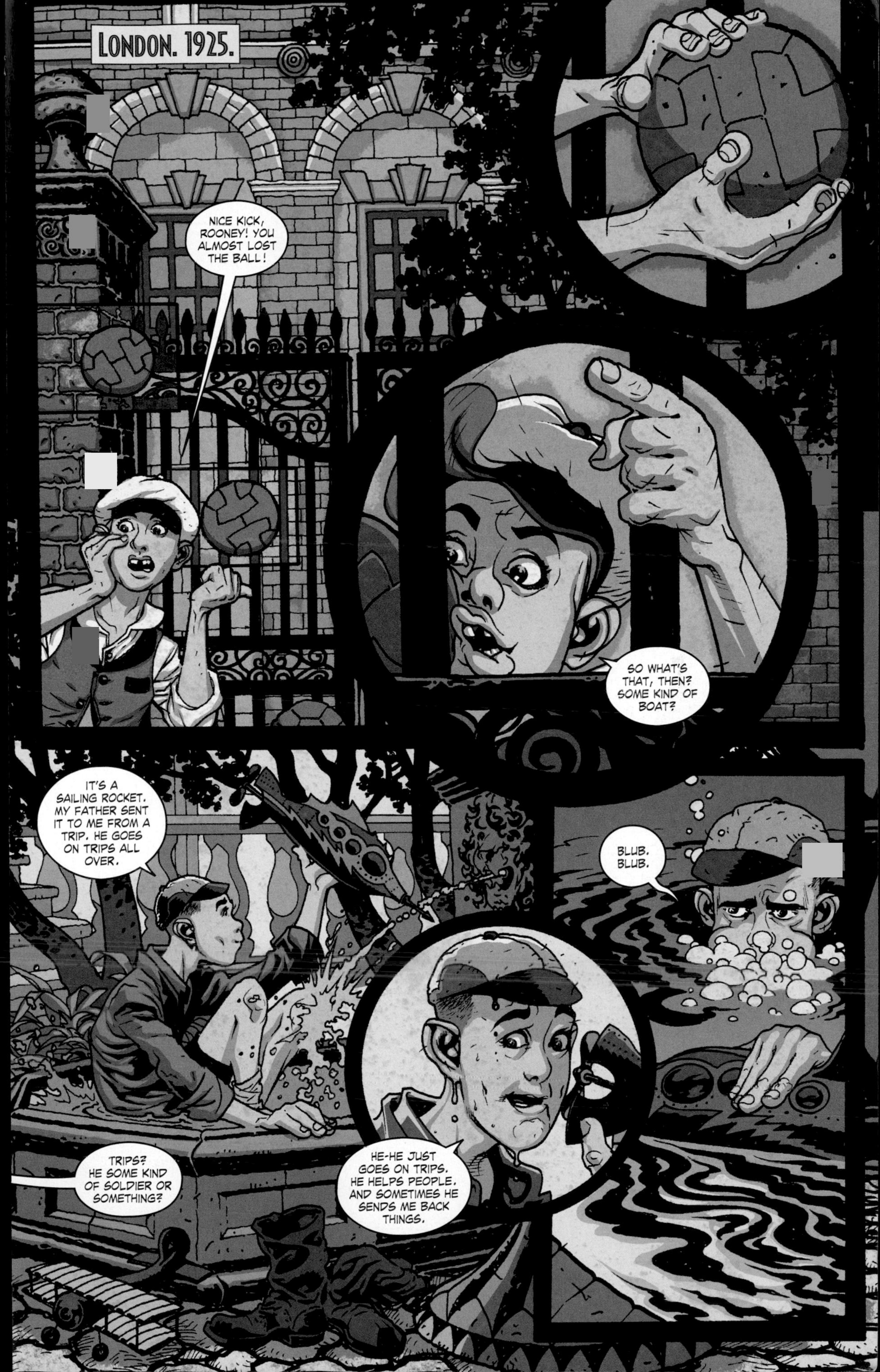
LONDON. 1925.
NICE KICK, ROONEY! YOU ALMOST LOST THE BALL!
SO WHAT'S THAT, THEN? SOME KIND OF BOAT?
IT'S A SAILING ROCKET. MY FATHER SENT IT TO ME FROM A TRIP. HE GOES ON TRIPS ALL OVER.
BLUB. BLUB.
TRIPS? HE SOME KIND OF SOLDIER OR SOMETHING?
HE-HE JUST GOES ON TRIPS. HE HELPS PEOPLE. AND SOMETIMES HE SENDS ME BACK THINGS.

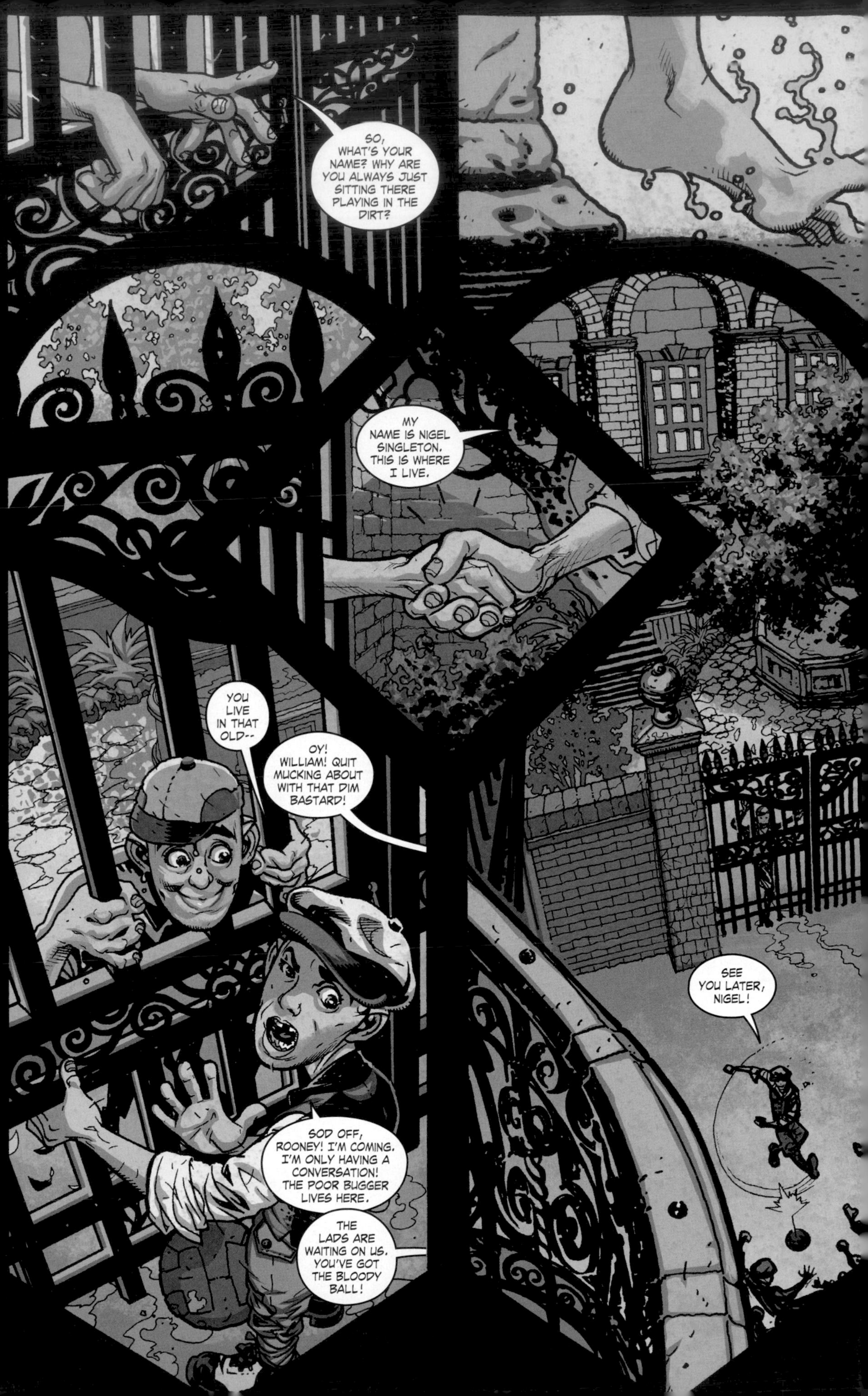
SO, WHAT'S YOUR NAME? WHY ARE YOU ALWAYS JUST SITTING THERE PLAYING IN THE DIRT?
MY NAME IS NIGEL SINGLETON. THIS IS WHERE I LIVE.
YOU LIVE IN THAT OLD--
OY! WILLIAM! QUIT MUCKING ABOUT WITH THAT DIM BASTARD!
SOD OFF, ROONEY! I'M COMING. I'M ONLY HAVING A CONVERSATION! THE POOR BUGGER LIVES HERE.
THE LADS ARE WAITING ON US. YOU'VE GOT THE BLOODY BALL!
SEE YOU LATER, NIGEL!

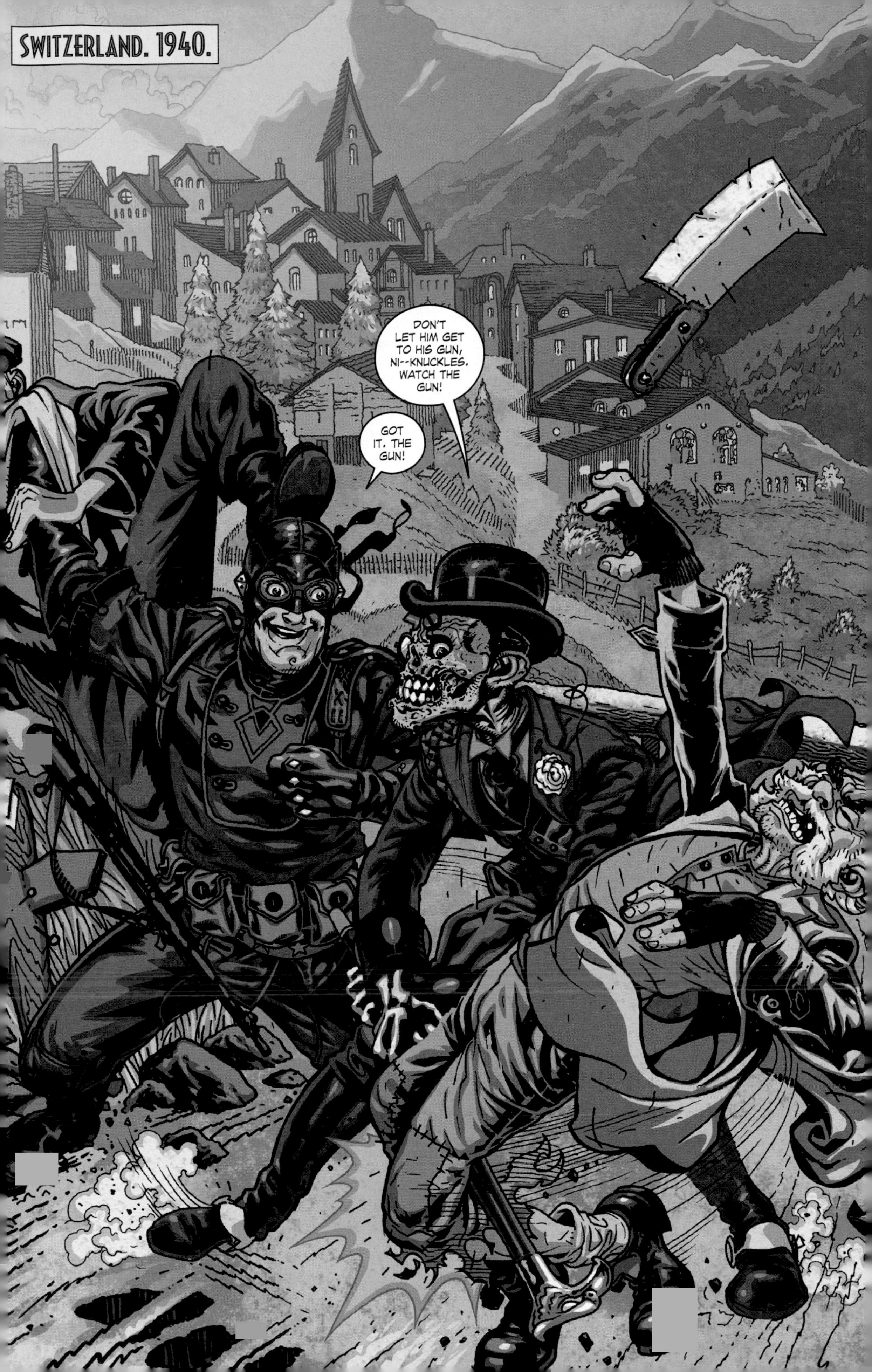

SWITZERLAND. 1940.
DON'T LET HIM GET TO HIS GUN, NI--KNUCKLES. WATCH THE GUN!
GOT IT. THE GUN!

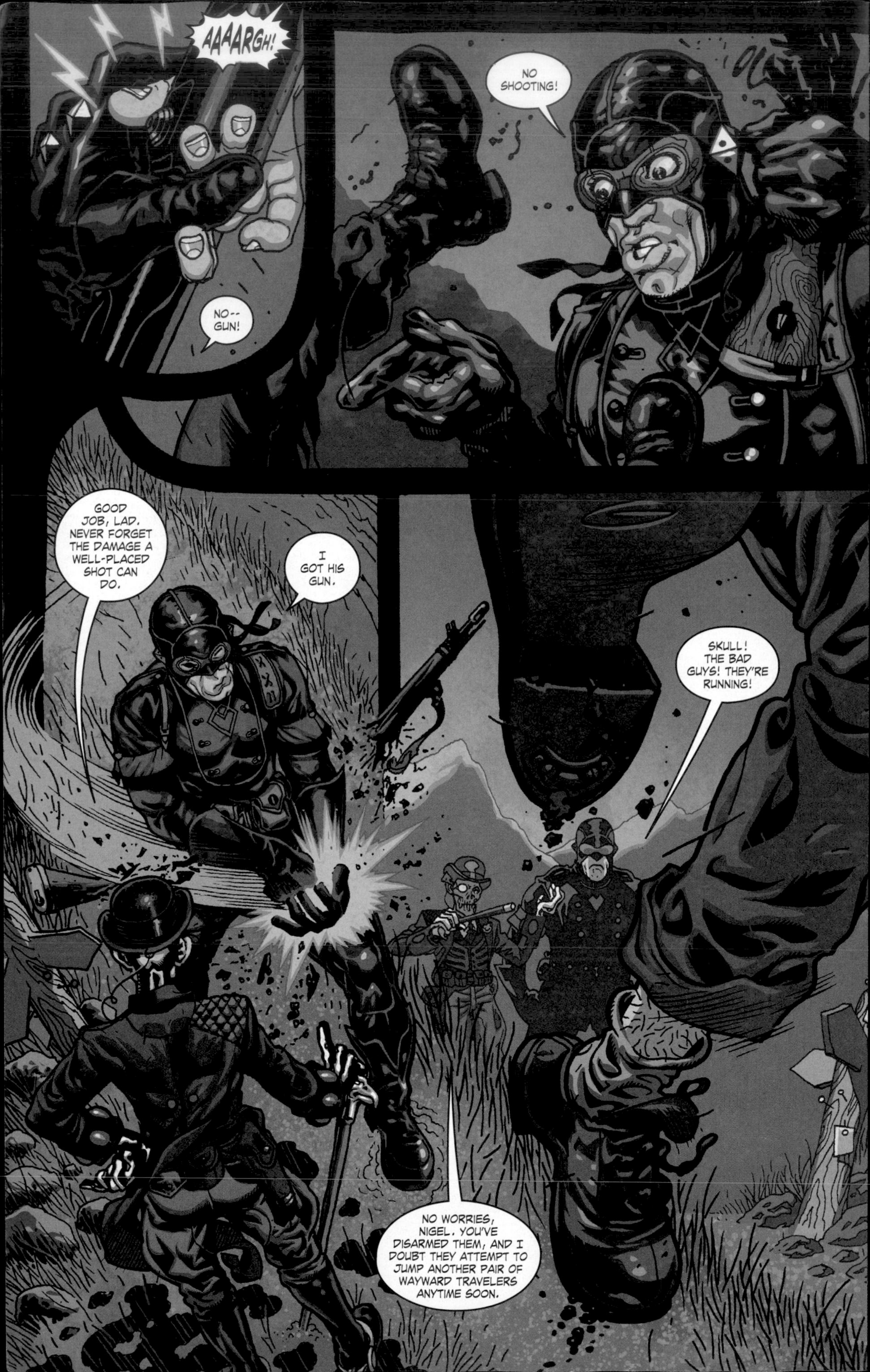

AAAARGH!
NO-- GUN!
NO SHOOTING!
GOOD JOB, LAD. NEVER FORGET THE DAMAGE A WELL-PLACED SHOT CAN DO.
I GOT HIS GUN.
SKULL! THE BAD GUYS! THEY'RE RUNNING!
NO WORRIES, NIGEL. YOU'VE DISARMED THEM, AND I DOUBT THEY ATTEMPT TO JUMP ANOTHER PAIR OF WAYWARD TRAVELERS ANYTIME SOON.

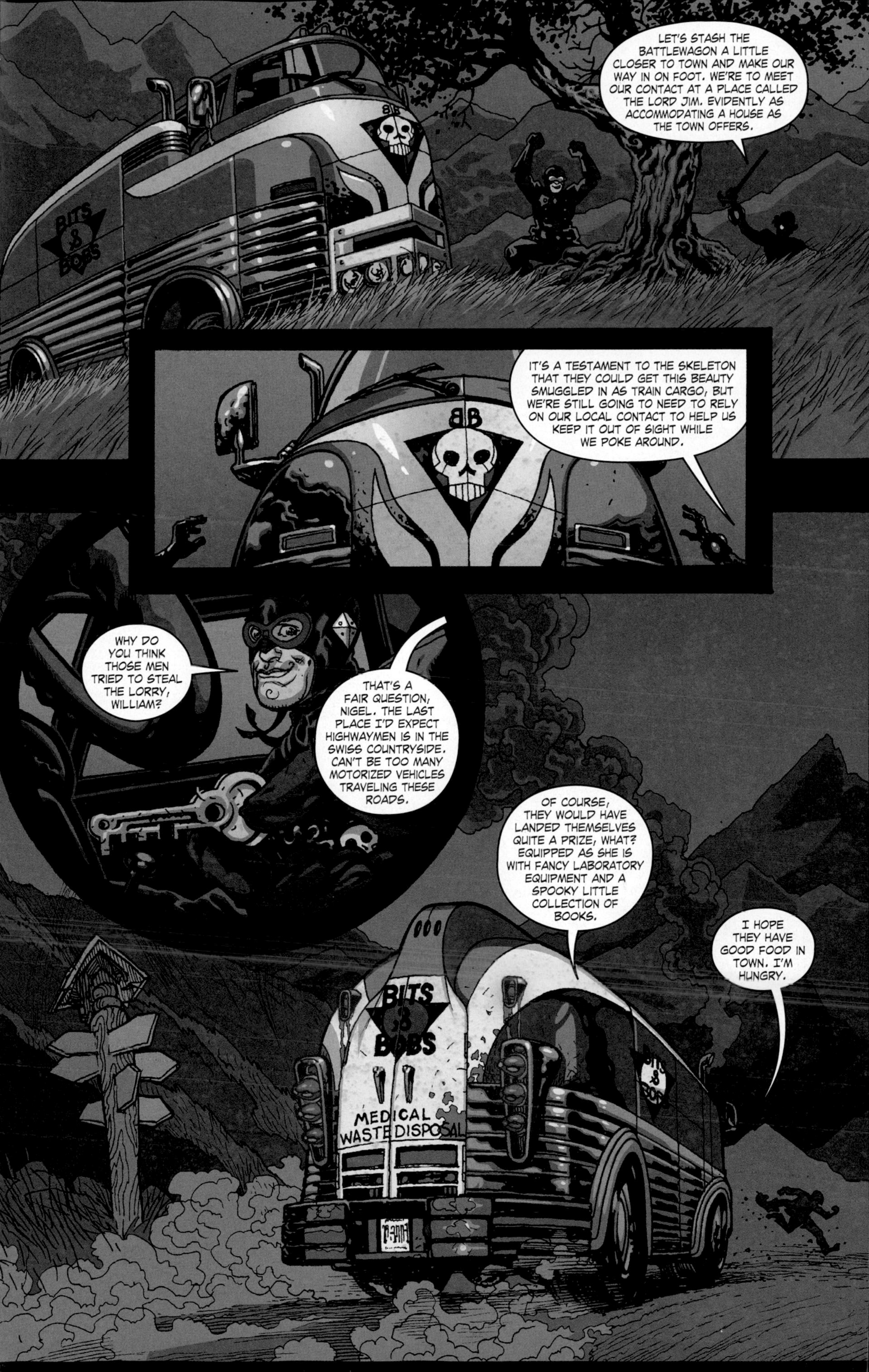
LET'S STASH THE BATTLEWAGON A LITTLE CLOSER TO TOWN AND MAKE OUR WAY IN ON FOOT. WE'RE TO MEET OUR CONTACT AT A PLACE CALLED THE LORD JIM. EVIDENTLY AS ACCOMMODATING A HOUSE AS THE TOWN OFFERS.
BITS & BOBS
IT'S A TESTAMENT TO THE SKELETON THAT THEY COULD GET THIS BEAUTY SMUGGLED IN AS TRAIN CARGO, BUT WE'RE STILL GOING TO NEED TO RELY ON OUR LOCAL CONTACT TO HELP US KEEP IT OUT OF SIGHT WHILE WE POKE AROUND.
WHY DO YOU THINK THOSE MEN TRIED TO STEAL THE LORRY, WILLIAM?
THAT'S A FAIR QUESTION, NIGEL. THE LAST PLACE I'D EXPECT HIGHWAYMEN IS IN THE SWISS COUNTRYSIDE. CAN'T BE TOO MANY MOTORIZED VEHICLES TRAVELING THESE ROADS.
OF COURSE, THEY WOULD HAVE LANDED THEMSELVES QUITE A PRIZE, WHAT? EQUIPPED AS SHE IS WITH FANCY LABORATORY EQUIPMENT AND A SPOOKY LITTLE COLLECTION OF BOOKS.
I HOPE THEY HAVE GOOD FOOD IN TOWN. I'M HUNGRY.
BITS & BOBS
MEDICAL WASTE DISPOSAL

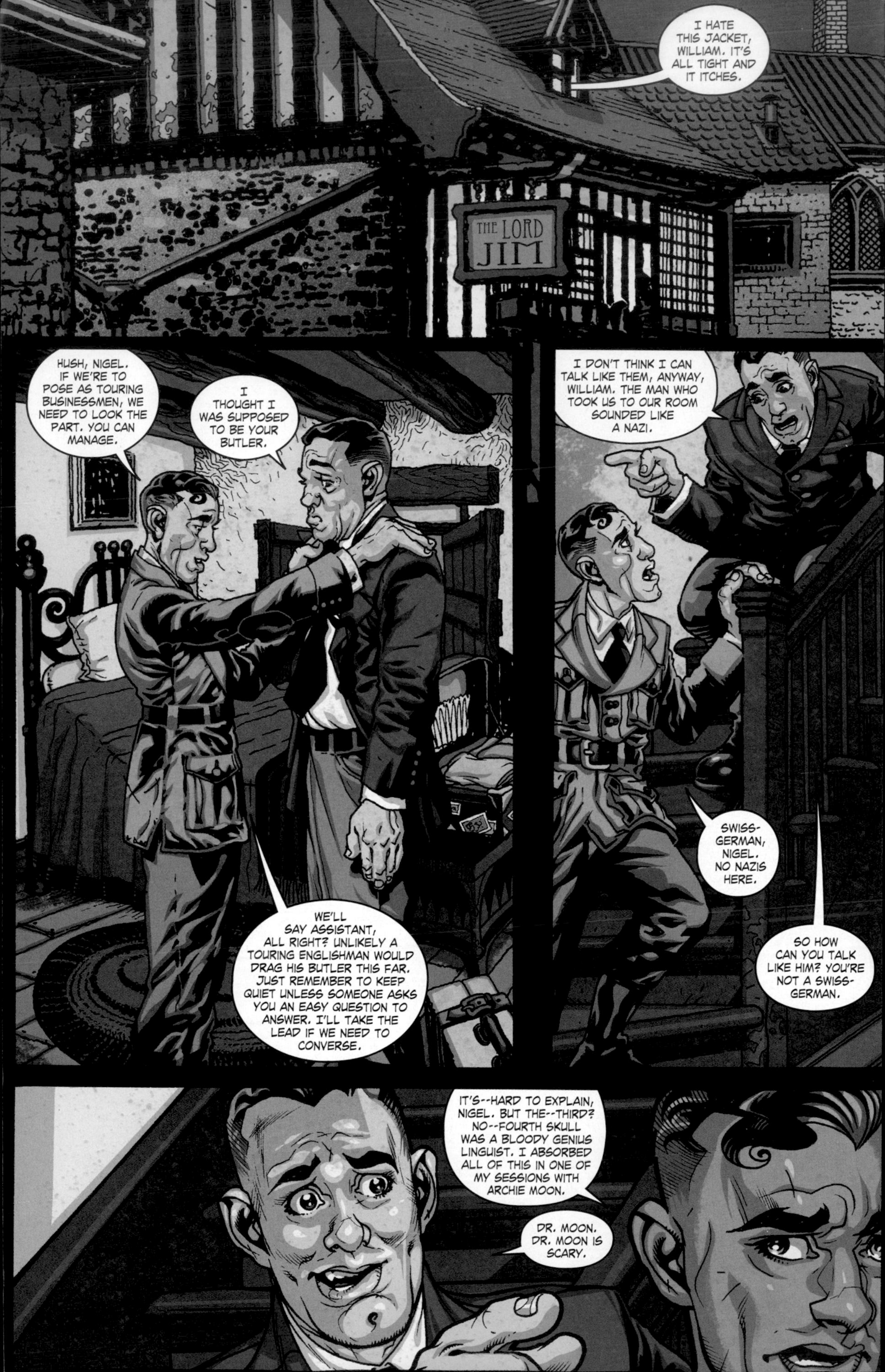
I HATE THIS JACKET, WILLIAM. IT'S ALL TIGHT AND IT ITCHES.
THE LORD JIM
HUSH, NIGEL. IF WE'RE TO POSE AS TOURING BUSINESSMEN, WE NEED TO LOOK THE PART. YOU CAN MANAGE.
I THOUGHT I WAS SUPPOSED TO BE YOUR BUTLER.
WE'LL SAY ASSISTANT, ALL RIGHT? UNLIKELY A TOURING ENGLISHMAN WOULD DRAG HIS BUTLER THIS FAR. JUST REMEMBER TO KEEP QUIET UNLESS SOMEONE ASKS YOU AN EASY QUESTION TO ANSWER. I'LL TAKE THE LEAD IF WE NEED TO CONVERSE.
I DON'T THINK I CAN TALK LIKE THEM, ANYWAY, WILLIAM. THE MAN WHO TOOK US TO OUR ROOM SOUNDED LIKE A NAZI.
SWISS-GERMAN, NIGEL. NO NAZIS HERE.
SO HOW CAN YOU TALK LIKE HIM? YOU'RE NOT A SWISS-GERMAN.
IT'S--HARD TO EXPLAIN, NIGEL. BUT THE--THIRD? NO--FOURTH SKULL WAS A BLOODY GENIUS LINGUIST. I ABSORBED ALL OF THIS IN ONE OF MY SESSIONS WITH ARCHIE MOON.
DR. MOON. DR. MOON IS SCARY.

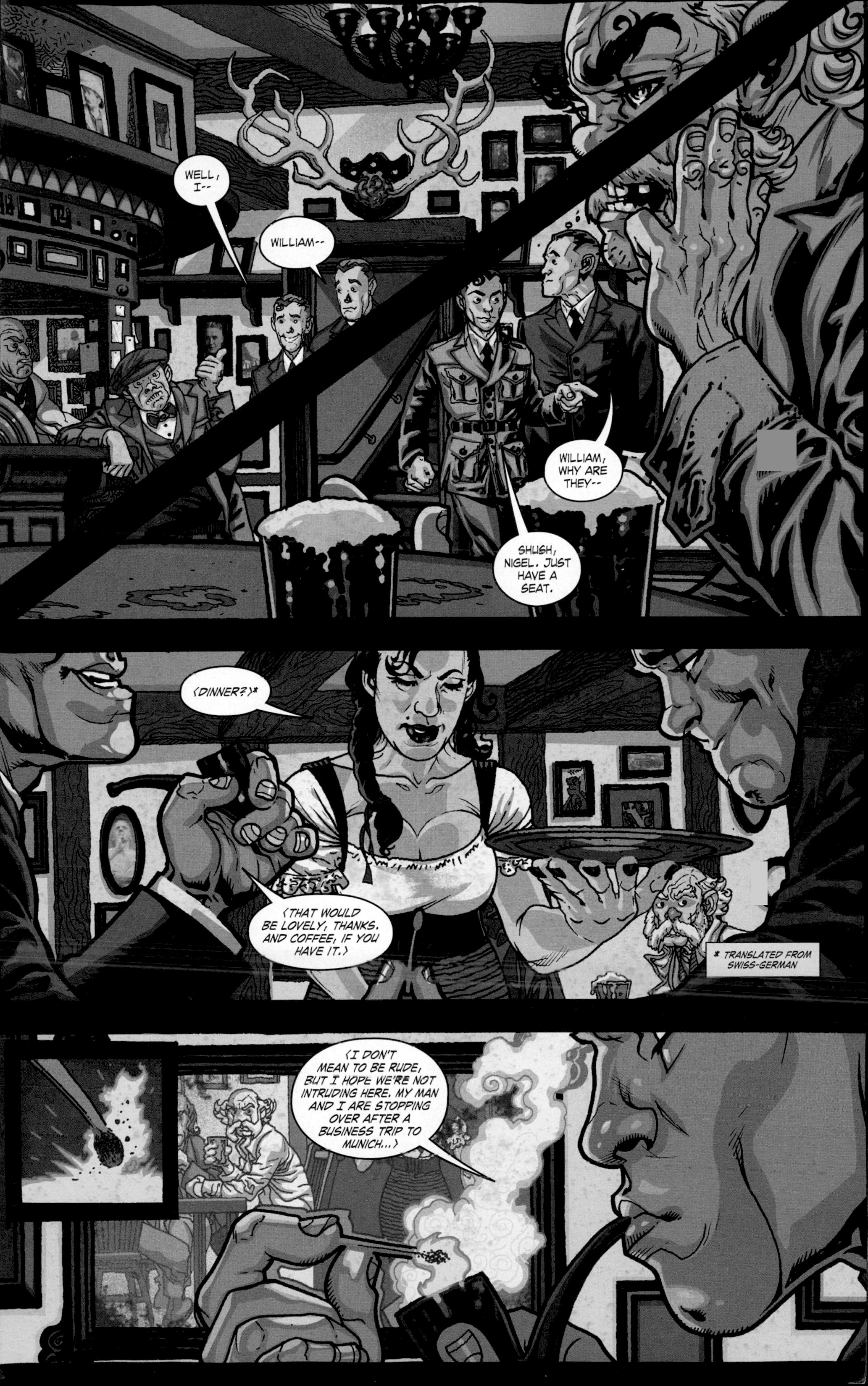
WELL, I--
WILLIAM--
WILLIAM, WHY ARE THEY--
SHUSH, NIGEL. JUST HAVE A SEAT.
<DINNER?>*
<THAT WOULD BE LOVELY, THANKS. AND COFFEE, IF YOU HAVE IT.>
* TRANSLATED FROM SWISS-GERMAN
<I DON'T MEAN TO BE RUDE, BUT I HOPE WE'RE NOT INTRUDING HERE. MY MAN AND I ARE STOPPING OVER AFTER A BUSINESS TRIP TO MUNICH...>

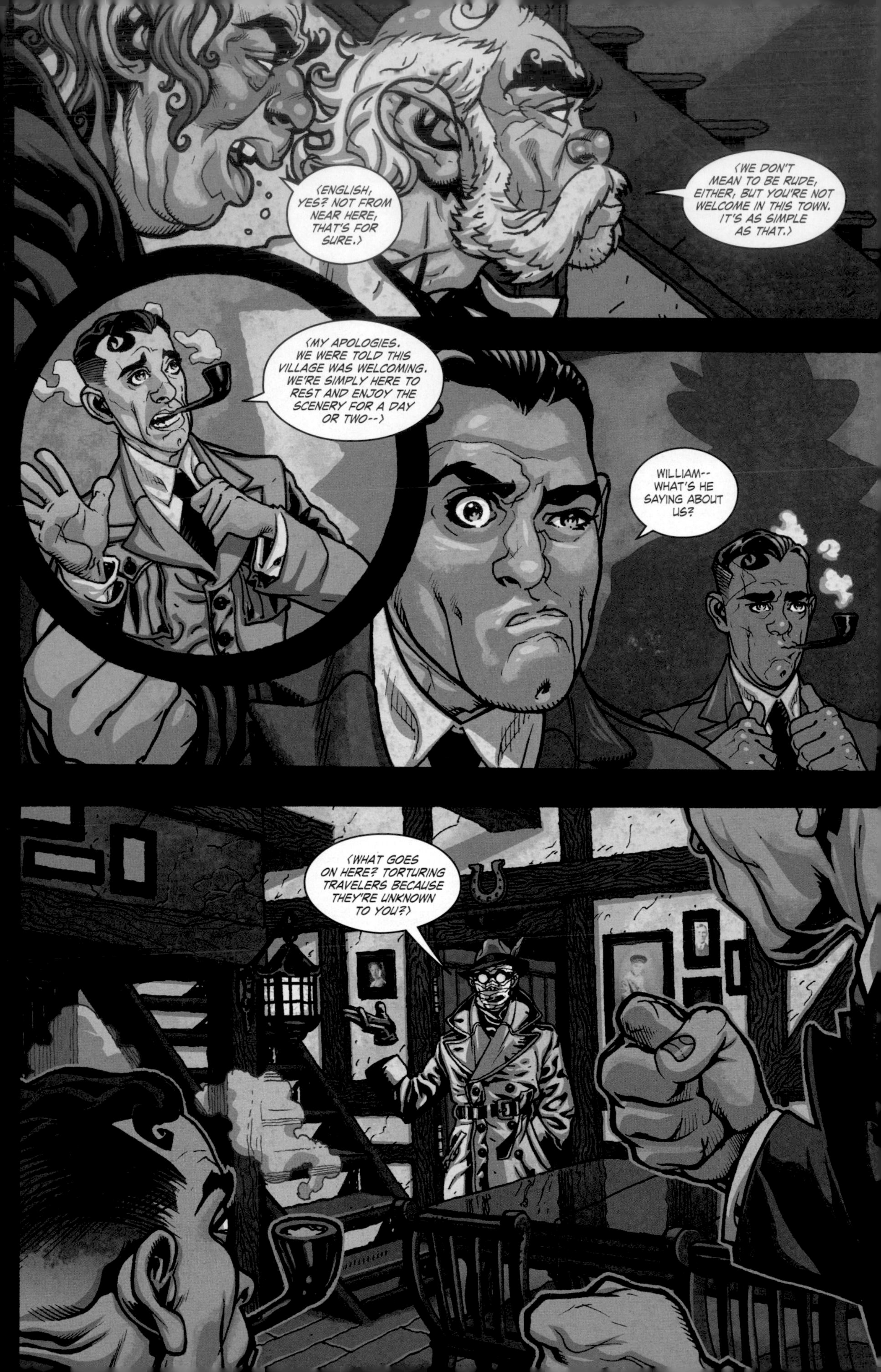

‹ENGLISH, YES? NOT FROM NEAR HERE, THAT'S FOR SURE.›
‹WE DON'T MEAN TO BE RUDE, EITHER, BUT YOU'RE NOT WELCOME IN THIS TOWN. IT'S AS SIMPLE AS THAT.›
‹MY APOLOGIES. WE WERE TOLD THIS VILLAGE WAS WELCOMING. WE'RE SIMPLY HERE TO REST AND ENJOY THE SCENERY FOR A DAY OR TWO--›
WILLIAM-- WHAT'S HE SAYING ABOUT US?
‹WHAT GOES ON HERE? TORTURING TRAVELERS BECAUSE THEY'RE UNKNOWN TO YOU?›

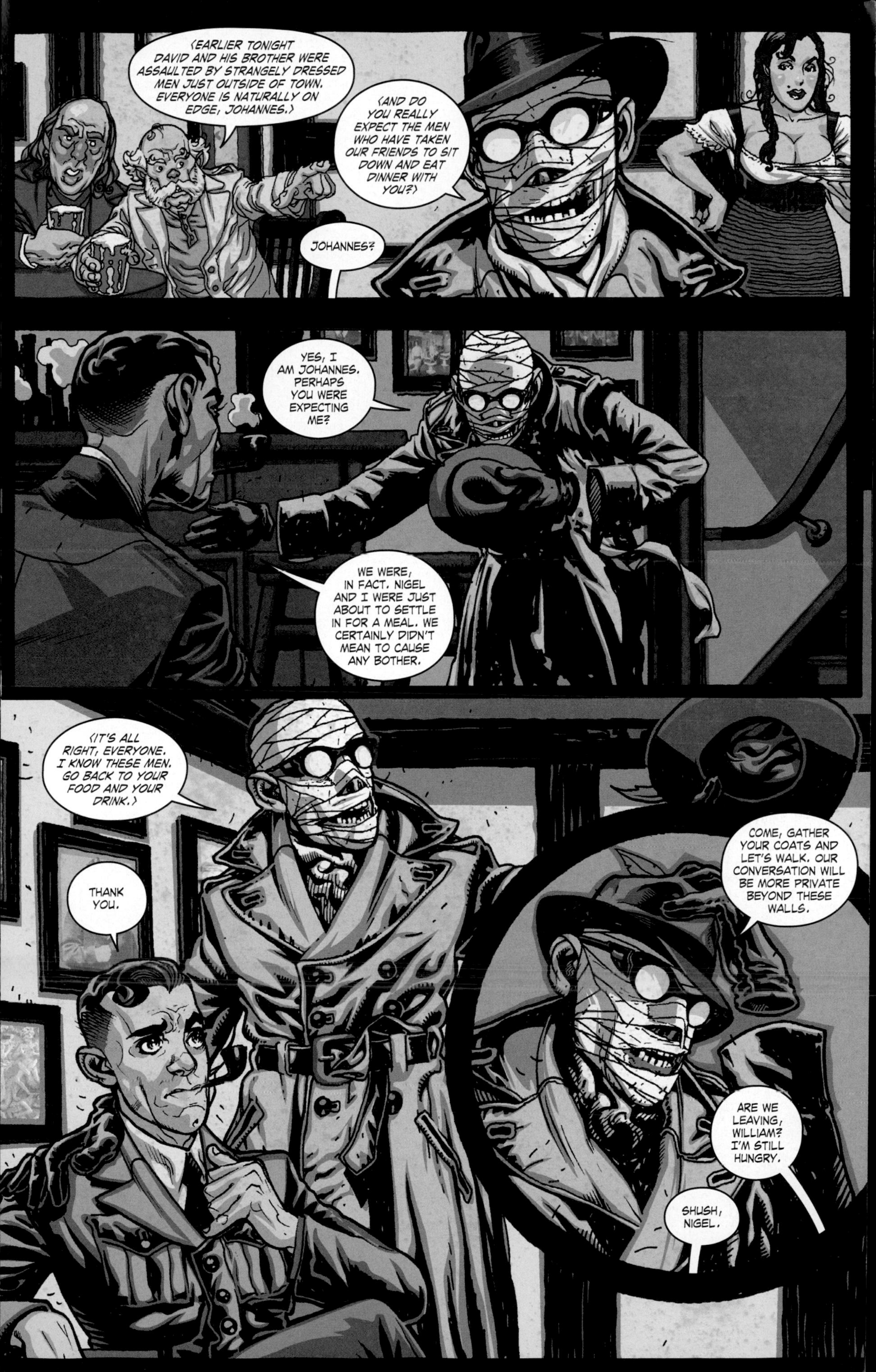

‹EARLIER TONIGHT DAVID AND HIS BROTHER WERE ASSAULTED BY STRANGELY DRESSED MEN JUST OUTSIDE OF TOWN. EVERYONE IS NATURALLY ON EDGE, JOHANNES.›
‹AND DO YOU REALLY EXPECT THE MEN WHO HAVE TAKEN OUR FRIENDS TO SIT DOWN AND EAT DINNER WITH YOU?›
JOHANNES?
YES, I AM JOHANNES. PERHAPS YOU WERE EXPECTING ME?
WE WERE, IN FACT. NIGEL AND I WERE JUST ABOUT TO SETTLE IN FOR A MEAL. WE CERTAINLY DIDN'T MEAN TO CAUSE ANY BOTHER.
‹IT'S ALL RIGHT, EVERYONE. I KNOW THESE MEN. GO BACK TO YOUR FOOD AND YOUR DRINK.›
THANK YOU.
COME, GATHER YOUR COATS AND LET'S WALK. OUR CONVERSATION WILL BE MORE PRIVATE BEYOND THESE WALLS.
ARE WE LEAVING, WILLIAM? I'M STILL HUNGRY.
SHUSH, NIGEL.

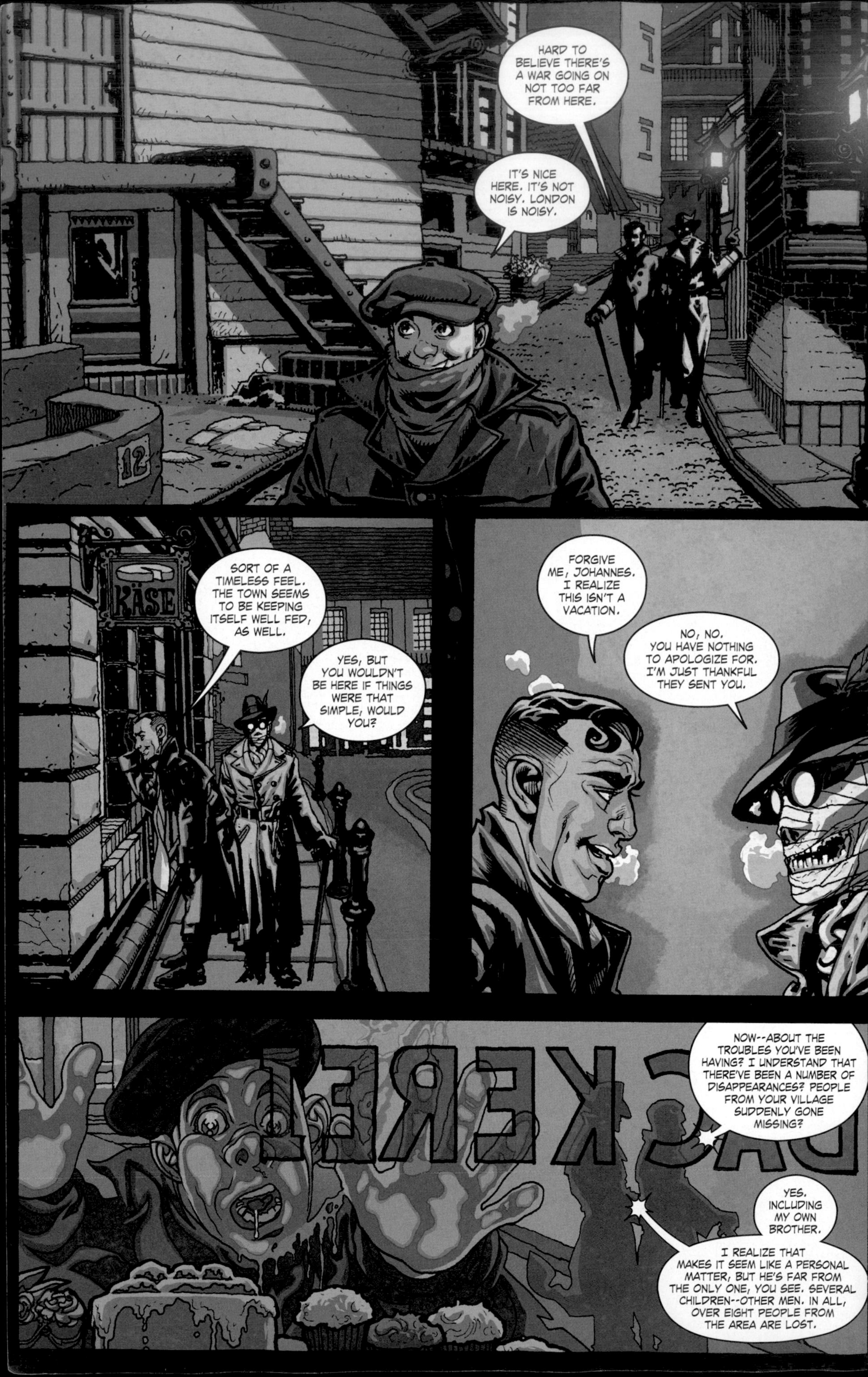
HARD TO BELIEVE THERE'S A WAR GOING ON NOT TOO FAR FROM HERE.
IT'S NICE HERE. IT'S NOT NOISY. LONDON IS NOISY.
12
KÄSE
SORT OF A TIMELESS FEEL. THE TOWN SEEMS TO BE KEEPING ITSELF WELL FED, AS WELL.
YES, BUT YOU WOULDN'T BE HERE IF THINGS WERE THAT SIMPLE, WOULD YOU?
FORGIVE ME, JOHANNES. I REALIZE THIS ISN'T A VACATION.
NO, NO. YOU HAVE NOTHING TO APOLOGIZE FOR. I'M JUST THANKFUL THEY SENT YOU.
NOW--ABOUT THE TROUBLES YOU'VE BEEN HAVING? I UNDERSTAND THAT THERE'VE BEEN A NUMBER OF DISAPPEARANCES? PEOPLE FROM YOUR VILLAGE SUDDENLY GONE MISSING?
YES. INCLUDING MY OWN BROTHER.
I REALIZE THAT MAKES IT SEEM LIKE A PERSONAL MATTER, BUT HE'S FAR FROM THE ONLY ONE, YOU SEE. SEVERAL CHILDREN--OTHER MEN. IN ALL, OVER EIGHT PEOPLE FROM THE AREA ARE LOST.

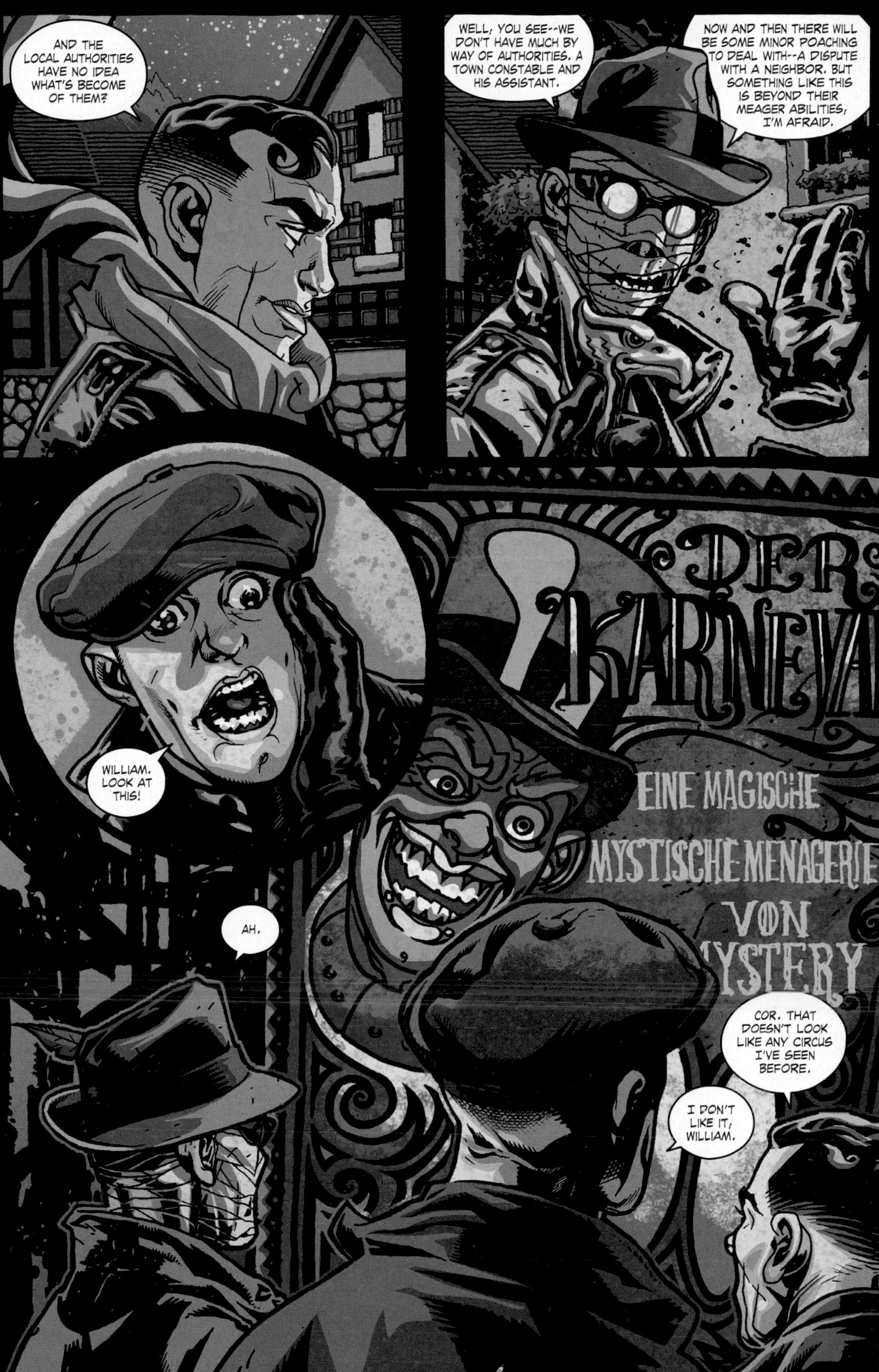
AND THE LOCAL AUTHORITIES HAVE NO IDEA WHAT'S BECOME OF THEM?
WELL, YOU SEE--WE DON'T HAVE MUCH BY WAY OF AUTHORITIES. A TOWN CONSTABLE AND HIS ASSISTANT.
NOW AND THEN THERE WILL BE SOME MINOR POACHING TO DEAL WITH--A DISPUTE WITH A NEIGHBOR. BUT SOMETHING LIKE THIS IS BEYOND THEIR MEAGER ABILITIES, I'M AFRAID.
DER KARNEVAL
EINE MAGISCHE
MYSTISCHE MENAGERIE
VON
MYSTERY
WILLIAM. LOOK AT THIS!
AH.
COR. THAT DOESN'T LOOK LIKE ANY CIRCUS I'VE SEEN BEFORE.
I DON'T LIKE IT, WILLIAM.

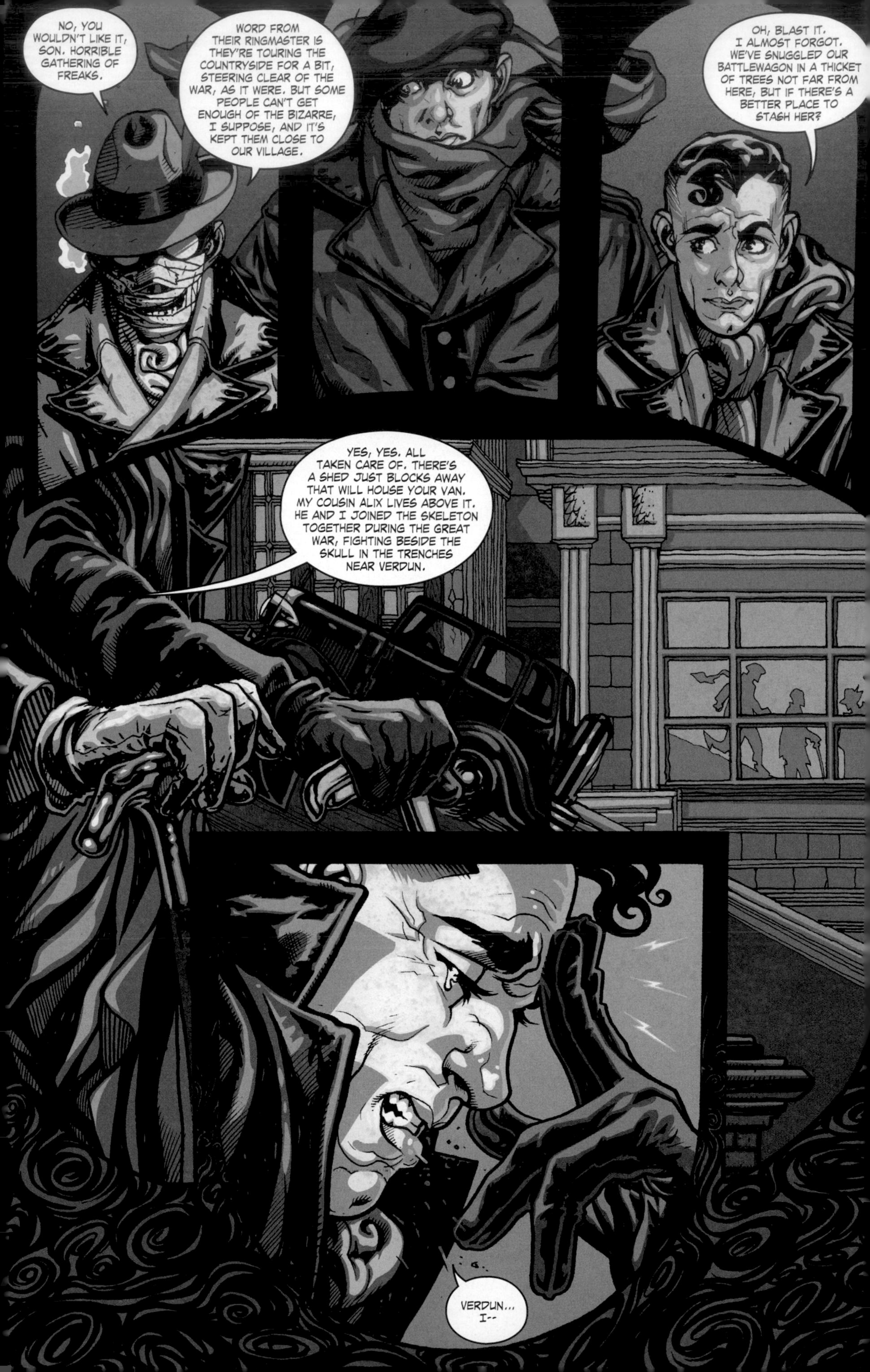
NO, YOU WOULDN'T LIKE IT, SON. HORRIBLE GATHERING OF FREAKS.
WORD FROM THEIR RINGMASTER IS THEY'RE TOURING THE COUNTRYSIDE FOR A BIT, STEERING CLEAR OF THE WAR, AS IT WERE. BUT SOME PEOPLE CAN'T GET ENOUGH OF THE BIZARRE, I SUPPOSE, AND IT'S KEPT THEM CLOSE TO OUR VILLAGE.
OH, BLAST IT. I ALMOST FORGOT. WE'VE SNUGGLED OUR BATTLEWAGON IN A THICKET OF TREES NOT FAR FROM HERE, BUT IF THERE'S A BETTER PLACE TO STASH HER?
YES, YES. ALL TAKEN CARE OF. THERE'S A SHED JUST BLOCKS AWAY THAT WILL HOUSE YOUR VAN. MY COUSIN ALIX LIVES ABOVE IT. HE AND I JOINED THE SKELETON TOGETHER DURING THE GREAT WAR, FIGHTING BESIDE THE SKULL IN THE TRENCHES NEAR VERDUN.
VERDUN... I--

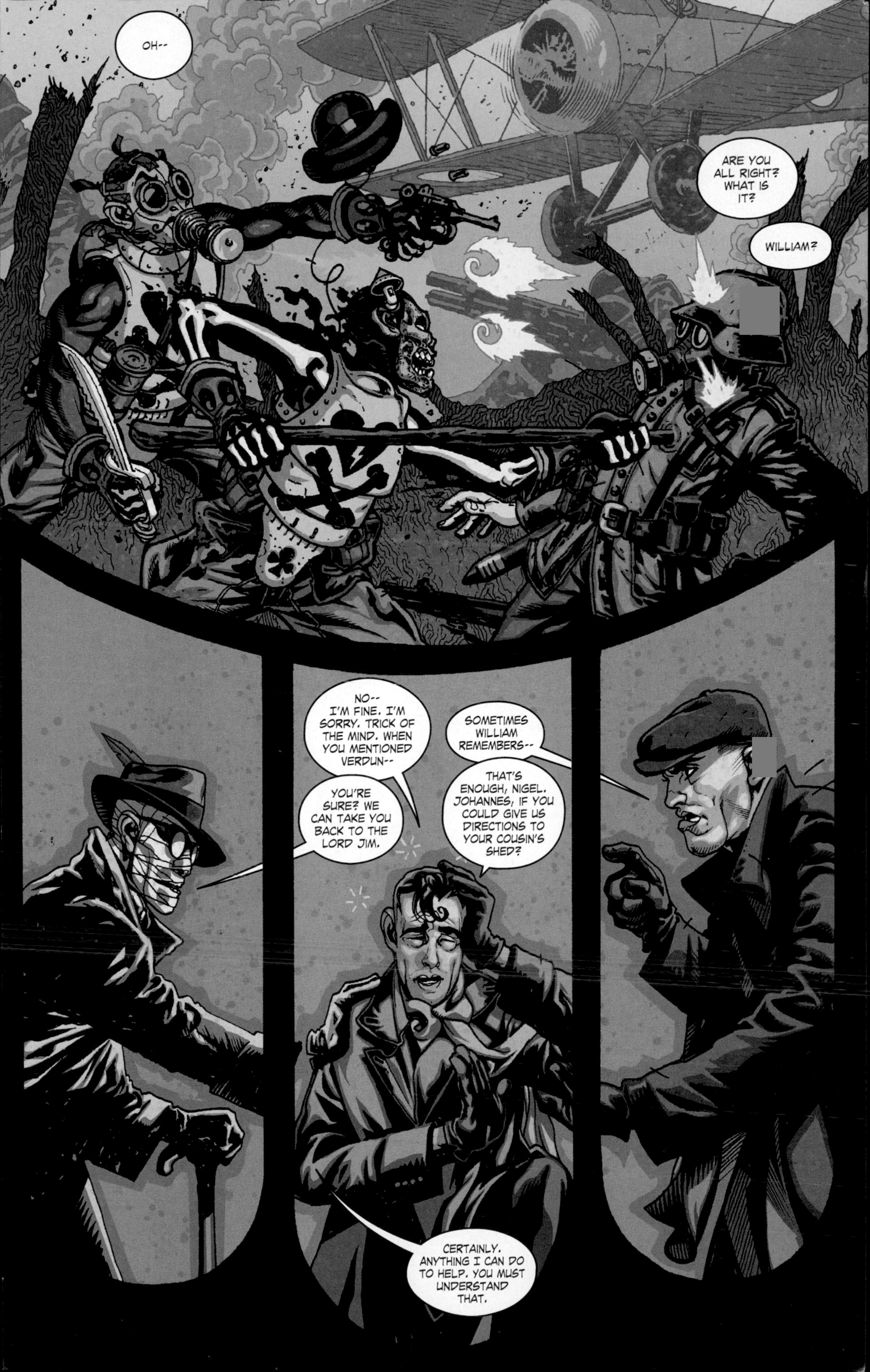
OH--
ARE YOU ALL RIGHT? WHAT IS IT?
WILLIAM?
NO-- I'M FINE. I'M SORRY. TRICK OF THE MIND. WHEN YOU MENTIONED VERDUN--
YOU'RE SURE? WE CAN TAKE YOU BACK TO THE LORD JIM.
SOMETIMES WILLIAM REMEMBERS--
THAT'S ENOUGH, NIGEL. JOHANNES, IF YOU COULD GIVE US DIRECTIONS TO YOUR COUSIN'S SHED?
CERTAINLY. ANYTHING I CAN DO TO HELP. YOU MUST UNDERSTAND THAT.

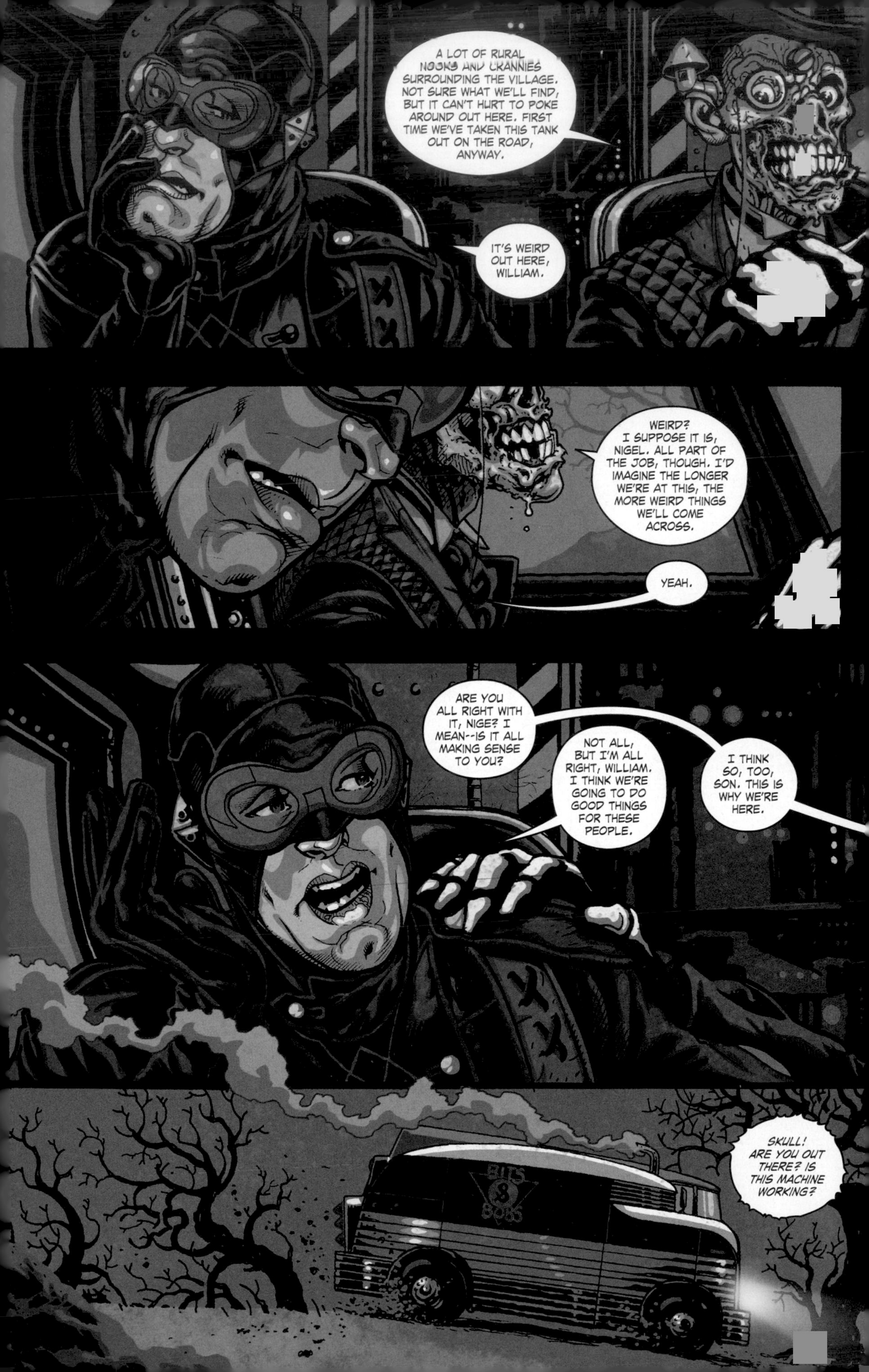
A LOT OF RURAL NOOKS AND CRANNIES SURROUNDING THE VILLAGE. NOT SURE WHAT WE'LL FIND, BUT IT CAN'T HURT TO POKE AROUND OUT HERE. FIRST TIME WE'VE TAKEN THIS TANK OUT ON THE ROAD, ANYWAY.
IT'S WEIRD OUT HERE, WILLIAM.
WEIRD? I SUPPOSE IT IS, NIGEL. ALL PART OF THE JOB, THOUGH. I'D IMAGINE THE LONGER WE'RE AT THIS, THE MORE WEIRD THINGS WE'LL COME ACROSS.
YEAH.
ARE YOU ALL RIGHT WITH IT, NIGE? I MEAN--IS IT ALL MAKING SENSE TO YOU?
NOT ALL, BUT I'M ALL RIGHT, WILLIAM. I THINK WE'RE GOING TO DO GOOD THINGS FOR THESE PEOPLE.
I THINK SO, TOO, SON. THIS IS WHY WE'RE HERE.
SKULL! ARE YOU OUT THERE? IS THIS MACHINE WORKING?

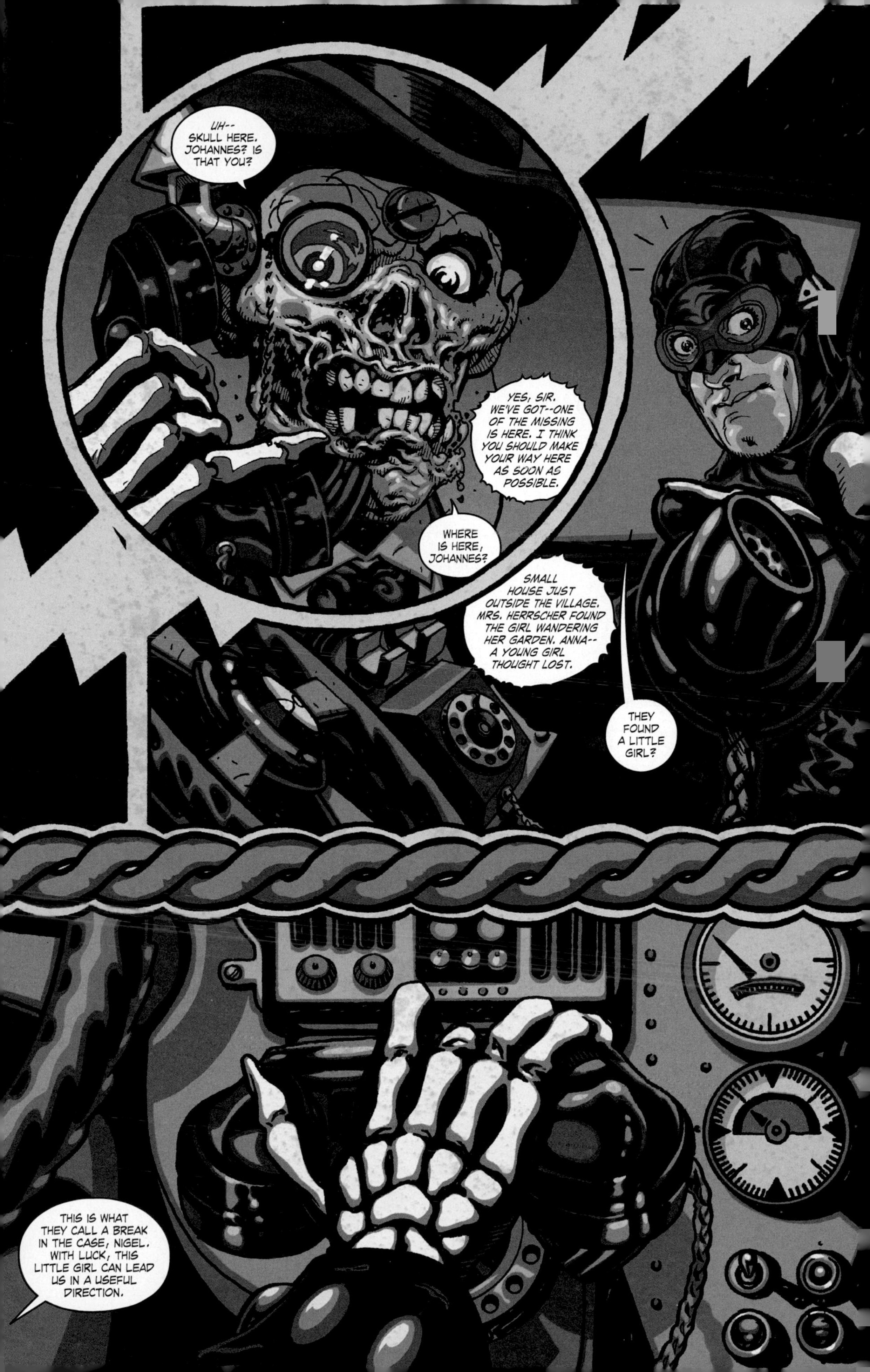
UH-- SKULL HERE. JOHANNES? IS THAT YOU?
YES, SIR. WE'VE GOT--ONE OF THE MISSING IS HERE. I THINK YOU SHOULD MAKE YOUR WAY HERE AS SOON AS POSSIBLE.
WHERE IS HERE, JOHANNES?
SMALL HOUSE JUST OUTSIDE THE VILLAGE. MRS. HERRSCHER FOUND THE GIRL WANDERING HER GARDEN. ANNA-- A YOUNG GIRL THOUGHT LOST.
THEY FOUND A LITTLE GIRL?
THIS IS WHAT THEY CALL A BREAK IN THE CASE, NIGEL. WITH LUCK, THIS LITTLE GIRL CAN LEAD US IN A USEFUL DIRECTION.

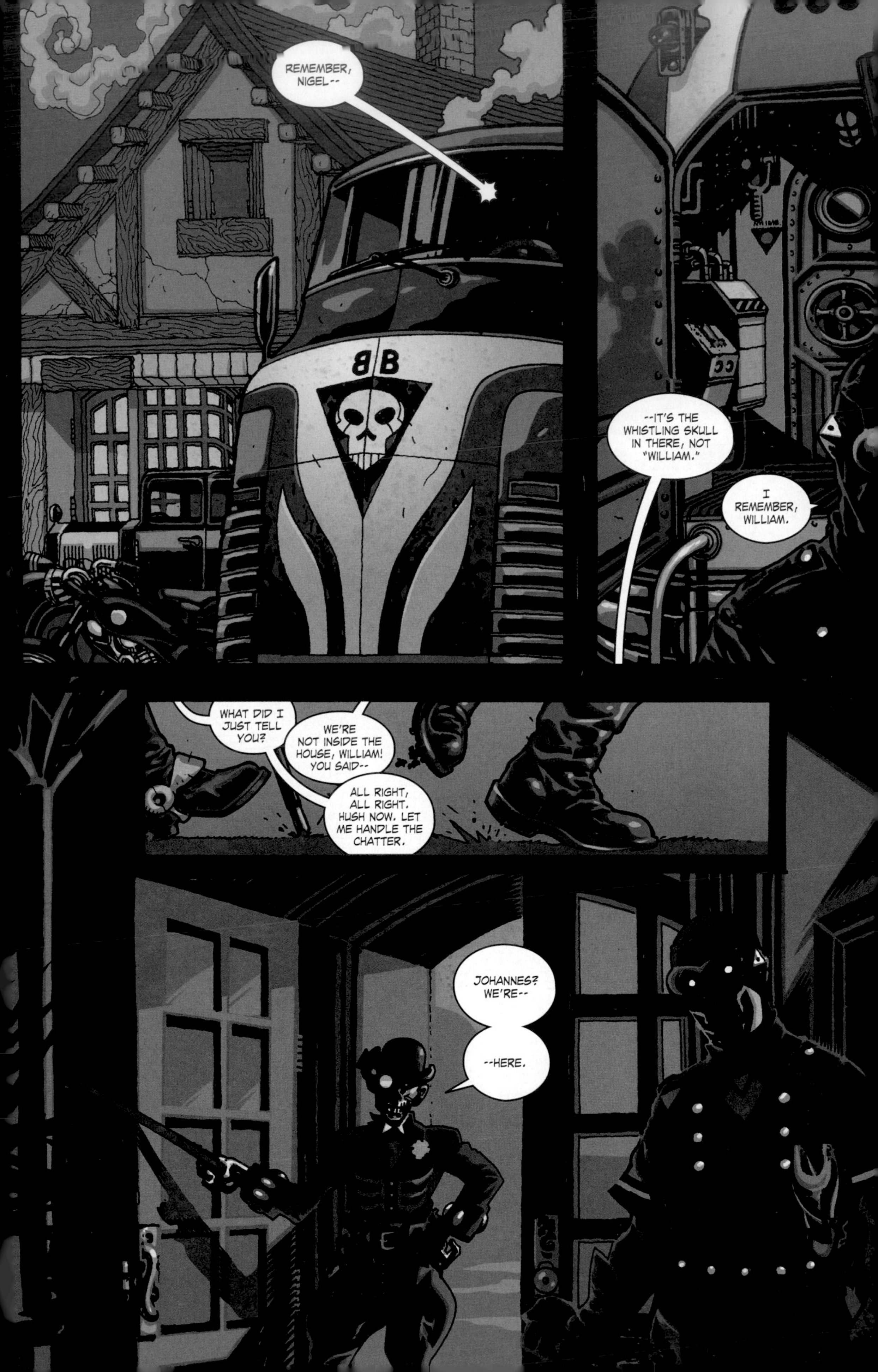
REMEMBER, NIGEL--
--IT'S THE WHISTLING SKULL IN THERE, NOT "WILLIAM."
I REMEMBER, WILLIAM.
WHAT DID I JUST TELL YOU?
WE'RE NOT INSIDE THE HOUSE, WILLIAM! YOU SAID--
ALL RIGHT, ALL RIGHT. HUSH NOW. LET ME HANDLE THE CHATTER.
JOHANNES? WE'RE--
--HERE.

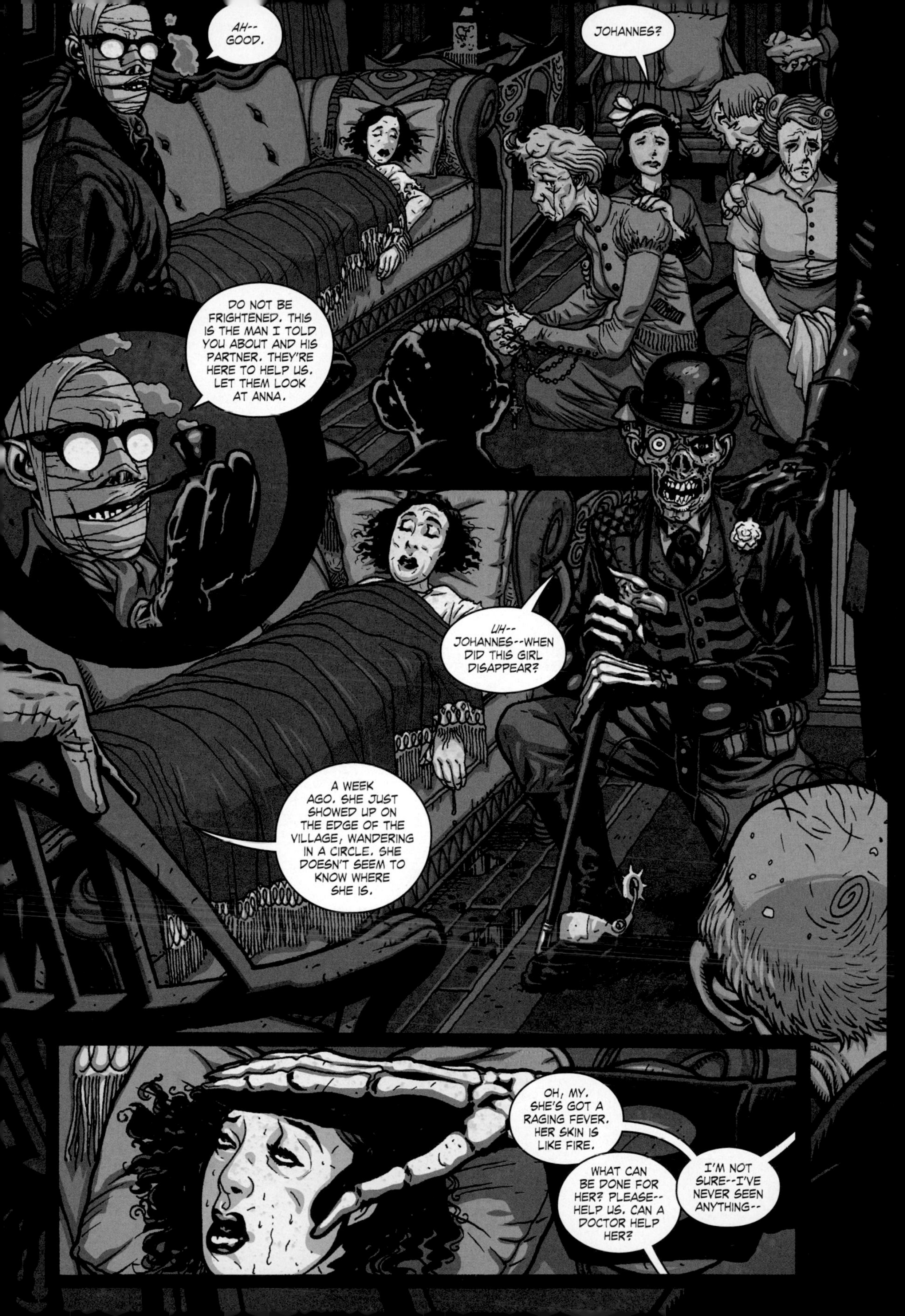
AH--
GOOD.
JOHANNES?
DO NOT BE FRIGHTENED. THIS IS THE MAN I TOLD YOU ABOUT AND HIS PARTNER. THEY'RE HERE TO HELP US. LET THEM LOOK AT ANNA.
UH--
JOHANNES--WHEN DID THIS GIRL DISAPPEAR?
A WEEK AGO. SHE JUST SHOWED UP ON THE EDGE OF THE VILLAGE, WANDERING IN A CIRCLE. SHE DOESN'T SEEM TO KNOW WHERE SHE IS.
OH, MY. SHE'S GOT A RAGING FEVER. HER SKIN IS LIKE FIRE.
WHAT CAN BE DONE FOR HER? PLEASE--HELP US. CAN A DOCTOR HELP HER?
I'M NOT SURE--I'VE NEVER SEEN ANYTHING--

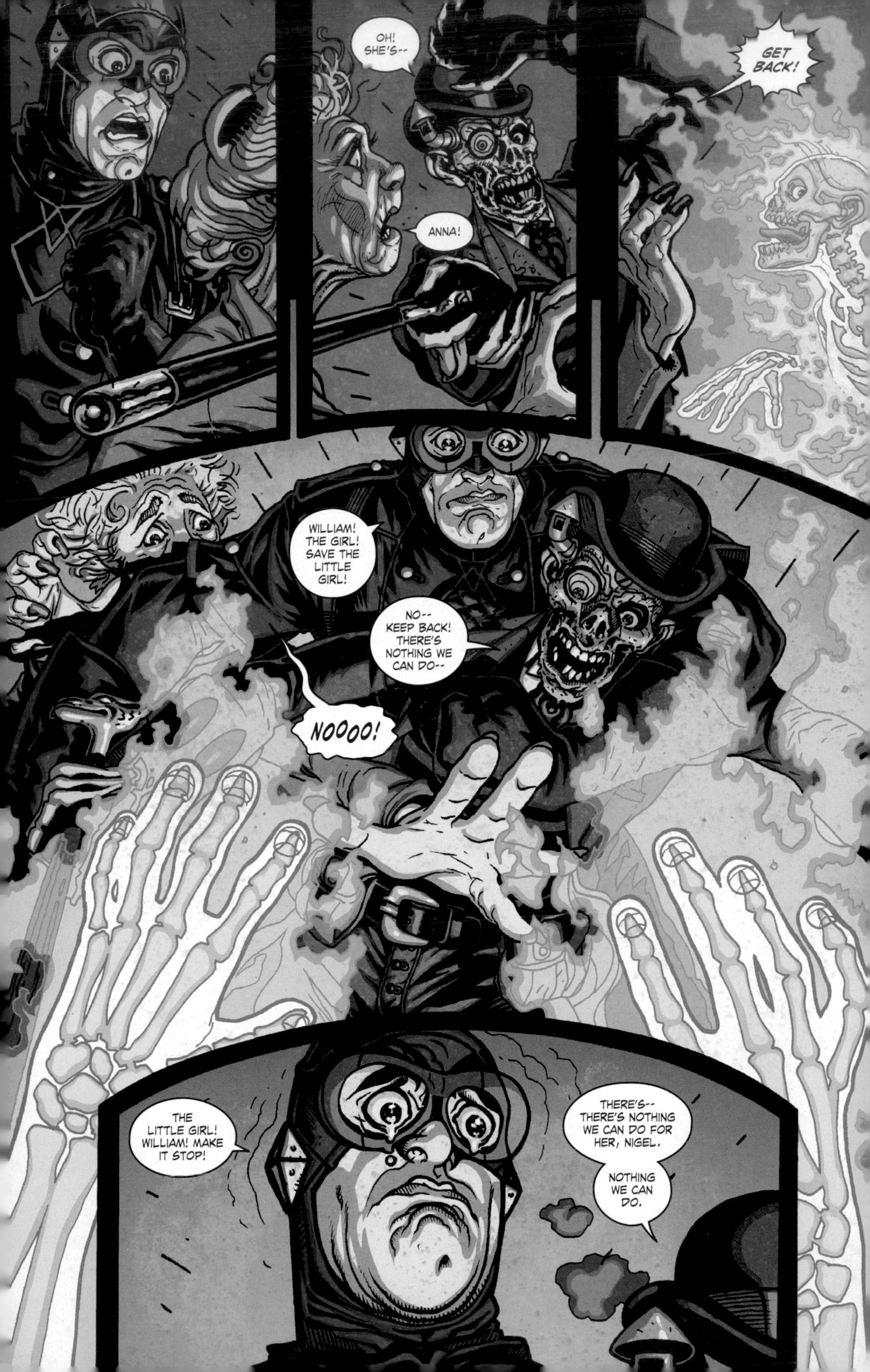
OH! SHE'S--
ANNA!
GET BACK!
WILLIAM! THE GIRL! SAVE THE LITTLE GIRL!
NO-- KEEP BACK! THERE'S NOTHING WE CAN DO--
NOOOO!
THE LITTLE GIRL! WILLIAM! MAKE IT STOP!
THERE'S-- THERE'S NOTHING WE CAN DO FOR HER, NIGEL.
NOTHING WE CAN DO.

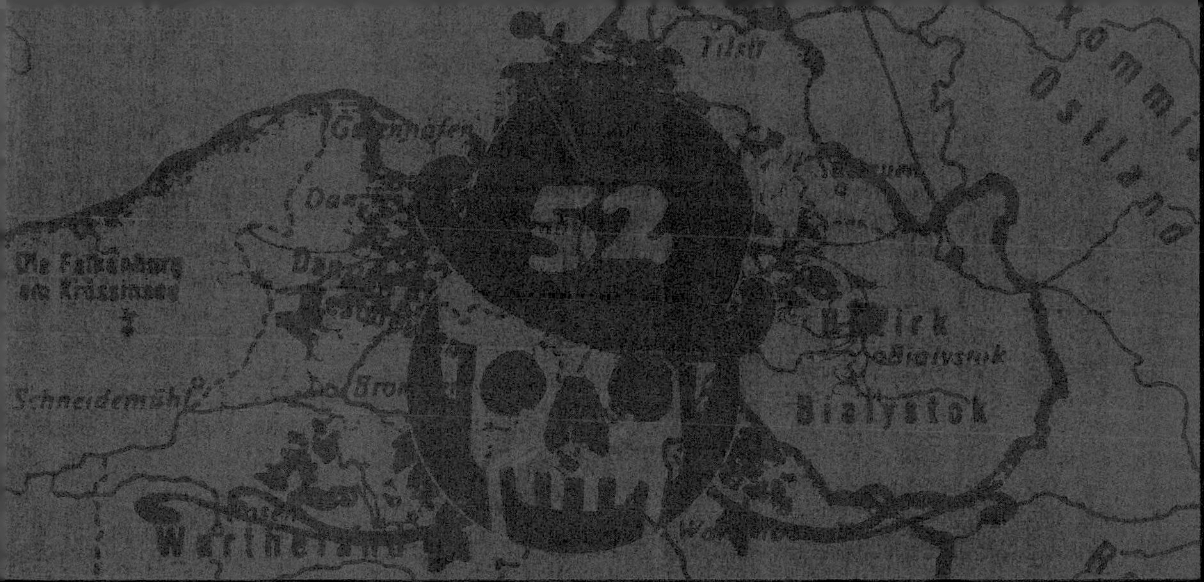
32
Schneidemühl
Bialystok

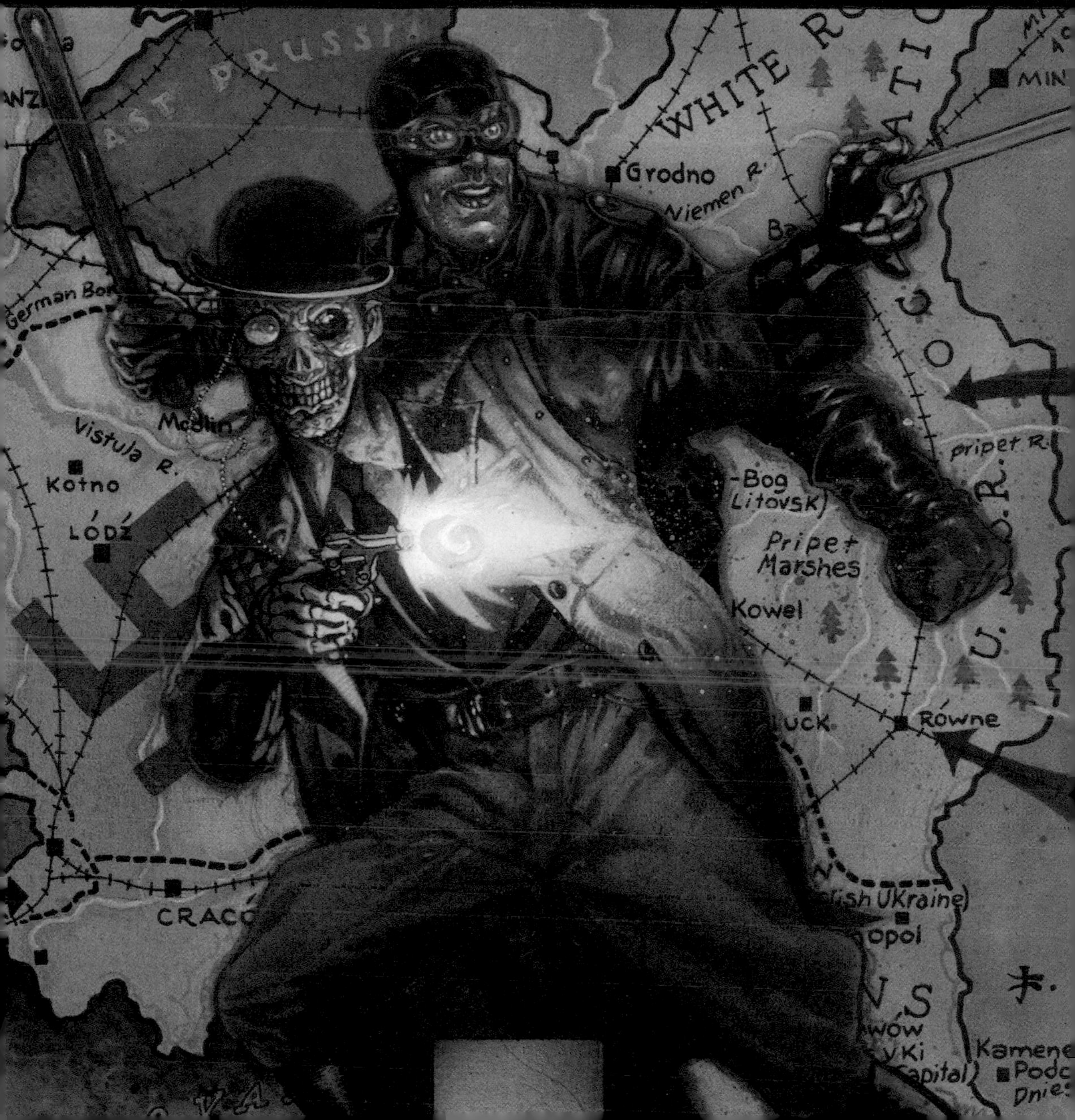
WHITE
Grodno
Niemen R.
Modlin
Vistula R.
Kotno
LÓDŹ
Pripet R.
Litovsk
Pripet Marshes
Kowel
Równe

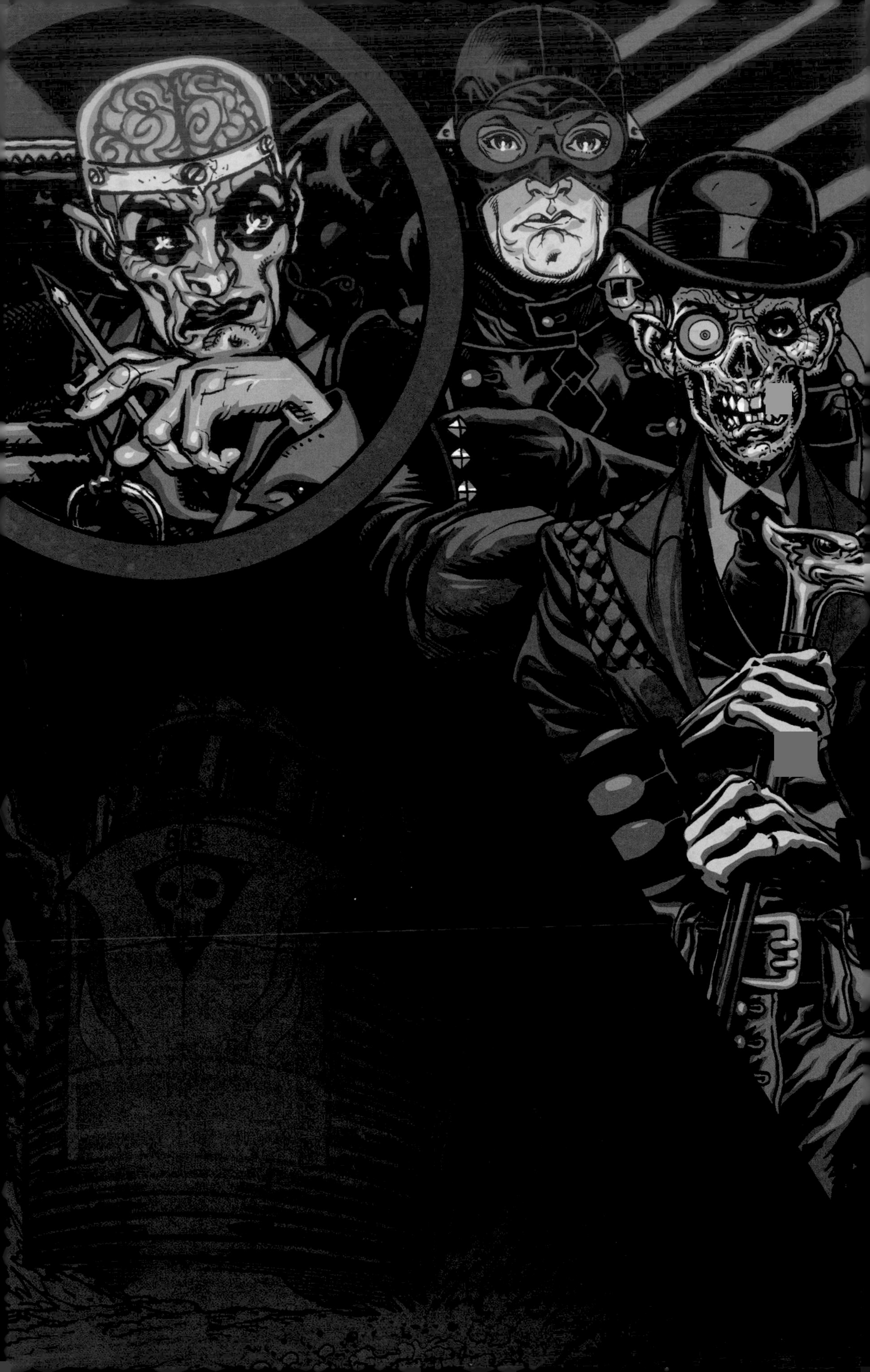

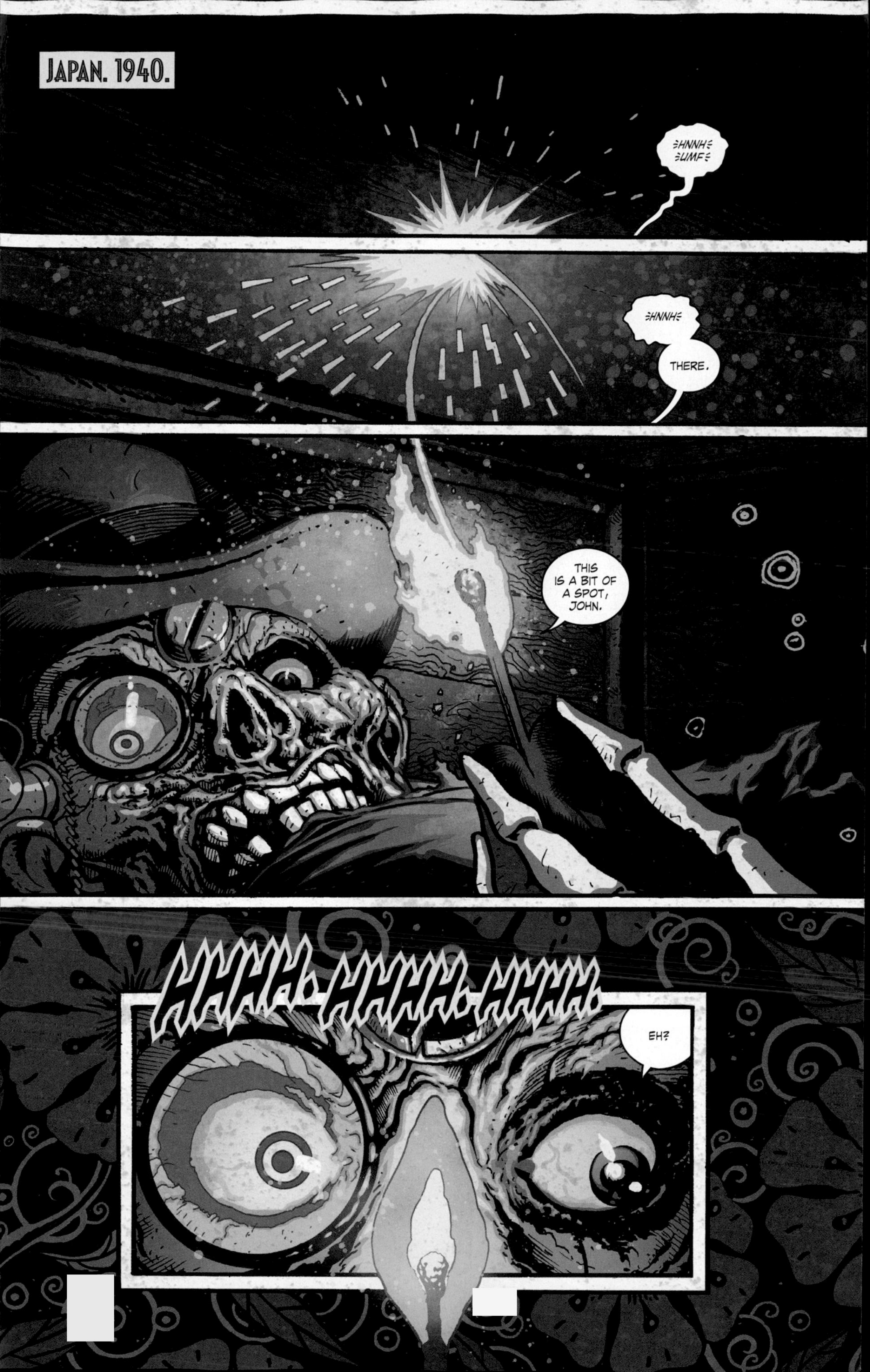
JAPAN. 1940.
HNNH UMF
HNNH
THERE.
THIS IS A BIT OF A SPOT, JOHN.
HHHH HHHH HHHH
EH?

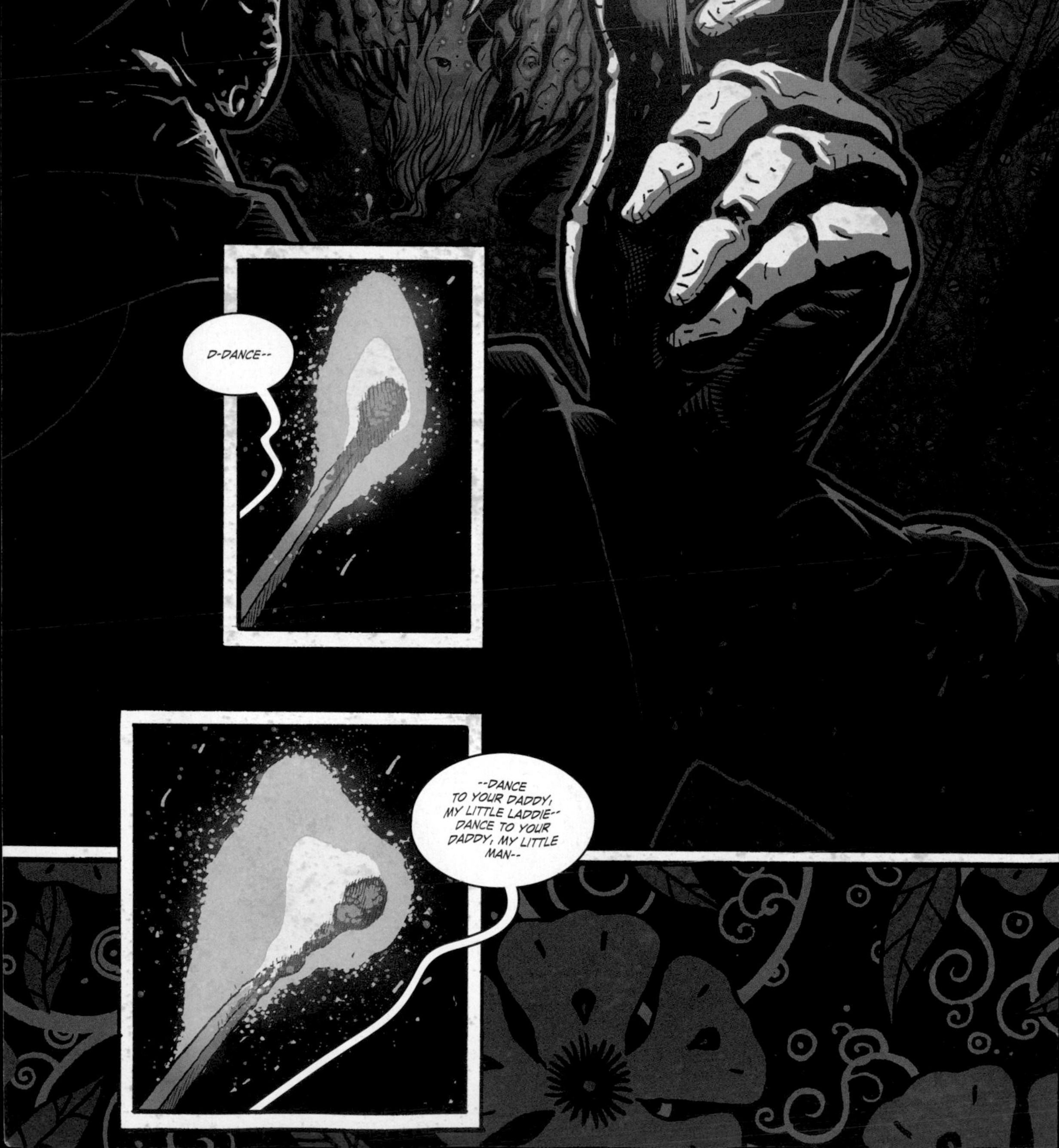
D-DANCE--
--DANCE TO YOUR DADDY, MY LITTLE LADDIE-- DANCE TO YOUR DADDY, MY LITTLE MAN--

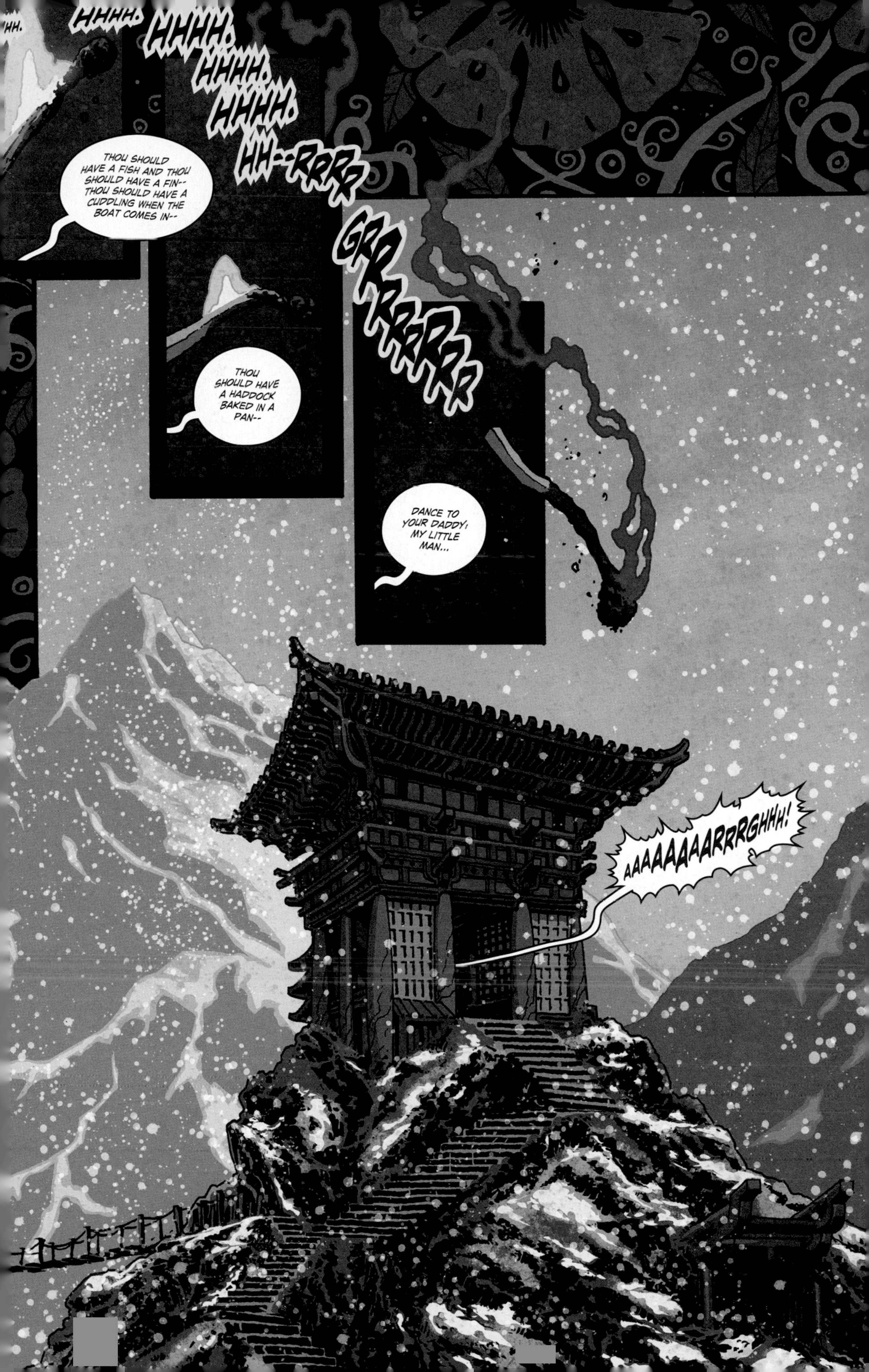
HH.
HHHH. HHHH.
HHHH.
HHHH.
HH--RRRR
THOU SHOULD HAVE A FISH AND THOU SHOULD HAVE A FIN-- THOU SHOULD HAVE A CUDDLING WHEN THE BOAT COMES IN--
THOU SHOULD HAVE A HADDOCK BAKED IN A PAN--
GRRRRRRRR
DANCE TO YOUR DADDY, MY LITTLE MAN...
AAAAAAAARRRGHHH!

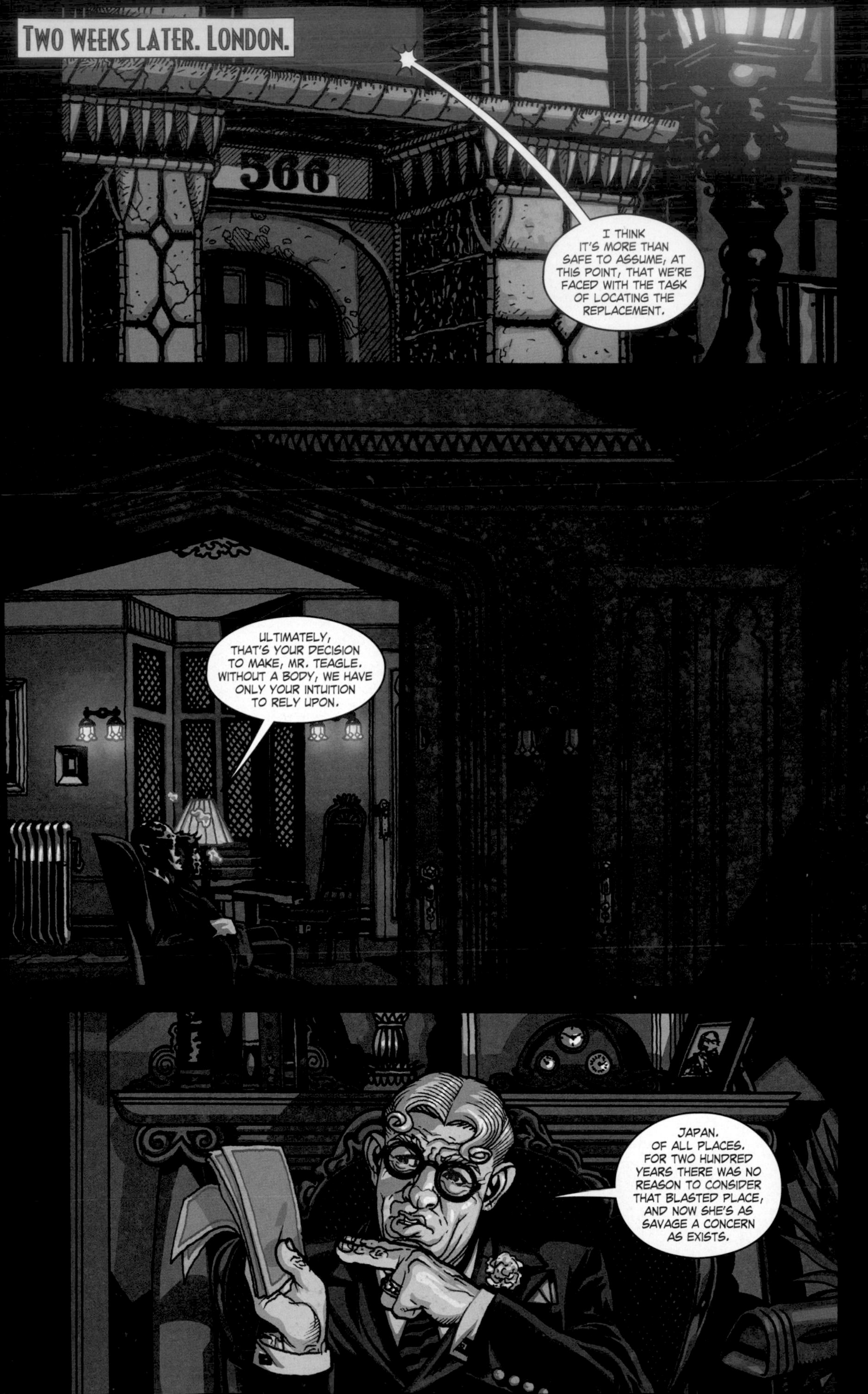
TWO WEEKS LATER. LONDON.
566
I THINK IT'S MORE THAN SAFE TO ASSUME, AT THIS POINT, THAT WE'RE FACED WITH THE TASK OF LOCATING THE REPLACEMENT.
ULTIMATELY, THAT'S YOUR DECISION TO MAKE, MR. TEAGLE. WITHOUT A BODY, WE HAVE ONLY YOUR INTUITION TO RELY UPON.
JAPAN. OF ALL PLACES. FOR TWO HUNDRED YEARS THERE WAS NO REASON TO CONSIDER THAT BLASTED PLACE, AND NOW SHE'S AS SAVAGE A CONCERN AS EXISTS.

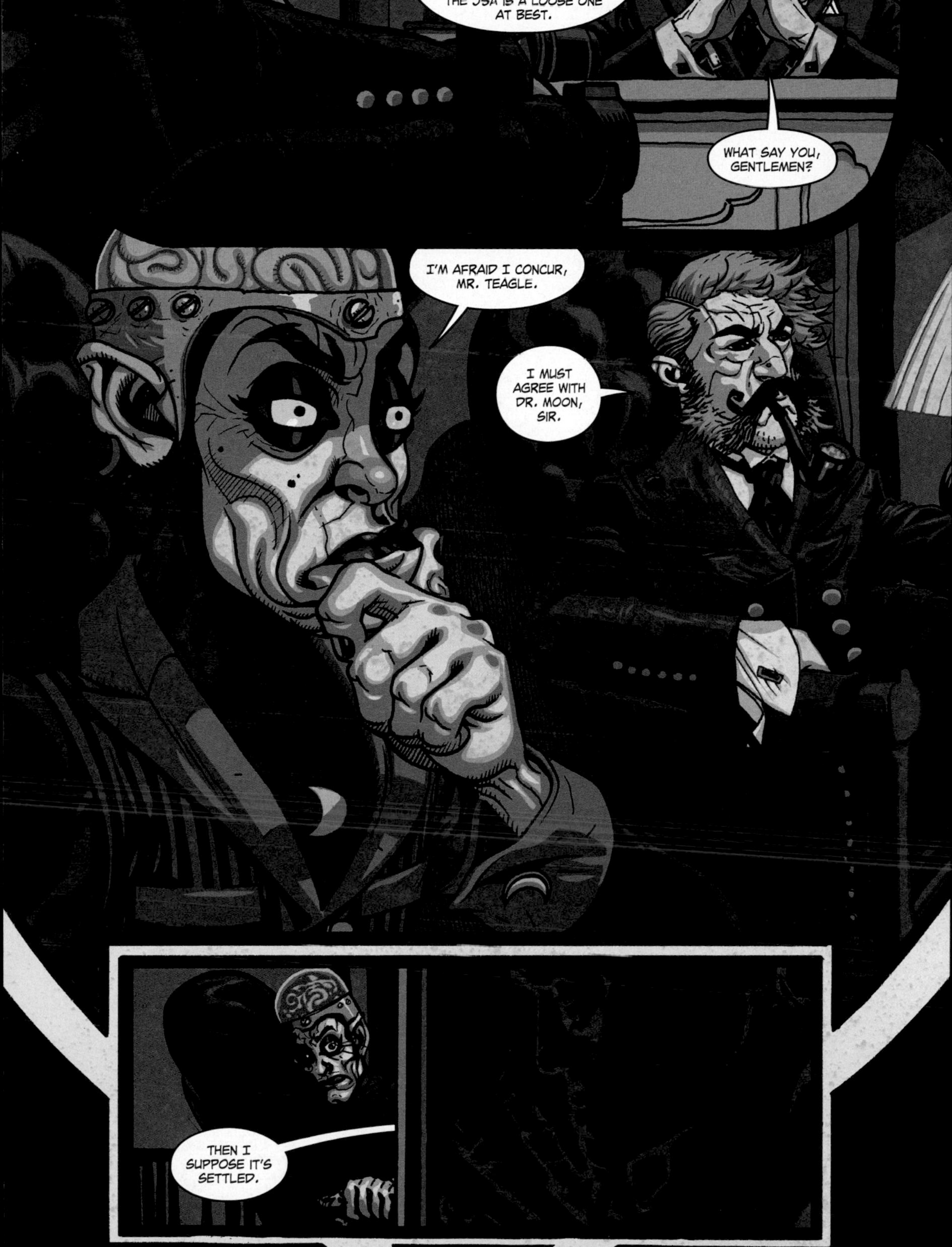
THE JSA IS A LOOSE ONE AT BEST.
WHAT SAY YOU, GENTLEMEN?
I'M AFRAID I CONCUR, MR. TEAGLE.
I MUST AGREE WITH DR. MOON, SIR.
THEN I SUPPOSE IT'S SETTLED.

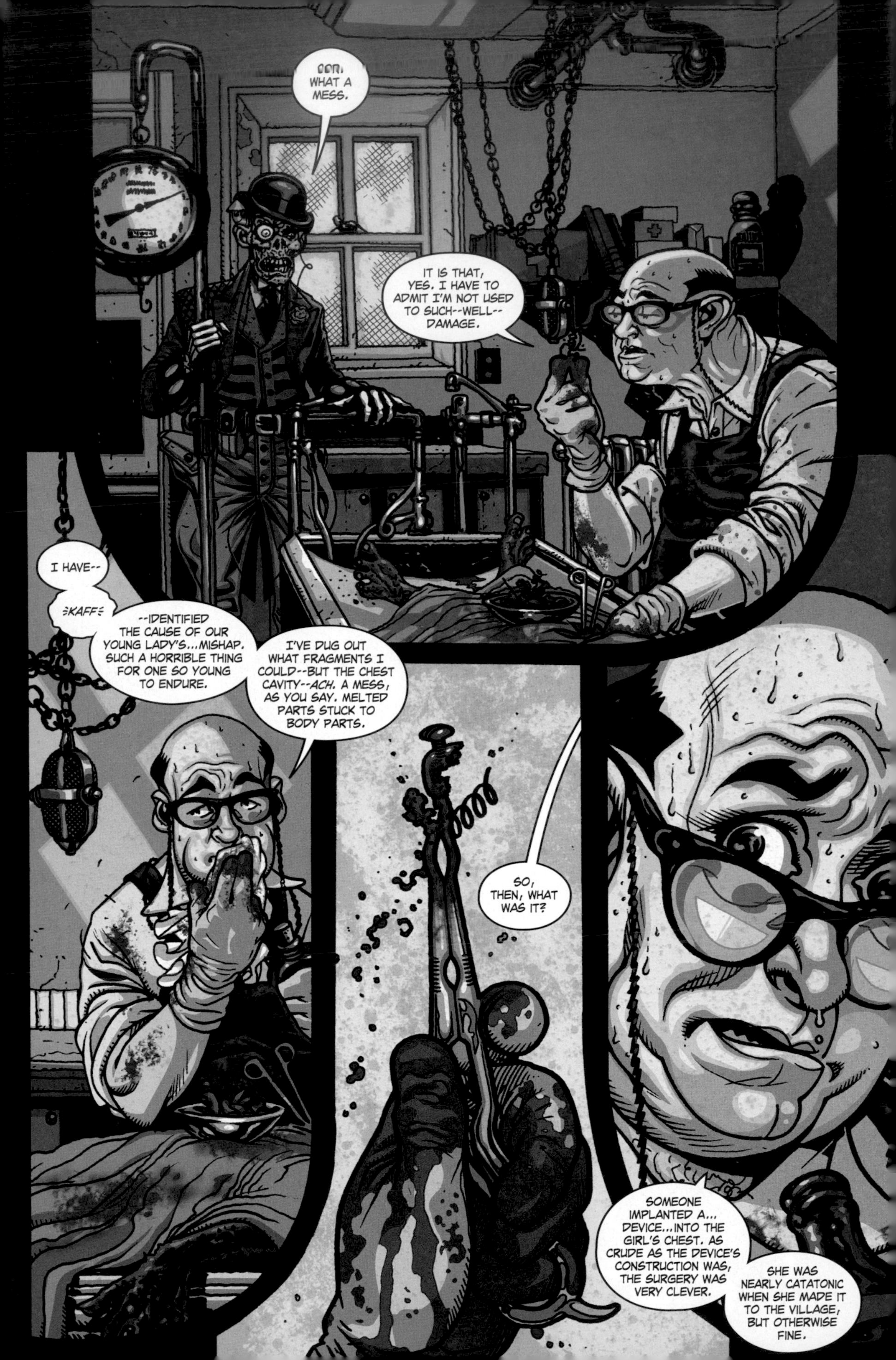

OOH. WHAT A MESS.
IT IS THAT, YES. I HAVE TO ADMIT I'M NOT USED TO SUCH--WELL--DAMAGE.
I HAVE--
KAFF
--IDENTIFIED THE CAUSE OF OUR YOUNG LADY'S...MISHAP. SUCH A HORRIBLE THING FOR ONE SO YOUNG TO ENDURE.
I'VE DUG OUT WHAT FRAGMENTS I COULD--BUT THE CHEST CAVITY--*ACH.* A MESS, AS YOU SAY. MELTED PARTS STUCK TO BODY PARTS.
SO, THEN, WHAT WAS IT?
SOMEONE IMPLANTED A... DEVICE...INTO THE GIRL'S CHEST. AS CRUDE AS THE DEVICE'S CONSTRUCTION WAS, THE SURGERY WAS VERY CLEVER.
SHE WAS NEARLY CATATONIC WHEN SHE MADE IT TO THE VILLAGE, BUT OTHERWISE FINE.

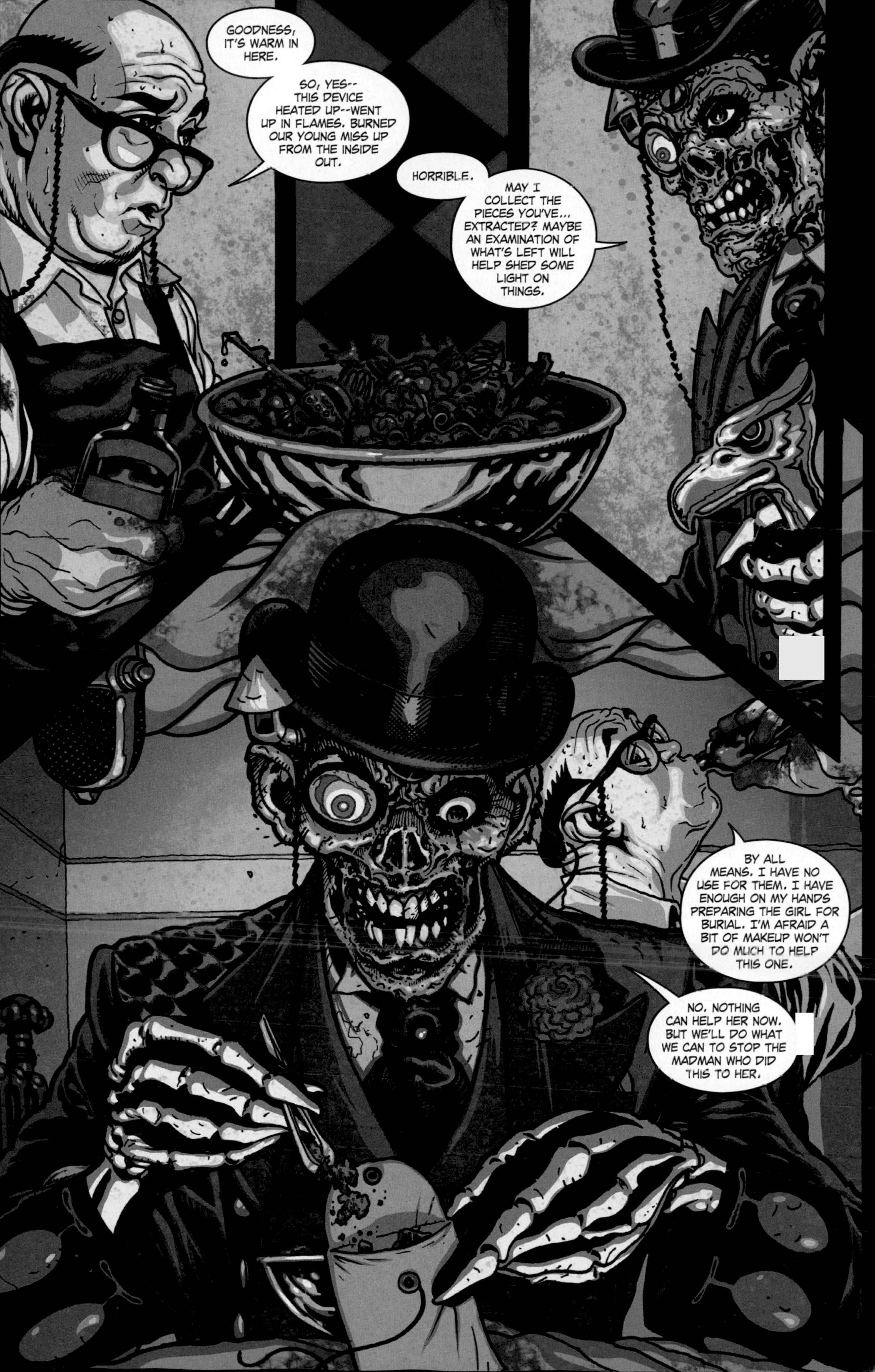
GOODNESS, IT'S WARM IN HERE.
SO, YES-- THIS DEVICE HEATED UP--WENT UP IN FLAMES. BURNED OUR YOUNG MISS UP FROM THE INSIDE OUT.
HORRIBLE.
MAY I COLLECT THE PIECES YOU'VE... EXTRACTED? MAYBE AN EXAMINATION OF WHAT'S LEFT WILL HELP SHED SOME LIGHT ON THINGS.
BY ALL MEANS. I HAVE NO USE FOR THEM. I HAVE ENOUGH ON MY HANDS PREPARING THE GIRL FOR BURIAL. I'M AFRAID A BIT OF MAKEUP WON'T DO MUCH TO HELP THIS ONE.
NO. NOTHING CAN HELP HER NOW. BUT WE'LL DO WHAT WE CAN TO STOP THE MADMAN WHO DID THIS TO HER.

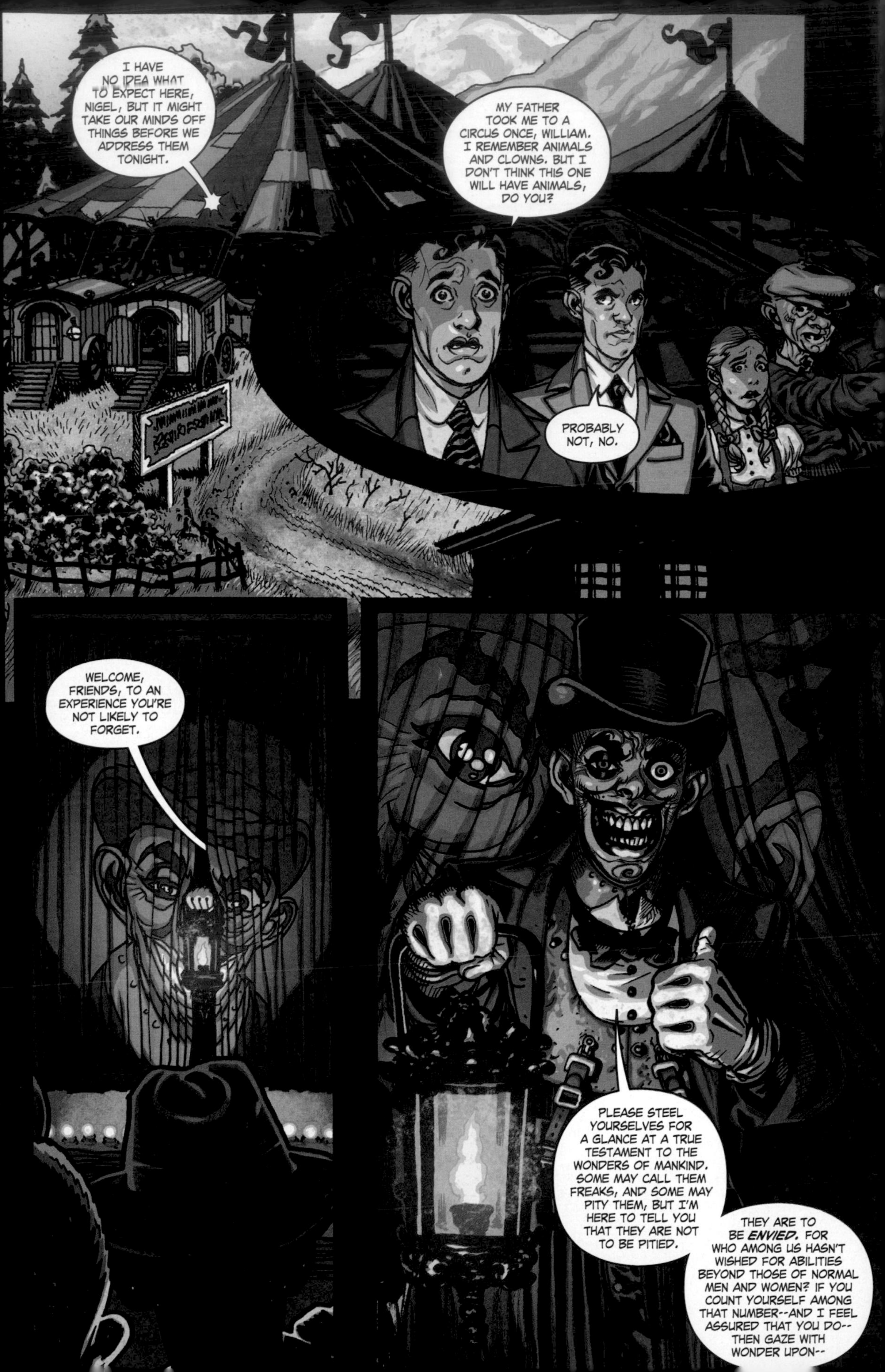
I HAVE NO IDEA WHAT TO EXPECT HERE, NIGEL, BUT IT MIGHT TAKE OUR MINDS OFF THINGS BEFORE WE ADDRESS THEM TONIGHT.
MY FATHER TOOK ME TO A CIRCUS ONCE, WILLIAM. I REMEMBER ANIMALS AND CLOWNS. BUT I DON'T THINK THIS ONE WILL HAVE ANIMALS, DO YOU?
PROBABLY NOT, NO.
WELCOME, FRIENDS, TO AN EXPERIENCE YOU'RE NOT LIKELY TO FORGET.
PLEASE STEEL YOURSELVES FOR A GLANCE AT A TRUE TESTAMENT TO THE WONDERS OF MANKIND. SOME MAY CALL THEM FREAKS, AND SOME MAY PITY THEM, BUT I'M HERE TO TELL YOU THAT THEY ARE NOT TO BE PITIED.
THEY ARE TO BE ENVIED. FOR WHO AMONG US HASN'T WISHED FOR ABILITIES BEYOND THOSE OF NORMAL MEN AND WOMEN? IF YOU COUNT YOURSELF AMONG THAT NUMBER--AND I FEEL ASSURED THAT YOU DO--THEN GAZE WITH WONDER UPON--

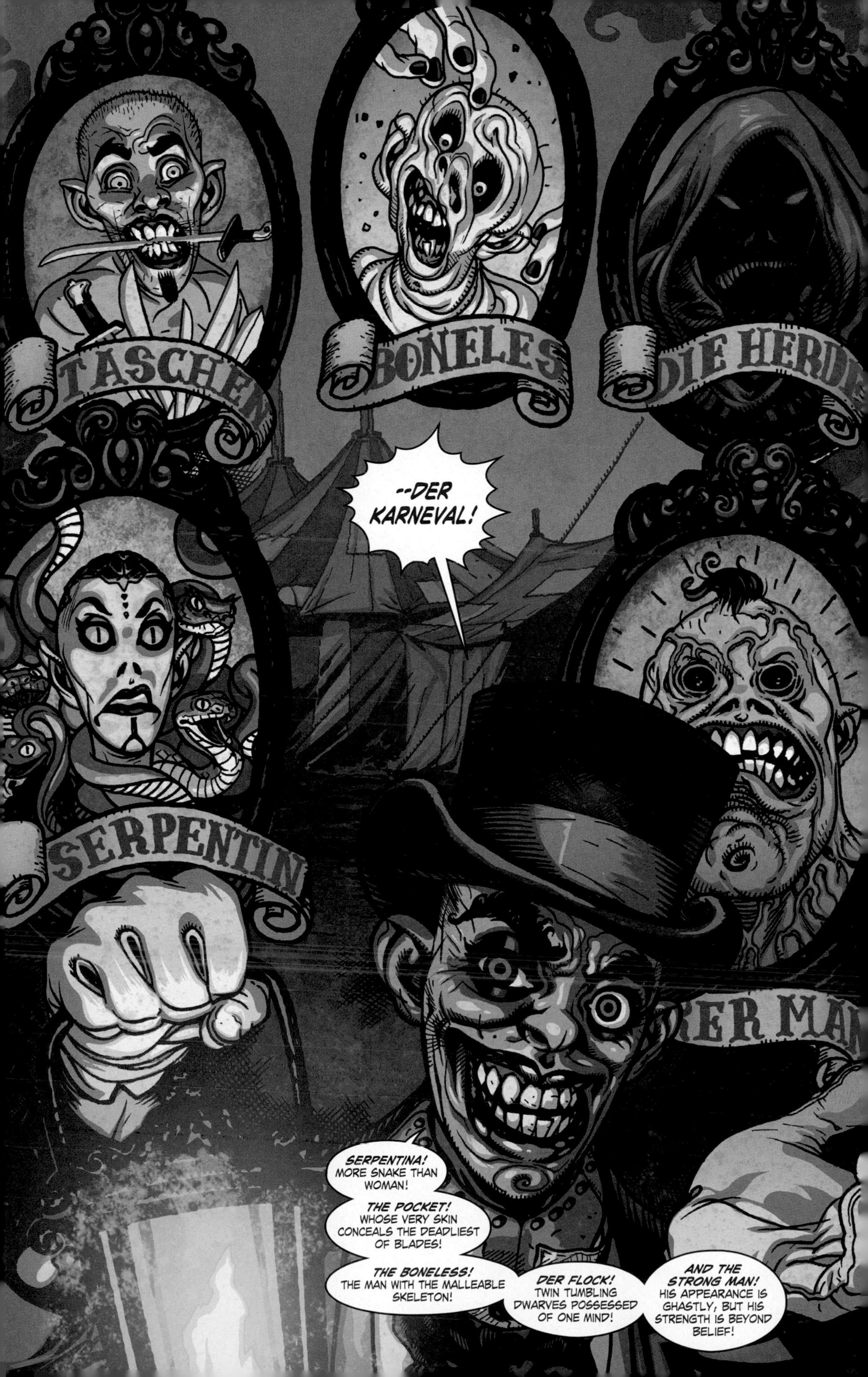
TASCHEN
BONELES
DIE HERDE
--DER KARNEVAL!
SERPENTIN
RER MAN
SERPENTINA! MORE SNAKE THAN WOMAN!
THE POCKET! WHOSE VERY SKIN CONCEALS THE DEADLIEST OF BLADES!
THE BONELESS! THE MAN WITH THE MALLEABLE SKELETON!
DER FLOCK! TWIN TUMBLING DWARVES POSSESSED OF ONE MIND!
AND THE STRONG MAN! HIS APPEARANCE IS GHASTLY, BUT HIS STRENGTH IS BEYOND BELIEF!

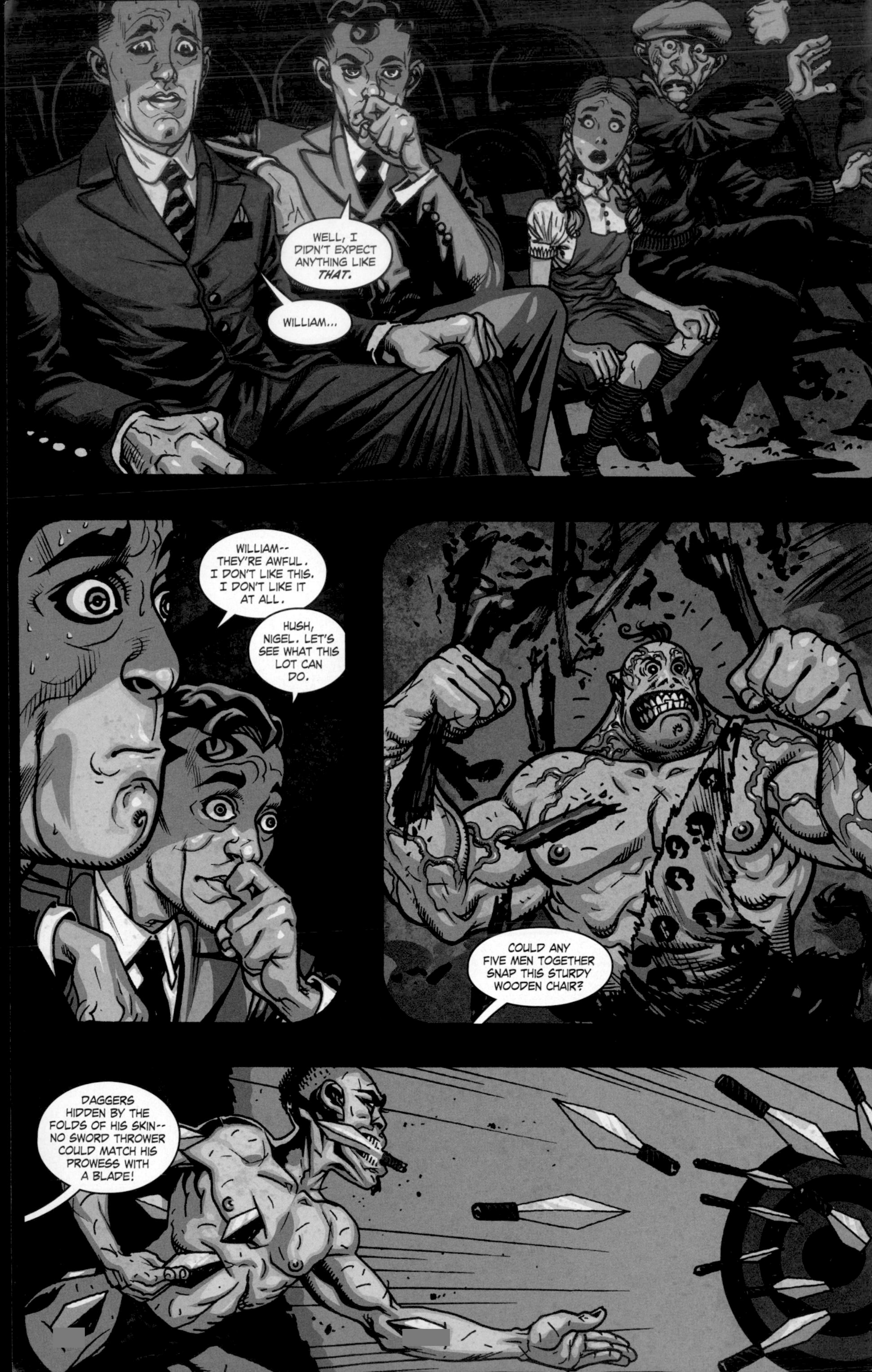
WELL, I DIDN'T EXPECT ANYTHING LIKE *THAT*.
WILLIAM...
WILLIAM-- THEY'RE AWFUL. I DON'T LIKE THIS. I DON'T LIKE IT AT ALL.
HUSH, NIGEL. LET'S SEE WHAT THIS LOT CAN DO.
COULD ANY FIVE MEN TOGETHER SNAP THIS STURDY WOODEN CHAIR?
DAGGERS HIDDEN BY THE FOLDS OF HIS SKIN-- NO SWORD THROWER COULD MATCH HIS PROWESS WITH A BLADE!

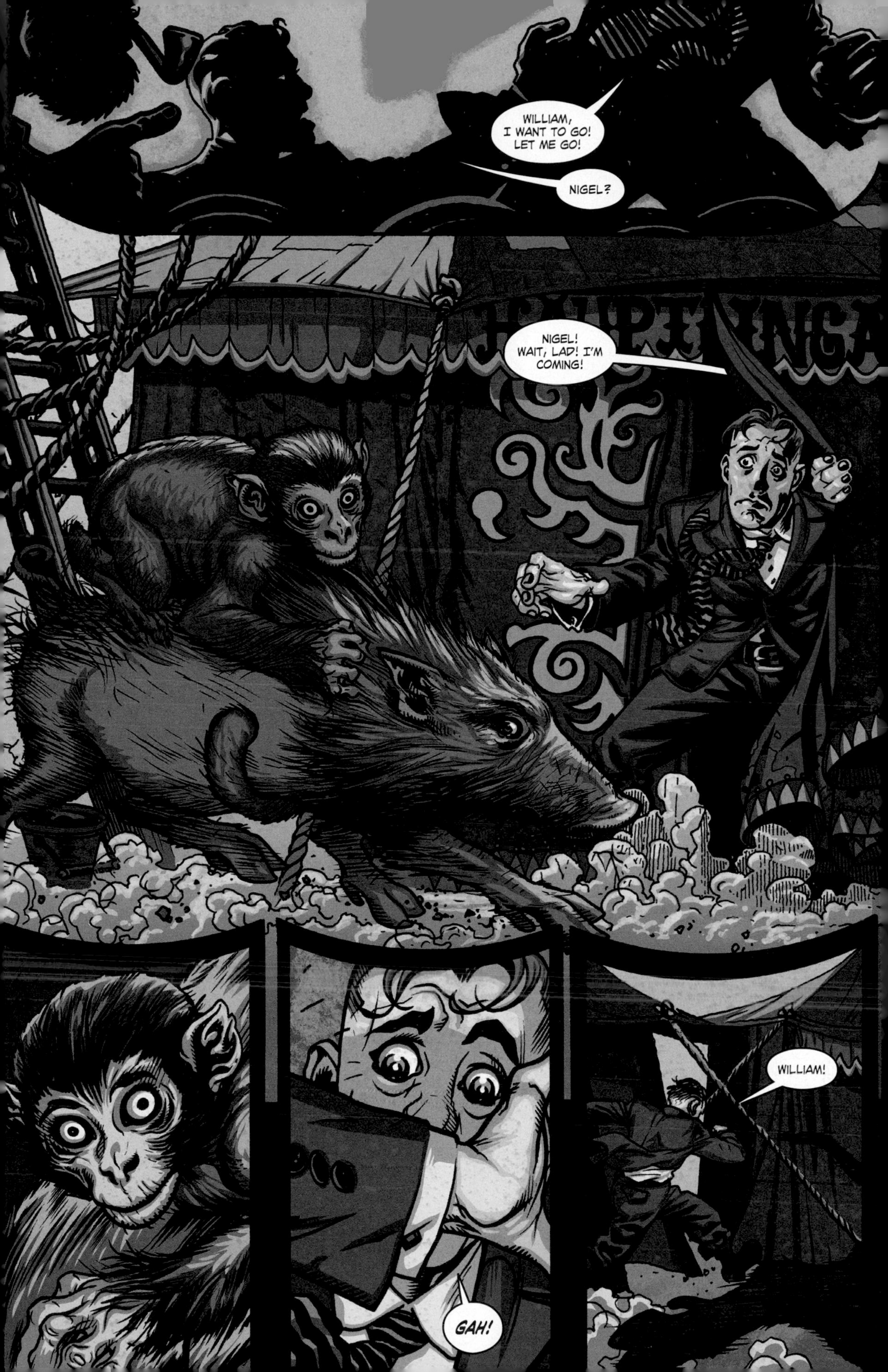
WILLIAM, I WANT TO GO! LET ME GO!
NIGEL?
NIGEL! WAIT, LAD! I'M COMING!
GAH!
WILLIAM!

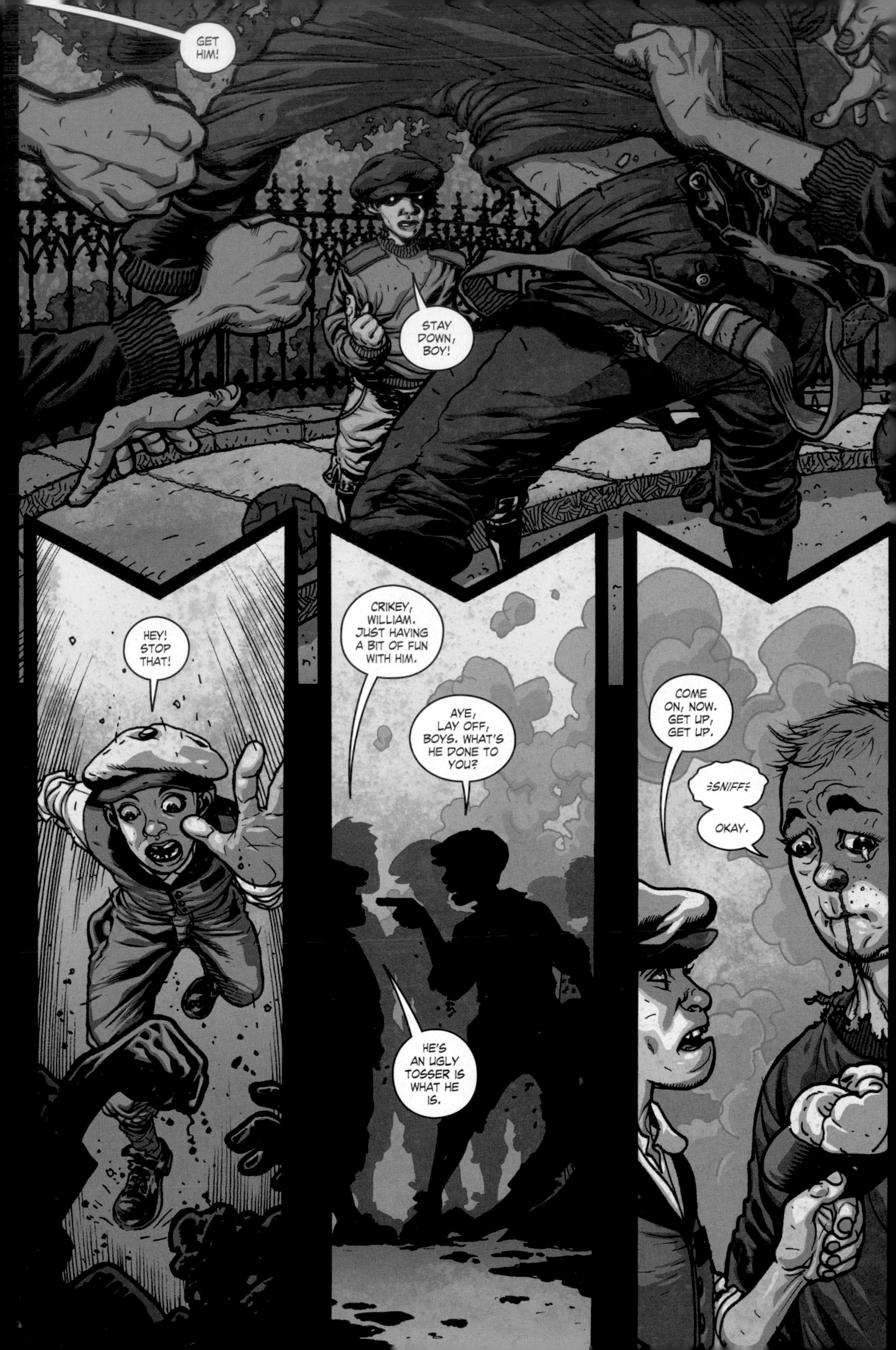
GET HIM!
STAY DOWN, BOY!
HEY! STOP THAT!
CRIKEY, WILLIAM. JUST HAVING A BIT OF FUN WITH HIM.
AYE, LAY OFF, BOYS. WHAT'S HE DONE TO YOU?
HE'S AN UGLY TOSSER IS WHAT HE IS.
COME ON, NOW. GET UP, GET UP.
SNIFF
OKAY.

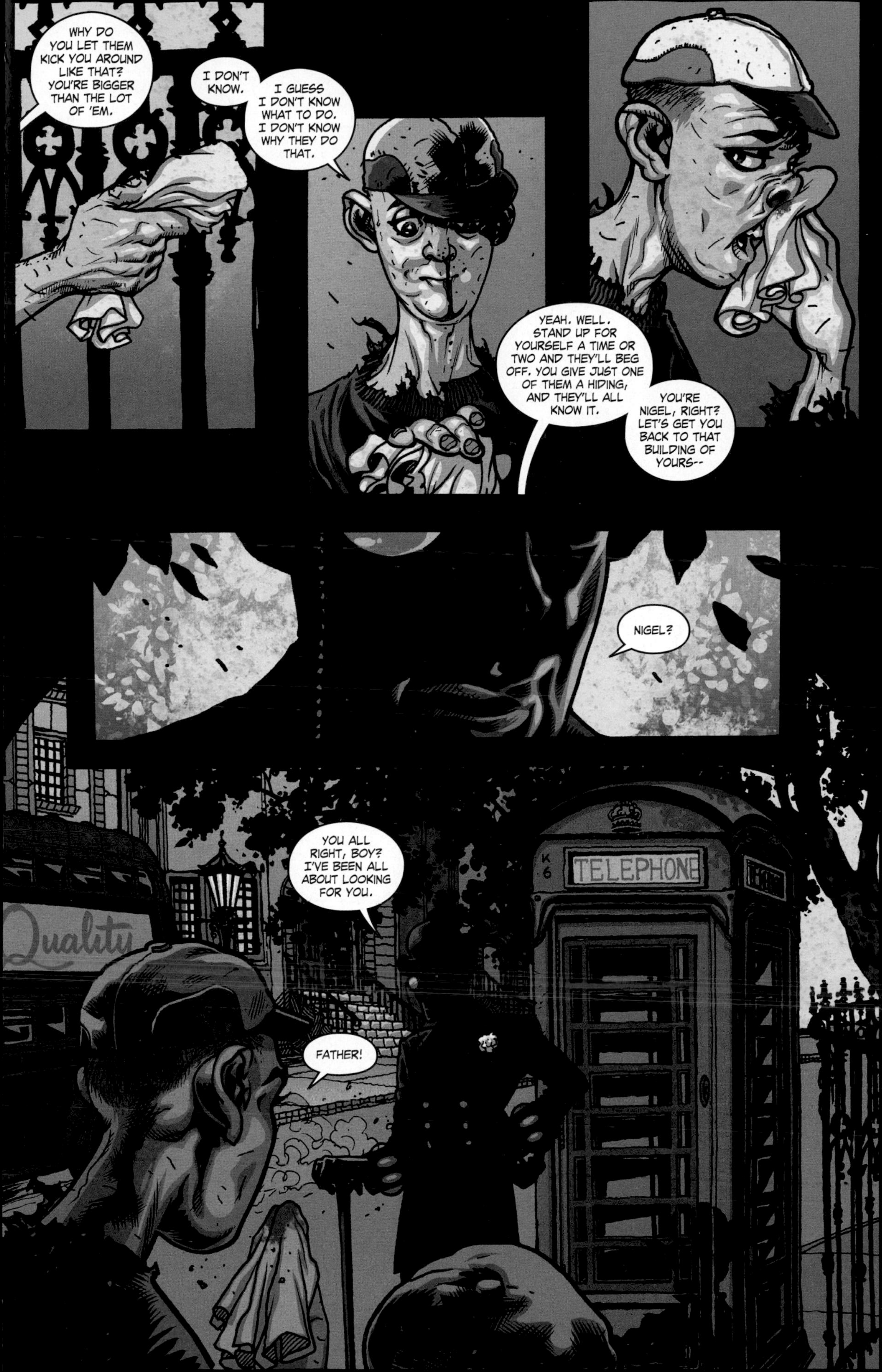
WHY DO YOU LET THEM KICK YOU AROUND LIKE THAT? YOU'RE BIGGER THAN THE LOT OF 'EM.
I DON'T KNOW.
I GUESS I DON'T KNOW WHAT TO DO. I DON'T KNOW WHY THEY DO THAT.
YEAH. WELL. STAND UP FOR YOURSELF A TIME OR TWO AND THEY'LL BEG OFF. YOU GIVE JUST ONE OF THEM A HIDING, AND THEY'LL ALL KNOW IT.
YOU'RE NIGEL, RIGHT? LET'S GET YOU BACK TO THAT BUILDING OF YOURS--
NIGEL?
Quality
YOU ALL RIGHT, BOY? I'VE BEEN ALL ABOUT LOOKING FOR YOU.
K 6
TELEPHONE
FATHER!

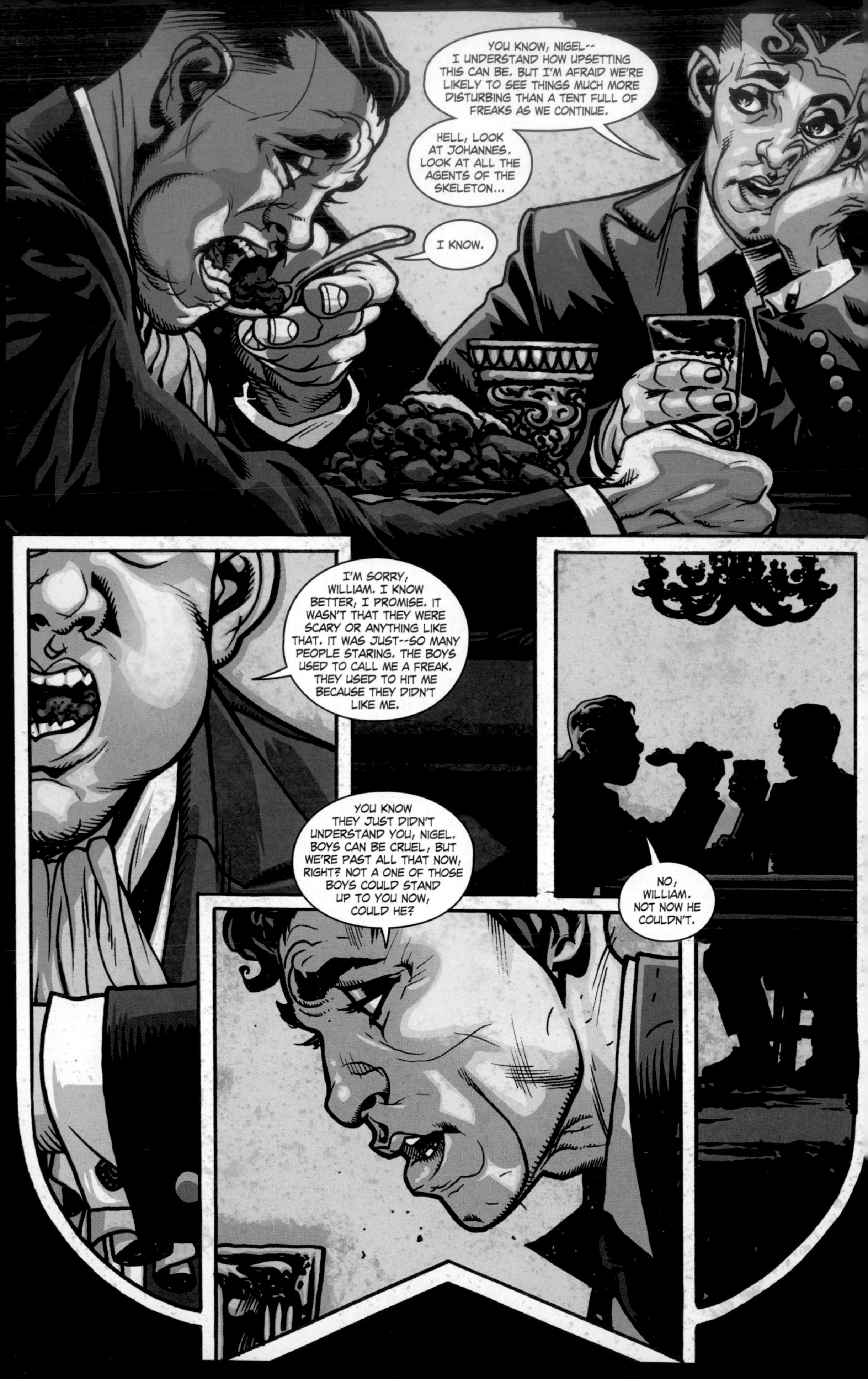
YOU KNOW, NIGEL-- I UNDERSTAND HOW UPSETTING THIS CAN BE. BUT I'M AFRAID WE'RE LIKELY TO SEE THINGS MUCH MORE DISTURBING THAN A TENT FULL OF FREAKS AS WE CONTINUE.
HELL, LOOK AT JOHANNES. LOOK AT ALL THE AGENTS OF THE SKELETON...
I KNOW.
I'M SORRY, WILLIAM. I KNOW BETTER, I PROMISE. IT WASN'T THAT THEY WERE SCARY OR ANYTHING LIKE THAT. IT WAS JUST--SO MANY PEOPLE STARING. THE BOYS USED TO CALL ME A FREAK. THEY USED TO HIT ME BECAUSE THEY DIDN'T LIKE ME.
YOU KNOW THEY JUST DIDN'T UNDERSTAND YOU, NIGEL. BOYS CAN BE CRUEL, BUT WE'RE PAST ALL THAT NOW, RIGHT? NOT A ONE OF THOSE BOYS COULD STAND UP TO YOU NOW, COULD HE?
NO, WILLIAM. NOT NOW HE COULDN'T.

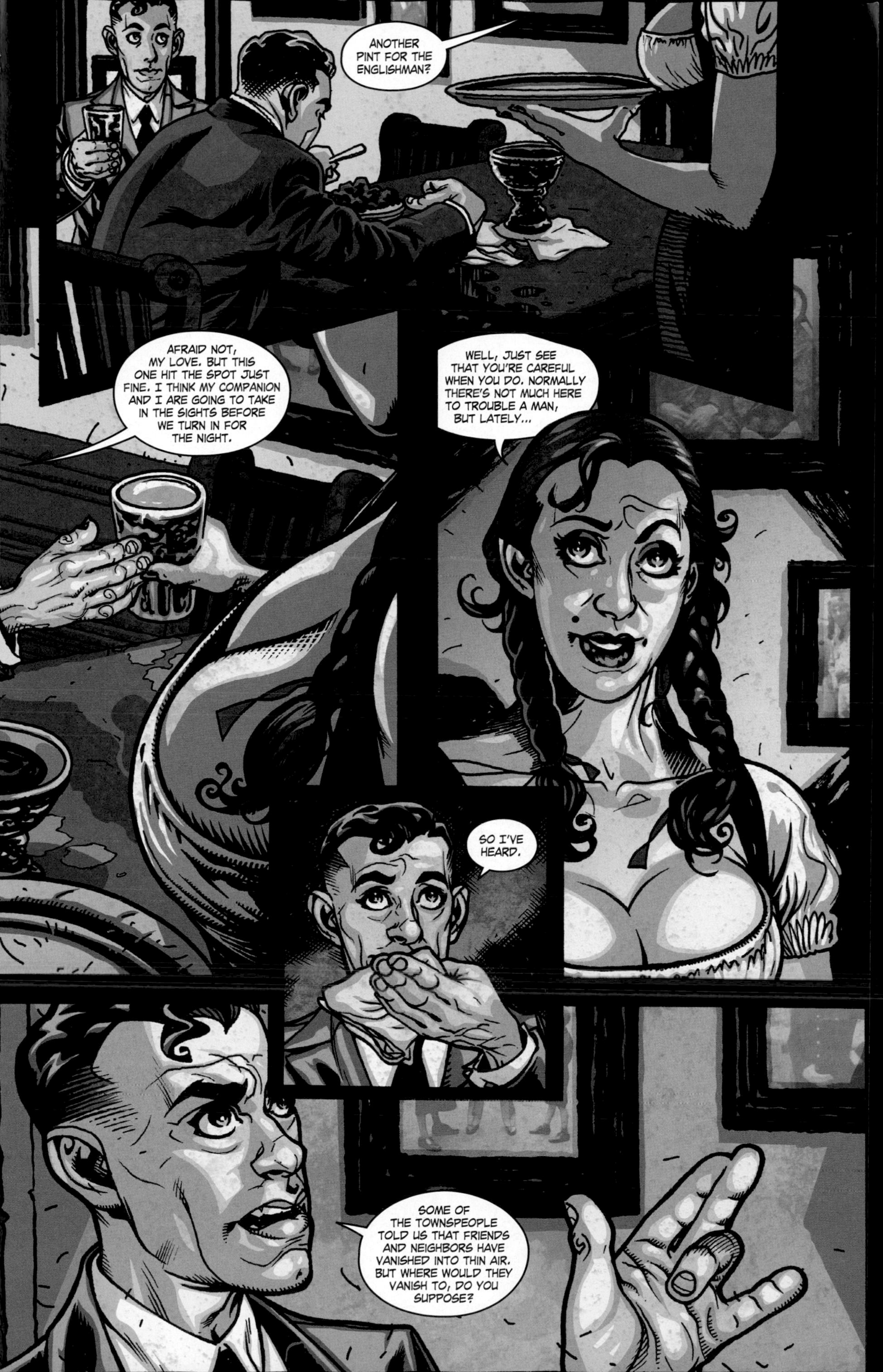
ANOTHER PINT FOR THE ENGLISHMAN?
AFRAID NOT, MY LOVE. BUT THIS ONE HIT THE SPOT JUST FINE. I THINK MY COMPANION AND I ARE GOING TO TAKE IN THE SIGHTS BEFORE WE TURN IN FOR THE NIGHT.
WELL, JUST SEE THAT YOU'RE CAREFUL WHEN YOU DO. NORMALLY THERE'S NOT MUCH HERE TO TROUBLE A MAN, BUT LATELY...
SO I'VE HEARD.
SOME OF THE TOWNSPEOPLE TOLD US THAT FRIENDS AND NEIGHBORS HAVE VANISHED INTO THIN AIR. BUT WHERE WOULD THEY VANISH TO, DO YOU SUPPOSE?

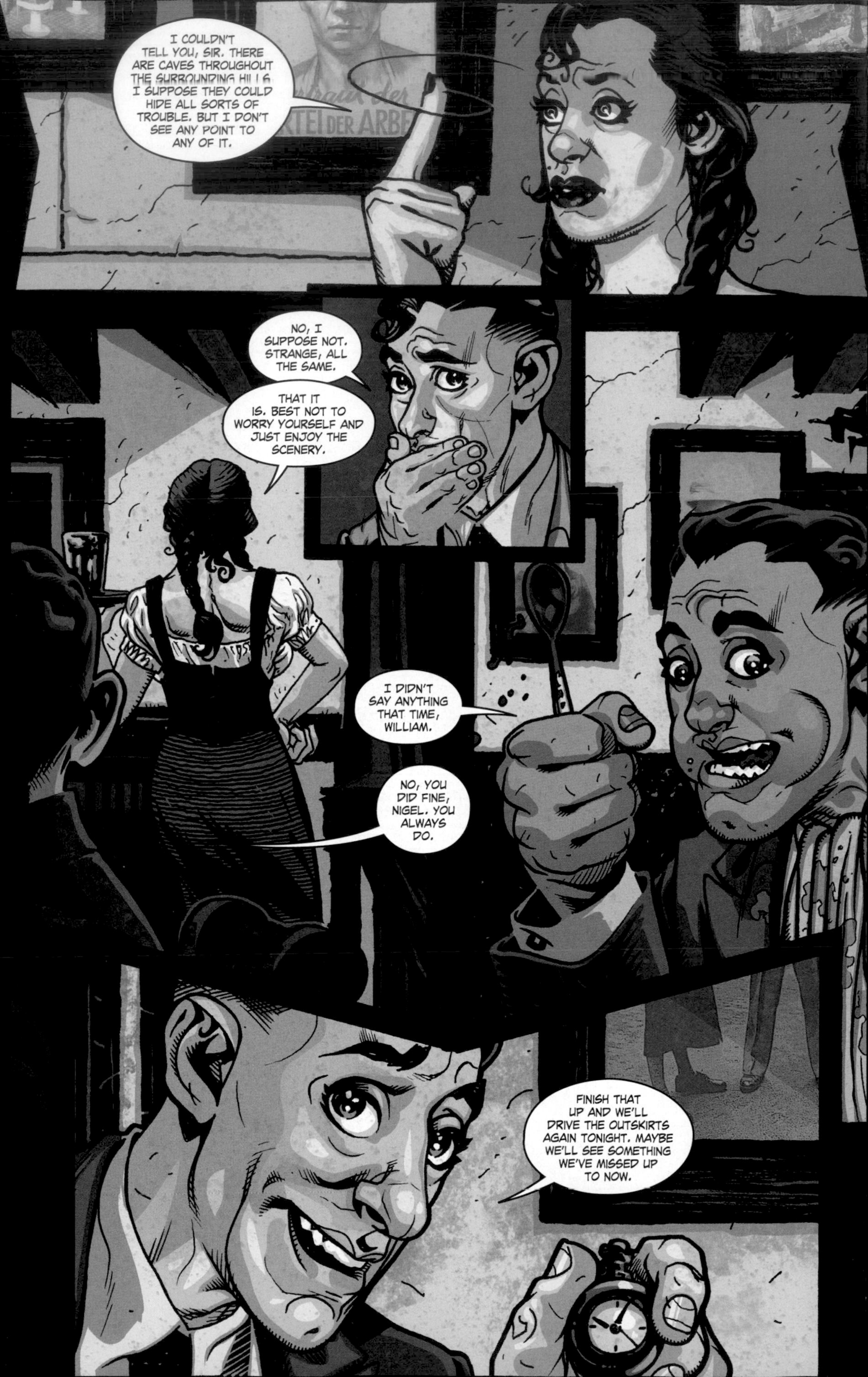
I COULDN'T TELL YOU, SIR. THERE ARE CAVES THROUGHOUT THE SURROUNDING HILLS. I SUPPOSE THEY COULD HIDE ALL SORTS OF TROUBLE. BUT I DON'T SEE ANY POINT TO ANY OF IT.
NO, I SUPPOSE NOT. STRANGE, ALL THE SAME.
THAT IT IS. BEST NOT TO WORRY YOURSELF AND JUST ENJOY THE SCENERY.
I DIDN'T SAY ANYTHING THAT TIME, WILLIAM.
NO, YOU DID FINE, NIGEL. YOU ALWAYS DO.
FINISH THAT UP AND WE'LL DRIVE THE OUTSKIRTS AGAIN TONIGHT. MAYBE WE'LL SEE SOMETHING WE'VE MISSED UP TO NOW.

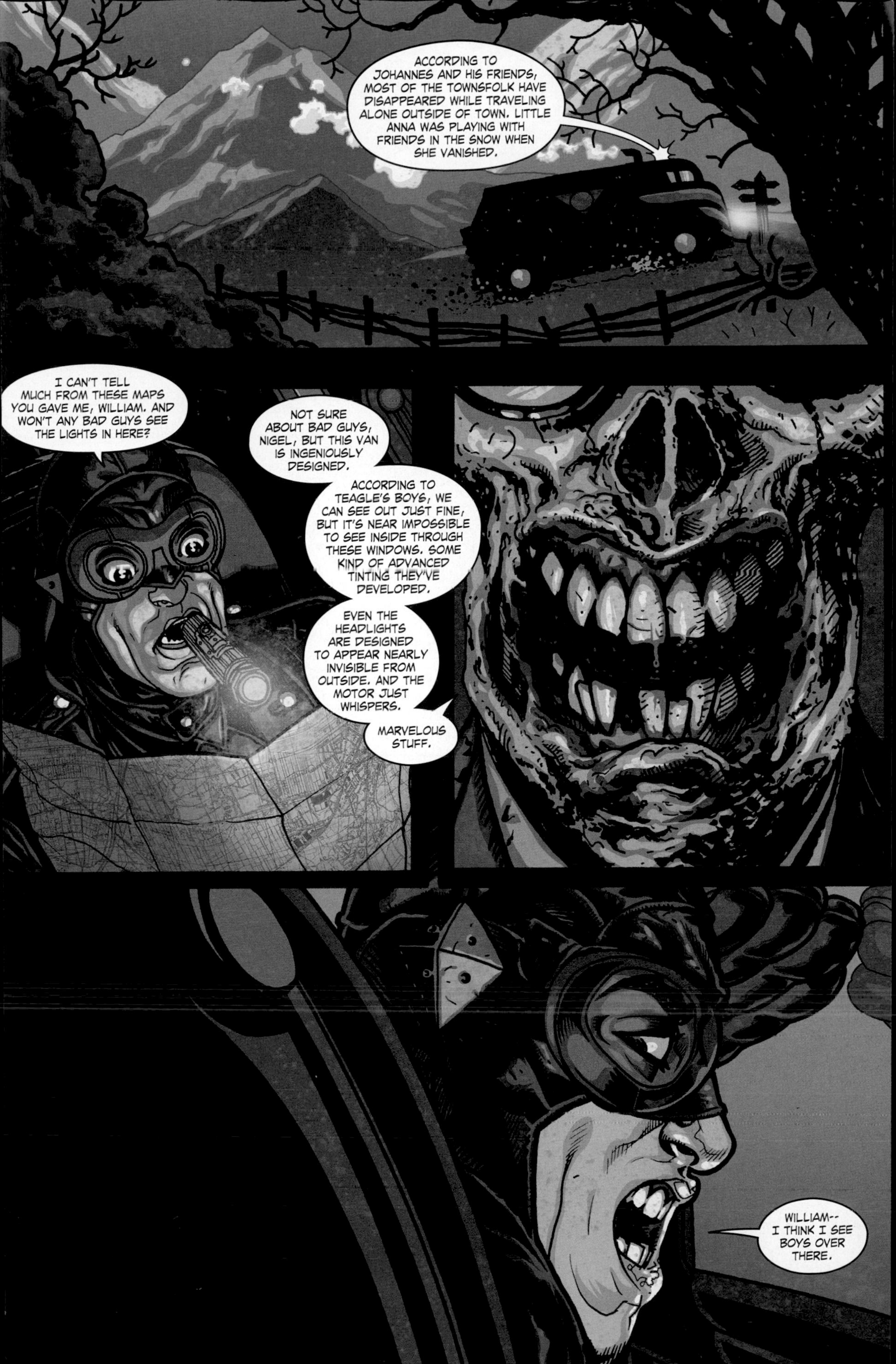
ACCORDING TO JOHANNES AND HIS FRIENDS, MOST OF THE TOWNSFOLK HAVE DISAPPEARED WHILE TRAVELING ALONE OUTSIDE OF TOWN. LITTLE ANNA WAS PLAYING WITH FRIENDS IN THE SNOW WHEN SHE VANISHED.
I CAN'T TELL MUCH FROM THESE MAPS YOU GAVE ME, WILLIAM. AND WON'T ANY BAD GUYS SEE THE LIGHTS IN HERE?
NOT SURE ABOUT BAD GUYS, NIGEL, BUT THIS VAN IS INGENIOUSLY DESIGNED.
ACCORDING TO TEAGLE'S BOYS, WE CAN SEE OUT JUST FINE, BUT IT'S NEAR IMPOSSIBLE TO SEE INSIDE THROUGH THESE WINDOWS. SOME KIND OF ADVANCED TINTING THEY'VE DEVELOPED.
EVEN THE HEADLIGHTS ARE DESIGNED TO APPEAR NEARLY INVISIBLE FROM OUTSIDE. AND THE MOTOR JUST WHISPERS.
MARVELOUS STUFF.
WILLIAM-- I THINK I SEE BOYS OVER THERE.

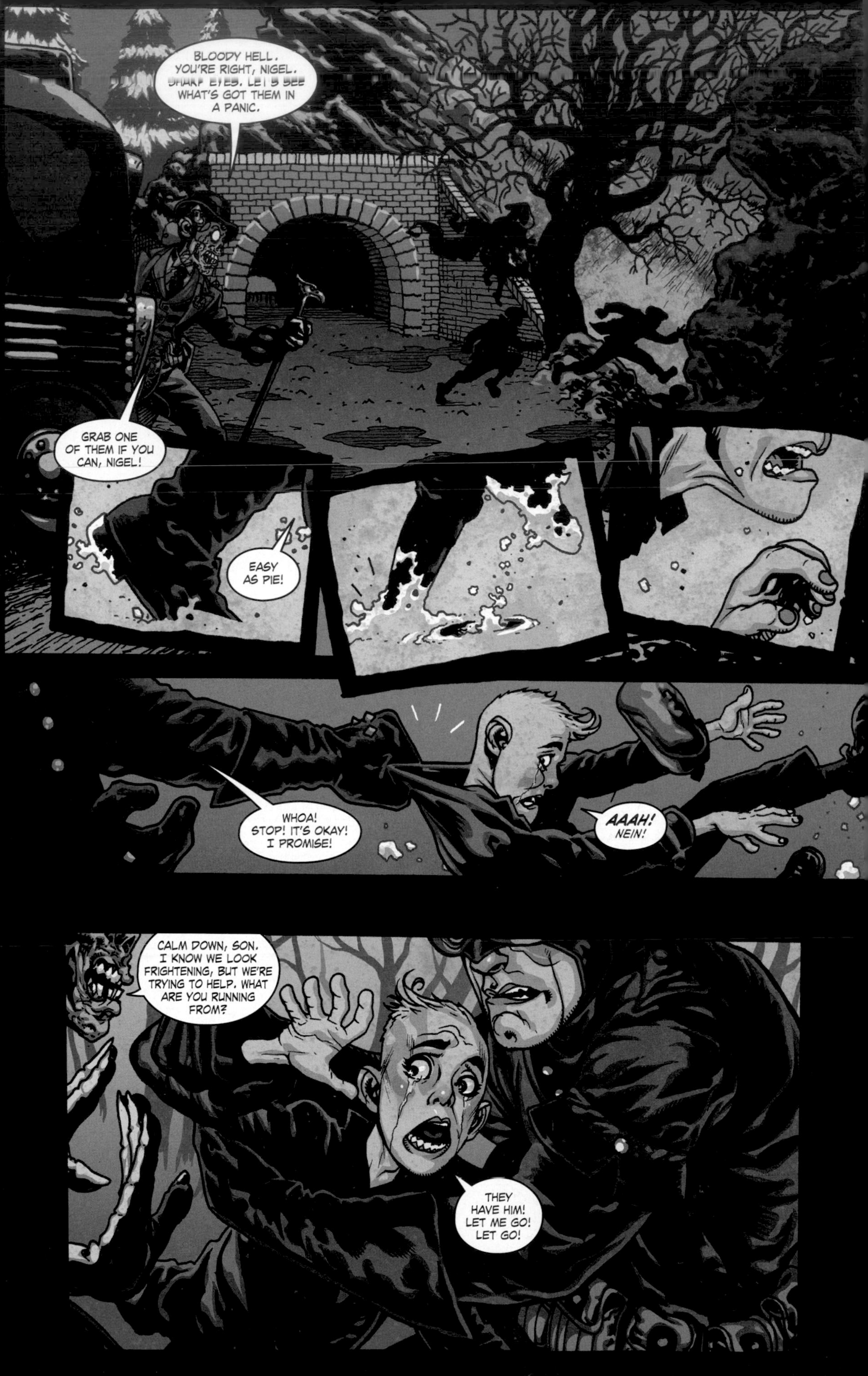
BLOODY HELL. YOU'RE RIGHT, NIGEL. SHARP EYES. LET'S SEE WHAT'S GOT THEM IN A PANIC.
GRAB ONE OF THEM IF YOU CAN, NIGEL!
EASY AS PIE!
WHOA! STOP! IT'S OKAY! I PROMISE!
AAAH! NEIN!
CALM DOWN, SON. I KNOW WE LOOK FRIGHTENING, BUT WE'RE TRYING TO HELP. WHAT ARE YOU RUNNING FROM?
THEY HAVE HIM! LET ME GO! LET GO!

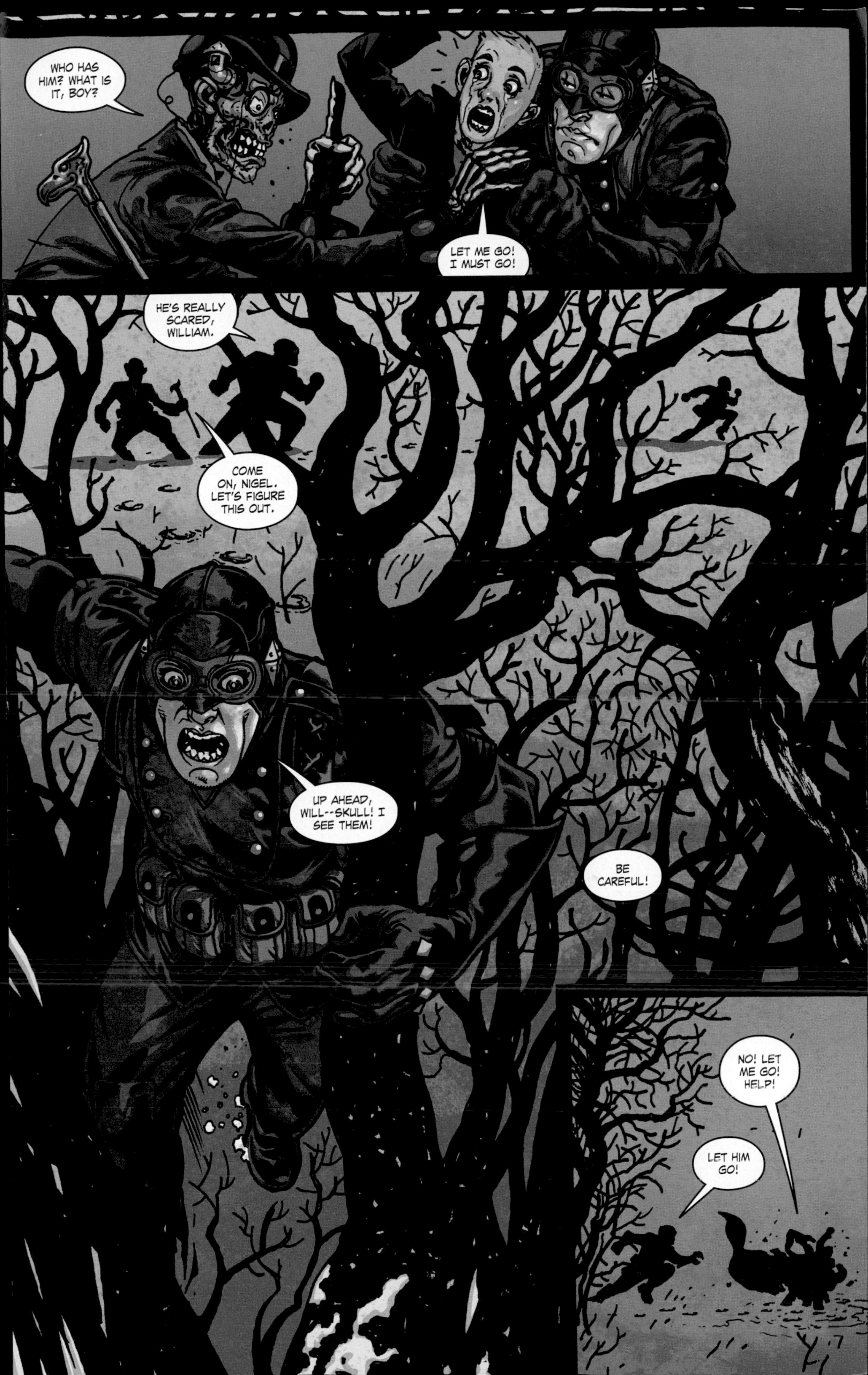
WHO HAS HIM? WHAT IS IT, BOY?
LET ME GO! I MUST GO!
HE'S REALLY SCARED, WILLIAM.
COME ON, NIGEL. LET'S FIGURE THIS OUT.
UP AHEAD, WILL--SKULL! I SEE THEM!
BE CAREFUL!
NO! LET ME GO! HELP!
LET HIM GO!

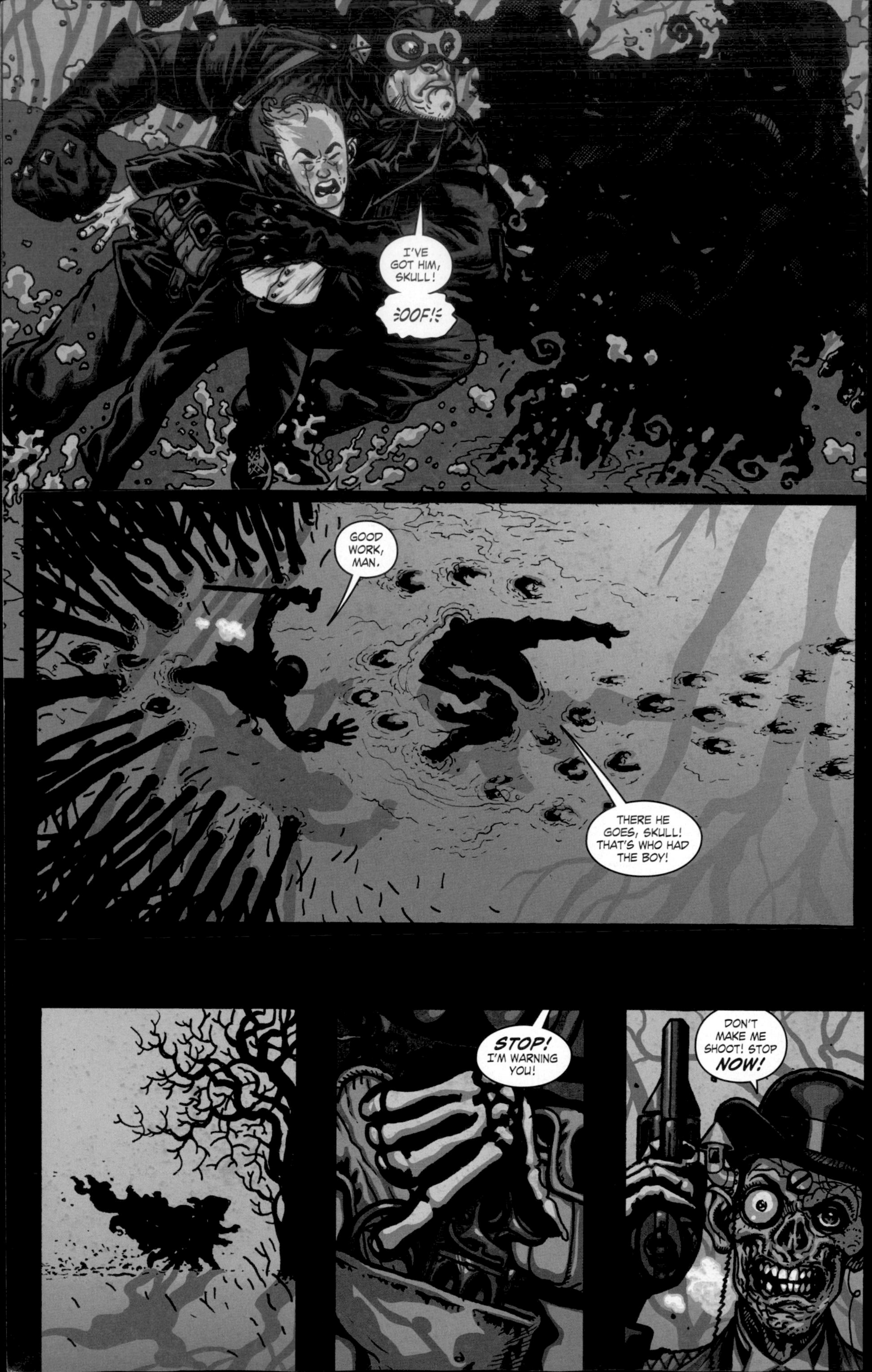
I'VE GOT HIM, SKULL!
OOF!
GOOD WORK, MAN.
THERE HE GOES, SKULL! THAT'S WHO HAD THE BOY!
STOP! I'M WARNING YOU!
DON'T MAKE ME SHOOT! STOP NOW!

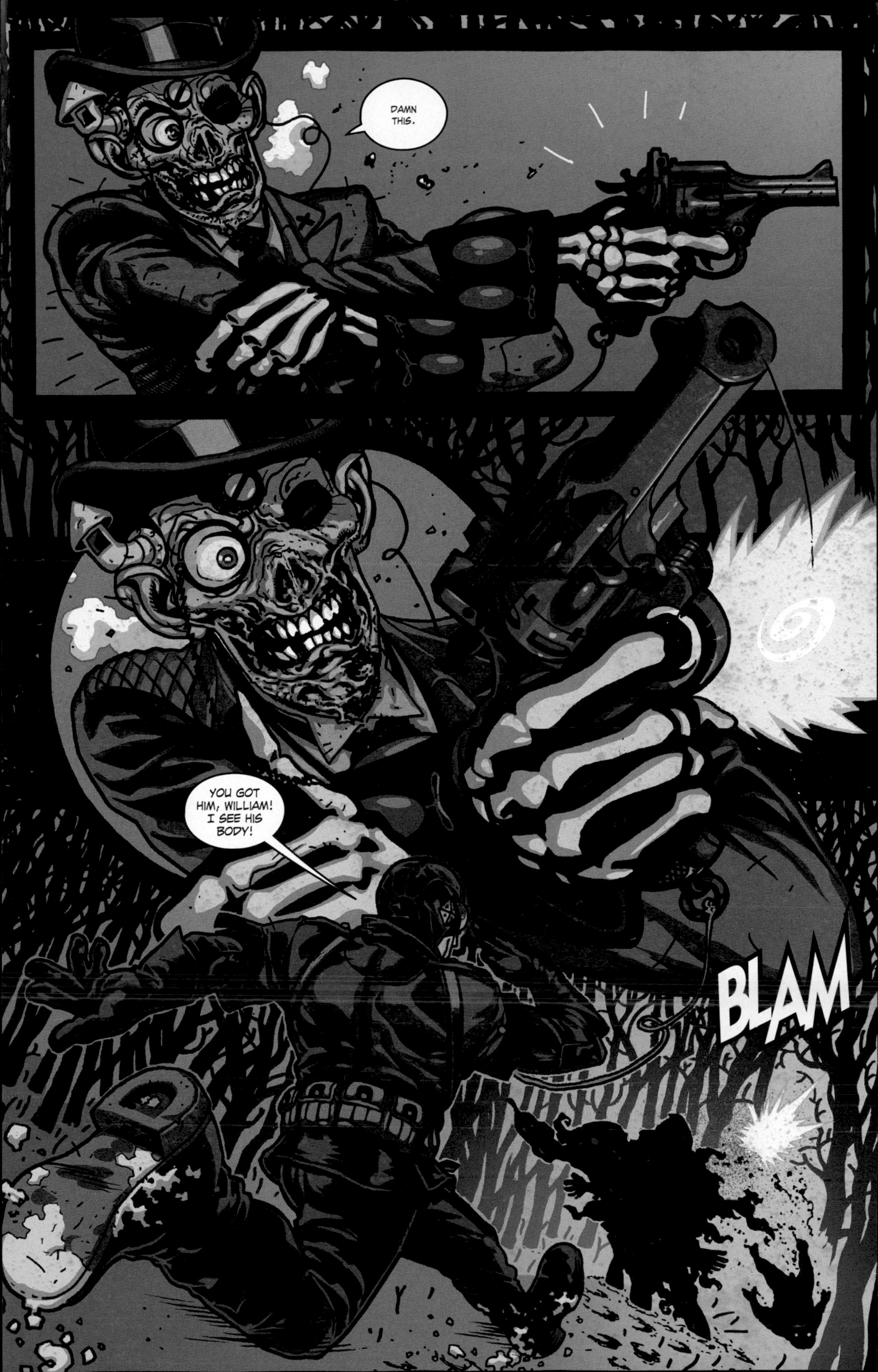
DAMN THIS.
YOU GOT HIM, WILLIAM! I SEE HIS BODY!
BLAM

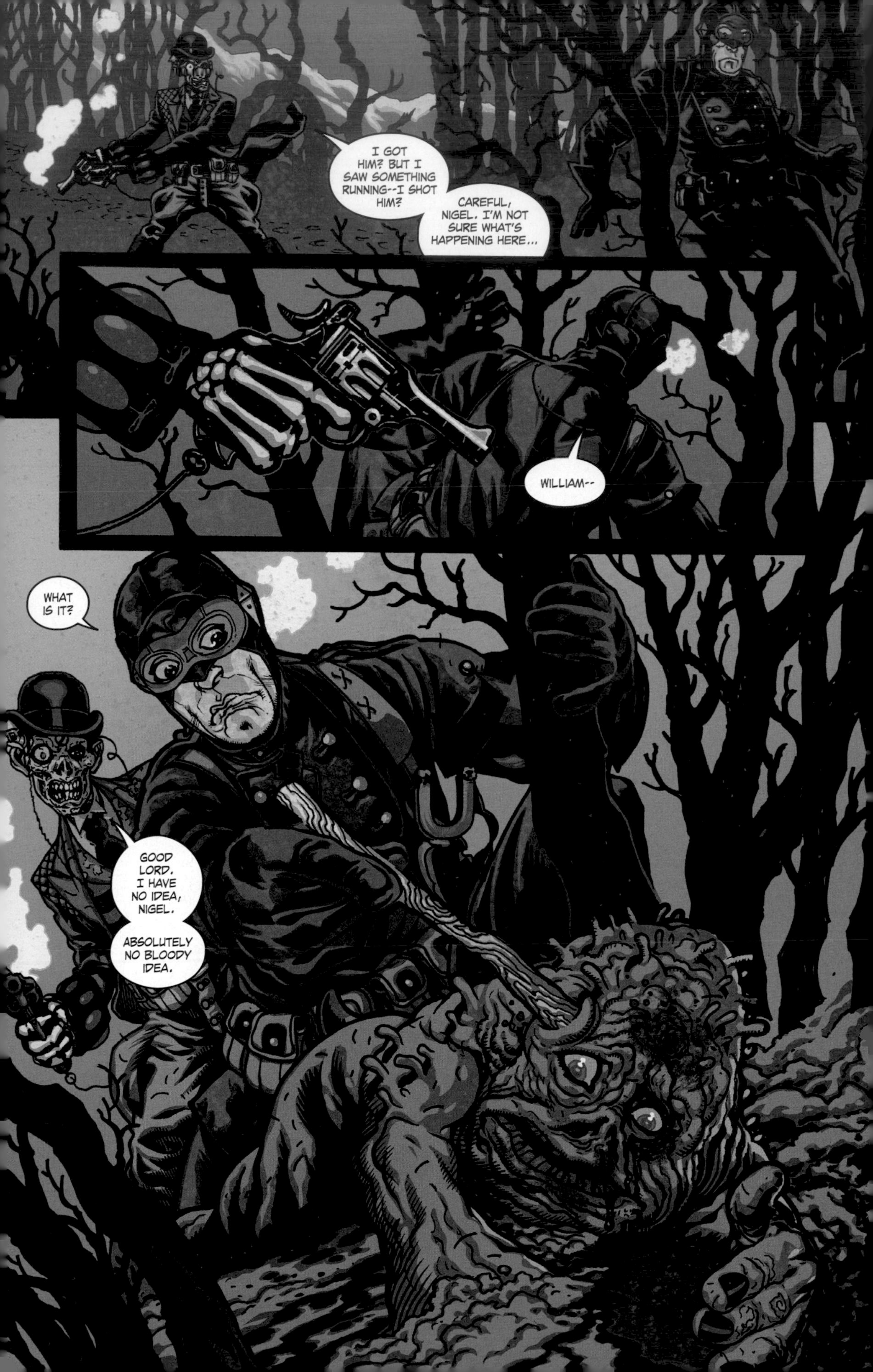
I GOT HIM? BUT I SAW SOMETHING RUNNING--I SHOT HIM?
CAREFUL, NIGEL. I'M NOT SURE WHAT'S HAPPENING HERE...
WILLIAM--
WHAT IS IT?
GOOD LORD. I HAVE NO IDEA, NIGEL.
ABSOLUTELY NO BLOODY IDEA.

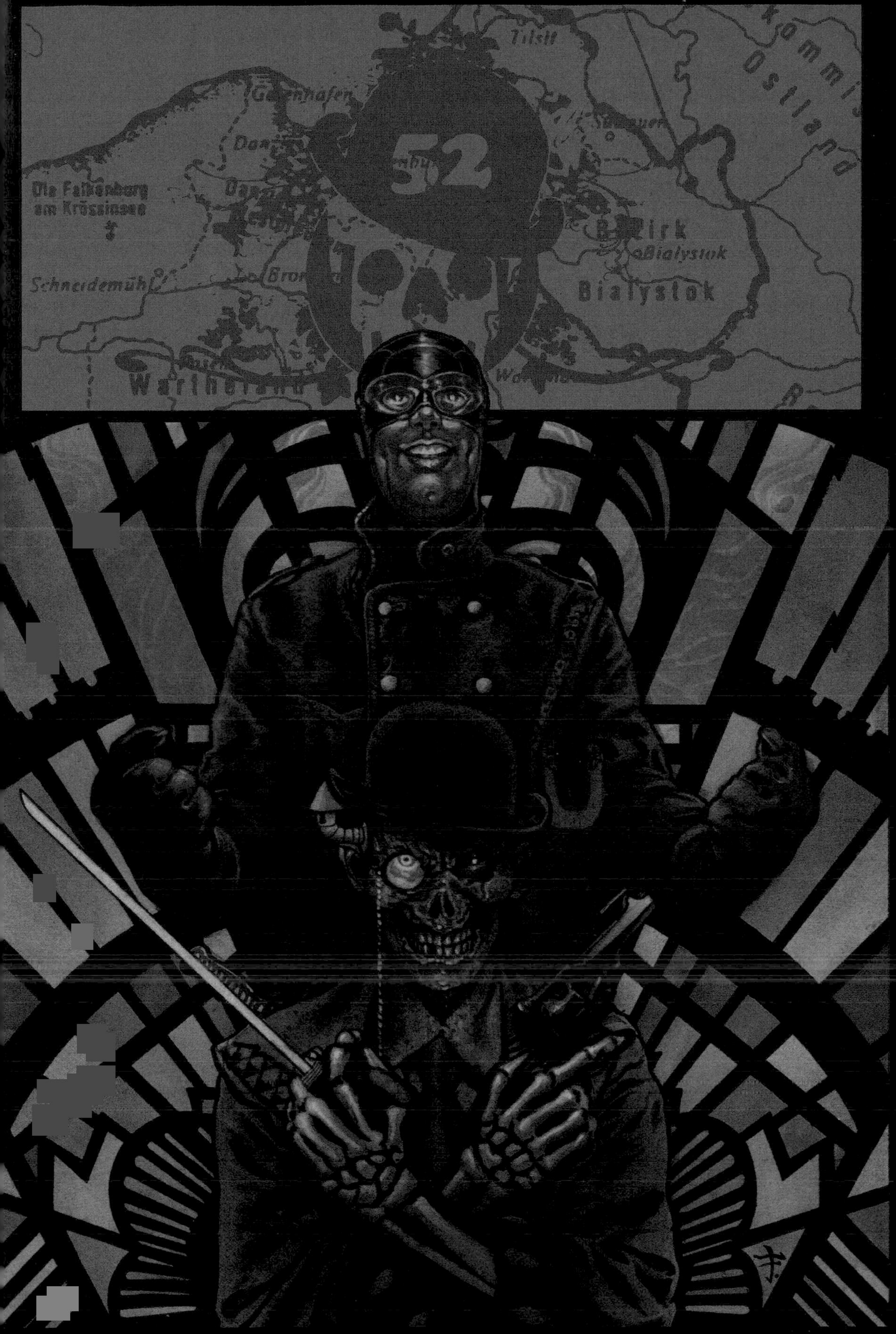
52
Tilsit
Die Falkenburg am Krössinsee
Schneidemühl
Bialystok
Bialystok
Ostland
Wartheland

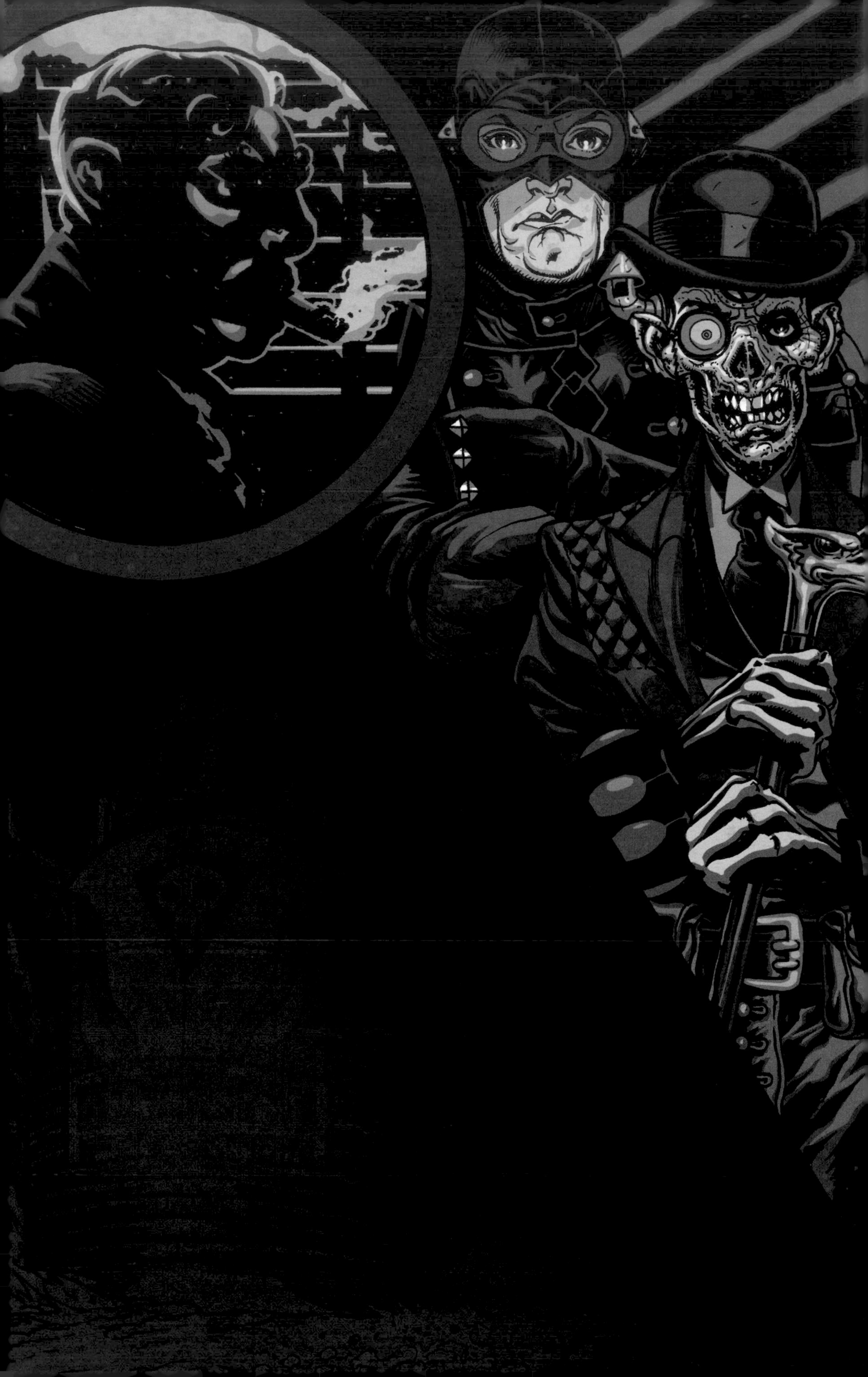

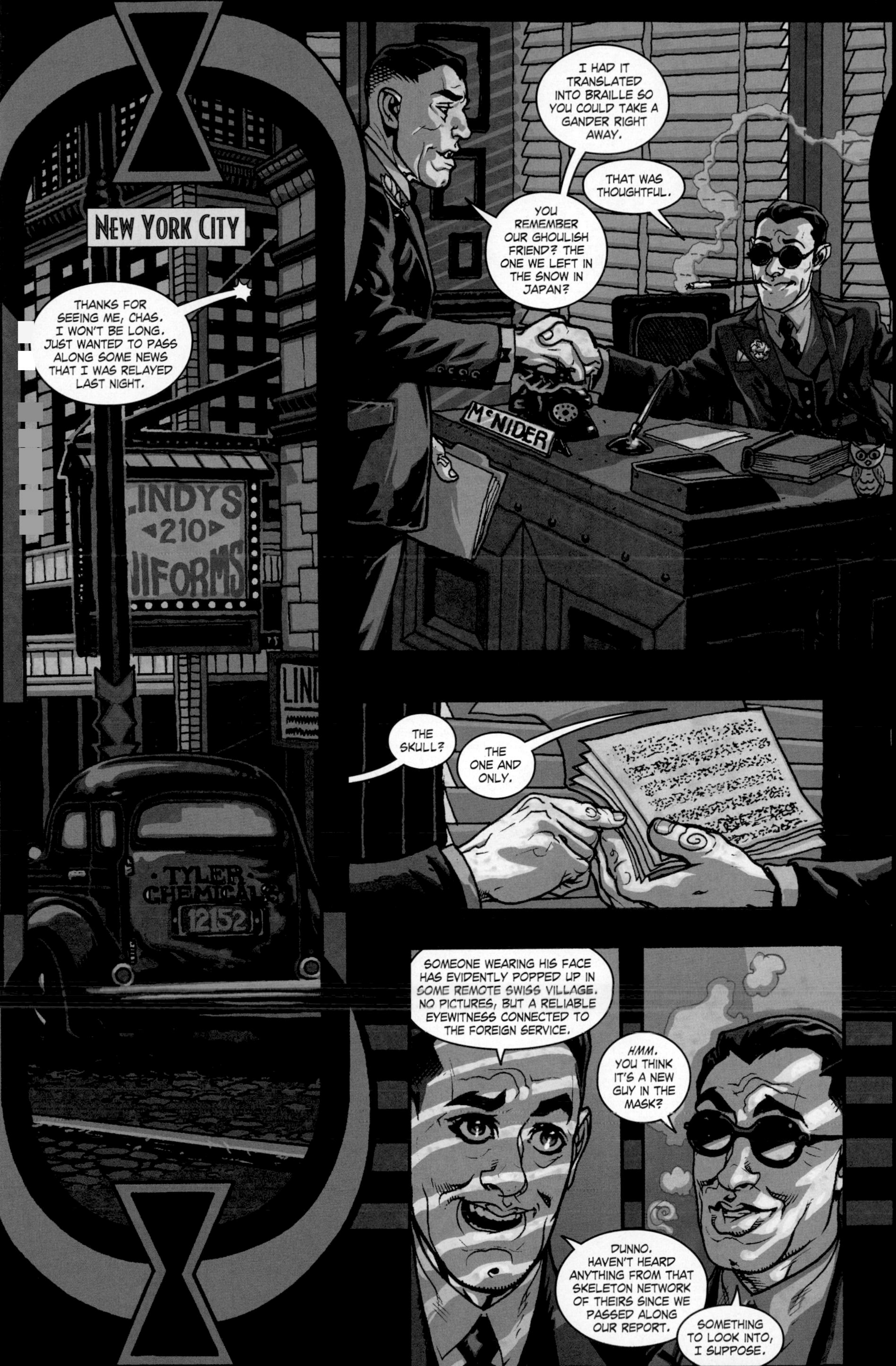
NEW YORK CITY
THANKS FOR SEEING ME, CHAS. I WON'T BE LONG. JUST WANTED TO PASS ALONG SOME NEWS THAT I WAS RELAYED LAST NIGHT.
LINDYS 210 UNIFORMS
TYLER CHEMICALS 12152
YOU REMEMBER OUR GHOULISH FRIEND? THE ONE WE LEFT IN THE SNOW IN JAPAN?
I HAD IT TRANSLATED INTO BRAILLE SO YOU COULD TAKE A GANDER RIGHT AWAY.
THAT WAS THOUGHTFUL.
McNIDER
THE SKULL?
THE ONE AND ONLY.
SOMEONE WEARING HIS FACE HAS EVIDENTLY POPPED UP IN SOME REMOTE SWISS VILLAGE. NO PICTURES, BUT A RELIABLE EYEWITNESS CONNECTED TO THE FOREIGN SERVICE.
HMM. YOU THINK IT'S A NEW GUY IN THE MASK?
DUNNO. HAVEN'T HEARD ANYTHING FROM THAT SKELETON NETWORK OF THEIRS SINCE WE PASSED ALONG OUR REPORT.
SOMETHING TO LOOK INTO, I SUPPOSE.

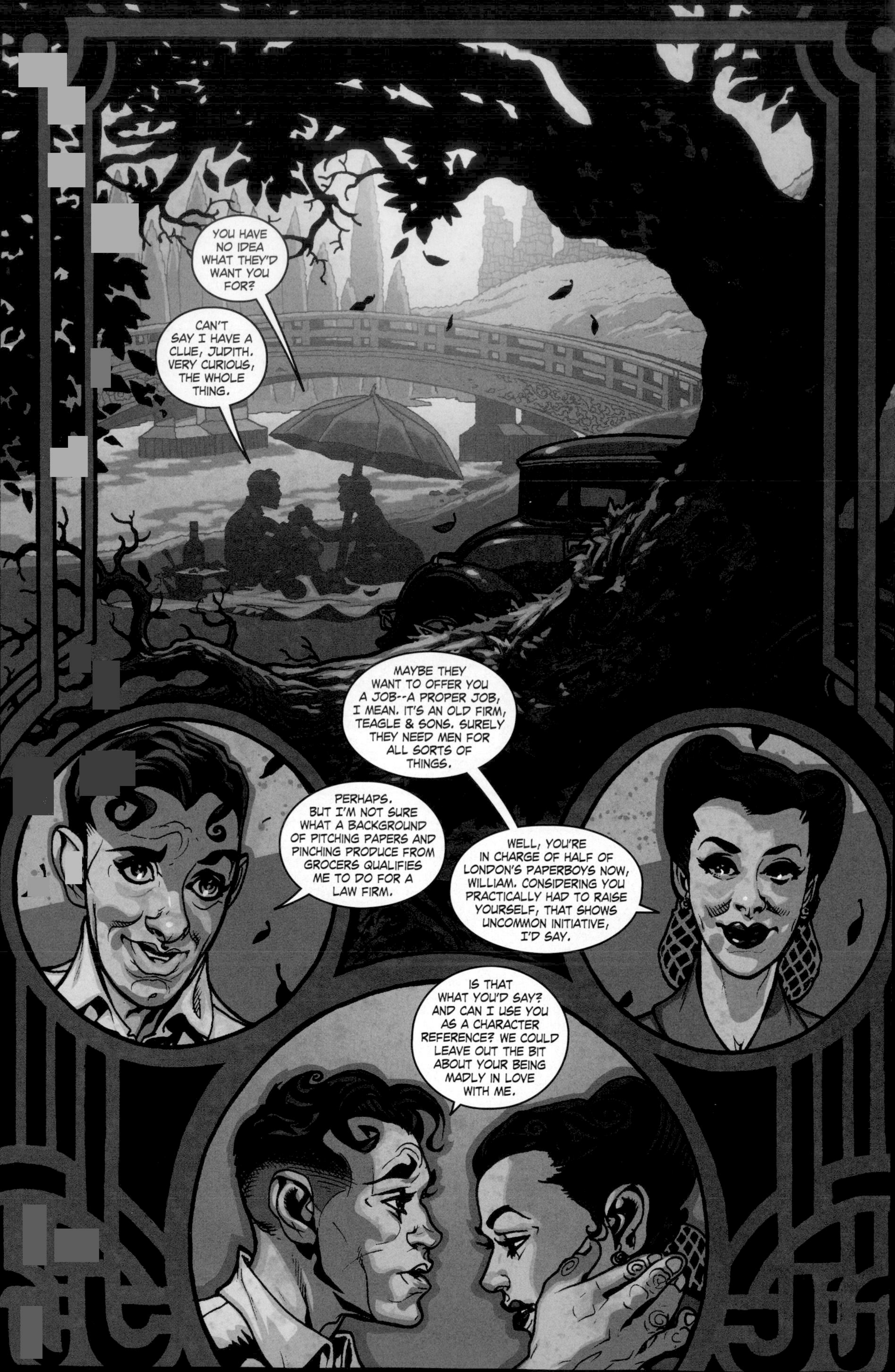
YOU HAVE NO IDEA WHAT THEY'D WANT YOU FOR?
CAN'T SAY I HAVE A CLUE, JUDITH. VERY CURIOUS, THE WHOLE THING.
MAYBE THEY WANT TO OFFER YOU A JOB--A PROPER JOB, I MEAN. IT'S AN OLD FIRM, TEAGLE & SONS. SURELY THEY NEED MEN FOR ALL SORTS OF THINGS.
PERHAPS. BUT I'M NOT SURE WHAT A BACKGROUND OF PITCHING PAPERS AND PINCHING PRODUCE FROM GROCERS QUALIFIES ME TO DO FOR A LAW FIRM.
WELL, YOU'RE IN CHARGE OF HALF OF LONDON'S PAPERBOYS NOW, WILLIAM. CONSIDERING YOU PRACTICALLY HAD TO RAISE YOURSELF, THAT SHOWS UNCOMMON INITIATIVE, I'D SAY.
IS THAT WHAT YOU'D SAY? AND CAN I USE YOU AS A CHARACTER REFERENCE? WE COULD LEAVE OUT THE BIT ABOUT YOUR BEING MADLY IN LOVE WITH ME.

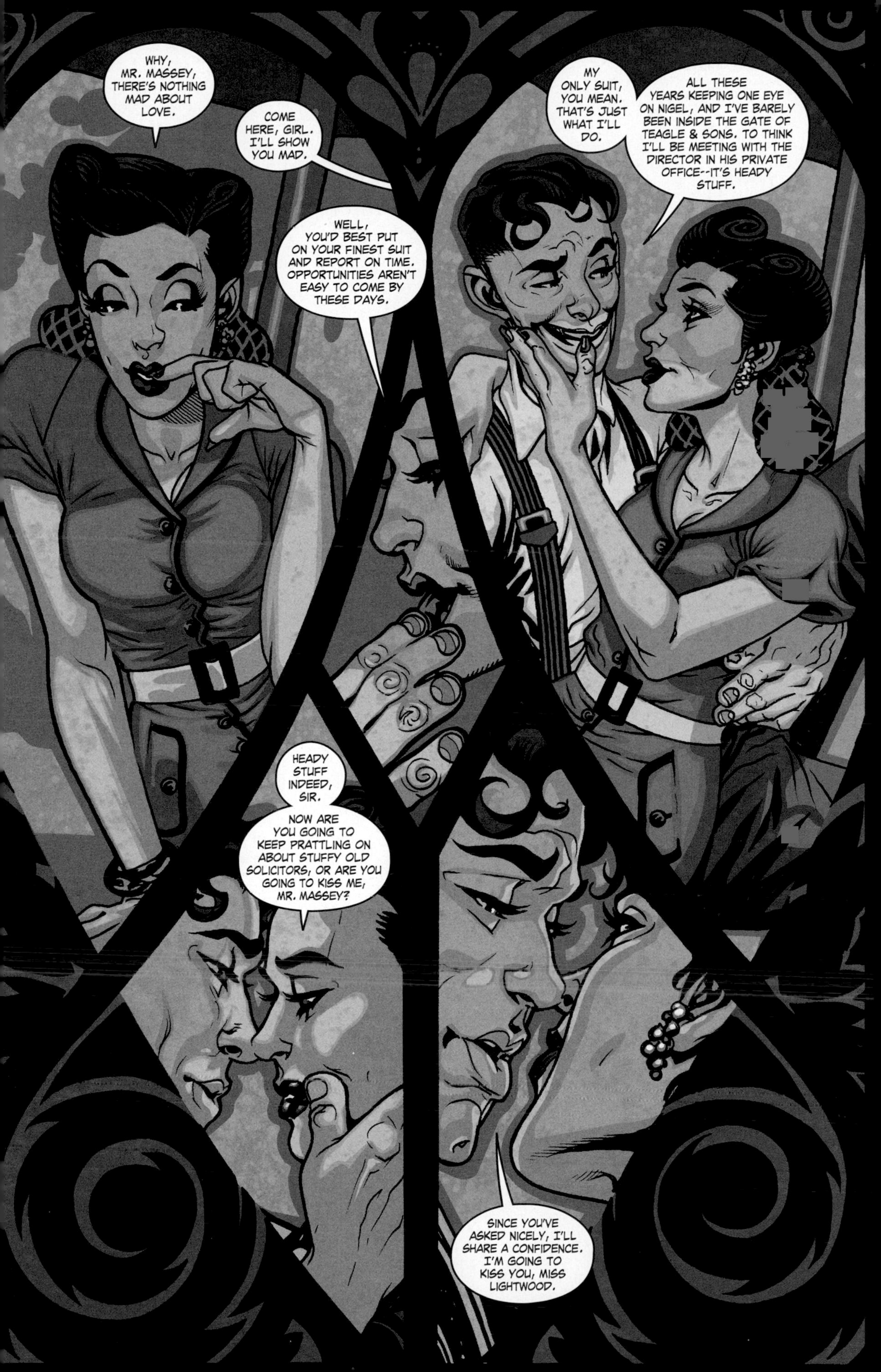
WHY, MR. MASSEY, THERE'S NOTHING MAD ABOUT LOVE.
COME HERE, GIRL. I'LL SHOW YOU MAD.
WELL, YOU'D BEST PUT ON YOUR FINEST SUIT AND REPORT ON TIME. OPPORTUNITIES AREN'T EASY TO COME BY THESE DAYS.
MY ONLY SUIT, YOU MEAN. THAT'S JUST WHAT I'LL DO.
ALL THESE YEARS KEEPING ONE EYE ON NIGEL, AND I'VE BARELY BEEN INSIDE THE GATE OF TEAGLE & SONS. TO THINK I'LL BE MEETING WITH THE DIRECTOR IN HIS PRIVATE OFFICE--IT'S HEADY STUFF.
HEADY STUFF INDEED, SIR.
NOW ARE YOU GOING TO KEEP PRATTLING ON ABOUT STUFFY OLD SOLICITORS, OR ARE YOU GOING TO KISS ME, MR. MASSEY?
SINCE YOU'VE ASKED NICELY, I'LL SHARE A CONFIDENCE. I'M GOING TO KISS YOU, MISS LIGHTWOOD.

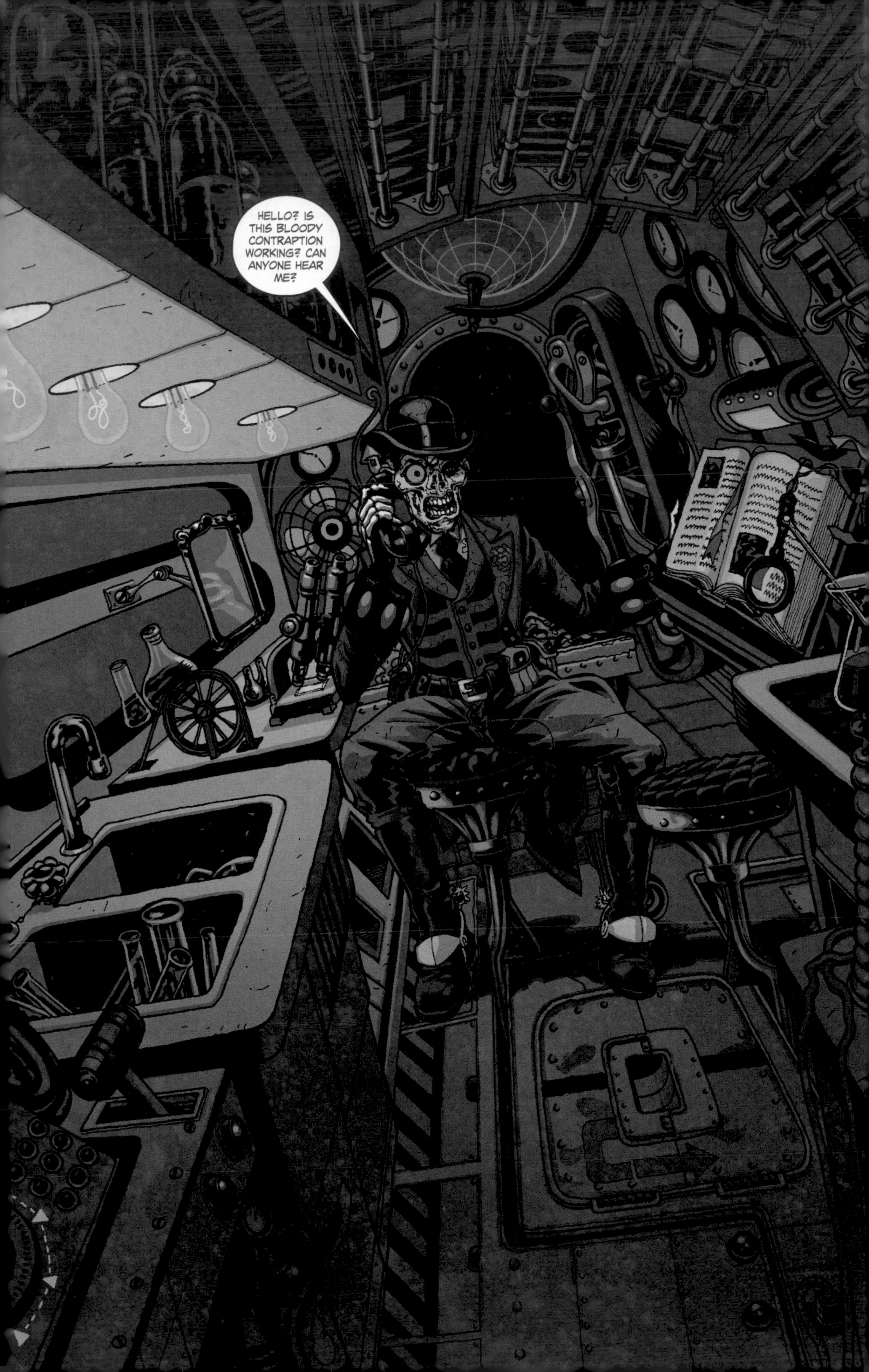
HELLO? IS THIS BLOODY CONTRAPTION WORKING? CAN ANYONE HEAR ME?

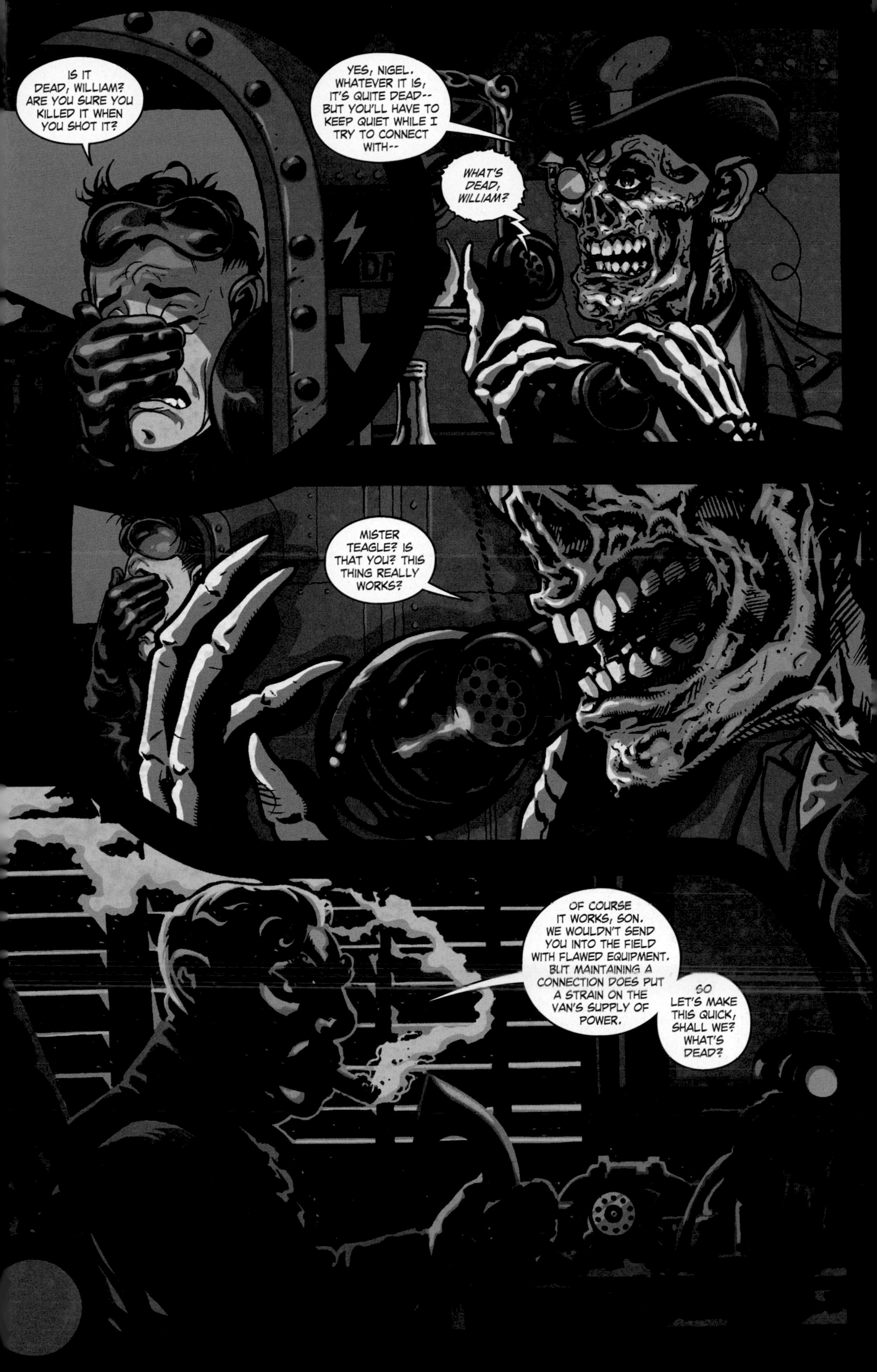
IS IT DEAD, WILLIAM? ARE YOU SURE YOU KILLED IT WHEN YOU SHOT IT?
YES, NIGEL. WHATEVER IT IS, IT'S QUITE DEAD-- BUT YOU'LL HAVE TO KEEP QUIET WHILE I TRY TO CONNECT WITH--
WHAT'S DEAD, WILLIAM?
MISTER TEAGLE? IS THAT YOU? THIS THING REALLY WORKS?
OF COURSE IT WORKS, SON. WE WOULDN'T SEND YOU INTO THE FIELD WITH FLAWED EQUIPMENT. BUT MAINTAINING A CONNECTION DOES PUT A STRAIN ON THE VAN'S SUPPLY OF POWER.
SO LET'S MAKE THIS QUICK, SHALL WE? WHAT'S DEAD?

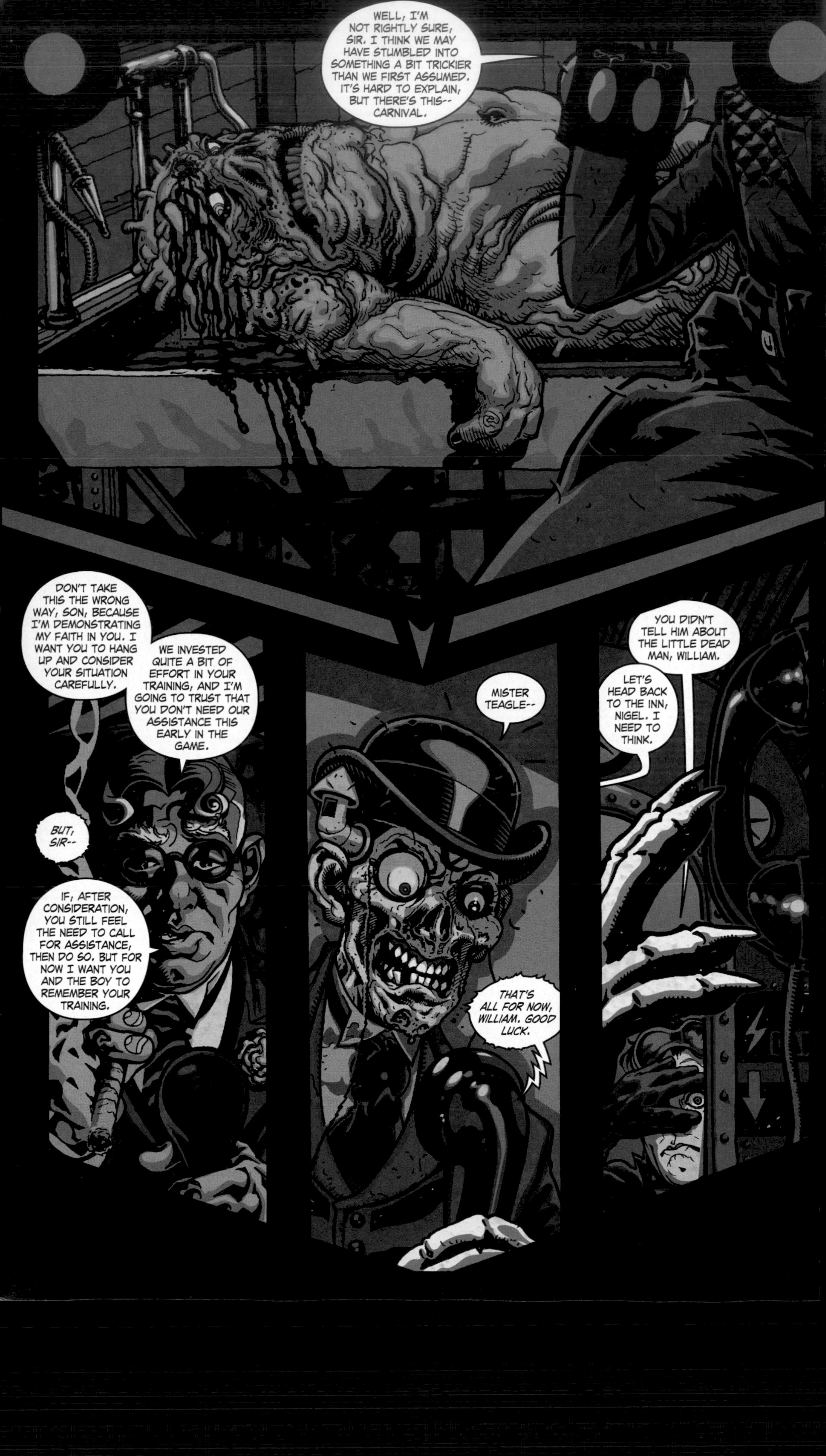

WELL, I'M NOT RIGHTLY SURE, SIR. I THINK WE MAY HAVE STUMBLED INTO SOMETHING A BIT TRICKIER THAN WE FIRST ASSUMED. IT'S HARD TO EXPLAIN, BUT THERE'S THIS-- CARNIVAL.
DON'T TAKE THIS THE WRONG WAY, SON, BECAUSE I'M DEMONSTRATING MY FAITH IN YOU. I WANT YOU TO HANG UP AND CONSIDER YOUR SITUATION CAREFULLY.
WE INVESTED QUITE A BIT OF EFFORT IN YOUR TRAINING, AND I'M GOING TO TRUST THAT YOU DON'T NEED OUR ASSISTANCE THIS EARLY IN THE GAME.
BUT, SIR--
IF, AFTER CONSIDERATION, YOU STILL FEEL THE NEED TO CALL FOR ASSISTANCE, THEN DO SO. BUT FOR NOW I WANT YOU AND THE BOY TO REMEMBER YOUR TRAINING.
MISTER TEAGLE--
THAT'S ALL FOR NOW, WILLIAM. GOOD LUCK.
YOU DIDN'T TELL HIM ABOUT THE LITTLE DEAD MAN, WILLIAM.
LET'S HEAD BACK TO THE INN, NIGEL. I NEED TO THINK.

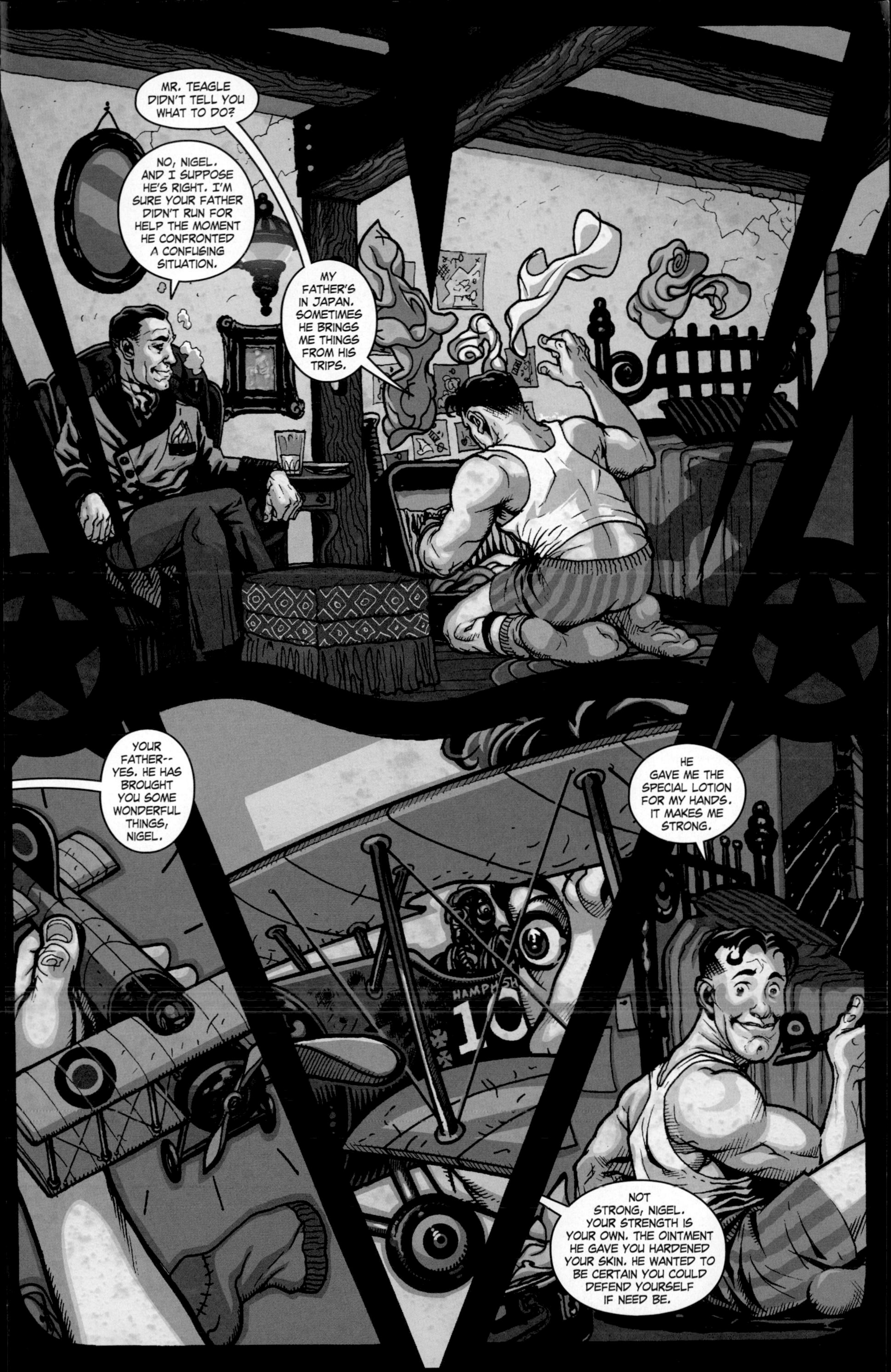
MR. TEAGLE DIDN'T TELL YOU WHAT TO DO?
NO, NIGEL. AND I SUPPOSE HE'S RIGHT. I'M SURE YOUR FATHER DIDN'T RUN FOR HELP THE MOMENT HE CONFRONTED A CONFUSING SITUATION.
MY FATHER'S IN JAPAN. SOMETIMES HE BRINGS ME THINGS FROM HIS TRIPS.
YOUR FATHER-- YES. HE HAS BROUGHT YOU SOME WONDERFUL THINGS, NIGEL.
HE GAVE ME THE SPECIAL LOTION FOR MY HANDS. IT MAKES ME STRONG.
NOT STRONG, NIGEL. YOUR STRENGTH IS YOUR OWN. THE OINTMENT HE GAVE YOU HARDENED YOUR SKIN. HE WANTED TO BE CERTAIN YOU COULD DEFEND YOURSELF IF NEED BE.

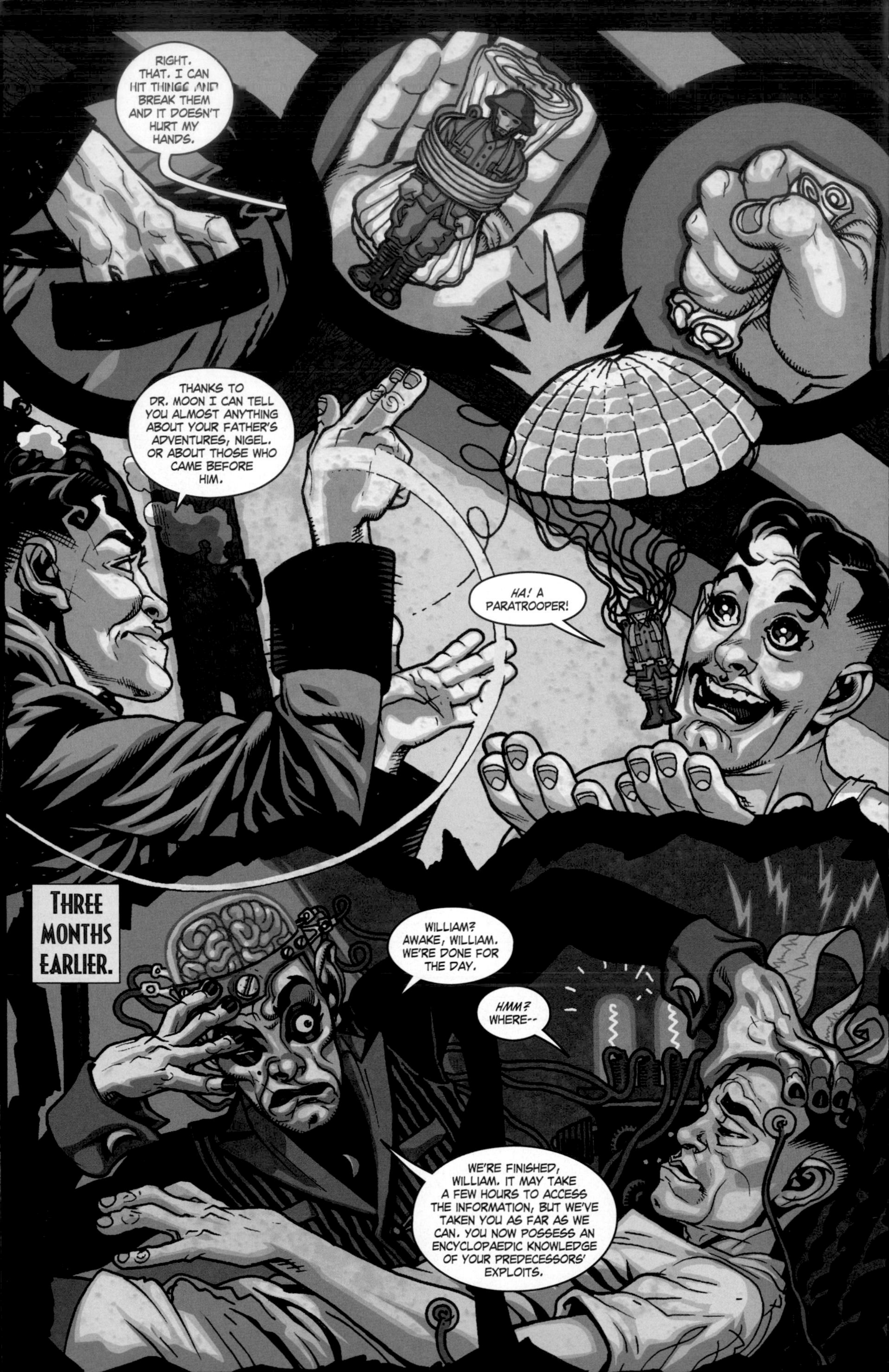

RIGHT. THAT. I CAN HIT THINGS AND BREAK THEM AND IT DOESN'T HURT MY HANDS.
THANKS TO DR. MOON I CAN TELL YOU ALMOST ANYTHING ABOUT YOUR FATHER'S ADVENTURES, NIGEL. OR ABOUT THOSE WHO CAME BEFORE HIM.
HA! A PARATROOPER!
THREE MONTHS EARLIER.
WILLIAM? AWAKE, WILLIAM. WE'RE DONE FOR THE DAY.
HMM? WHERE--
WE'RE FINISHED, WILLIAM. IT MAY TAKE A FEW HOURS TO ACCESS THE INFORMATION, BUT WE'VE TAKEN YOU AS FAR AS WE CAN. YOU NOW POSSESS AN ENCYCLOPAEDIC KNOWLEDGE OF YOUR PREDECESSORS' EXPLOITS.

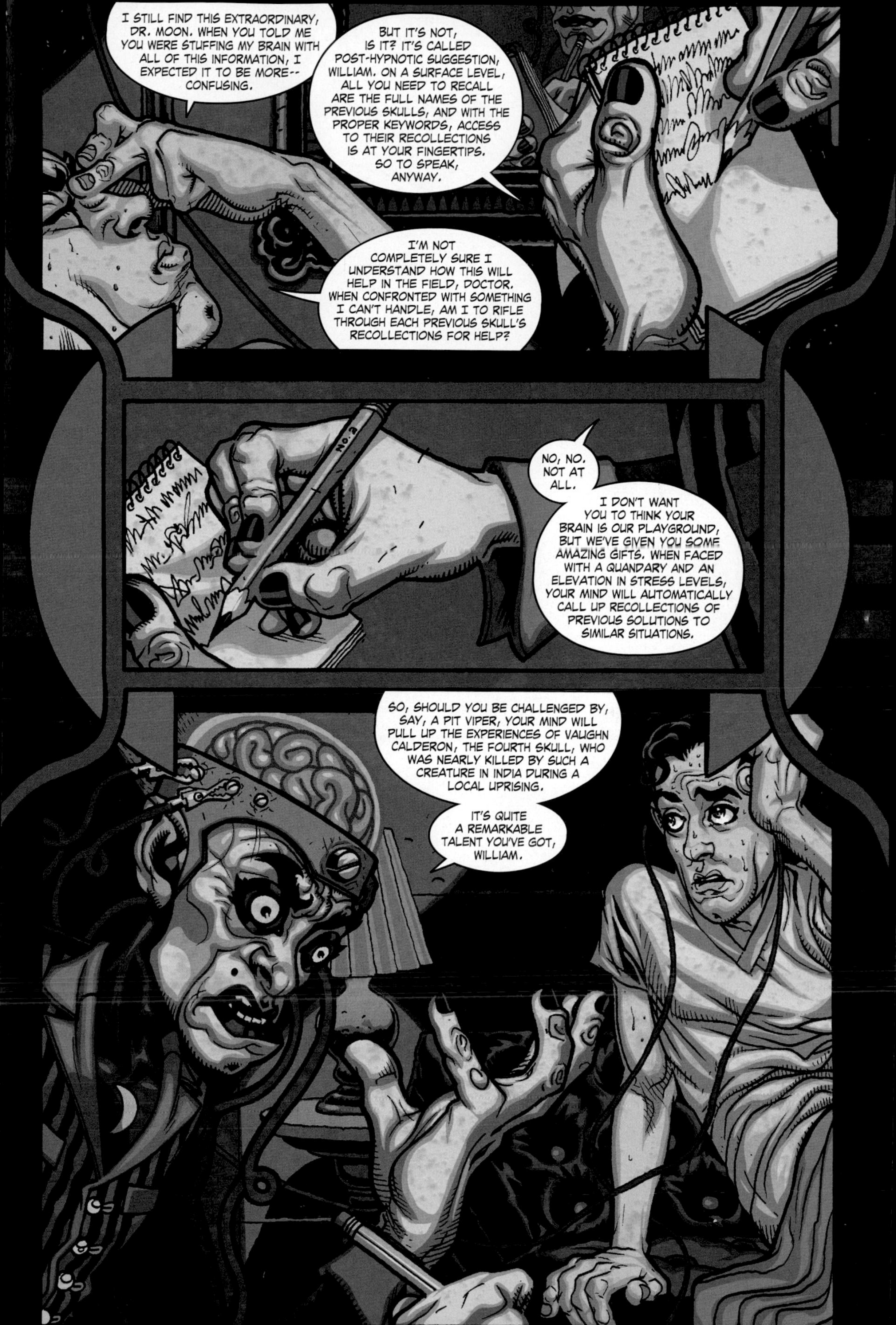
I STILL FIND THIS EXTRAORDINARY, DR. MOON. WHEN YOU TOLD ME YOU WERE STUFFING MY BRAIN WITH ALL OF THIS INFORMATION, I EXPECTED IT TO BE MORE-- CONFUSING.
BUT IT'S NOT, IS IT? IT'S CALLED POST-HYPNOTIC SUGGESTION, WILLIAM. ON A SURFACE LEVEL, ALL YOU NEED TO RECALL ARE THE FULL NAMES OF THE PREVIOUS SKULLS, AND WITH THE PROPER KEYWORDS, ACCESS TO THEIR RECOLLECTIONS IS AT YOUR FINGERTIPS. SO TO SPEAK, ANYWAY.
I'M NOT COMPLETELY SURE I UNDERSTAND HOW THIS WILL HELP IN THE FIELD, DOCTOR. WHEN CONFRONTED WITH SOMETHING I CAN'T HANDLE, AM I TO RIFLE THROUGH EACH PREVIOUS SKULL'S RECOLLECTIONS FOR HELP?
NO. 2
NO, NO. NOT AT ALL.
I DON'T WANT YOU TO THINK YOUR BRAIN IS OUR PLAYGROUND, BUT WE'VE GIVEN YOU SOME AMAZING GIFTS. WHEN FACED WITH A QUANDARY AND AN ELEVATION IN STRESS LEVELS, YOUR MIND WILL AUTOMATICALLY CALL UP RECOLLECTIONS OF PREVIOUS SOLUTIONS TO SIMILAR SITUATIONS.
SO, SHOULD YOU BE CHALLENGED BY, SAY, A PIT VIPER, YOUR MIND WILL PULL UP THE EXPERIENCES OF VAUGHN CALDERON, THE FOURTH SKULL, WHO WAS NEARLY KILLED BY SUCH A CREATURE IN INDIA DURING A LOCAL UPRISING.
IT'S QUITE A REMARKABLE TALENT YOU'VE GOT, WILLIAM.

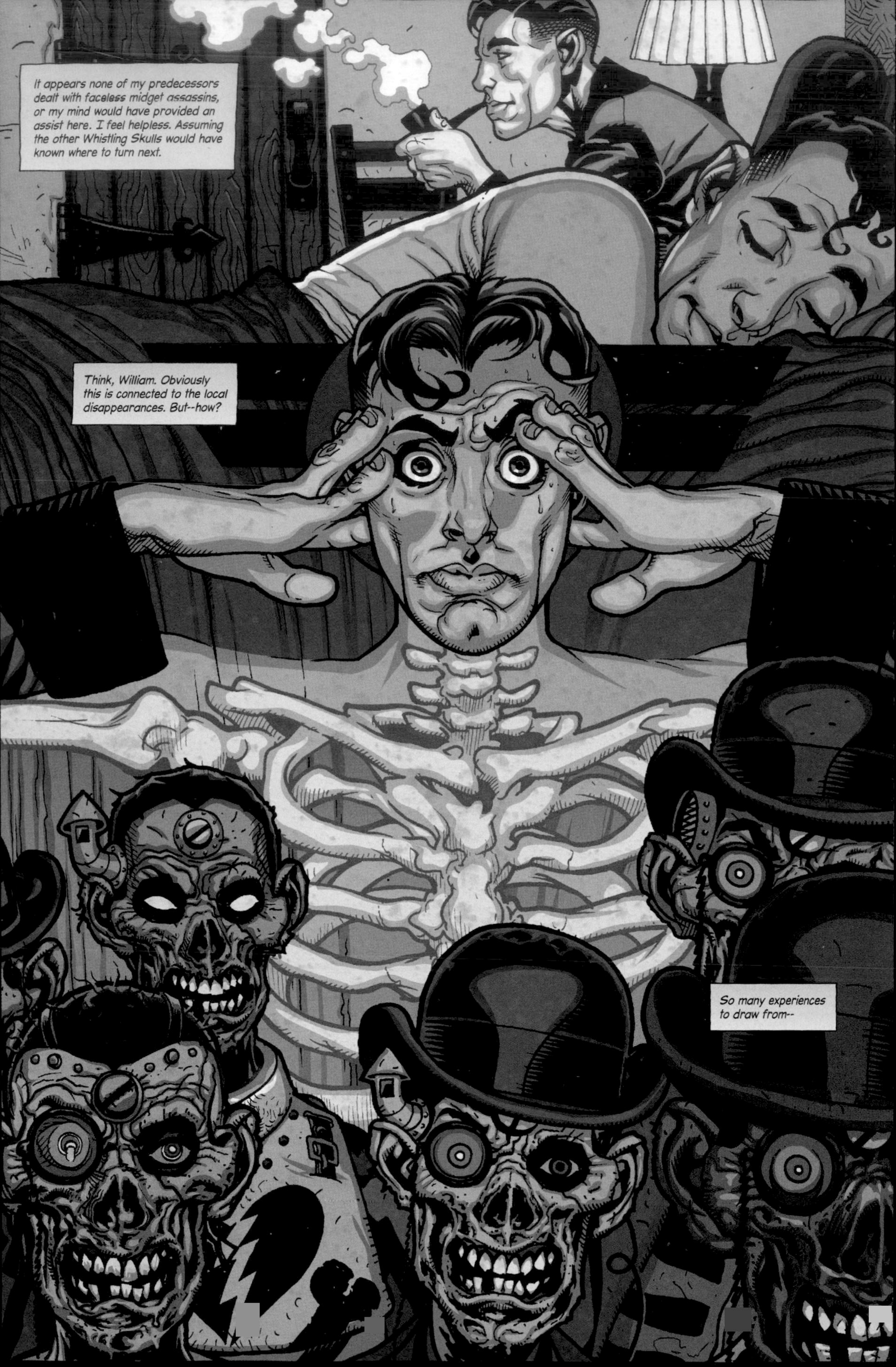

It appears none of my predecessors dealt with faceless midget assassins, or my mind would have provided an assist here. I feel helpless. Assuming the other Whistling Skulls would have known where to turn next.
Think, William. Obviously this is connected to the local disappearances. But--how?
So many experiences to draw from--

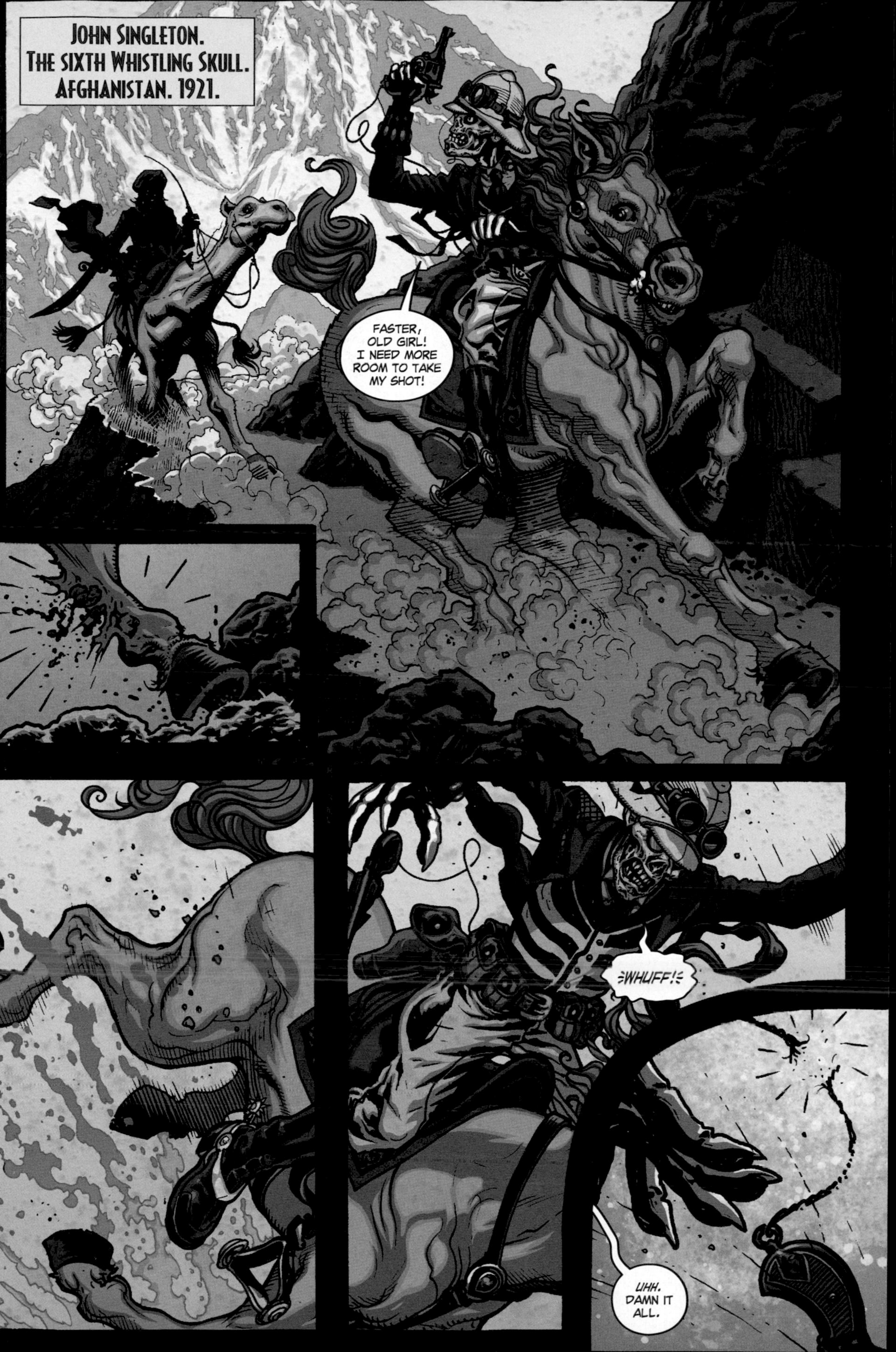
JOHN SINGLETON.
THE SIXTH WHISTLING SKULL.
AFGHANISTAN. 1921.
FASTER, OLD GIRL! I NEED MORE ROOM TO TAKE MY SHOT!
WHUFF!
UHH. DAMN IT ALL.

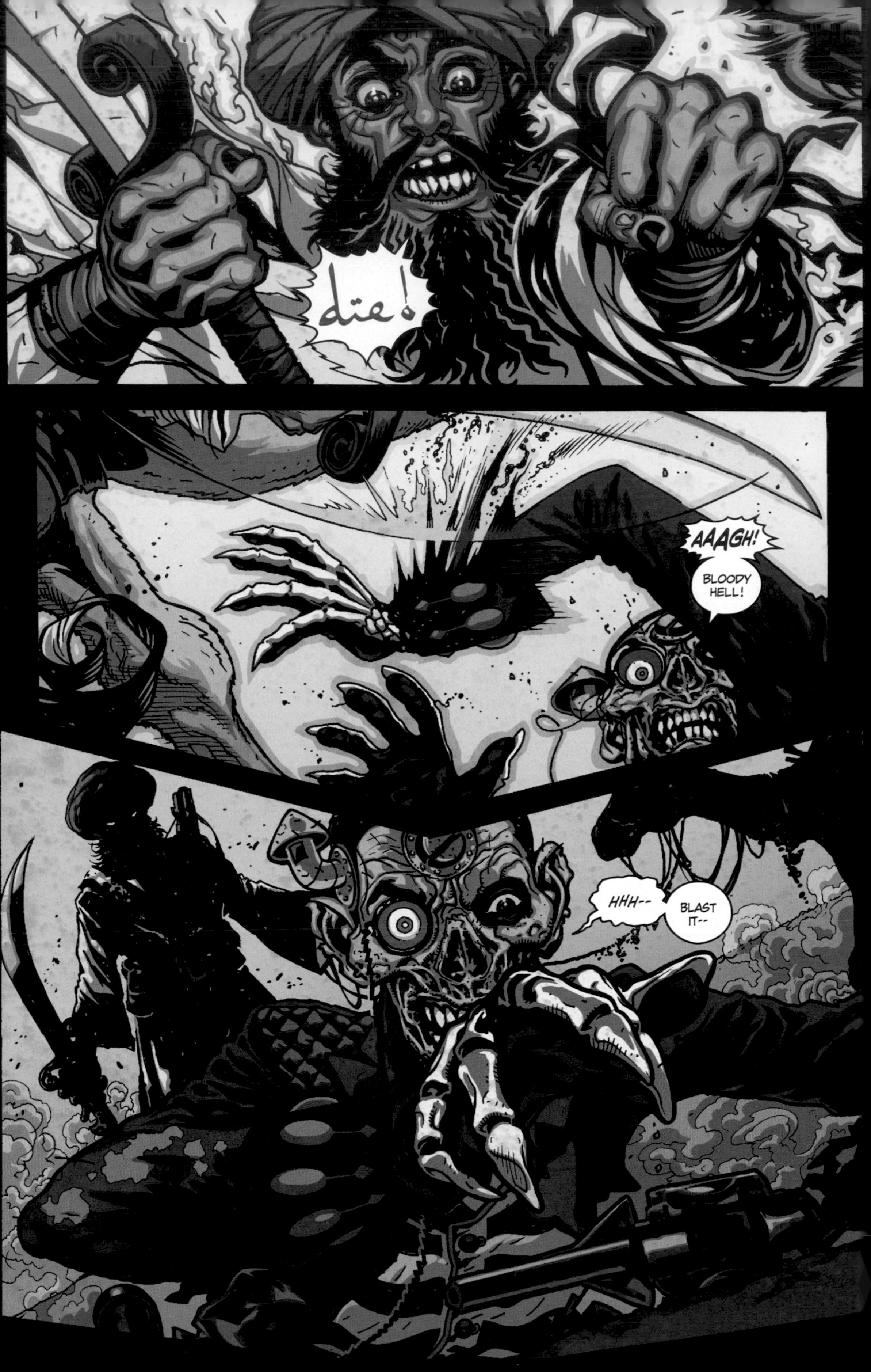
die!
AAAGH!
BLOODY HELL!
HHH--
BLAST IT--

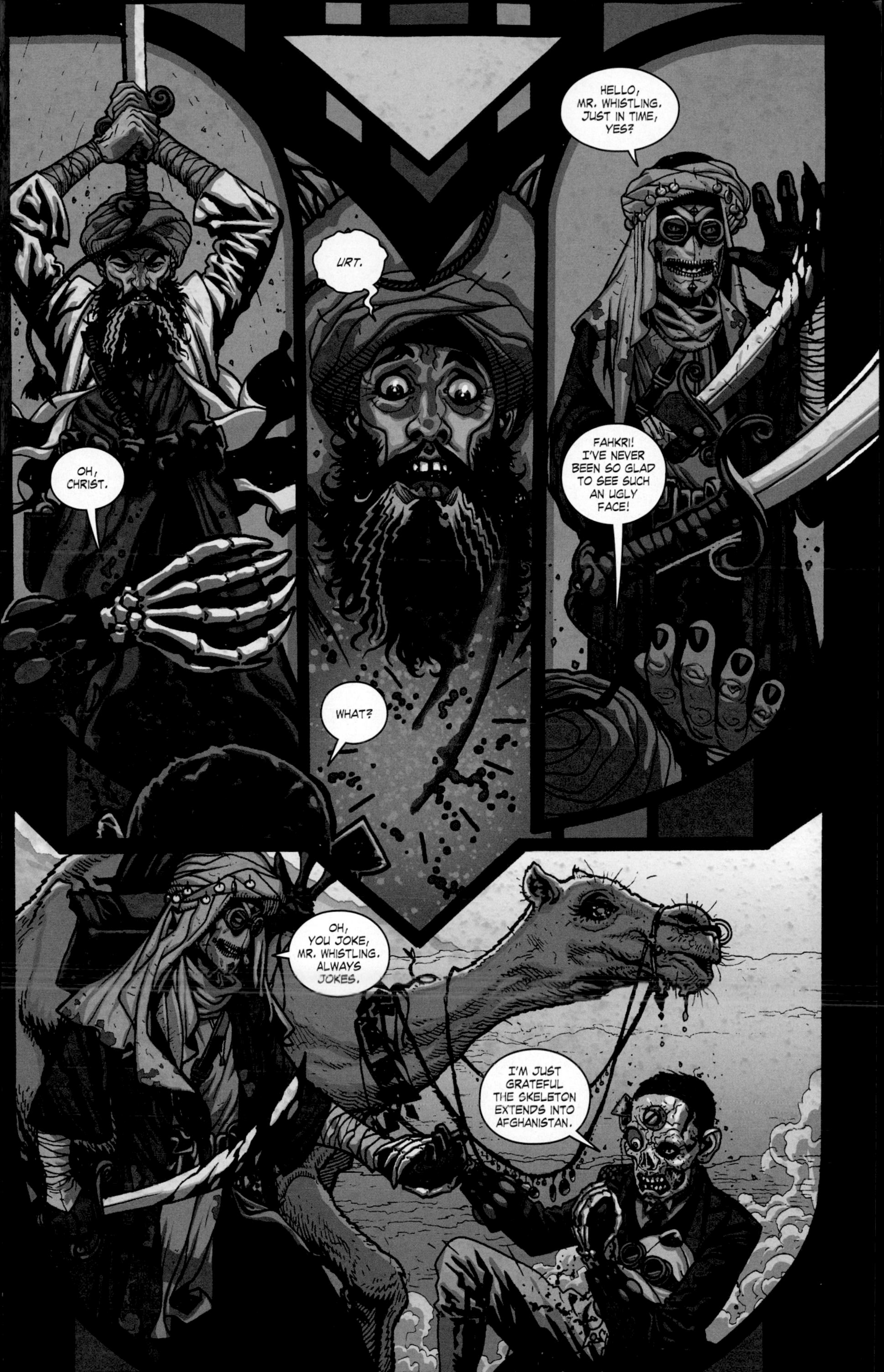

OH, CHRIST.
URT.
WHAT?
HELLO, MR. WHISTLING. JUST IN TIME, YES?
FAHKRI! I'VE NEVER BEEN SO GLAD TO SEE SUCH AN UGLY FACE!
OH, YOU JOKE, MR. WHISTLING. ALWAYS JOKES.
I'M JUST GRATEFUL THE SKELETON EXTENDS INTO AFGHANISTAN.

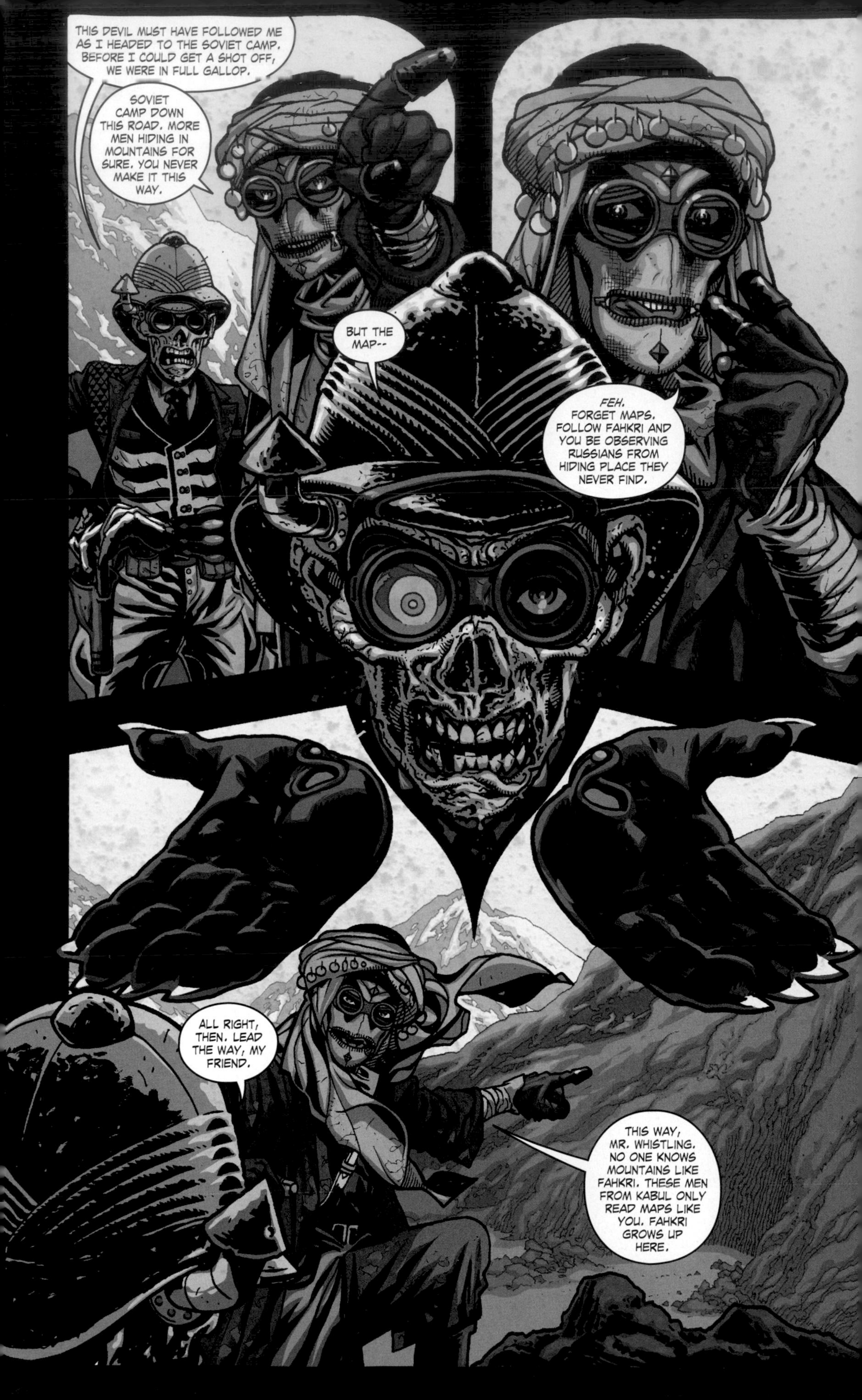
THIS DEVIL MUST HAVE FOLLOWED ME AS I HEADED TO THE SOVIET CAMP. BEFORE I COULD GET A SHOT OFF, WE WERE IN FULL GALLOP.
SOVIET CAMP DOWN THIS ROAD. MORE MEN HIDING IN MOUNTAINS FOR SURE. YOU NEVER MAKE IT THIS WAY.
BUT THE MAP--
FEH. FORGET MAPS. FOLLOW FAHKRI AND YOU BE OBSERVING RUSSIANS FROM HIDING PLACE THEY NEVER FIND.
ALL RIGHT, THEN. LEAD THE WAY, MY FRIEND.
THIS WAY, MR. WHISTLING. NO ONE KNOWS MOUNTAINS LIKE FAHKRI. THESE MEN FROM KABUL ONLY READ MAPS LIKE YOU. FAHKRI GROWS UP HERE.

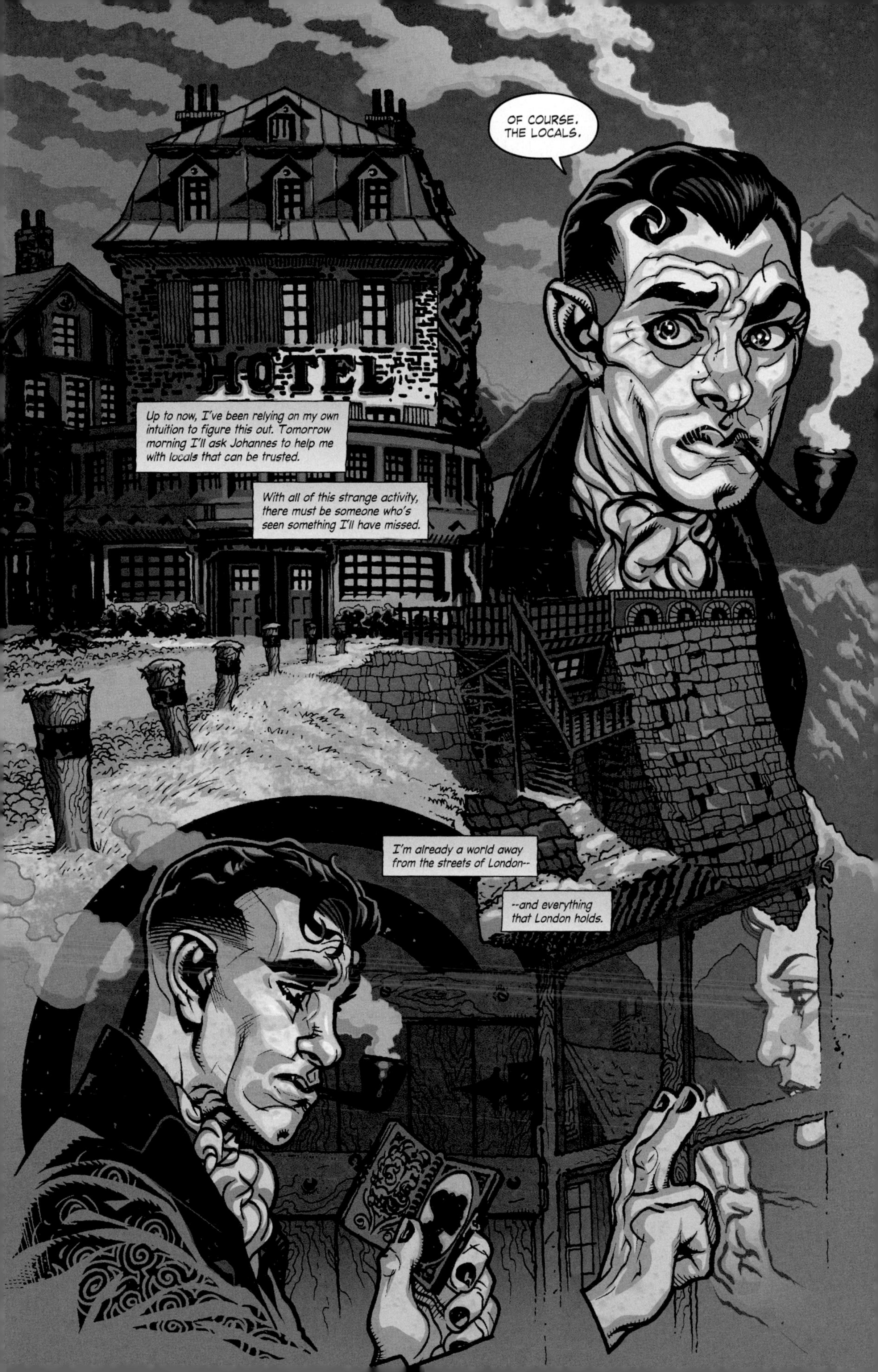
HOTEL
OF COURSE. THE LOCALS.
Up to now, I've been relying on my own intuition to figure this out. Tomorrow morning I'll ask Johannes to help me with locals that can be trusted.
With all of this strange activity, there must be someone who's seen something I'll have missed.
I'm already a world away from the streets of London--
--and everything that London holds.

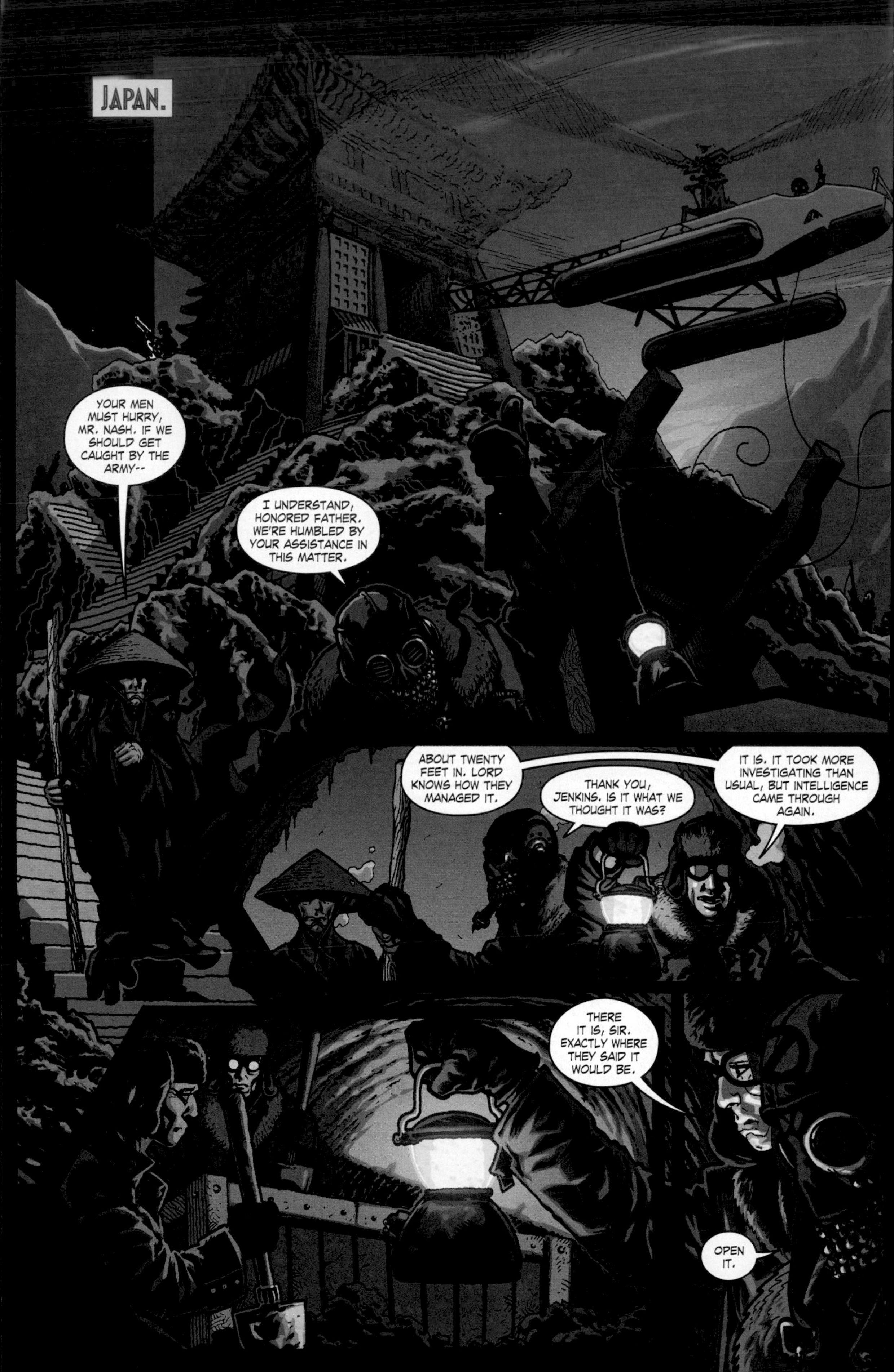
JAPAN.
YOUR MEN MUST HURRY, MR. NASH. IF WE SHOULD GET CAUGHT BY THE ARMY--
I UNDERSTAND, HONORED FATHER. WE'RE HUMBLED BY YOUR ASSISTANCE IN THIS MATTER.
ABOUT TWENTY FEET IN. LORD KNOWS HOW THEY MANAGED IT.
THANK YOU, JENKINS. IS IT WHAT WE THOUGHT IT WAS?
IT IS. IT TOOK MORE INVESTIGATING THAN USUAL, BUT INTELLIGENCE CAME THROUGH AGAIN.
THERE IT IS, SIR. EXACTLY WHERE THEY SAID IT WOULD BE.
OPEN IT.

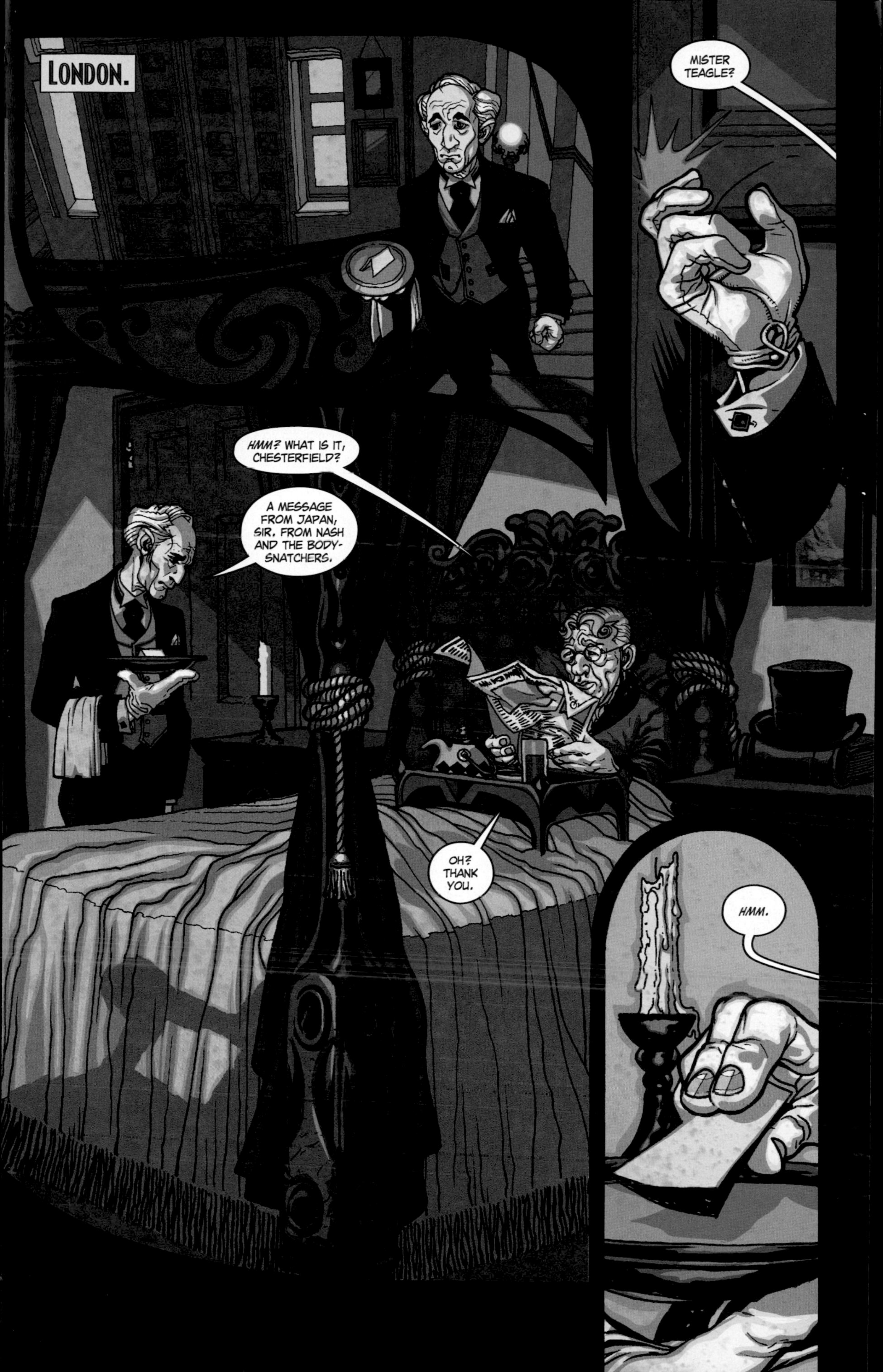
LONDON.
MISTER TEAGLE?
HMM? WHAT IS IT, CHESTERFIELD?
A MESSAGE FROM JAPAN, SIR. FROM NASH AND THE BODY-SNATCHERS.
OH? THANK YOU.
HMM.

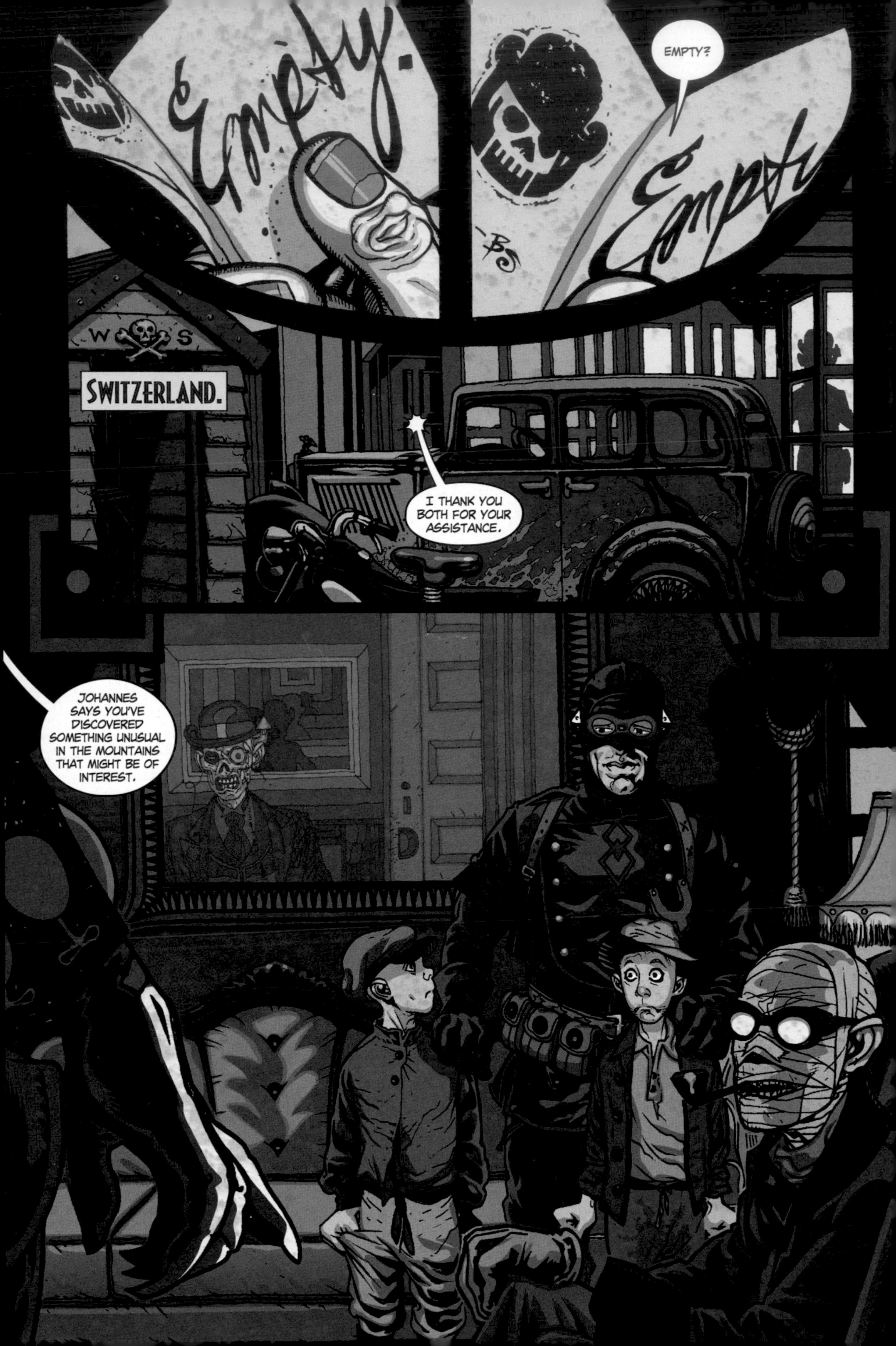
Empty.
Empty?
Empty
W S
SWITZERLAND.
I THANK YOU BOTH FOR YOUR ASSISTANCE.
JOHANNES SAYS YOU'VE DISCOVERED SOMETHING UNUSUAL IN THE MOUNTAINS THAT MIGHT BE OF INTEREST.

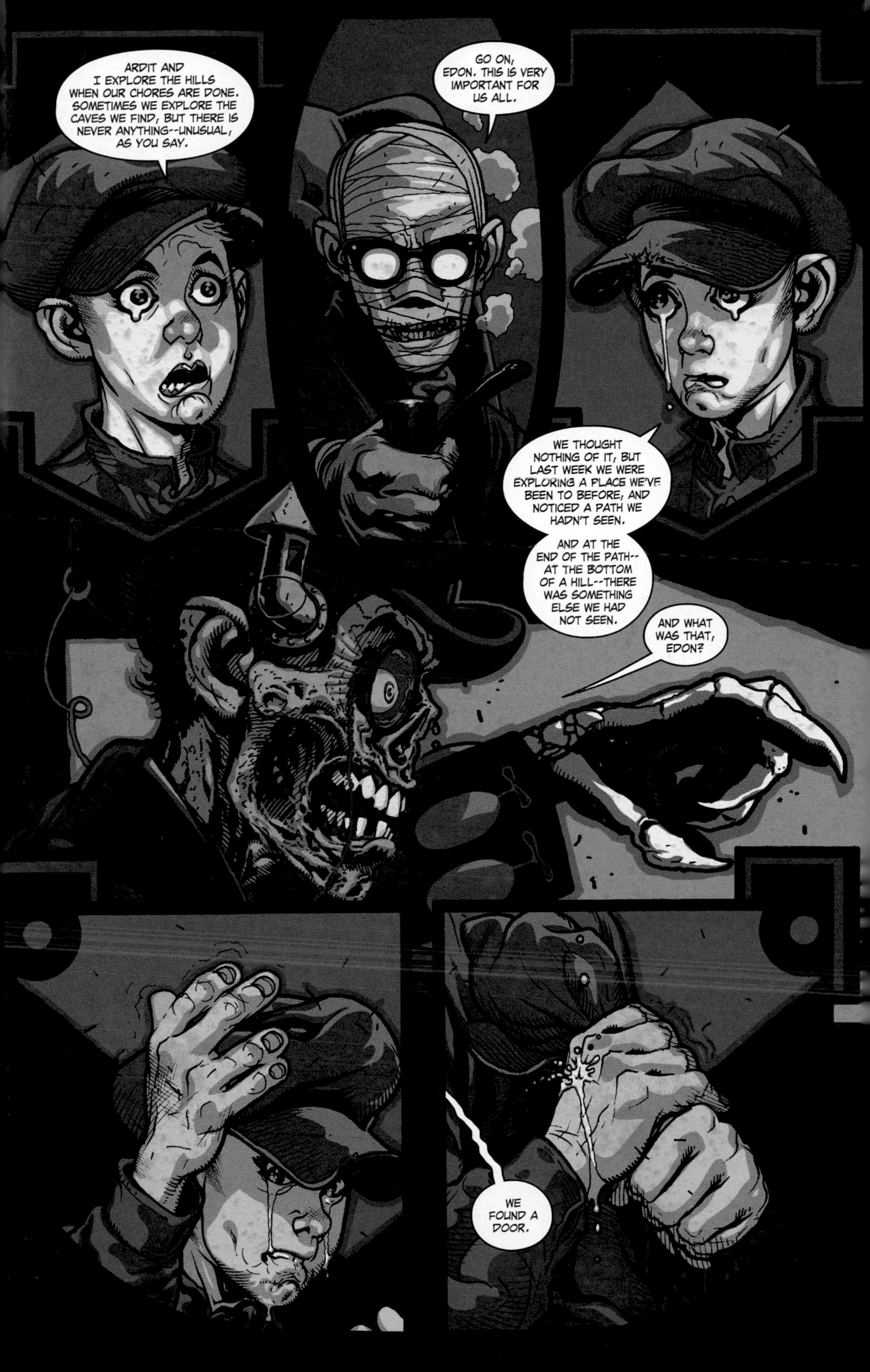
ARDIT AND I EXPLORE THE HILLS WHEN OUR CHORES ARE DONE. SOMETIMES WE EXPLORE THE CAVES WE FIND, BUT THERE IS NEVER ANYTHING--UNUSUAL, AS YOU SAY.
GO ON, EDON. THIS IS VERY IMPORTANT FOR US ALL.
WE THOUGHT NOTHING OF IT, BUT LAST WEEK WE WERE EXPLORING A PLACE WE'VE BEEN TO BEFORE, AND NOTICED A PATH WE HADN'T SEEN.
AND AT THE END OF THE PATH--AT THE BOTTOM OF A HILL--THERE WAS SOMETHING ELSE WE HAD NOT SEEN.
AND WHAT WAS THAT, EDON?
WE FOUND A DOOR.

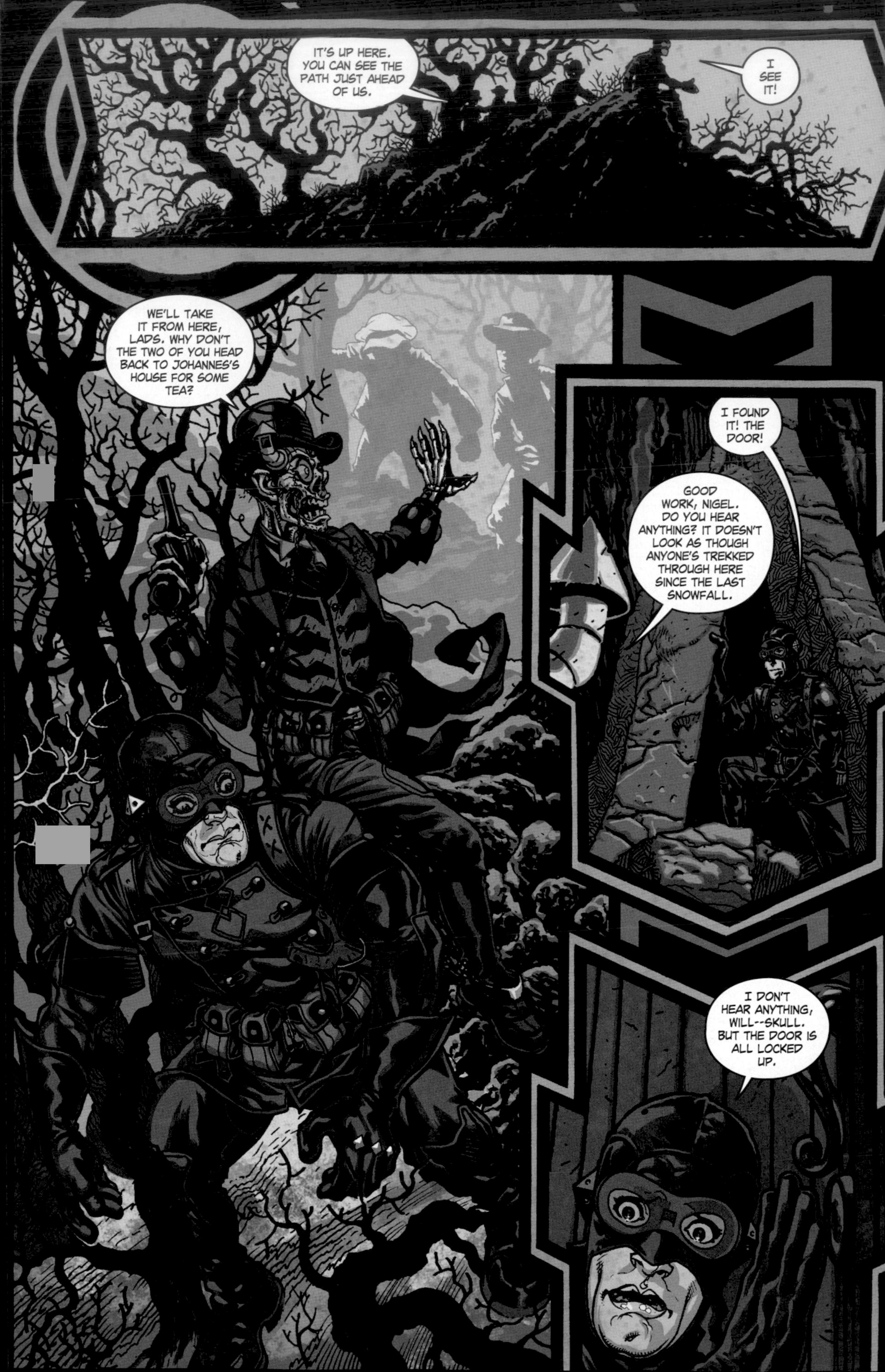
IT'S UP HERE. YOU CAN SEE THE PATH JUST AHEAD OF US.
I SEE IT!
WE'LL TAKE IT FROM HERE, LADS. WHY DON'T THE TWO OF YOU HEAD BACK TO JOHANNES'S HOUSE FOR SOME TEA?
I FOUND IT! THE DOOR!
GOOD WORK, NIGEL. DO YOU HEAR ANYTHING? IT DOESN'T LOOK AS THOUGH ANYONE'S TREKKED THROUGH HERE SINCE THE LAST SNOWFALL.
I DON'T HEAR ANYTHING, WILL--SKULL. BUT THE DOOR IS ALL LOCKED UP.

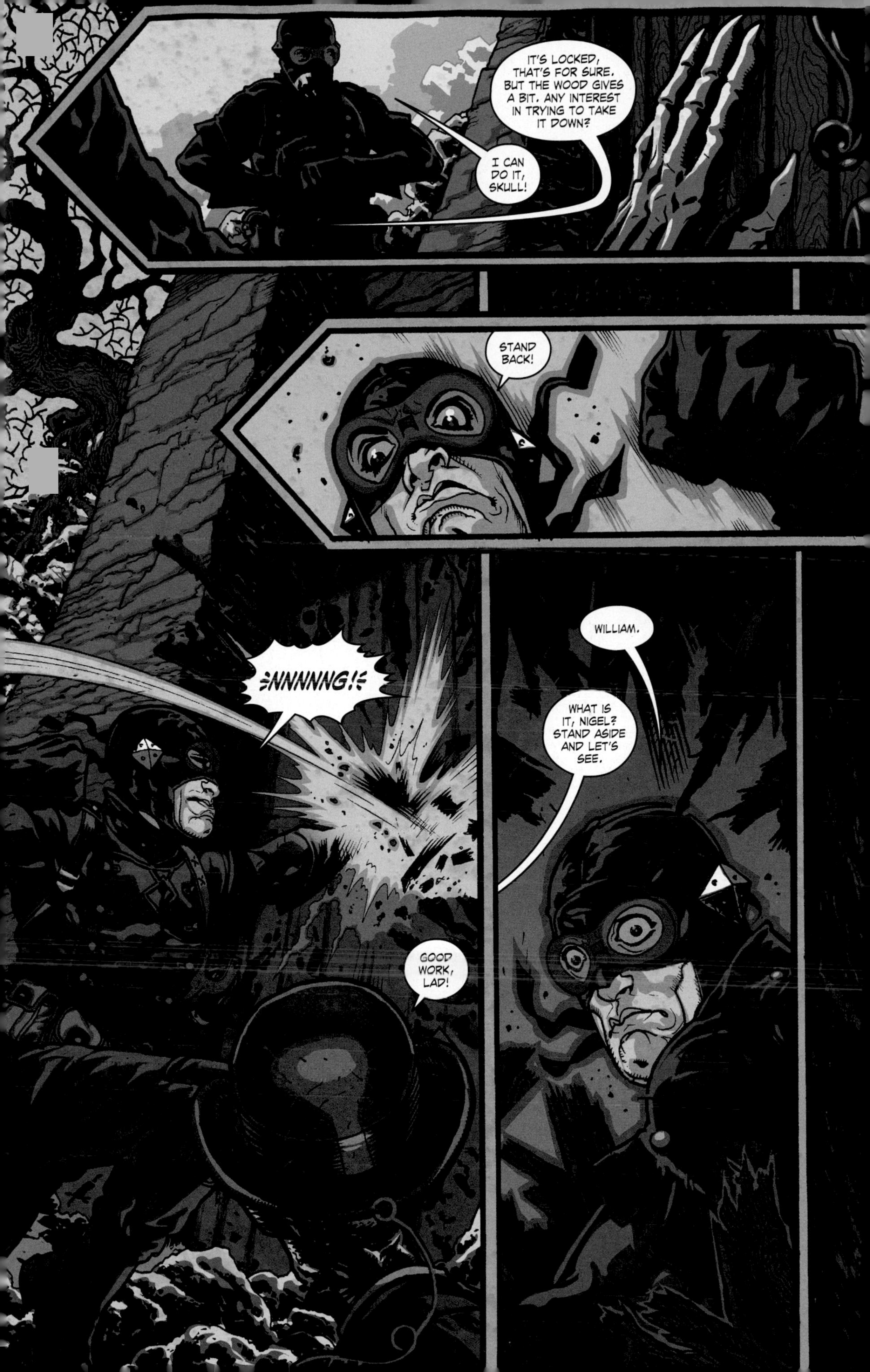
IT'S LOCKED, THAT'S FOR SURE. BUT THE WOOD GIVES A BIT. ANY INTEREST IN TRYING TO TAKE IT DOWN?
I CAN DO IT, SKULL!
STAND BACK!
NNNNNG!
GOOD WORK, LAD!
WILLIAM.
WHAT IS IT, NIGEL? STAND ASIDE AND LET'S SEE.

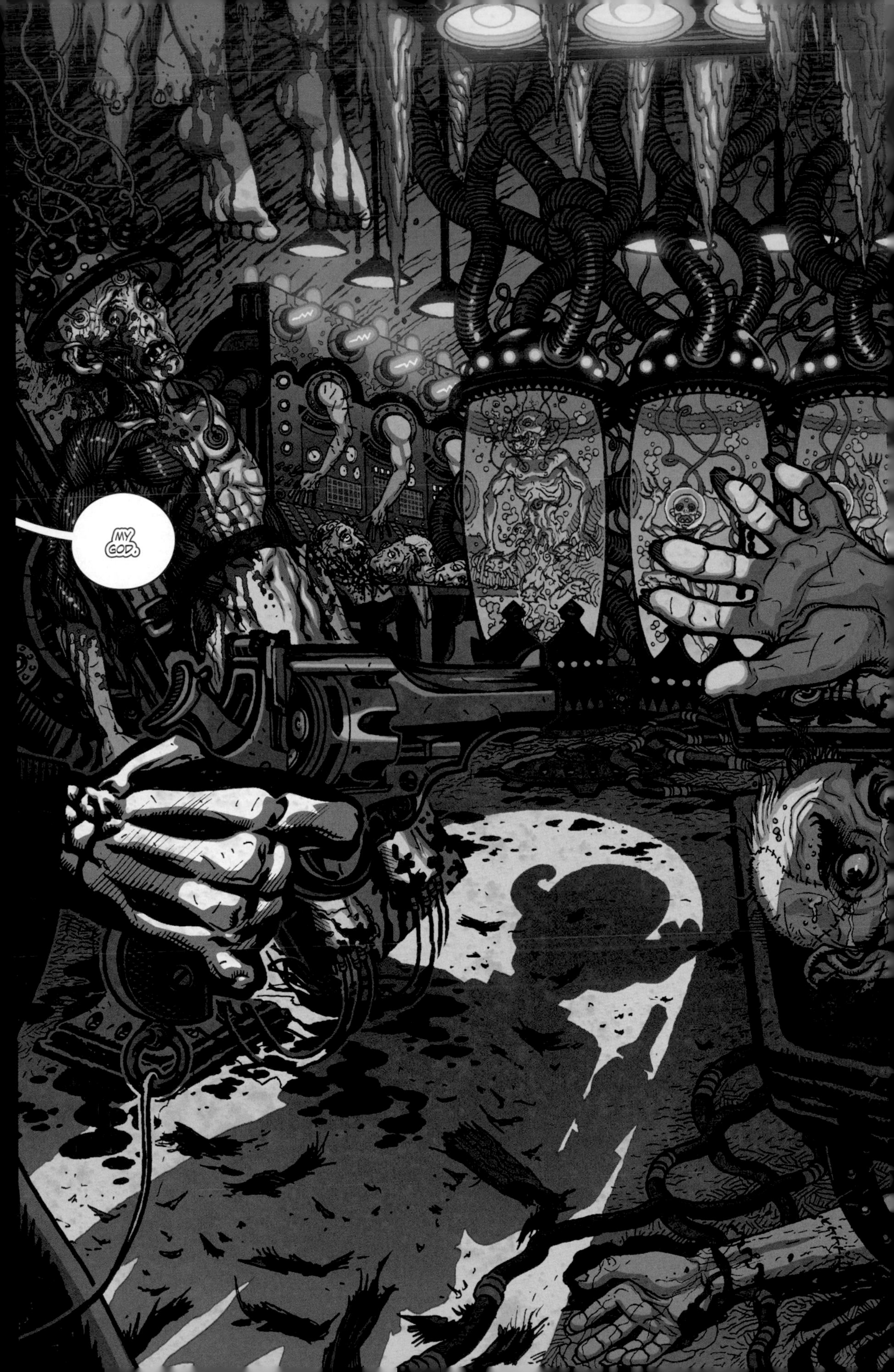
MY GOD.

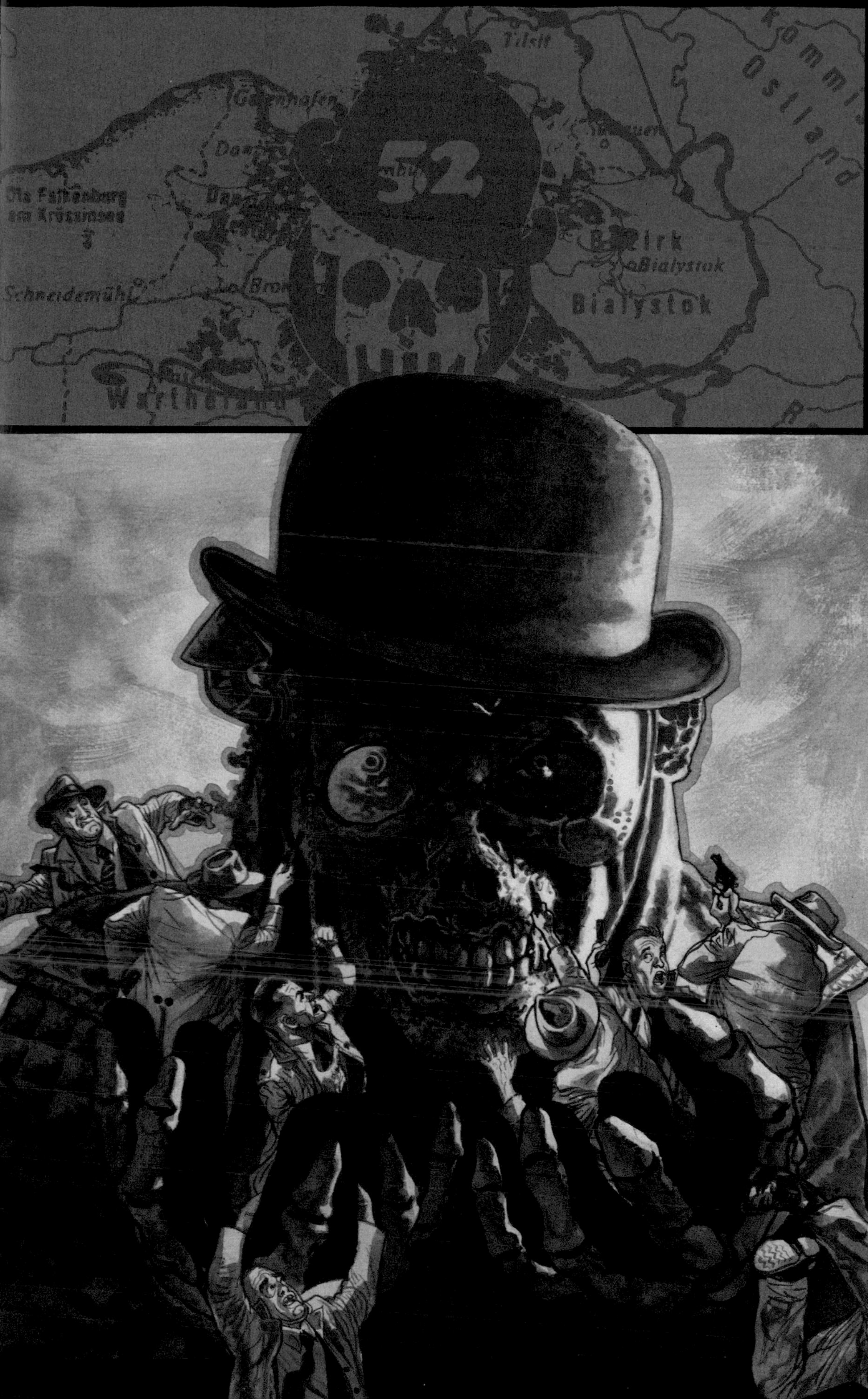
Tilsit
52
Bialystok
Bialystok
Schneidemühl
Ostland

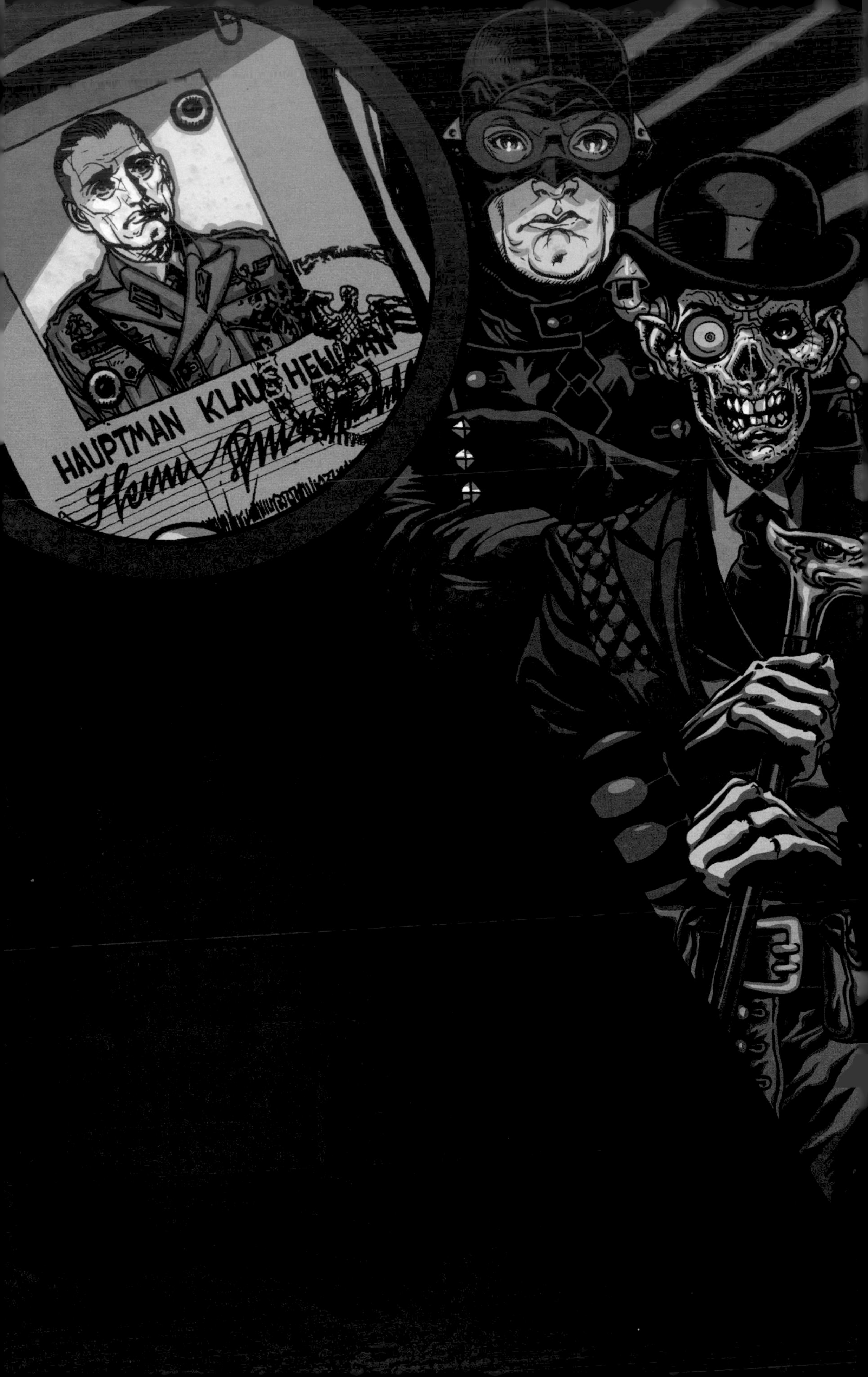
HAUPTMAN KLAUS

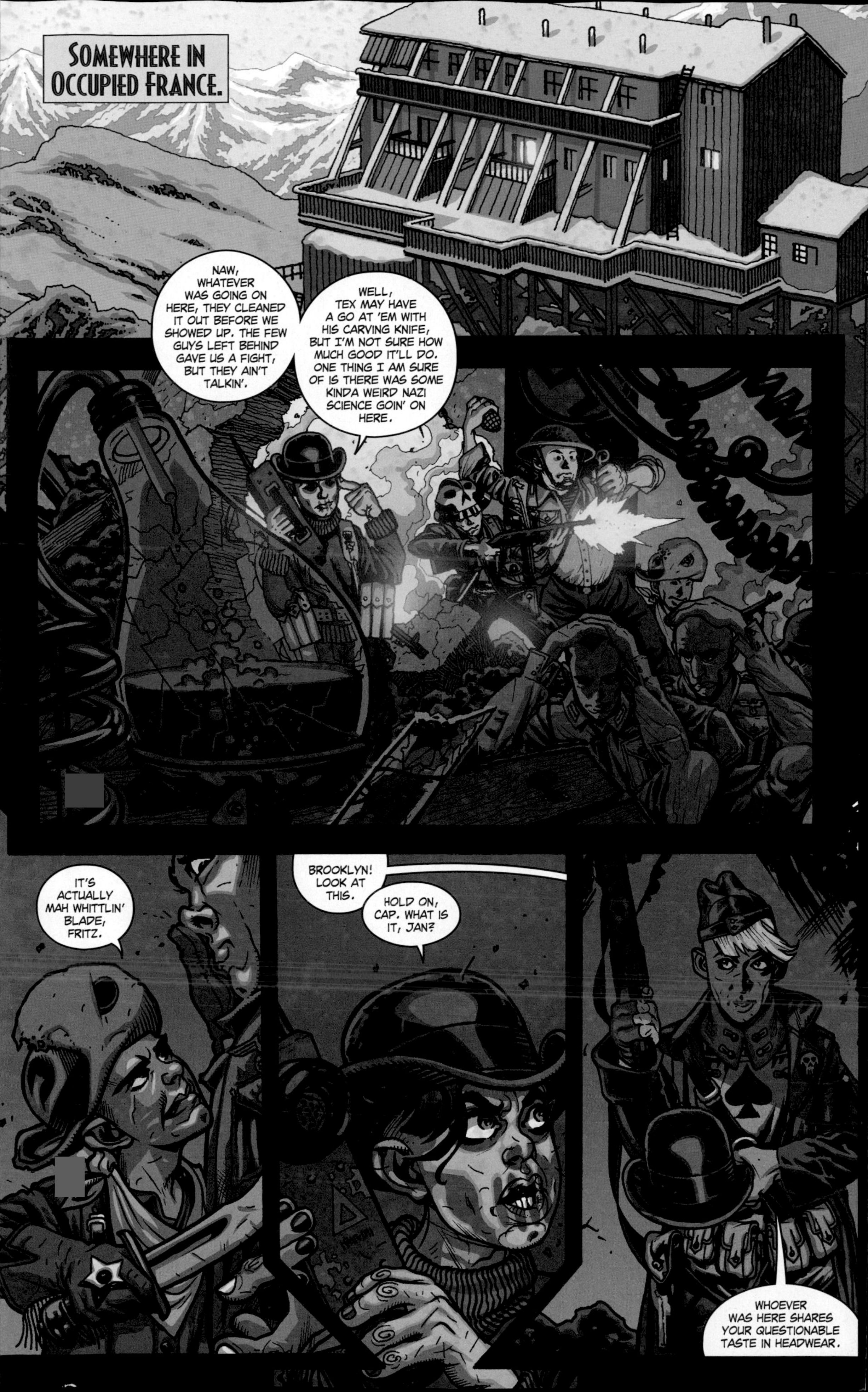
SOMEWHERE IN OCCUPIED FRANCE.
NAW, WHATEVER WAS GOING ON HERE, THEY CLEANED IT OUT BEFORE WE SHOWED UP. THE FEW GUYS LEFT BEHIND GAVE US A FIGHT, BUT THEY AIN'T TALKIN'.
WELL, TEX MAY HAVE A GO AT 'EM WITH HIS CARVING KNIFE, BUT I'M NOT SURE HOW MUCH GOOD IT'LL DO. ONE THING I AM SURE OF IS THERE WAS SOME KINDA WEIRD NAZI SCIENCE GOIN' ON HERE.
IT'S ACTUALLY MAH WHITTLIN' BLADE, FRITZ.
BROOKLYN! LOOK AT THIS.
HOLD ON, CAP. WHAT IS IT, JAN?
WHOEVER WAS HERE SHARES YOUR QUESTIONABLE TASTE IN HEADWEAR.

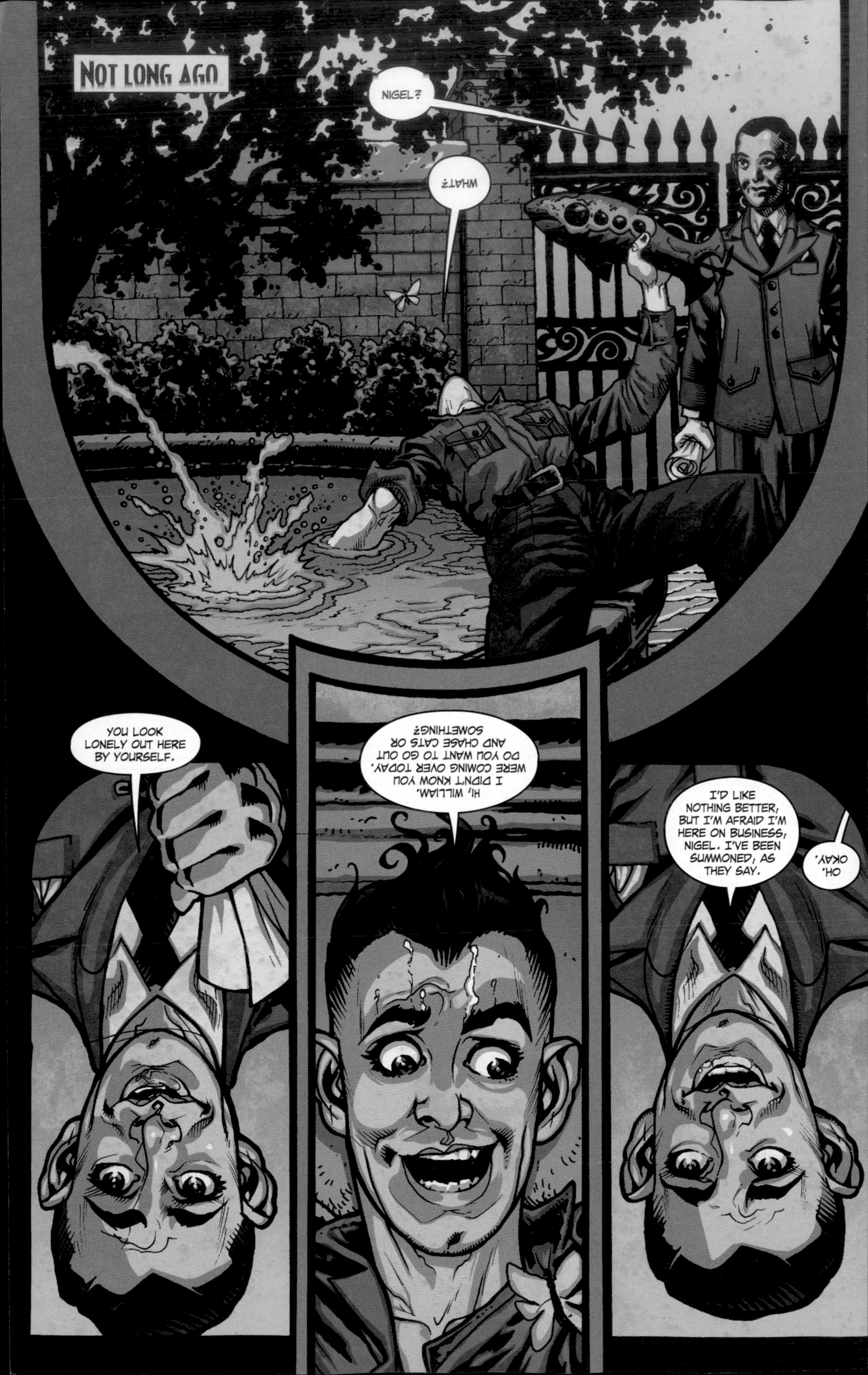
NOT LONG AGO
NIGEL?
WHAT?
YOU LOOK LONELY OUT HERE BY YOURSELF.
HI, WILLIAM. I DIDN'T KNOW YOU WERE COMING OVER TODAY. DO YOU WANT TO GO OUT AND CHASE CATS OR SOMETHING?
I'D LIKE NOTHING BETTER, BUT I'M AFRAID I'M HERE ON BUSINESS, NIGEL. I'VE BEEN SUMMONED, AS THEY SAY.
OH, OKAY.

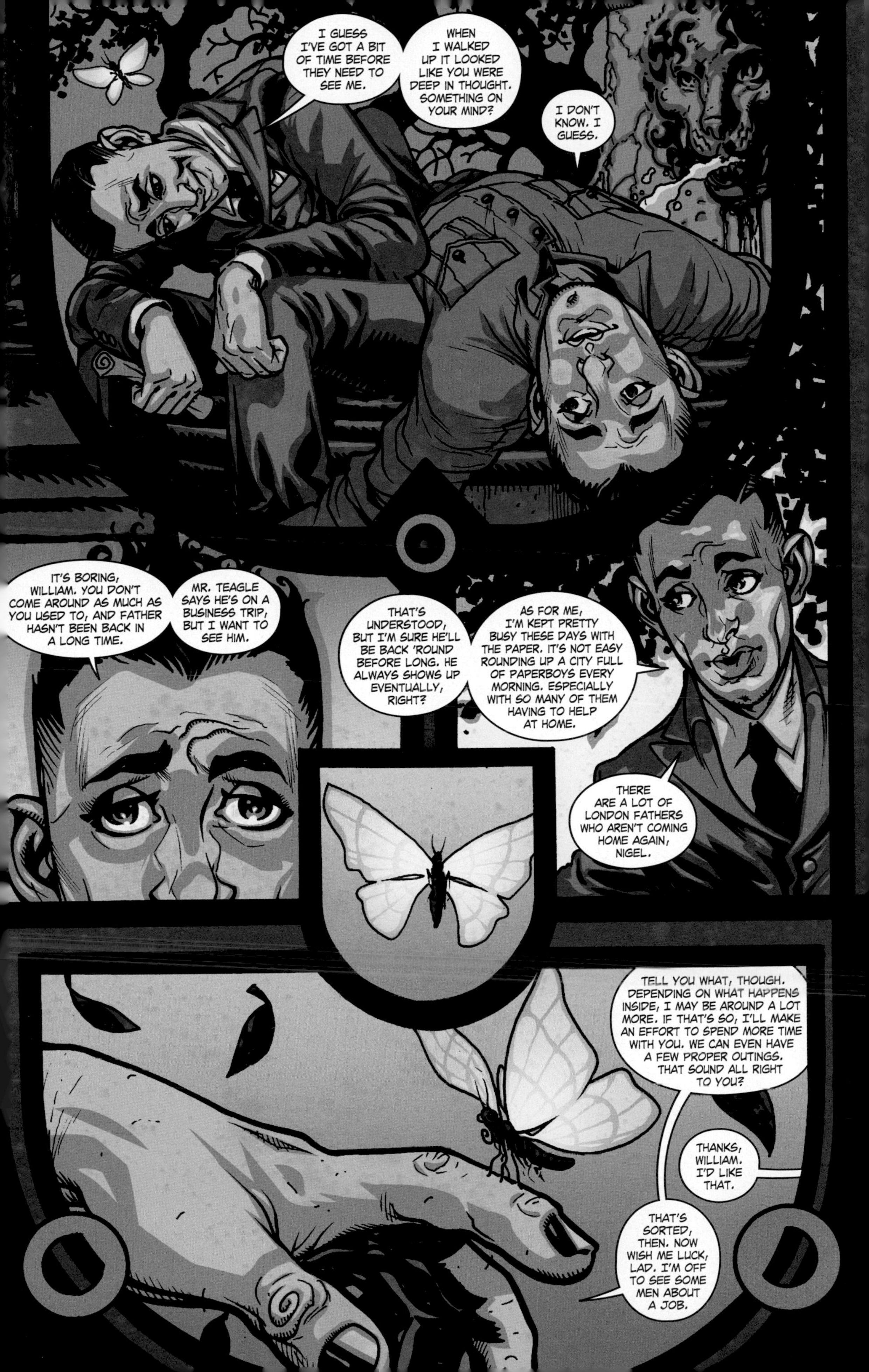
I GUESS I'VE GOT A BIT OF TIME BEFORE THEY NEED TO SEE ME.
WHEN I WALKED UP IT LOOKED LIKE YOU WERE DEEP IN THOUGHT. SOMETHING ON YOUR MIND?
I DON'T KNOW. I GUESS.
IT'S BORING, WILLIAM. YOU DON'T COME AROUND AS MUCH AS YOU USED TO, AND FATHER HASN'T BEEN BACK IN A LONG TIME.
MR. TEAGLE SAYS HE'S ON A BUSINESS TRIP, BUT I WANT TO SEE HIM.
THAT'S UNDERSTOOD, BUT I'M SURE HE'LL BE BACK 'ROUND BEFORE LONG. HE ALWAYS SHOWS UP EVENTUALLY, RIGHT?
AS FOR ME, I'M KEPT PRETTY BUSY THESE DAYS WITH THE PAPER. IT'S NOT EASY ROUNDING UP A CITY FULL OF PAPERBOYS EVERY MORNING. ESPECIALLY WITH SO MANY OF THEM HAVING TO HELP AT HOME.
THERE ARE A LOT OF LONDON FATHERS WHO AREN'T COMING HOME AGAIN, NIGEL.
TELL YOU WHAT, THOUGH. DEPENDING ON WHAT HAPPENS INSIDE, I MAY BE AROUND A LOT MORE. IF THAT'S SO, I'LL MAKE AN EFFORT TO SPEND MORE TIME WITH YOU. WE CAN EVEN HAVE A FEW PROPER OUTINGS. THAT SOUND ALL RIGHT TO YOU?
THANKS, WILLIAM. I'D LIKE THAT.
THAT'S SORTED, THEN. NOW WISH ME LUCK, LAD. I'M OFF TO SEE SOME MEN ABOUT A JOB.

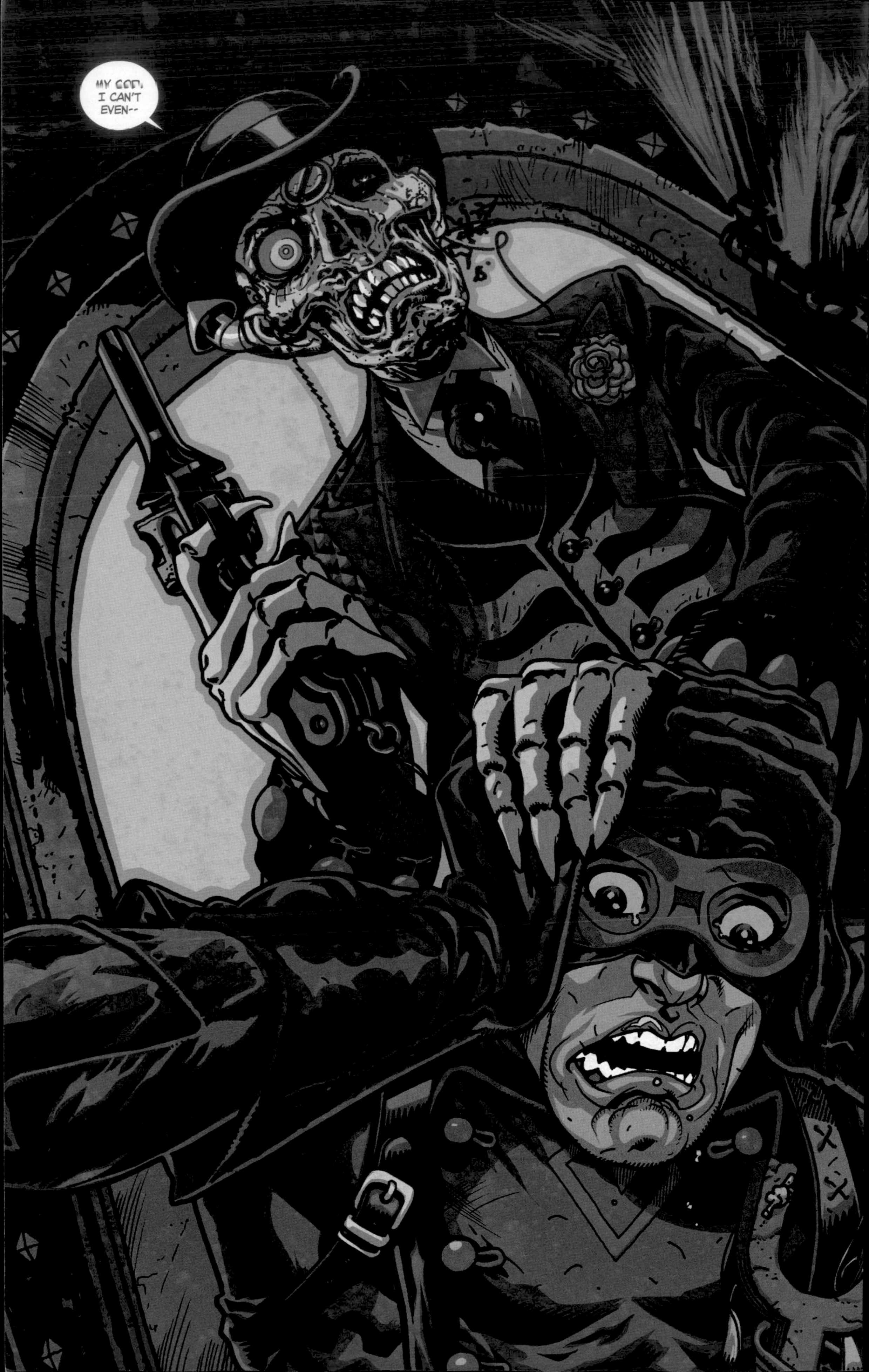
MY GOD, I CAN'T EVEN--

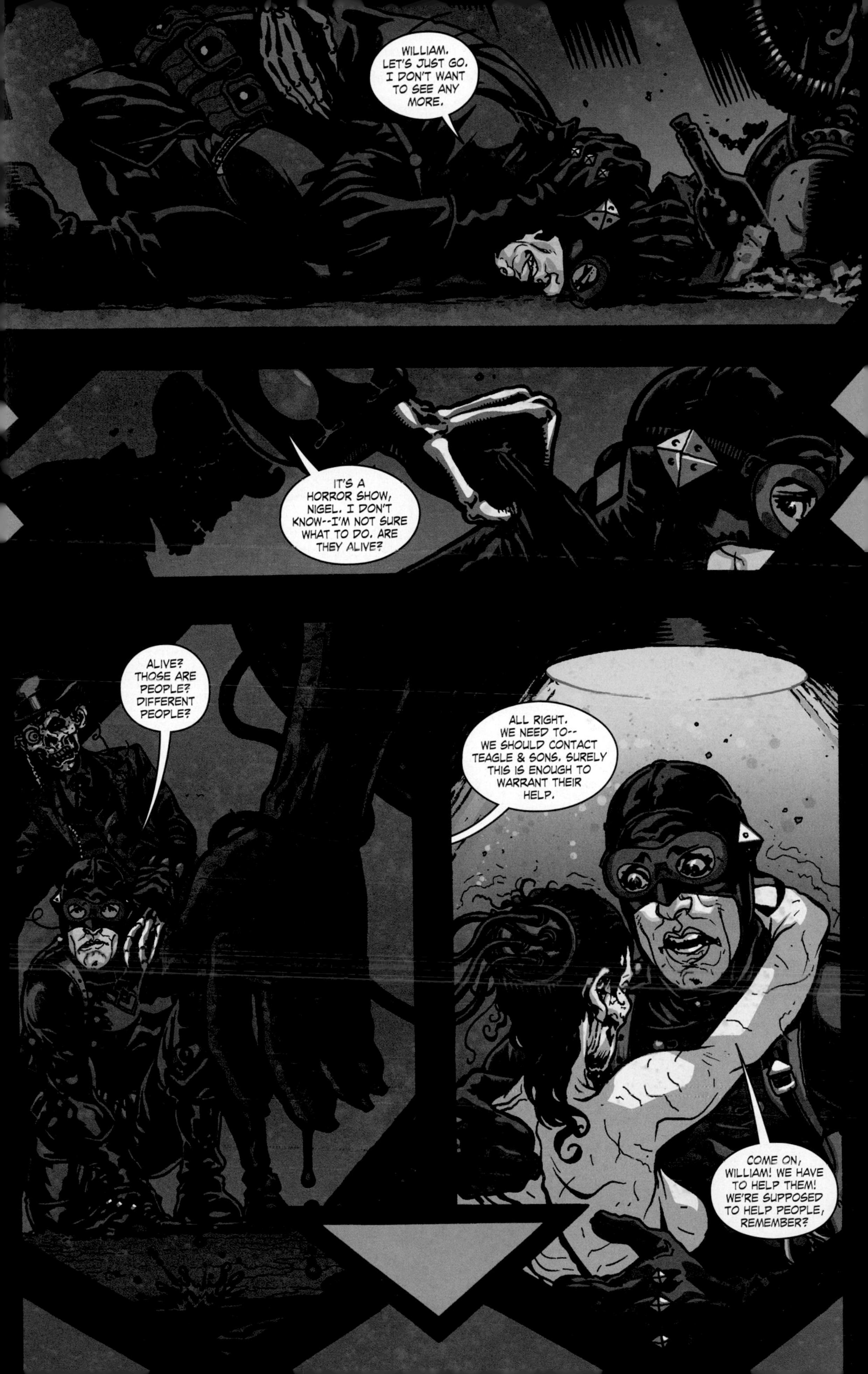
WILLIAM. LET'S JUST GO. I DON'T WANT TO SEE ANY MORE.
IT'S A HORROR SHOW, NIGEL. I DON'T KNOW--I'M NOT SURE WHAT TO DO. ARE THEY ALIVE?
ALIVE? THOSE ARE PEOPLE? DIFFERENT PEOPLE?
ALL RIGHT. WE NEED TO-- WE SHOULD CONTACT TEAGLE & SONS. SURELY THIS IS ENOUGH TO WARRANT THEIR HELP.
COME ON, WILLIAM! WE HAVE TO HELP THEM! WE'RE SUPPOSED TO HELP PEOPLE, REMEMBER?

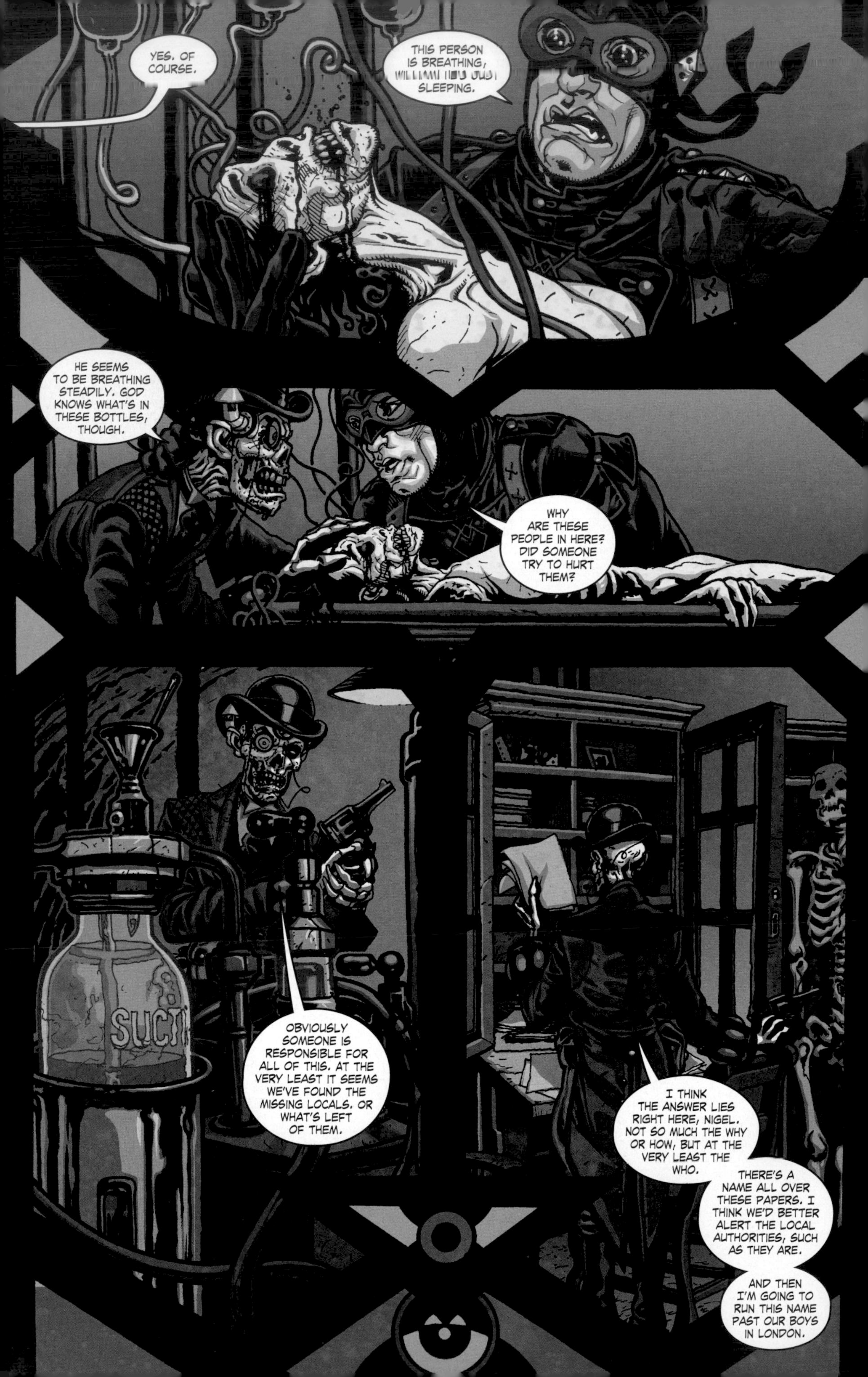
YES. OF COURSE.
THIS PERSON IS BREATHING,
SLEEPING.
HE SEEMS TO BE BREATHING STEADILY. GOD KNOWS WHAT'S IN THESE BOTTLES, THOUGH.
WHY ARE THESE PEOPLE IN HERE? DID SOMEONE TRY TO HURT THEM?
SUCTI
OBVIOUSLY SOMEONE IS RESPONSIBLE FOR ALL OF THIS. AT THE VERY LEAST IT SEEMS WE'VE FOUND THE MISSING LOCALS. OR WHAT'S LEFT OF THEM.
I THINK THE ANSWER LIES RIGHT HERE, NIGEL. NOT SO MUCH THE WHY OR HOW, BUT AT THE VERY LEAST THE WHO.
THERE'S A NAME ALL OVER THESE PAPERS. I THINK WE'D BETTER ALERT THE LOCAL AUTHORITIES, SUCH AS THEY ARE.
AND THEN I'M GOING TO RUN THIS NAME PAST OUR BOYS IN LONDON.

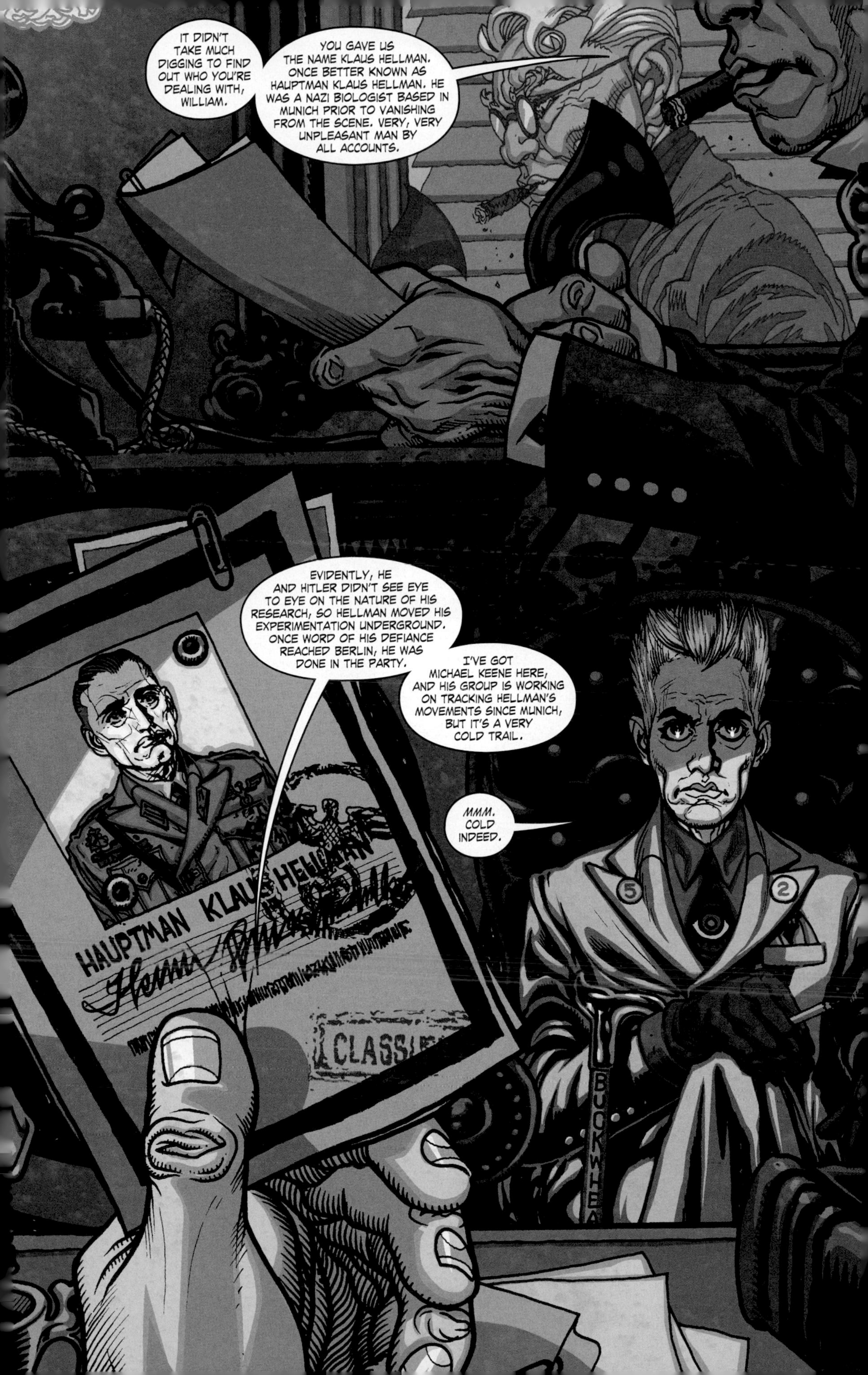
IT DIDN'T TAKE MUCH DIGGING TO FIND OUT WHO YOU'RE DEALING WITH, WILLIAM.
YOU GAVE US THE NAME KLAUS HELLMAN. ONCE BETTER KNOWN AS HAUPTMAN KLAUS HELLMAN. HE WAS A NAZI BIOLOGIST BASED IN MUNICH PRIOR TO VANISHING FROM THE SCENE. VERY, VERY UNPLEASANT MAN BY ALL ACCOUNTS.
EVIDENTLY, HE AND HITLER DIDN'T SEE EYE TO EYE ON THE NATURE OF HIS RESEARCH, SO HELLMAN MOVED HIS EXPERIMENTATION UNDERGROUND. ONCE WORD OF HIS DEFIANCE REACHED BERLIN, HE WAS DONE IN THE PARTY.
I'VE GOT MICHAEL KEENE HERE, AND HIS GROUP IS WORKING ON TRACKING HELLMAN'S MOVEMENTS SINCE MUNICH, BUT IT'S A VERY COLD TRAIL.
MMM. COLD INDEED.
HAUPTMAN KLAUS HELLMAN
CLASS
BUCKWHEA

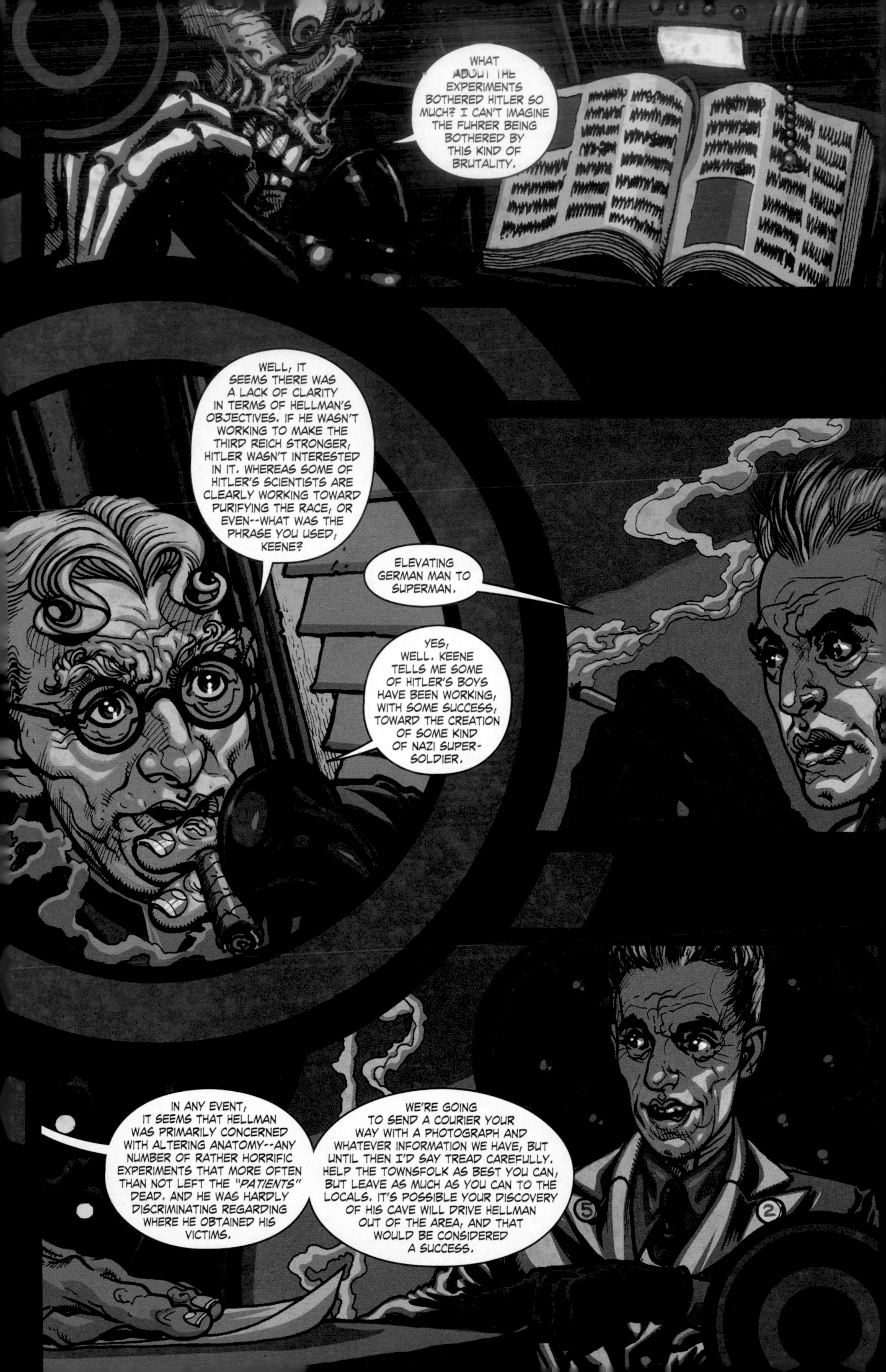
WHAT ABOUT THE EXPERIMENTS BOTHERED HITLER SO MUCH? I CAN'T IMAGINE THE FUHRER BEING BOTHERED BY THIS KIND OF BRUTALITY.
WELL, IT SEEMS THERE WAS A LACK OF CLARITY IN TERMS OF HELLMAN'S OBJECTIVES. IF HE WASN'T WORKING TO MAKE THE THIRD REICH STRONGER, HITLER WASN'T INTERESTED IN IT. WHEREAS SOME OF HITLER'S SCIENTISTS ARE CLEARLY WORKING TOWARD PURIFYING THE RACE, OR EVEN--WHAT WAS THE PHRASE YOU USED, KEENE?
ELEVATING GERMAN MAN TO SUPERMAN.
YES, WELL. KEENE TELLS ME SOME OF HITLER'S BOYS HAVE BEEN WORKING, WITH SOME SUCCESS, TOWARD THE CREATION OF SOME KIND OF NAZI SUPER-SOLDIER.
IN ANY EVENT, IT SEEMS THAT HELLMAN WAS PRIMARILY CONCERNED WITH ALTERING ANATOMY--ANY NUMBER OF RATHER HORRIFIC EXPERIMENTS THAT MORE OFTEN THAN NOT LEFT THE "PATIENTS" DEAD. AND HE WAS HARDLY DISCRIMINATING REGARDING WHERE HE OBTAINED HIS VICTIMS.
WE'RE GOING TO SEND A COURIER YOUR WAY WITH A PHOTOGRAPH AND WHATEVER INFORMATION WE HAVE, BUT UNTIL THEN I'D SAY TREAD CAREFULLY. HELP THE TOWNSFOLK AS BEST YOU CAN, BUT LEAVE AS MUCH AS YOU CAN TO THE LOCALS. IT'S POSSIBLE YOUR DISCOVERY OF HIS CAVE WILL DRIVE HELLMAN OUT OF THE AREA, AND THAT WOULD BE CONSIDERED A SUCCESS.

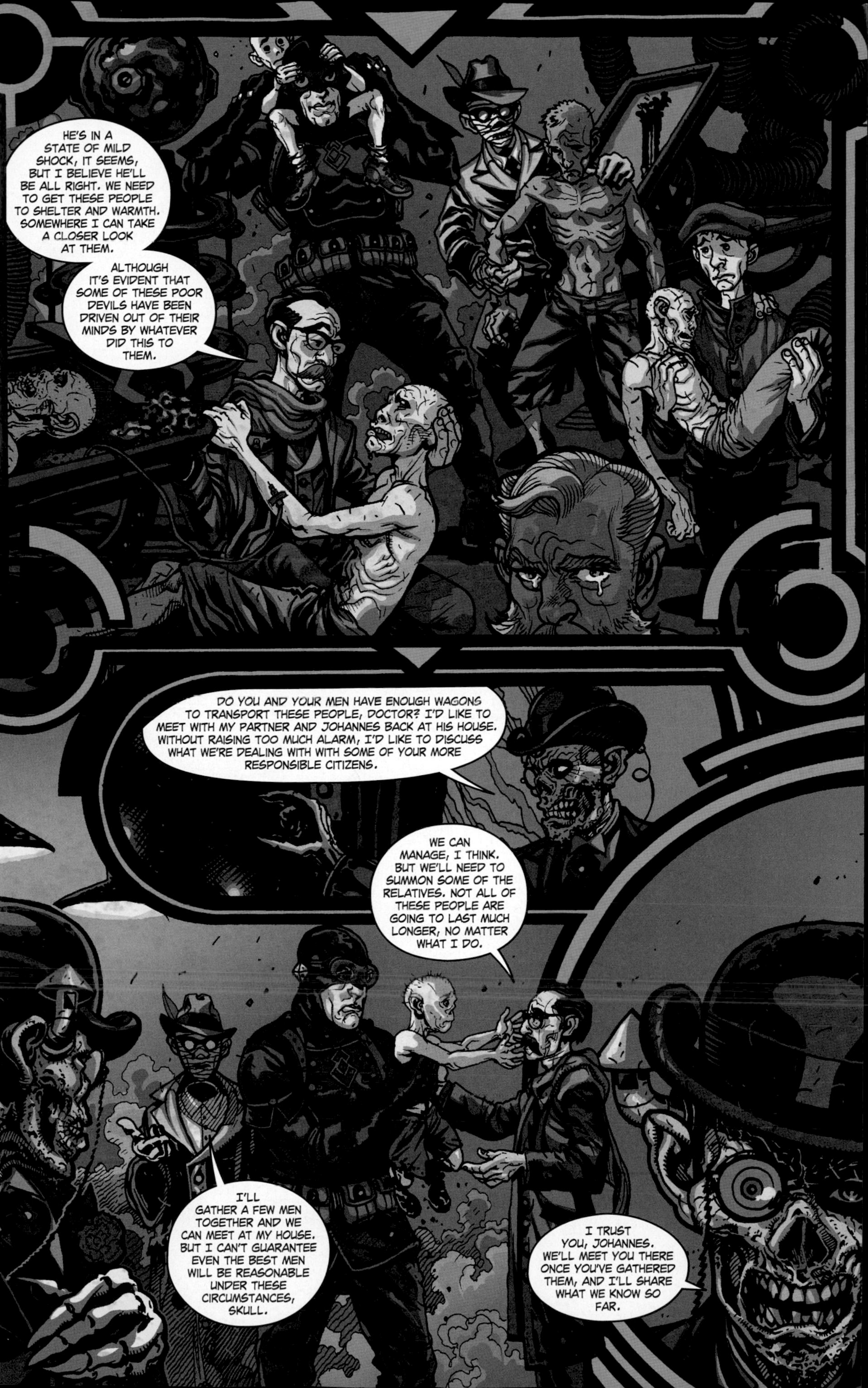
HE'S IN A STATE OF MILD SHOCK, IT SEEMS, BUT I BELIEVE HE'LL BE ALL RIGHT. WE NEED TO GET THESE PEOPLE TO SHELTER AND WARMTH. SOMEWHERE I CAN TAKE A CLOSER LOOK AT THEM.
ALTHOUGH IT'S EVIDENT THAT SOME OF THESE POOR DEVILS HAVE BEEN DRIVEN OUT OF THEIR MINDS BY WHATEVER DID THIS TO THEM.
DO YOU AND YOUR MEN HAVE ENOUGH WAGONS TO TRANSPORT THESE PEOPLE, DOCTOR? I'D LIKE TO MEET WITH MY PARTNER AND JOHANNES BACK AT HIS HOUSE. WITHOUT RAISING TOO MUCH ALARM, I'D LIKE TO DISCUSS WHAT WE'RE DEALING WITH WITH SOME OF YOUR MORE RESPONSIBLE CITIZENS.
WE CAN MANAGE, I THINK. BUT WE'LL NEED TO SUMMON SOME OF THE RELATIVES. NOT ALL OF THESE PEOPLE ARE GOING TO LAST MUCH LONGER, NO MATTER WHAT I DO.
I'LL GATHER A FEW MEN TOGETHER AND WE CAN MEET AT MY HOUSE. BUT I CAN'T GUARANTEE EVEN THE BEST MEN WILL BE REASONABLE UNDER THESE CIRCUMSTANCES, SKULL.
I TRUST YOU, JOHANNES. WE'LL MEET YOU THERE ONCE YOU'VE GATHERED THEM, AND I'LL SHARE WHAT WE KNOW SO FAR.

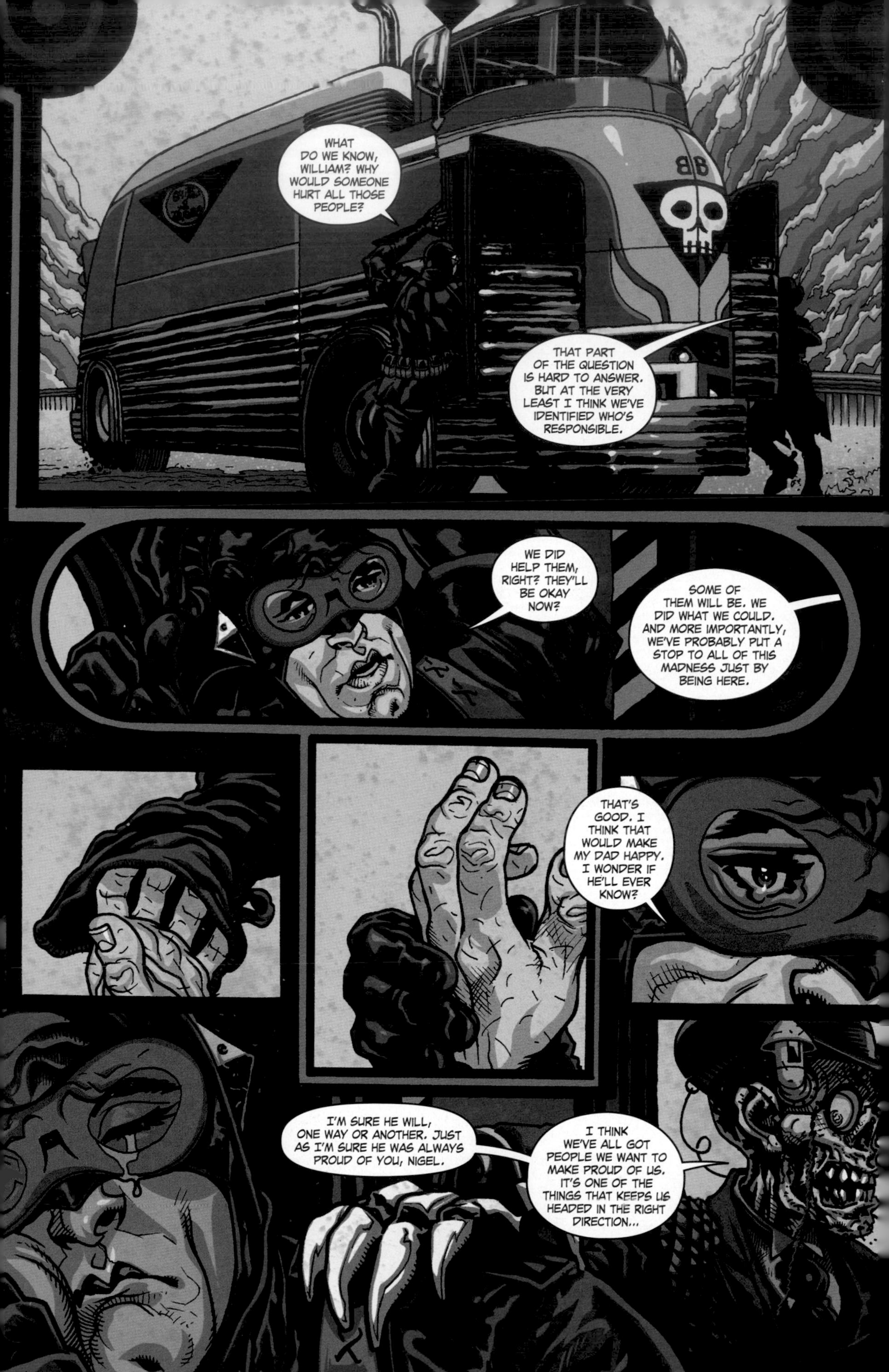
WHAT DO WE KNOW, WILLIAM? WHY WOULD SOMEONE HURT ALL THOSE PEOPLE?
THAT PART OF THE QUESTION IS HARD TO ANSWER. BUT AT THE VERY LEAST I THINK WE'VE IDENTIFIED WHO'S RESPONSIBLE.
WE DID HELP THEM, RIGHT? THEY'LL BE OKAY NOW?
SOME OF THEM WILL BE. WE DID WHAT WE COULD. AND MORE IMPORTANTLY, WE'VE PROBABLY PUT A STOP TO ALL OF THIS MADNESS JUST BY BEING HERE.
THAT'S GOOD. I THINK THAT WOULD MAKE MY DAD HAPPY. I WONDER IF HE'LL EVER KNOW?
I'M SURE HE WILL, ONE WAY OR ANOTHER. JUST AS I'M SURE HE WAS ALWAYS PROUD OF YOU, NIGEL.
I THINK WE'VE ALL GOT PEOPLE WE WANT TO MAKE PROUD OF US. IT'S ONE OF THE THINGS THAT KEEPS US HEADED IN THE RIGHT DIRECTION...

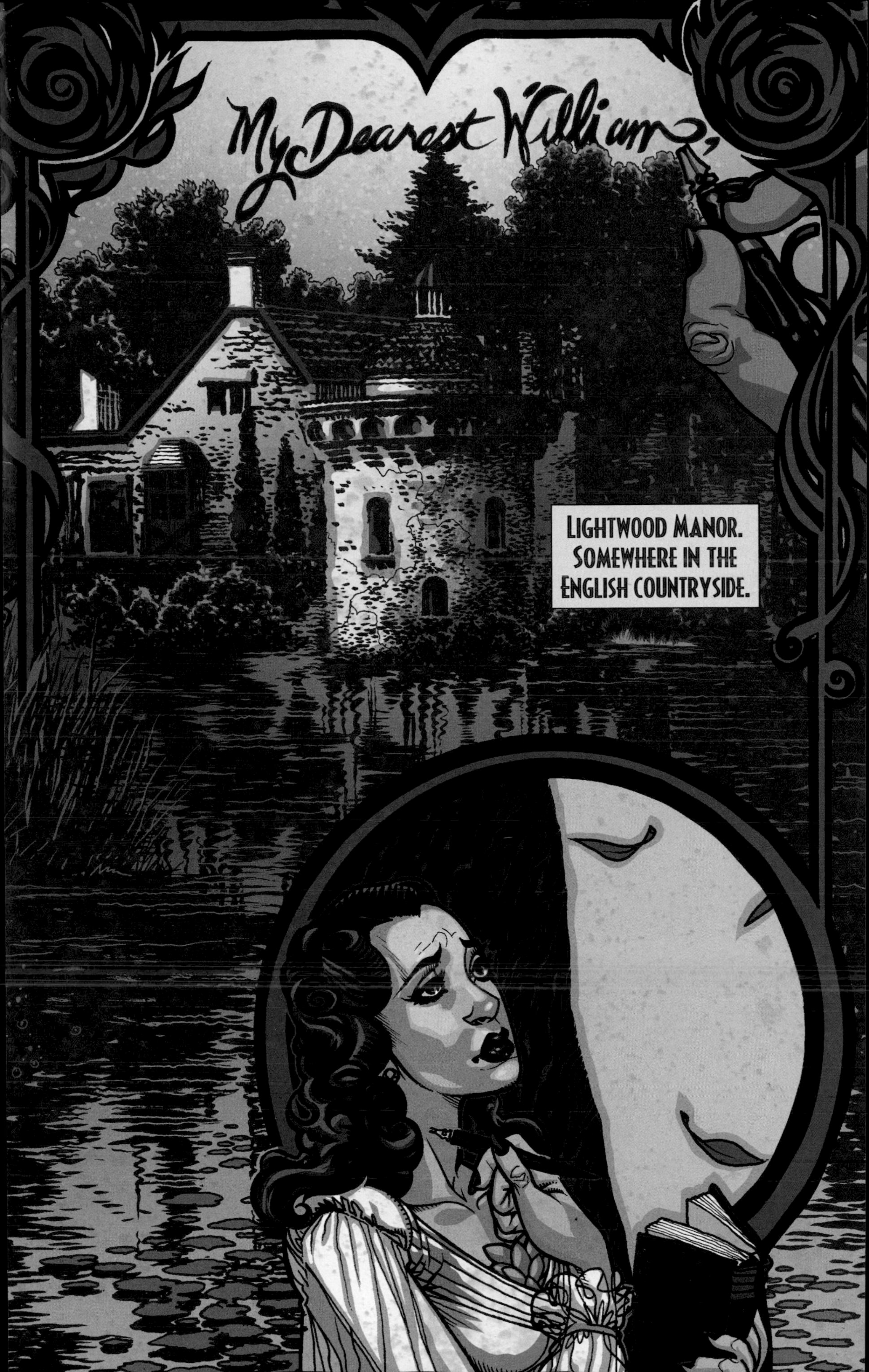
My Dearest William,
LIGHTWOOD MANOR. SOMEWHERE IN THE ENGLISH COUNTRYSIDE.

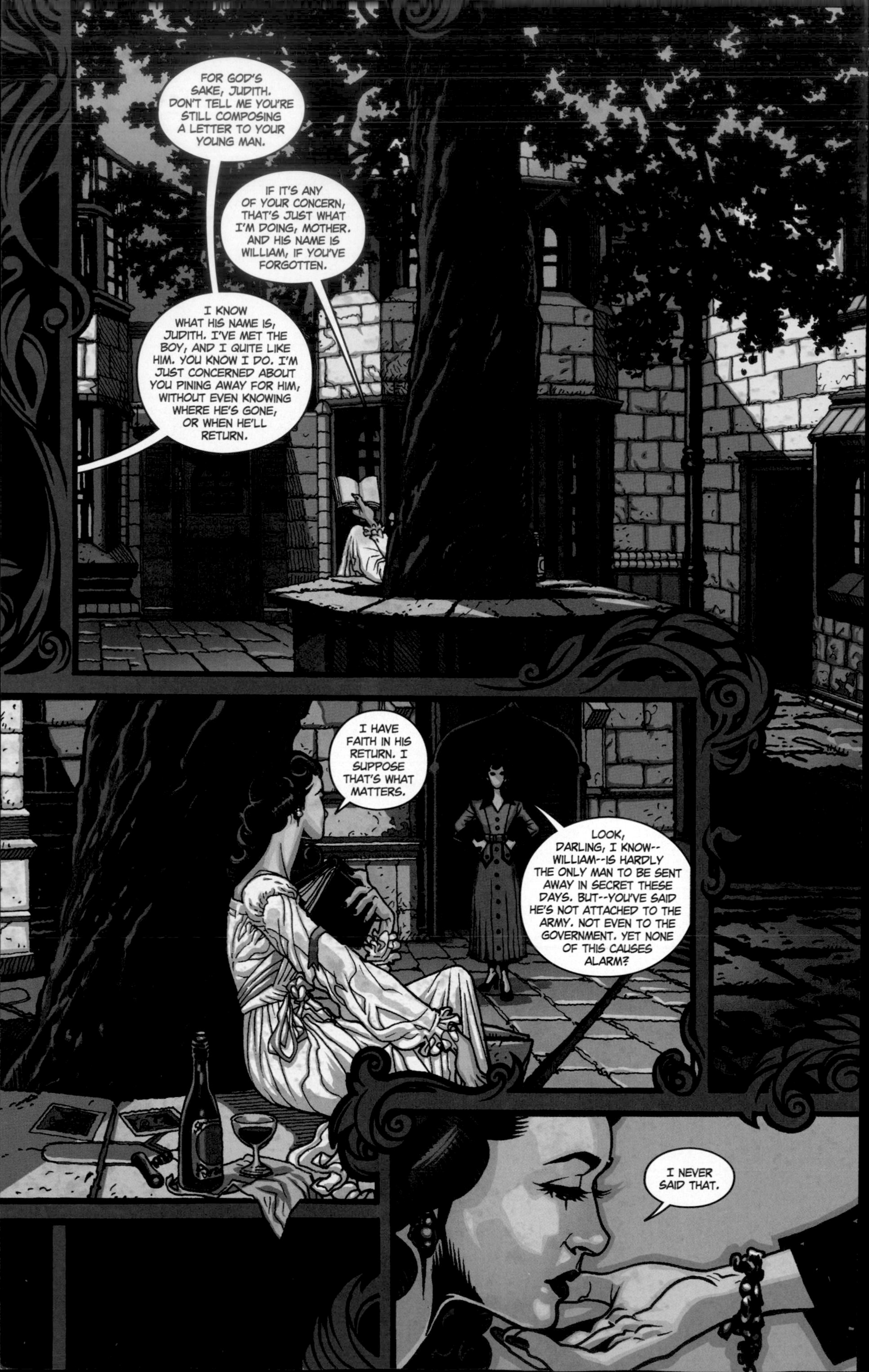
FOR GOD'S SAKE, JUDITH. DON'T TELL ME YOU'RE STILL COMPOSING A LETTER TO YOUR YOUNG MAN.
IF IT'S ANY OF YOUR CONCERN, THAT'S JUST WHAT I'M DOING, MOTHER. AND HIS NAME IS WILLIAM, IF YOU'VE FORGOTTEN.
I KNOW WHAT HIS NAME IS, JUDITH. I'VE MET THE BOY, AND I QUITE LIKE HIM. YOU KNOW I DO. I'M JUST CONCERNED ABOUT YOU PINING AWAY FOR HIM, WITHOUT EVEN KNOWING WHERE HE'S GONE, OR WHEN HE'LL RETURN.
I HAVE FAITH IN HIS RETURN. I SUPPOSE THAT'S WHAT MATTERS.
LOOK, DARLING, I KNOW--WILLIAM--IS HARDLY THE ONLY MAN TO BE SENT AWAY IN SECRET THESE DAYS. BUT--YOU'VE SAID HE'S NOT ATTACHED TO THE ARMY. NOT EVEN TO THE GOVERNMENT. YET NONE OF THIS CAUSES ALARM?
I NEVER SAID THAT.

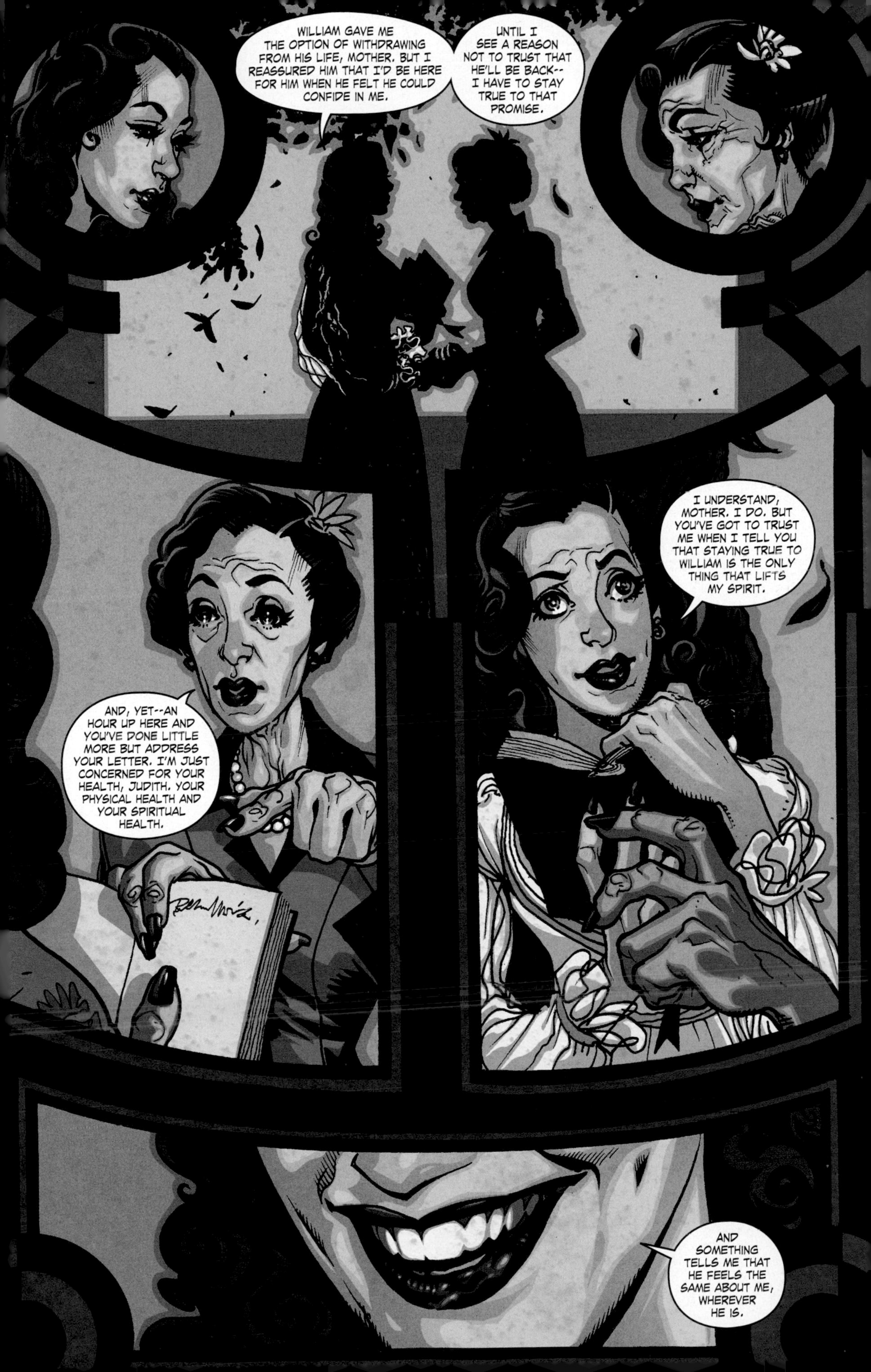
WILLIAM GAVE ME THE OPTION OF WITHDRAWING FROM HIS LIFE, MOTHER. BUT I REASSURED HIM THAT I'D BE HERE FOR HIM WHEN HE FELT HE COULD CONFIDE IN ME.
UNTIL I SEE A REASON NOT TO TRUST THAT HE'LL BE BACK-- I HAVE TO STAY TRUE TO THAT PROMISE.
AND, YET--AN HOUR UP HERE AND YOU'VE DONE LITTLE MORE BUT ADDRESS YOUR LETTER. I'M JUST CONCERNED FOR YOUR HEALTH, JUDITH. YOUR PHYSICAL HEALTH AND YOUR SPIRITUAL HEALTH.
I UNDERSTAND, MOTHER. I DO. BUT YOU'VE GOT TO TRUST ME WHEN I TELL YOU THAT STAYING TRUE TO WILLIAM IS THE ONLY THING THAT LIFTS MY SPIRIT.
AND SOMETHING TELLS ME THAT HE FEELS THE SAME ABOUT ME, WHEREVER HE IS.

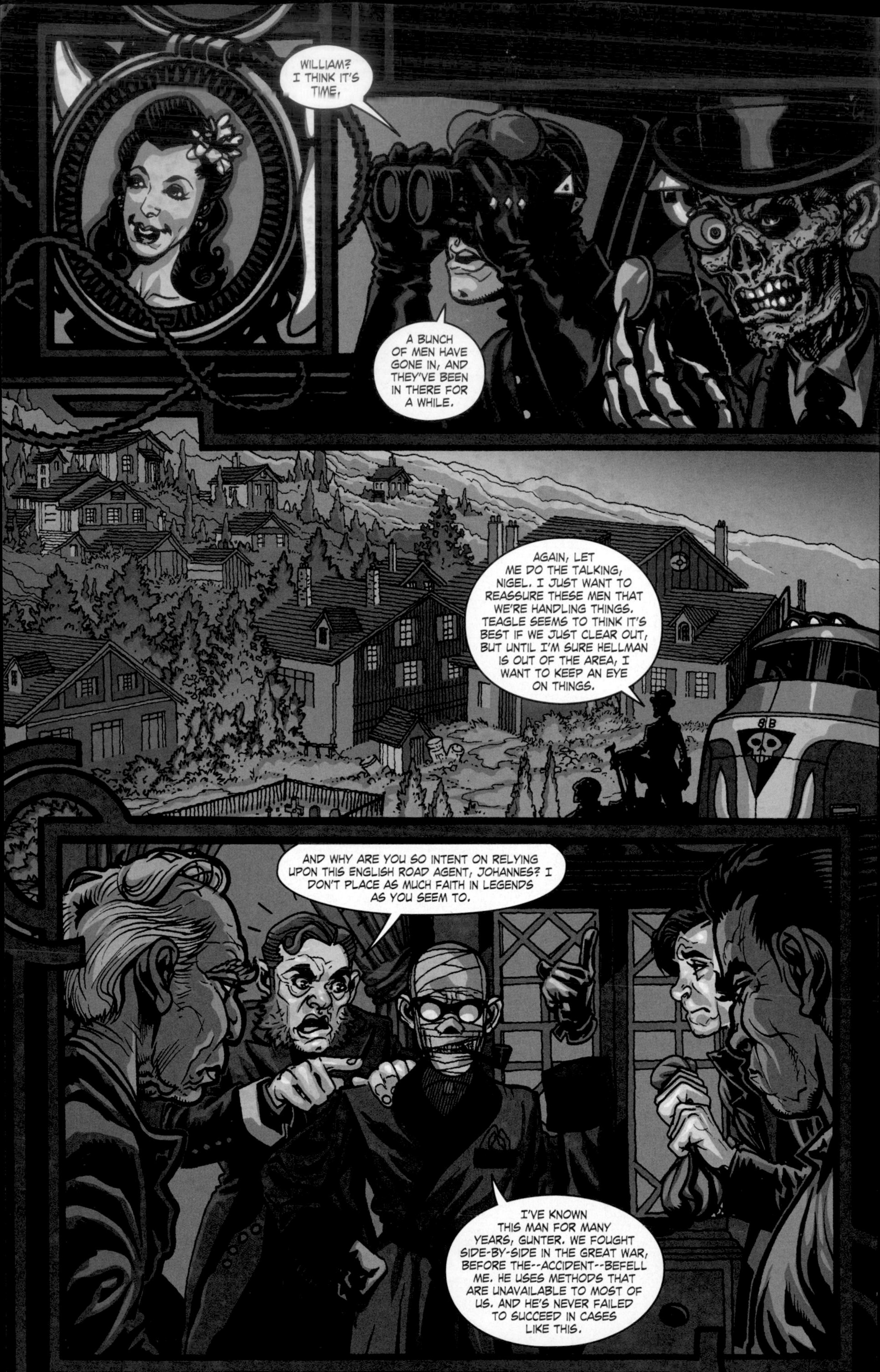
WILLIAM? I THINK IT'S TIME.
A BUNCH OF MEN HAVE GONE IN, AND THEY'VE BEEN IN THERE FOR A WHILE.
AGAIN, LET ME DO THE TALKING, NIGEL. I JUST WANT TO REASSURE THESE MEN THAT WE'RE HANDLING THINGS. TEAGLE SEEMS TO THINK IT'S BEST IF WE JUST CLEAR OUT, BUT UNTIL I'M SURE HELLMAN IS OUT OF THE AREA, I WANT TO KEEP AN EYE ON THINGS.
AND WHY ARE YOU SO INTENT ON RELYING UPON THIS ENGLISH ROAD AGENT, JOHANNES? I DON'T PLACE AS MUCH FAITH IN LEGENDS AS YOU SEEM TO.
I'VE KNOWN THIS MAN FOR MANY YEARS, GUNTER. WE FOUGHT SIDE-BY-SIDE IN THE GREAT WAR, BEFORE THE--ACCIDENT--BEFELL ME. HE USES METHODS THAT ARE UNAVAILABLE TO MOST OF US. AND HE'S NEVER FAILED TO SUCCEED IN CASES LIKE THIS.

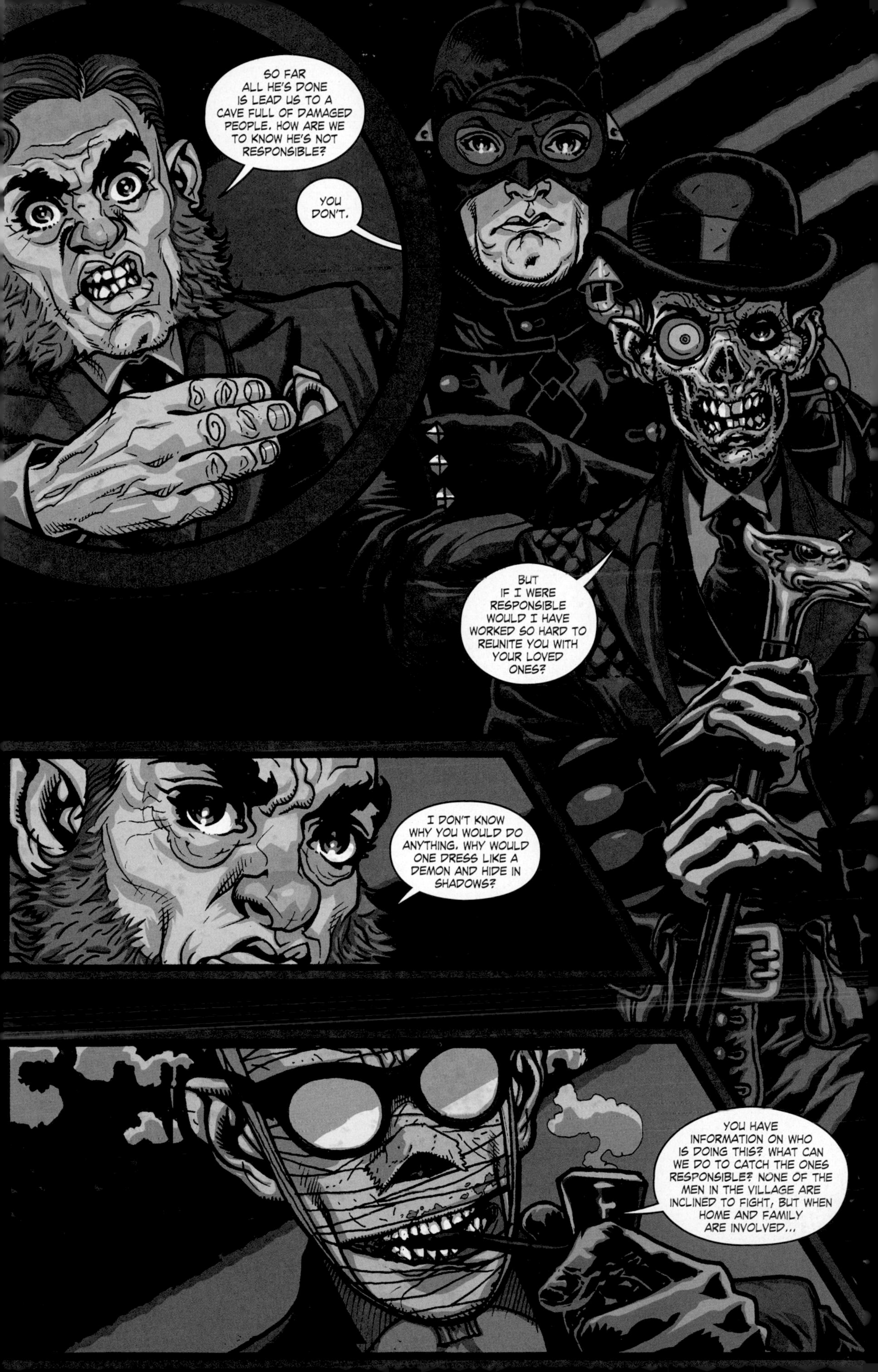
SO FAR ALL HE'S DONE IS LEAD US TO A CAVE FULL OF DAMAGED PEOPLE. HOW ARE WE TO KNOW HE'S NOT RESPONSIBLE?
YOU DON'T.
BUT IF I WERE RESPONSIBLE WOULD I HAVE WORKED SO HARD TO REUNITE YOU WITH YOUR LOVED ONES?
I DON'T KNOW WHY YOU WOULD DO ANYTHING. WHY WOULD ONE DRESS LIKE A DEMON AND HIDE IN SHADOWS?
YOU HAVE INFORMATION ON WHO IS DOING THIS? WHAT CAN WE DO TO CATCH THE ONES RESPONSIBLE? NONE OF THE MEN IN THE VILLAGE ARE INCLINED TO FIGHT, BUT WHEN HOME AND FAMILY ARE INVOLVED...

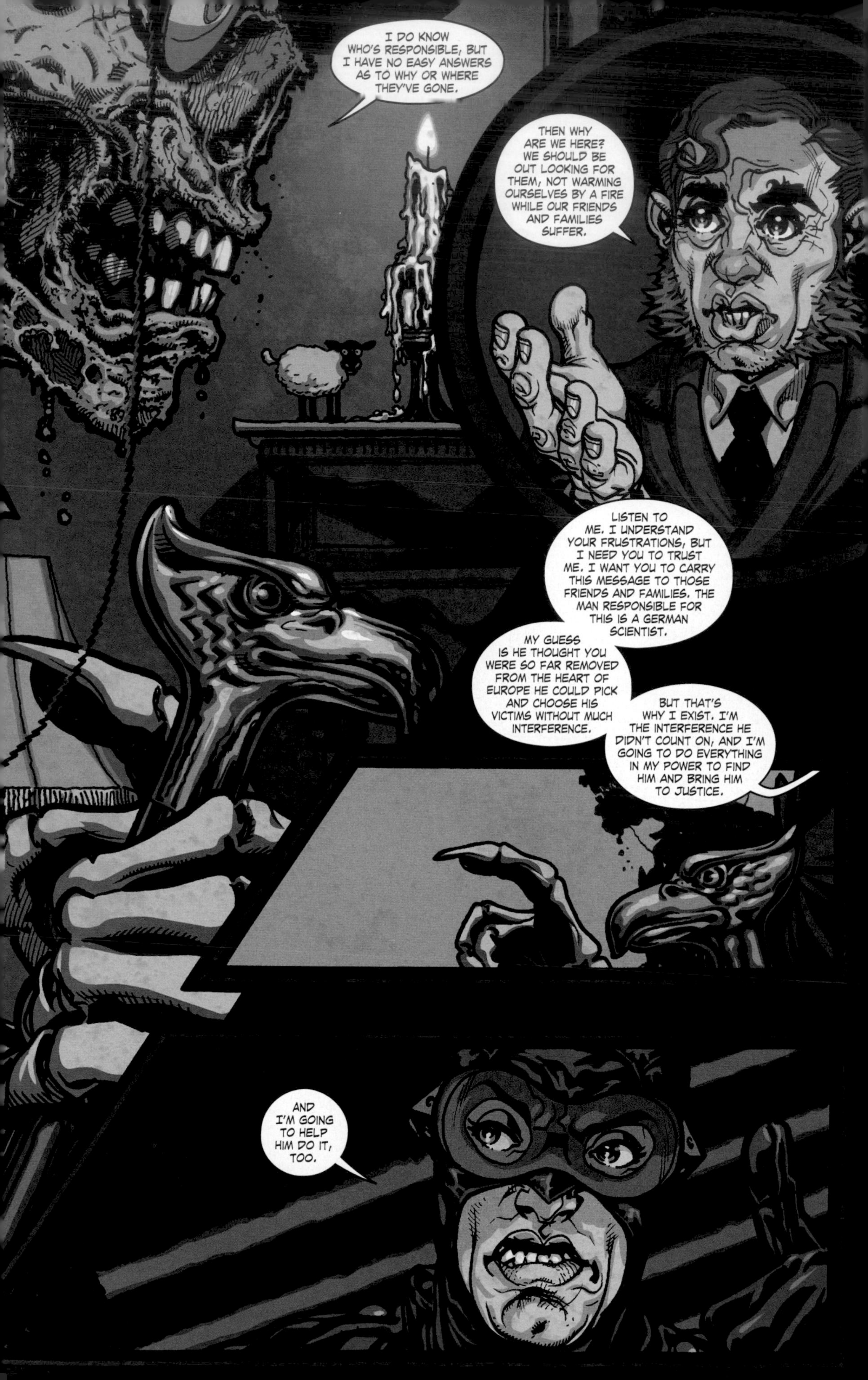
I DO KNOW WHO'S RESPONSIBLE, BUT I HAVE NO EASY ANSWERS AS TO WHY OR WHERE THEY'VE GONE.
THEN WHY ARE WE HERE? WE SHOULD BE OUT LOOKING FOR THEM, NOT WARMING OURSELVES BY A FIRE WHILE OUR FRIENDS AND FAMILIES SUFFER.
LISTEN TO ME. I UNDERSTAND YOUR FRUSTRATIONS, BUT I NEED YOU TO TRUST ME. I WANT YOU TO CARRY THIS MESSAGE TO THOSE FRIENDS AND FAMILIES. THE MAN RESPONSIBLE FOR THIS IS A GERMAN SCIENTIST.
MY GUESS IS HE THOUGHT YOU WERE SO FAR REMOVED FROM THE HEART OF EUROPE HE COULD PICK AND CHOOSE HIS VICTIMS WITHOUT MUCH INTERFERENCE.
BUT THAT'S WHY I EXIST. I'M THE INTERFERENCE HE DIDN'T COUNT ON, AND I'M GOING TO DO EVERYTHING IN MY POWER TO FIND HIM AND BRING HIM TO JUSTICE.
AND I'M GOING TO HELP HIM DO IT, TOO.

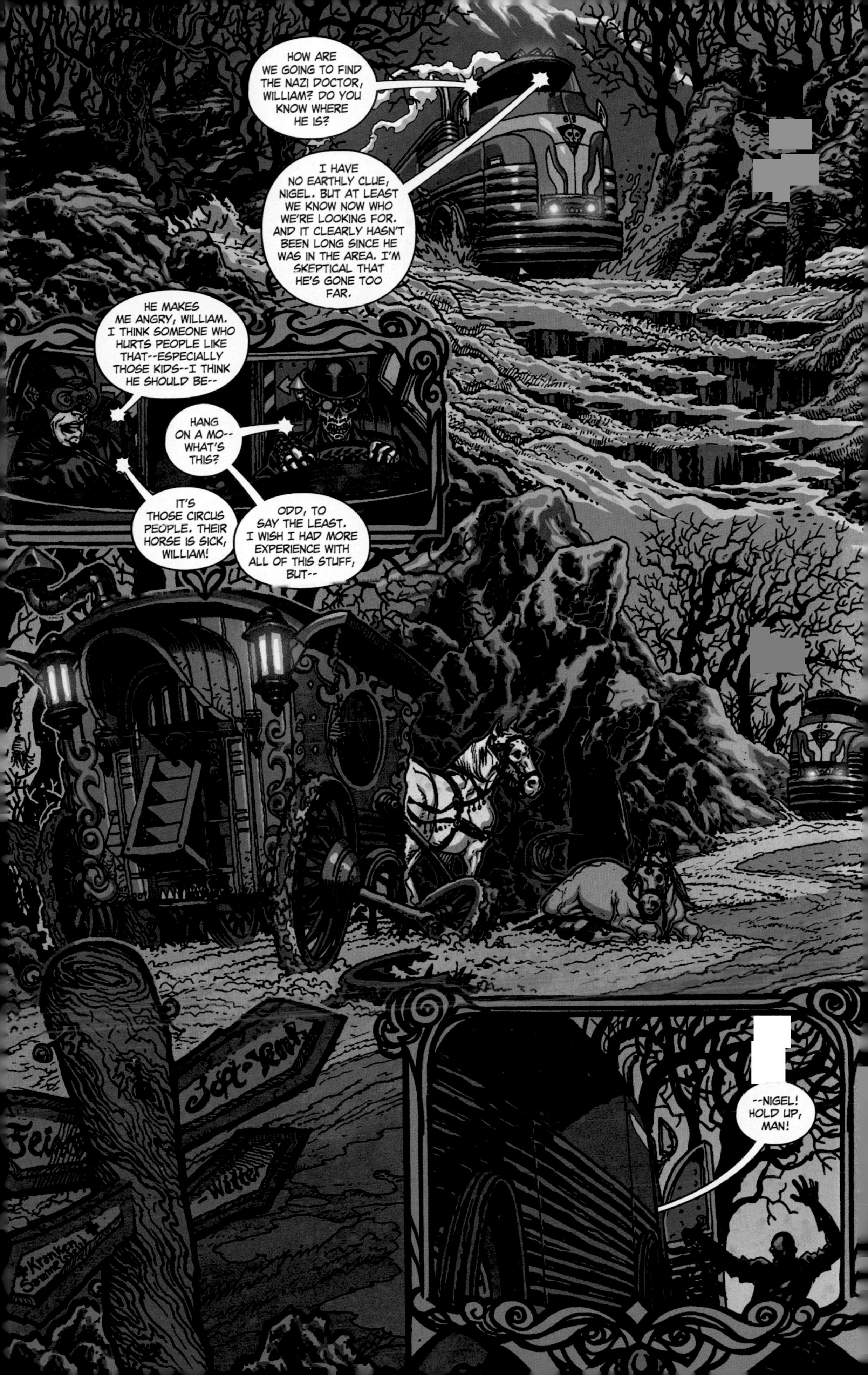
HOW ARE WE GOING TO FIND THE NAZI DOCTOR, WILLIAM? DO YOU KNOW WHERE HE IS?
I HAVE NO EARTHLY CLUE, NIGEL. BUT AT LEAST WE KNOW NOW WHO WE'RE LOOKING FOR. AND IT CLEARLY HASN'T BEEN LONG SINCE HE WAS IN THE AREA. I'M SKEPTICAL THAT HE'S GONE TOO FAR.
HE MAKES ME ANGRY, WILLIAM. I THINK SOMEONE WHO HURTS PEOPLE LIKE THAT--ESPECIALLY THOSE KIDS--I THINK HE SHOULD BE--
HANG ON A MO--WHAT'S THIS?
IT'S THOSE CIRCUS PEOPLE. THEIR HORSE IS SICK, WILLIAM!
ODD, TO SAY THE LEAST. I WISH I HAD MORE EXPERIENCE WITH ALL OF THIS STUFF, BUT--
--NIGEL! HOLD UP, MAN!

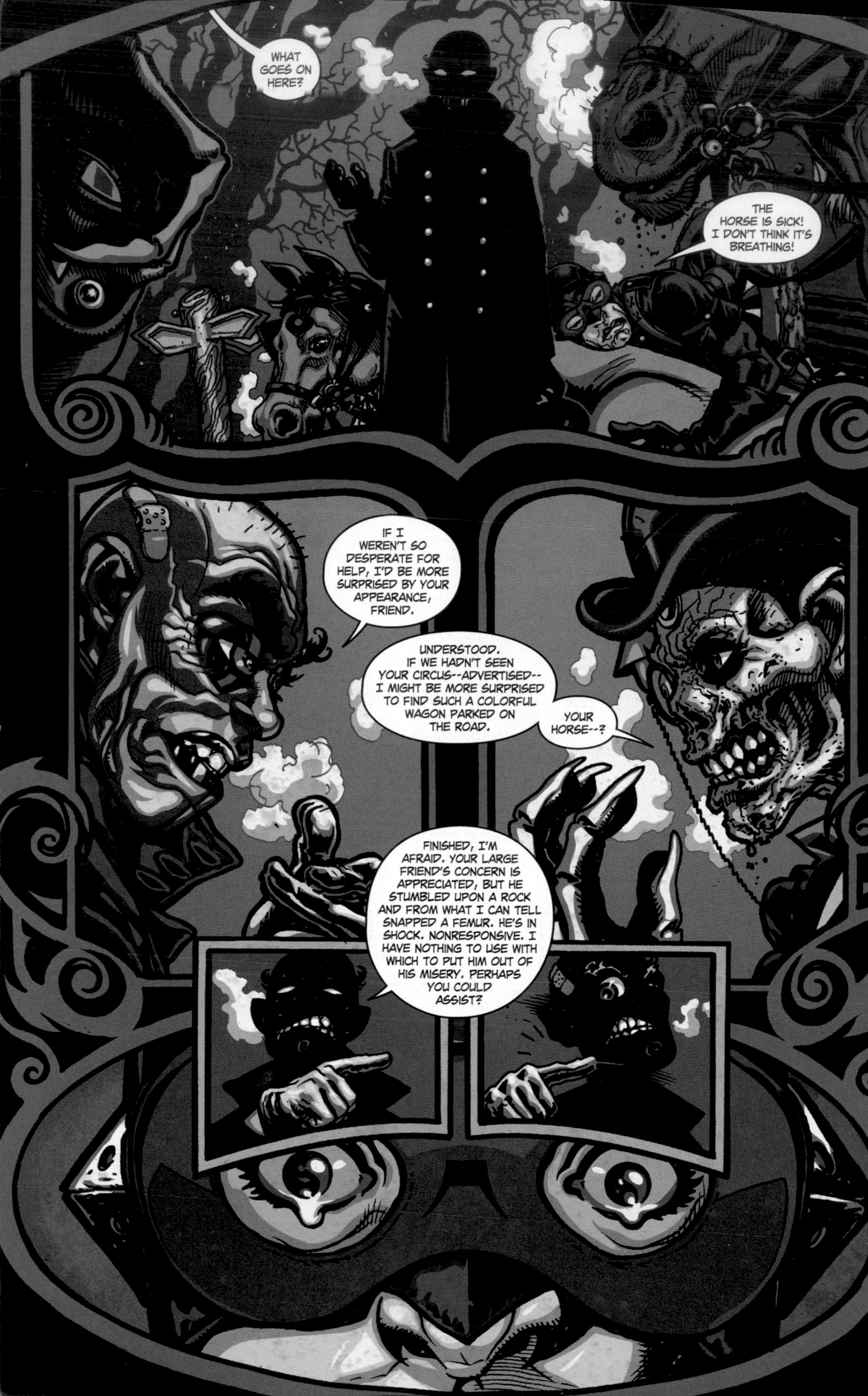
WHAT GOES ON HERE?
THE HORSE IS SICK! I DON'T THINK IT'S BREATHING!
IF I WEREN'T SO DESPERATE FOR HELP, I'D BE MORE SURPRISED BY YOUR APPEARANCE, FRIEND.
UNDERSTOOD. IF WE HADN'T SEEN YOUR CIRCUS--ADVERTISED-- I MIGHT BE MORE SURPRISED TO FIND SUCH A COLORFUL WAGON PARKED ON THE ROAD.
YOUR HORSE--?
FINISHED, I'M AFRAID. YOUR LARGE FRIEND'S CONCERN IS APPRECIATED, BUT HE STUMBLED UPON A ROCK AND FROM WHAT I CAN TELL SNAPPED A FEMUR. HE'S IN SHOCK. NONRESPONSIVE. I HAVE NOTHING TO USE WITH WHICH TO PUT HIM OUT OF HIS MISERY. PERHAPS YOU COULD ASSIST?

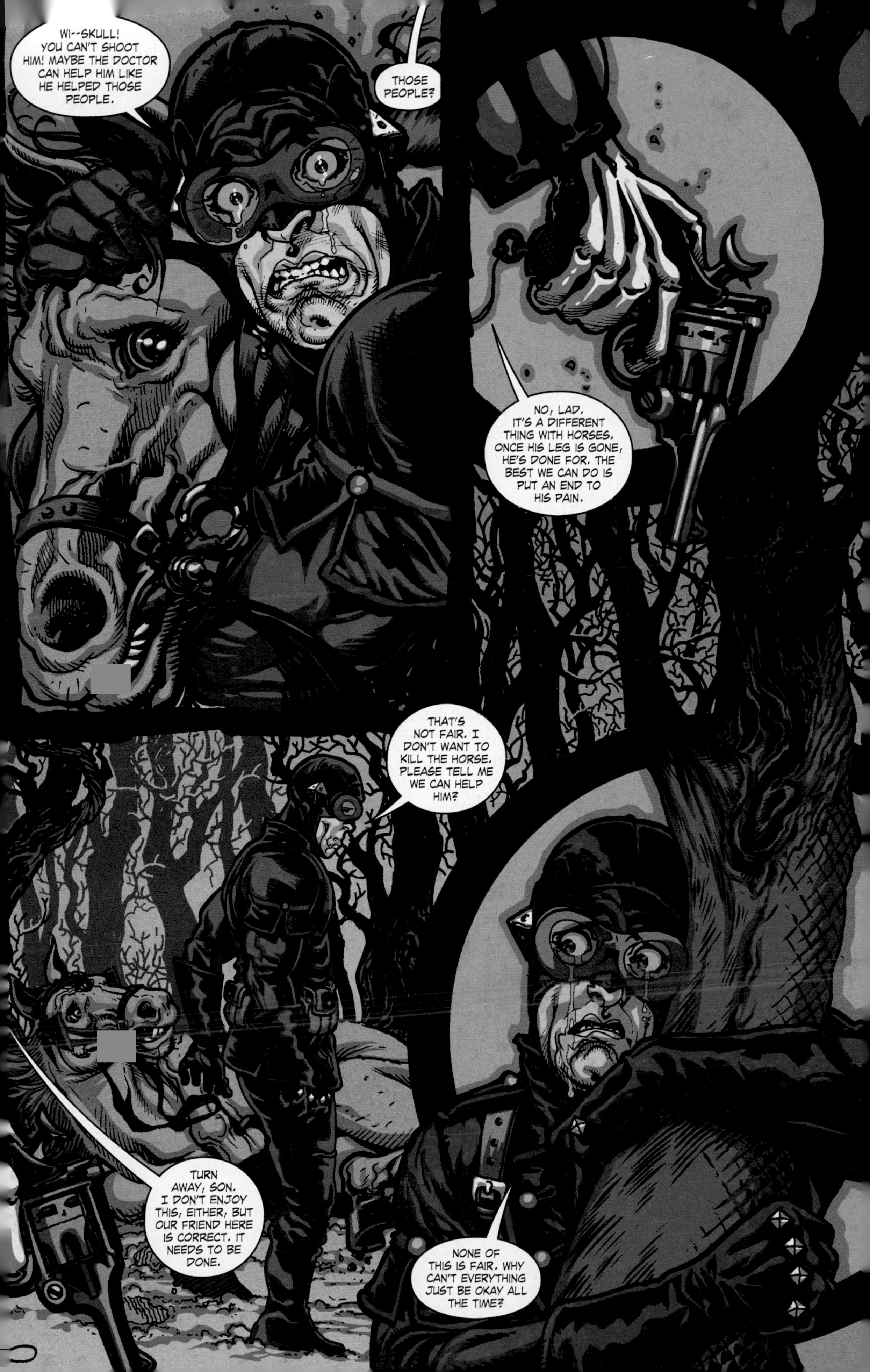
WI--SKULL! YOU CAN'T SHOOT HIM! MAYBE THE DOCTOR CAN HELP HIM LIKE HE HELPED THOSE PEOPLE.
THOSE PEOPLE?
NO, LAD. IT'S A DIFFERENT THING WITH HORSES. ONCE HIS LEG IS GONE, HE'S DONE FOR. THE BEST WE CAN DO IS PUT AN END TO HIS PAIN.
THAT'S NOT FAIR. I DON'T WANT TO KILL THE HORSE. PLEASE TELL ME WE CAN HELP HIM?
TURN AWAY, SON. I DON'T ENJOY THIS, EITHER, BUT OUR FRIEND HERE IS CORRECT. IT NEEDS TO BE DONE.
NONE OF THIS IS FAIR. WHY CAN'T EVERYTHING JUST BE OKAY ALL THE TIME?

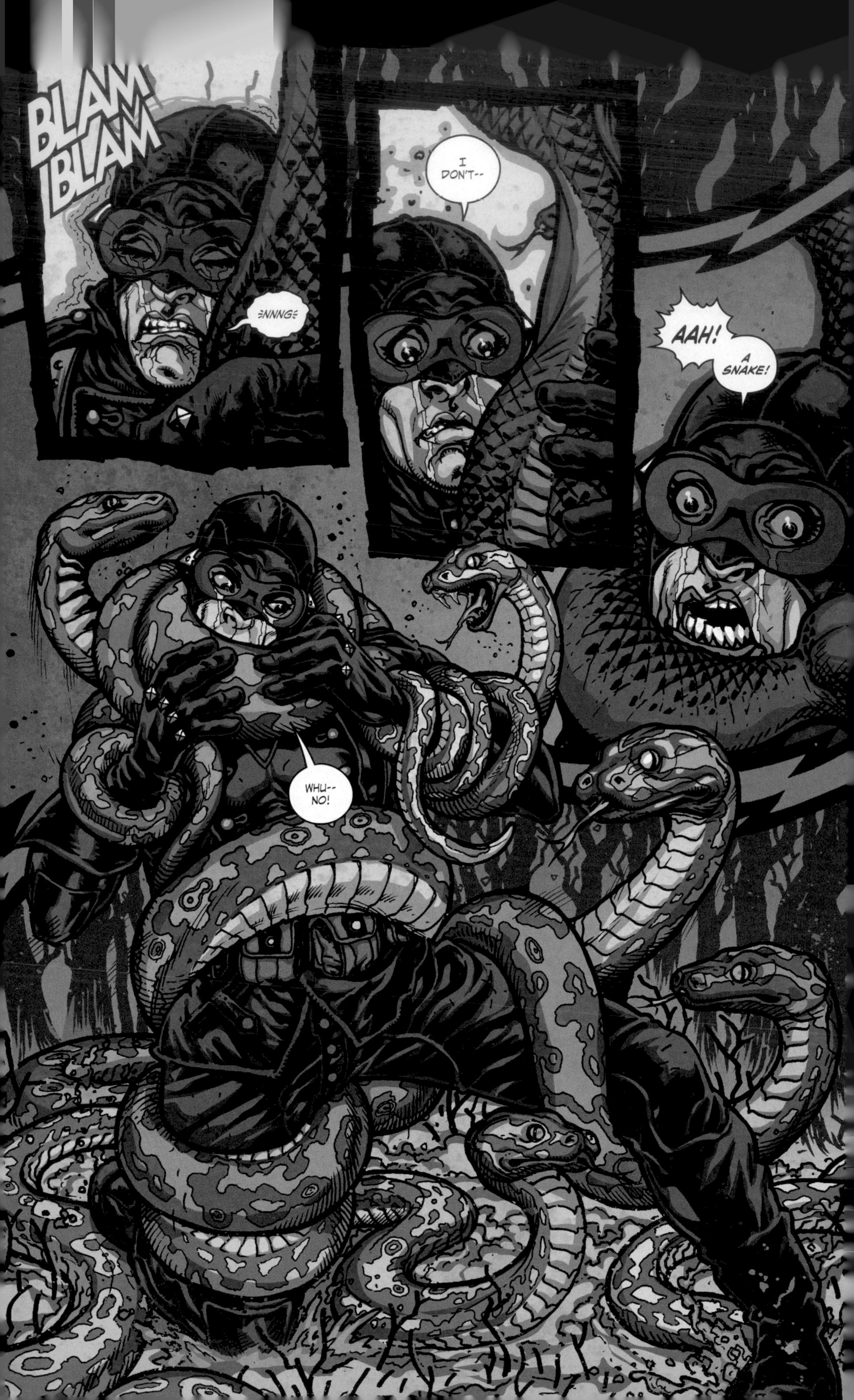
BLAM BLAM
NNNG
I DON'T--
AAH!
A SNAKE!
WHU-- NO!

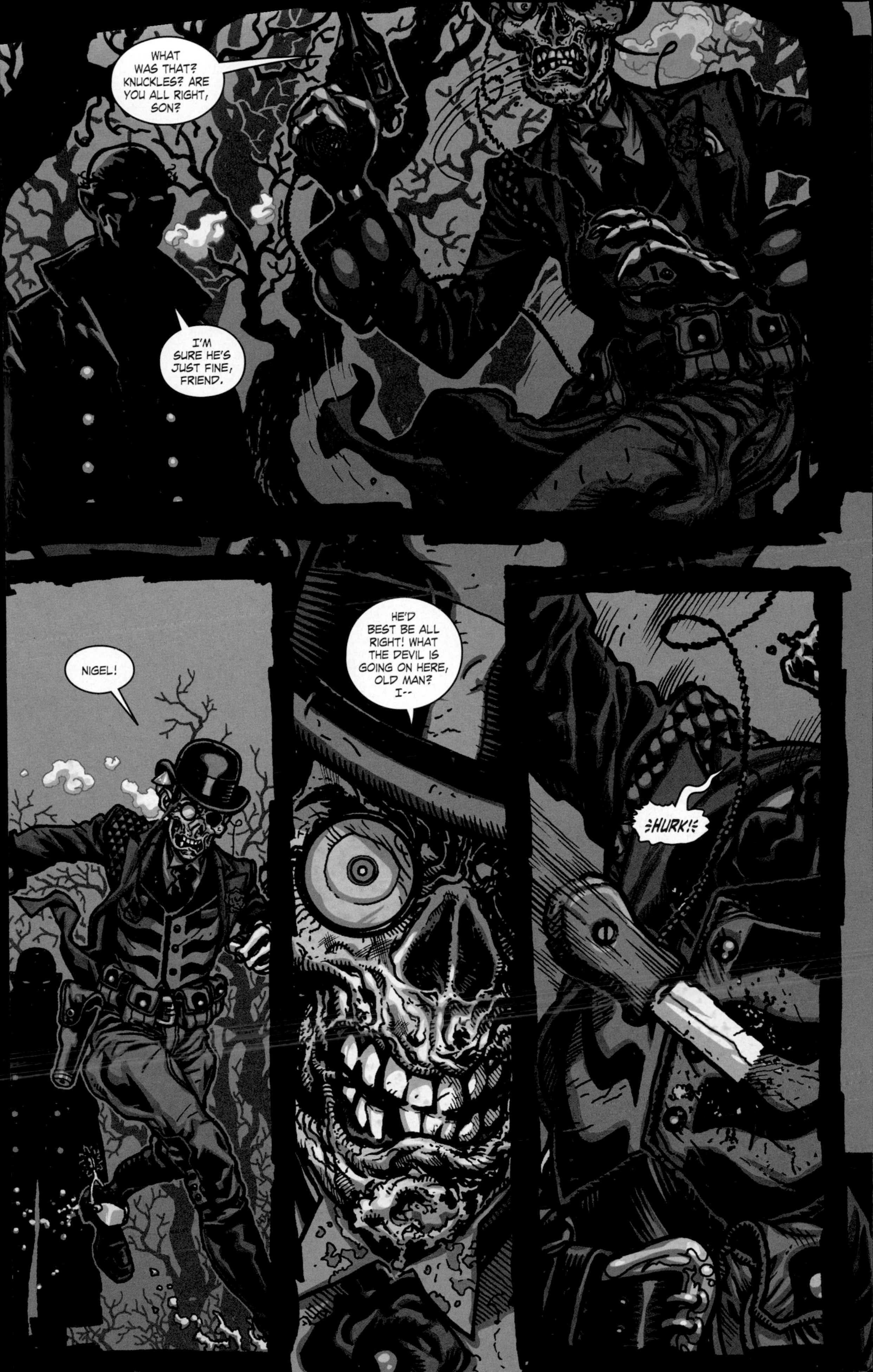
WHAT WAS THAT? KNUCKLES? ARE YOU ALL RIGHT, SON?
I'M SURE HE'S JUST FINE, FRIEND.
NIGEL!
HE'D BEST BE ALL RIGHT! WHAT THE DEVIL IS GOING ON HERE, OLD MAN? I--
HURK!

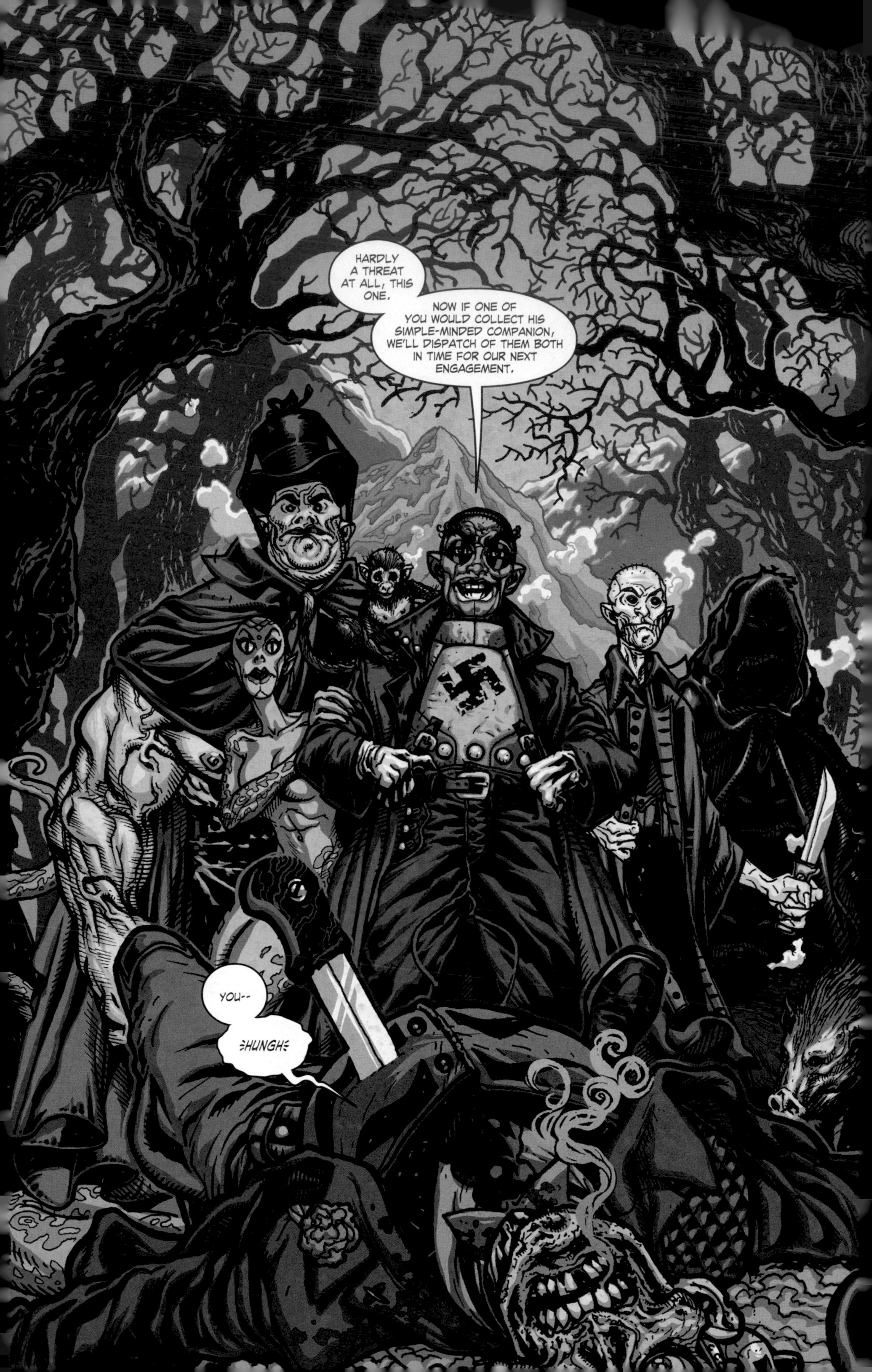
HARDLY A THREAT AT ALL, THIS ONE.
NOW IF ONE OF YOU WOULD COLLECT HIS SIMPLE-MINDED COMPANION, WE'LL DISPATCH OF THEM BOTH IN TIME FOR OUR NEXT ENGAGEMENT.
YOU--
HUNGH

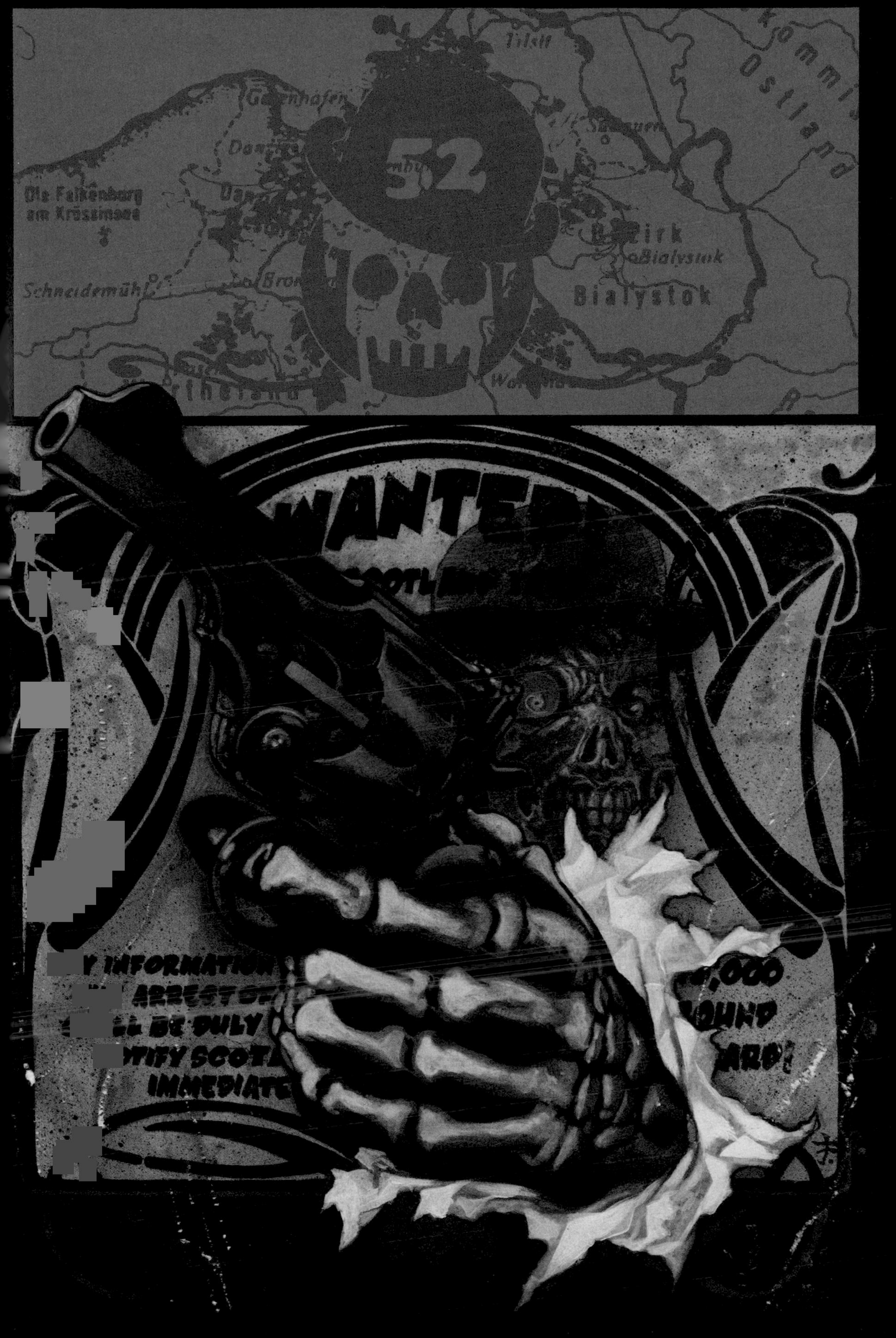
Tilsit
52
Die Falkenburg am Krössinsee
Schneidemühl
Bezirk
Bialystok
Bialystok
Ostland
INFORMATION

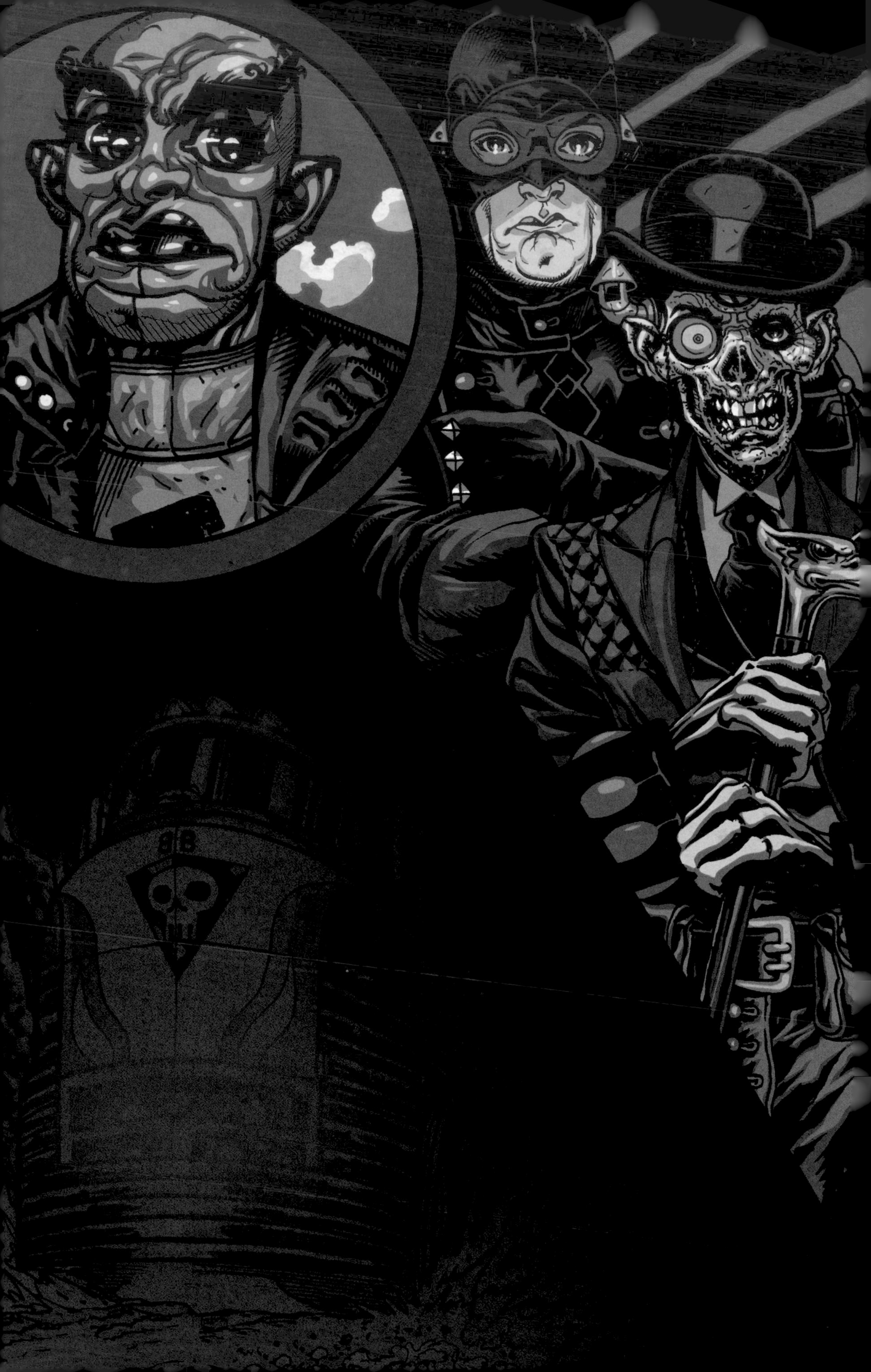

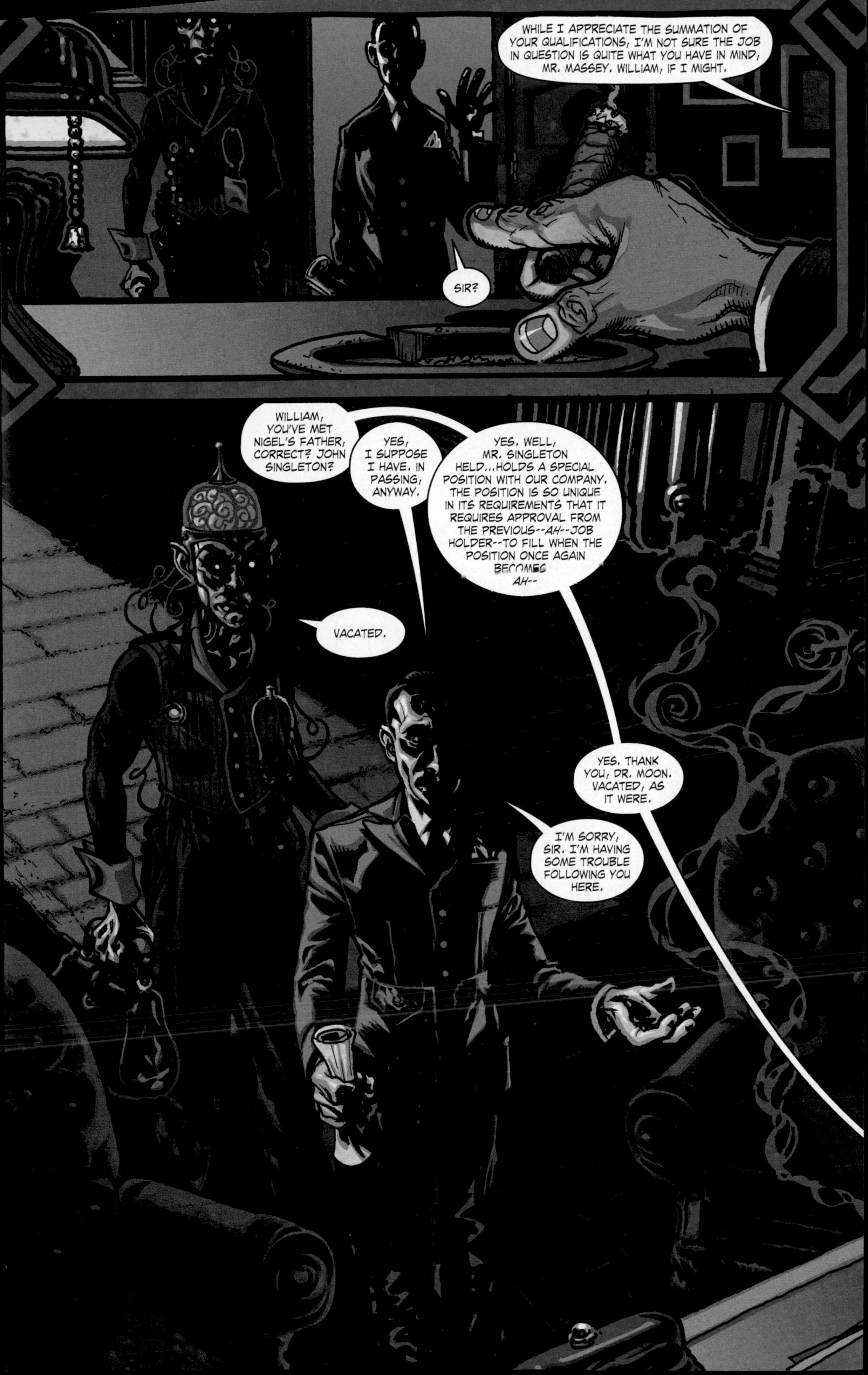
WHILE I APPRECIATE THE SUMMATION OF YOUR QUALIFICATIONS, I'M NOT SURE THE JOB IN QUESTION IS QUITE WHAT YOU HAVE IN MIND, MR. MASSEY. WILLIAM, IF I MIGHT.
SIR?
WILLIAM, YOU'VE MET NIGEL'S FATHER, CORRECT? JOHN SINGLETON?
YES, I SUPPOSE I HAVE. IN PASSING, ANYWAY.
YES. WELL, MR. SINGLETON HELD...HOLDS A SPECIAL POSITION WITH OUR COMPANY. THE POSITION IS SO UNIQUE IN ITS REQUIREMENTS THAT IT REQUIRES APPROVAL FROM THE PREVIOUS--AH--JOB HOLDER--TO FILL WHEN THE POSITION ONCE AGAIN BECOMES AH--
VACATED.
YES. THANK YOU, DR. MOON. VACATED, AS IT WERE.
I'M SORRY, SIR. I'M HAVING SOME TROUBLE FOLLOWING YOU HERE.

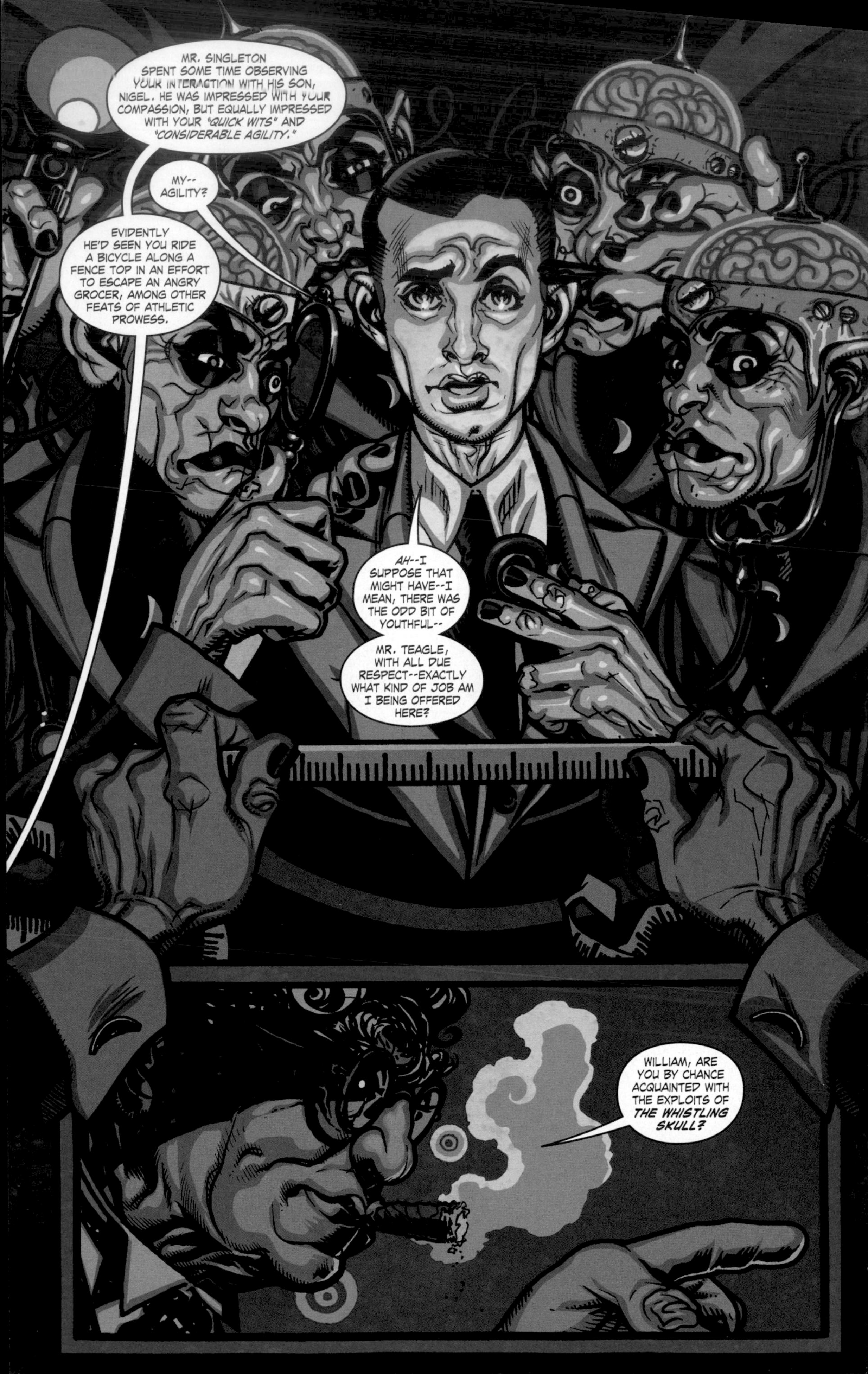
MR. SINGLETON SPENT SOME TIME OBSERVING YOUR INTERACTION WITH HIS SON, NIGEL. HE WAS IMPRESSED WITH YOUR COMPASSION, BUT EQUALLY IMPRESSED WITH YOUR "QUICK WITS" AND "CONSIDERABLE AGILITY."
MY--AGILITY?
EVIDENTLY HE'D SEEN YOU RIDE A BICYCLE ALONG A FENCE TOP IN AN EFFORT TO ESCAPE AN ANGRY GROCER, AMONG OTHER FEATS OF ATHLETIC PROWESS.
AH--I SUPPOSE THAT MIGHT HAVE--I MEAN, THERE WAS THE ODD BIT OF YOUTHFUL--
MR. TEAGLE, WITH ALL DUE RESPECT--EXACTLY WHAT KIND OF JOB AM I BEING OFFERED HERE?
WILLIAM, ARE YOU BY CHANCE ACQUAINTED WITH THE EXPLOITS OF THE WHISTLING SKULL?

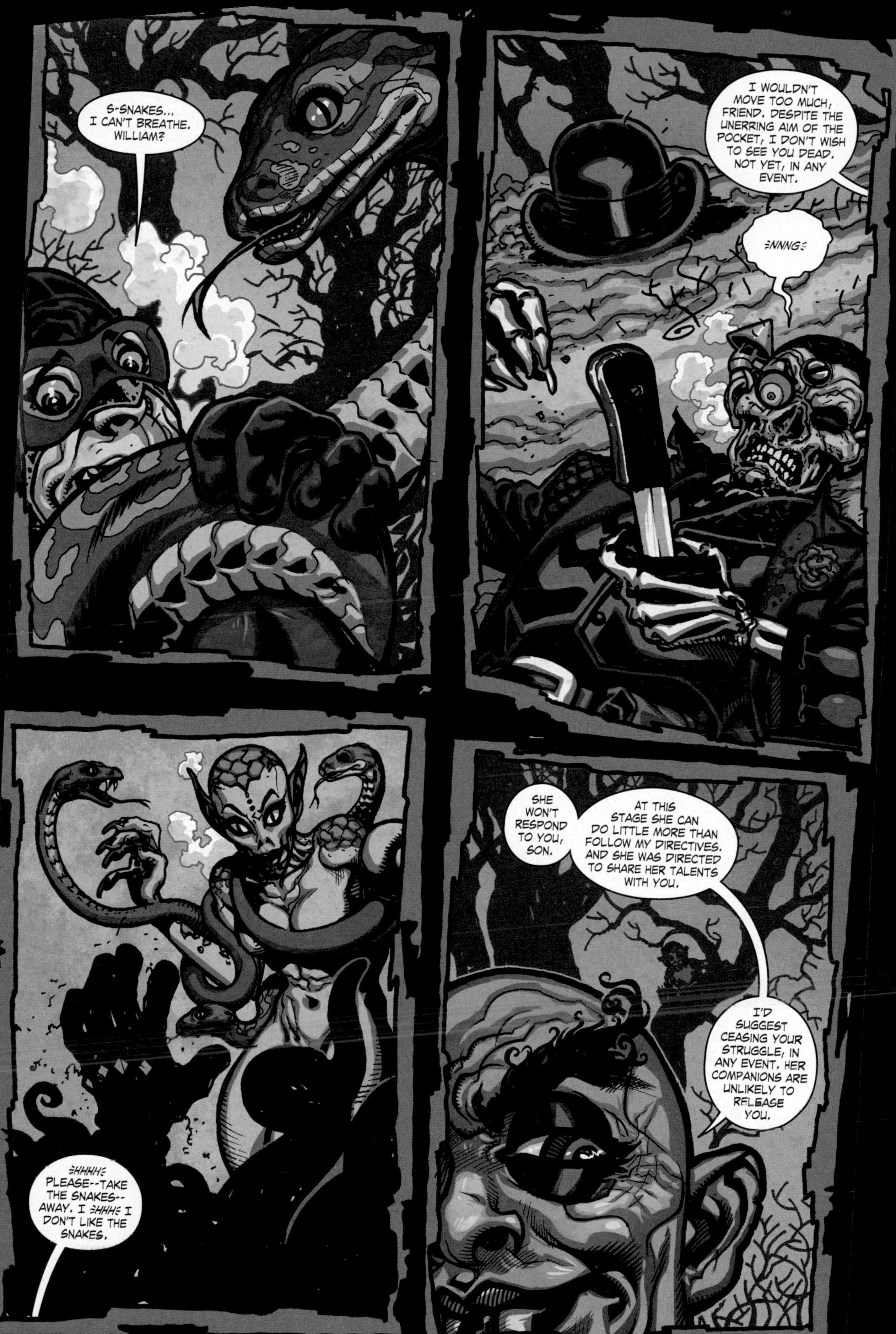
S-SNAKES... I CAN'T BREATHE. WILLIAM?
I WOULDN'T MOVE TOO MUCH, FRIEND. DESPITE THE UNERRING AIM OF THE POCKET, I DON'T WISH TO SEE YOU DEAD. NOT YET, IN ANY EVENT.
NNNG
SHHHH PLEASE--TAKE THE SNAKES--AWAY. I SHHHH I DON'T LIKE THE SNAKES.
SHE WON'T RESPOND TO YOU, SON.
AT THIS STAGE SHE CAN DO LITTLE MORE THAN FOLLOW MY DIRECTIVES. AND SHE WAS DIRECTED TO SHARE HER TALENTS WITH YOU.
I'D SUGGEST CEASING YOUR STRUGGLE, IN ANY EVENT. HER COMPANIONS ARE UNLIKELY TO RELEASE YOU.

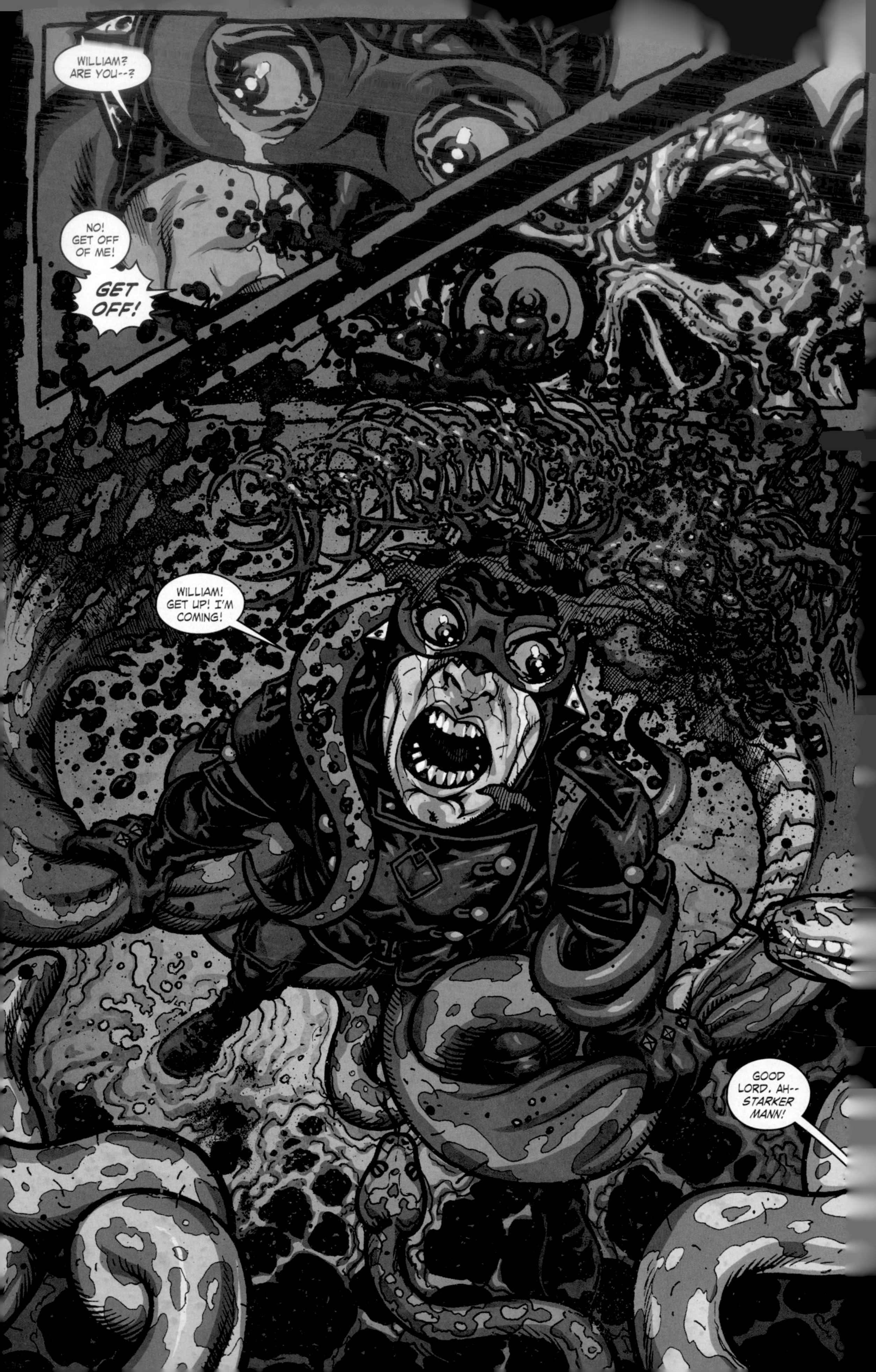
WILLIAM? ARE YOU--?
NO! GET OFF OF ME!
GET OFF!
WILLIAM! GET UP! I'M COMING!
GOOD LORD. AH-- STARKER MANN!

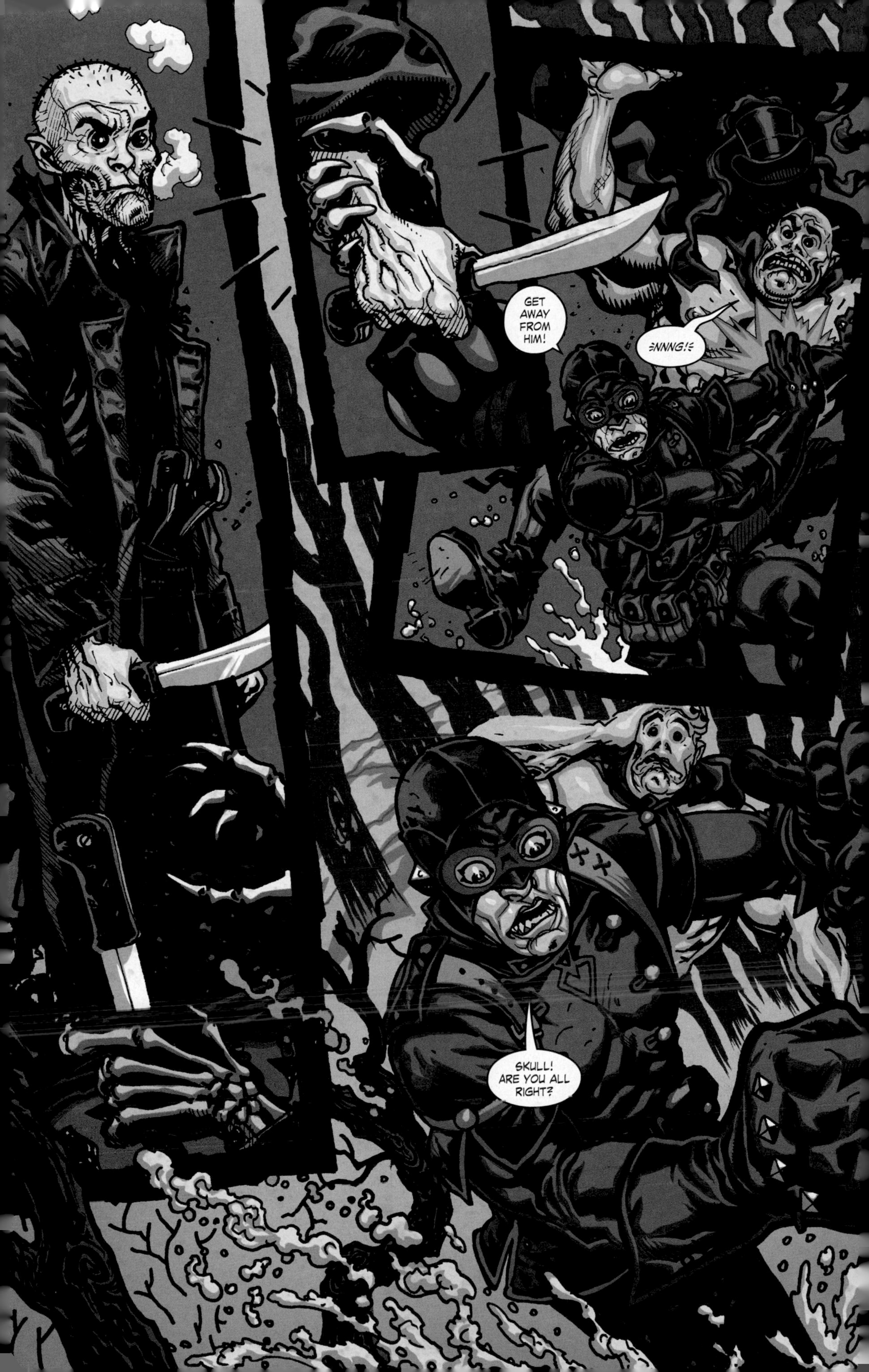
GET AWAY FROM HIM!
NNNG!
SKULL! ARE YOU ALL RIGHT?

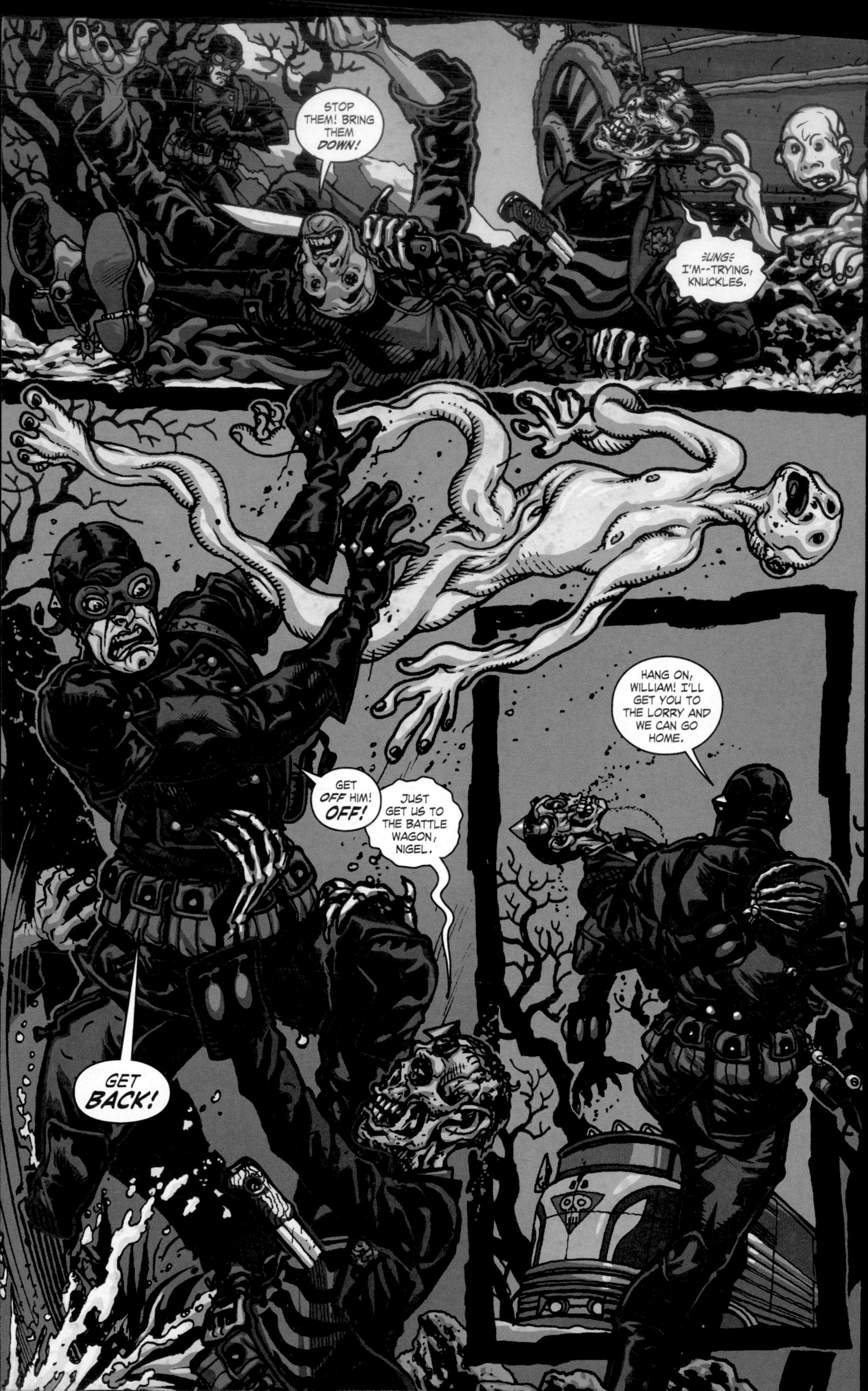
STOP THEM! BRING THEM DOWN!
=UNG= I'M--TRYING, KNUCKLES.
HANG ON, WILLIAM! I'LL GET YOU TO THE LORRY AND WE CAN GO HOME.
GET OFF HIM! OFF!
JUST GET US TO THE BATTLE WAGON, NIGEL.
GET BACK!

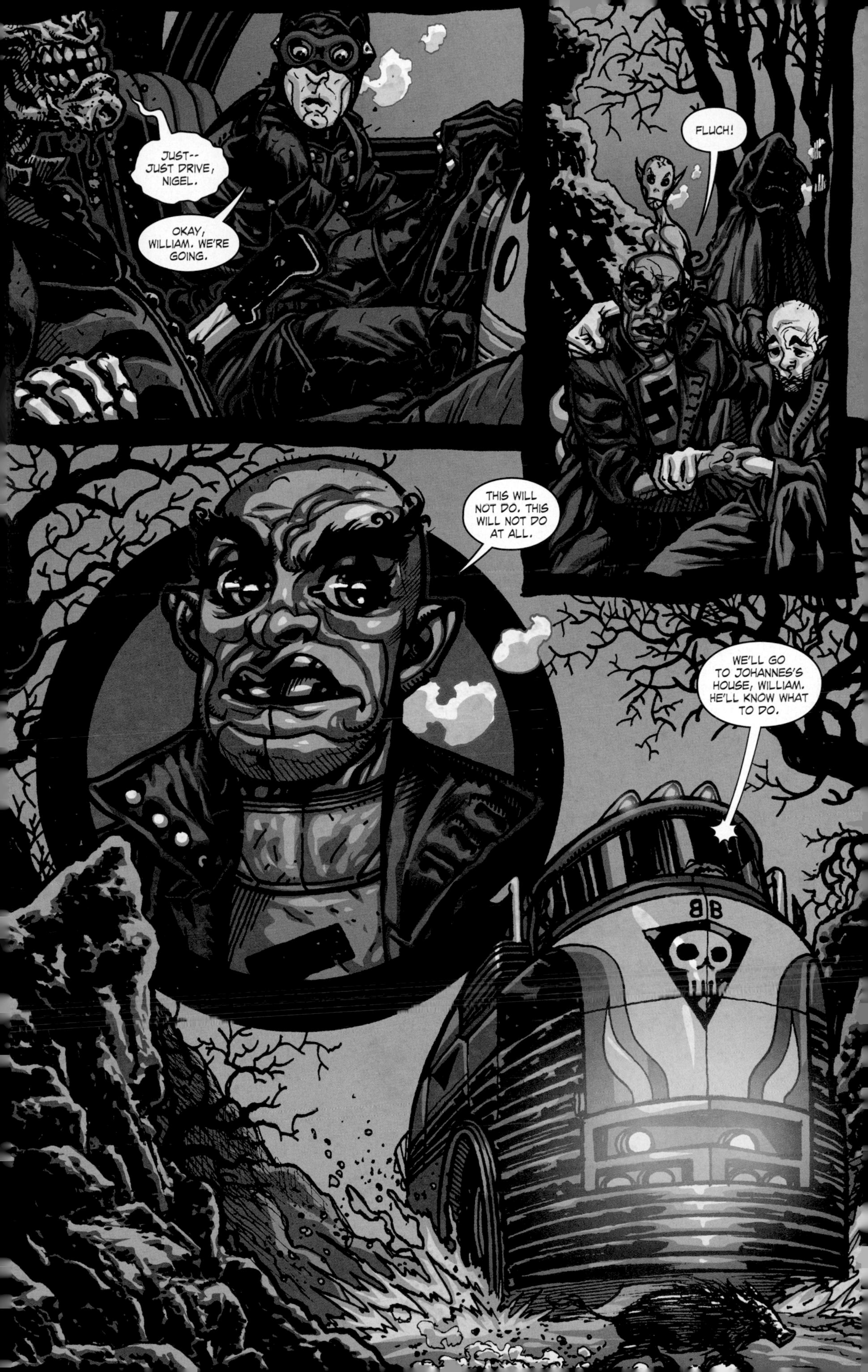
JUST--
JUST DRIVE, NIGEL.
OKAY, WILLIAM. WE'RE GOING.
FLUCH!
THIS WILL NOT DO. THIS WILL NOT DO AT ALL.
WE'LL GO TO JOHANNES'S HOUSE, WILLIAM. HE'LL KNOW WHAT TO DO.
BB

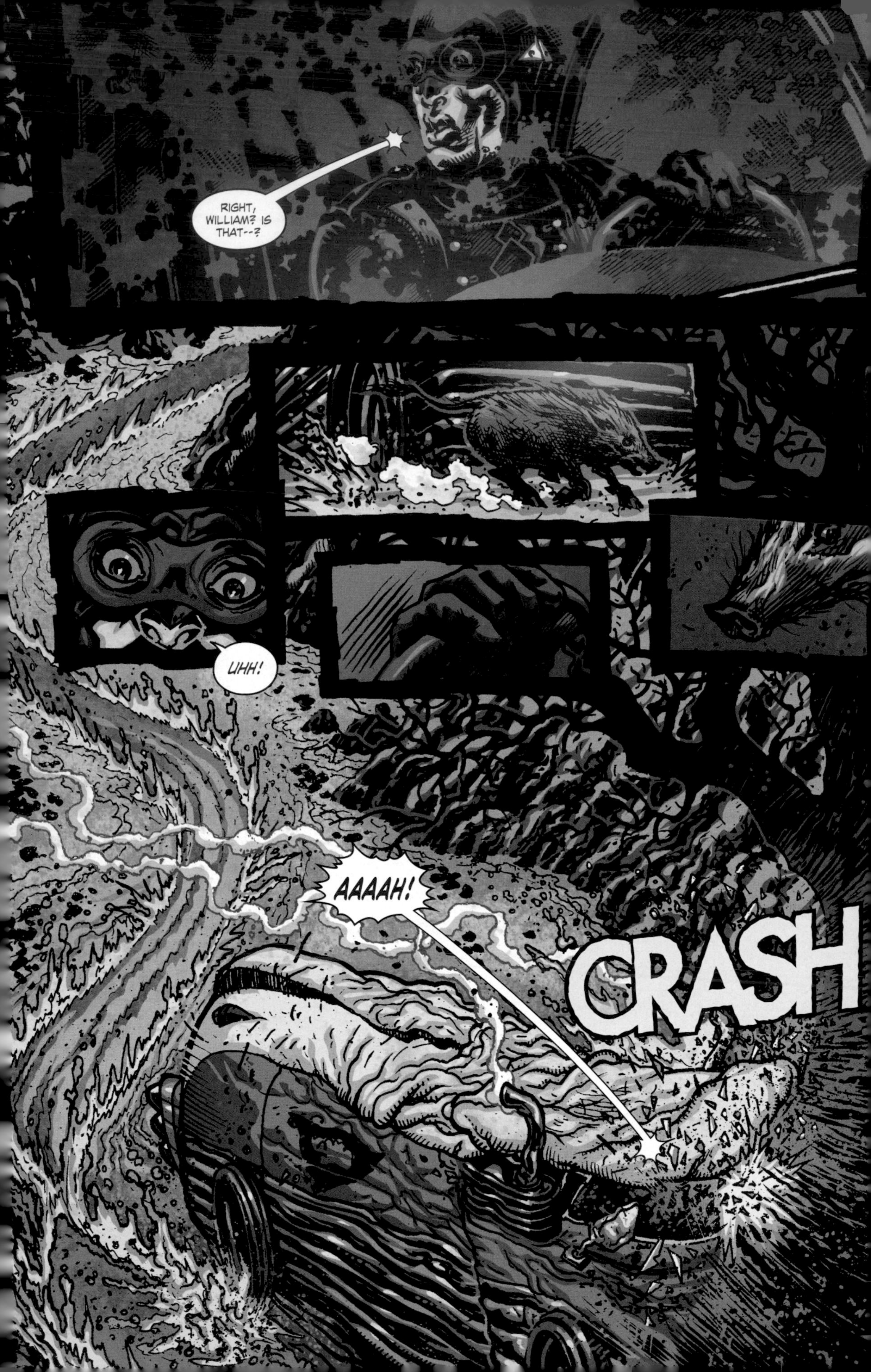
RIGHT, WILLIAM? IS THAT--?
UHH!
AAAAH!
CRASH

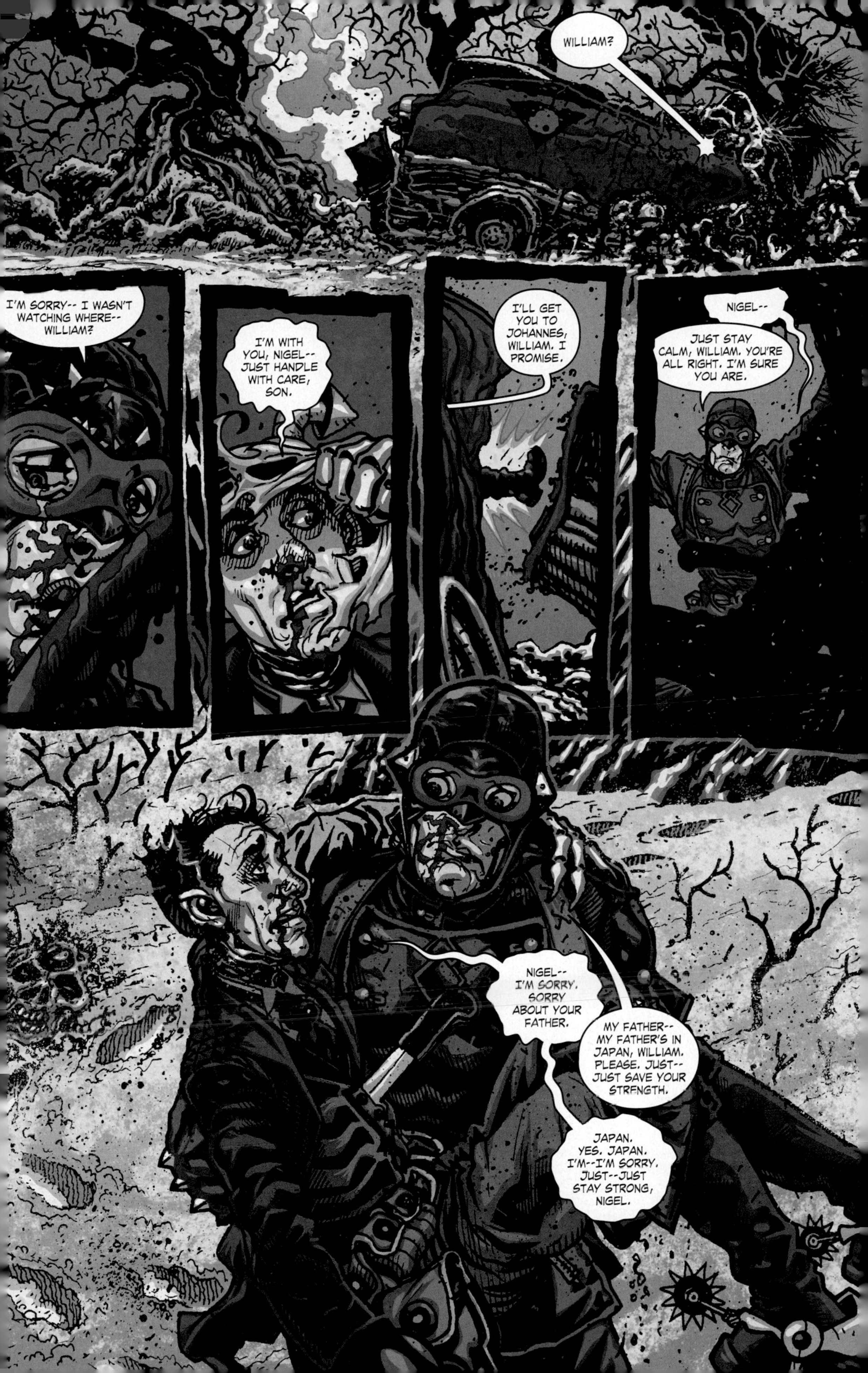
WILLIAM?
I'M SORRY-- I WASN'T WATCHING WHERE-- WILLIAM?
I'M WITH YOU, NIGEL-- JUST HANDLE WITH CARE, SON.
I'LL GET YOU TO JOHANNES, WILLIAM. I PROMISE.
NIGEL--
JUST STAY CALM, WILLIAM. YOU'RE ALL RIGHT. I'M SURE YOU ARE.
NIGEL-- I'M SORRY. SORRY ABOUT YOUR FATHER.
MY FATHER-- MY FATHER'S IN JAPAN, WILLIAM. PLEASE. JUST-- JUST SAVE YOUR STRENGTH.
JAPAN. YES. JAPAN. I'M--I'M SORRY. JUST--JUST STAY STRONG, NIGEL.

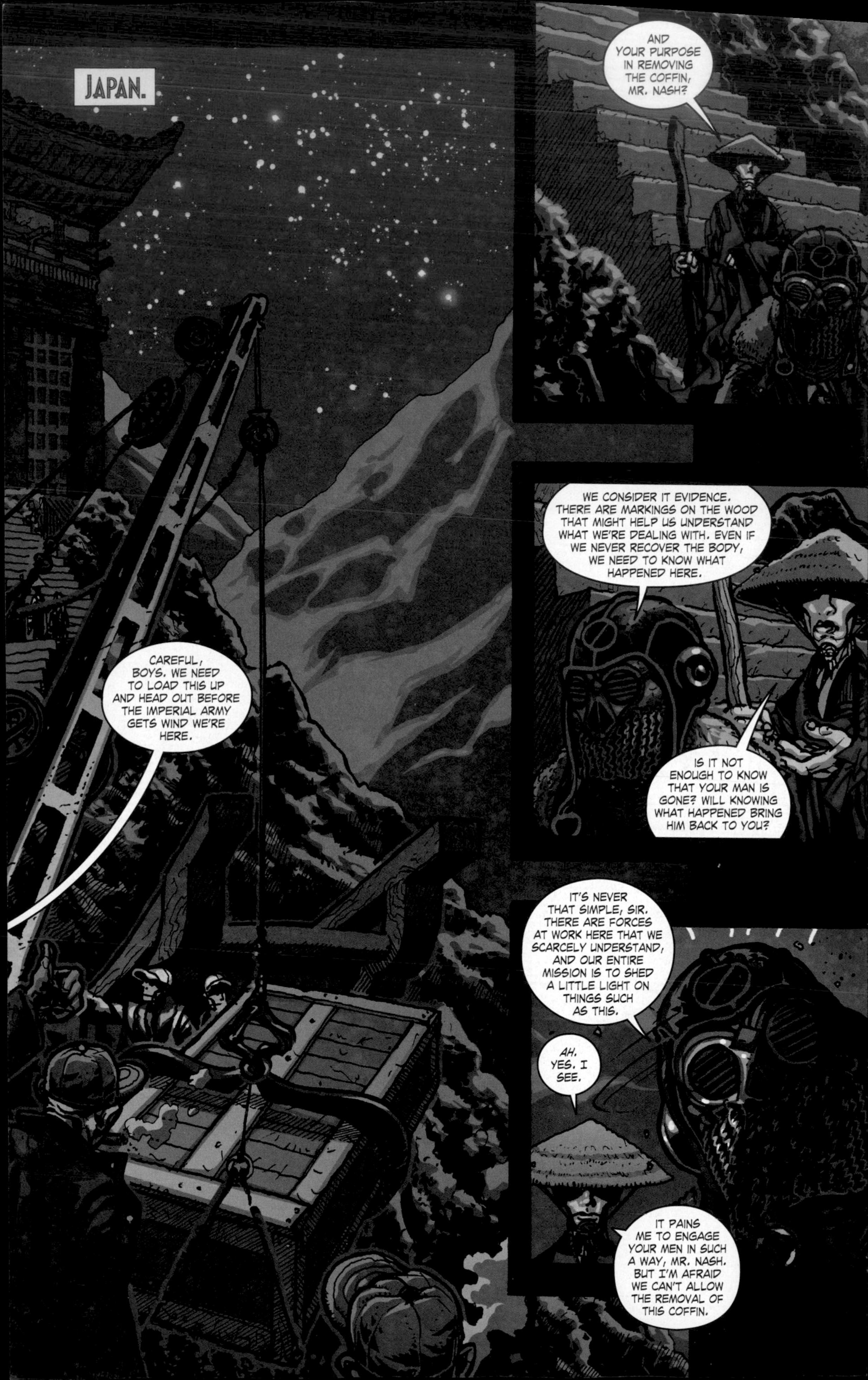
JAPAN.
CAREFUL, BOYS. WE NEED TO LOAD THIS UP AND HEAD OUT BEFORE THE IMPERIAL ARMY GETS WIND WE'RE HERE.
AND YOUR PURPOSE IN REMOVING THE COFFIN, MR. NASH?
WE CONSIDER IT EVIDENCE. THERE ARE MARKINGS ON THE WOOD THAT MIGHT HELP US UNDERSTAND WHAT WE'RE DEALING WITH. EVEN IF WE NEVER RECOVER THE BODY, WE NEED TO KNOW WHAT HAPPENED HERE.
IS IT NOT ENOUGH TO KNOW THAT YOUR MAN IS GONE? WILL KNOWING WHAT HAPPENED BRING HIM BACK TO YOU?
IT'S NEVER THAT SIMPLE, SIR. THERE ARE FORCES AT WORK HERE THAT WE SCARCELY UNDERSTAND, AND OUR ENTIRE MISSION IS TO SHED A LITTLE LIGHT ON THINGS SUCH AS THIS.
AH. YES. I SEE.
IT PAINS ME TO ENGAGE YOUR MEN IN SUCH A WAY, MR. NASH. BUT I'M AFRAID WE CAN'T ALLOW THE REMOVAL OF THIS COFFIN.

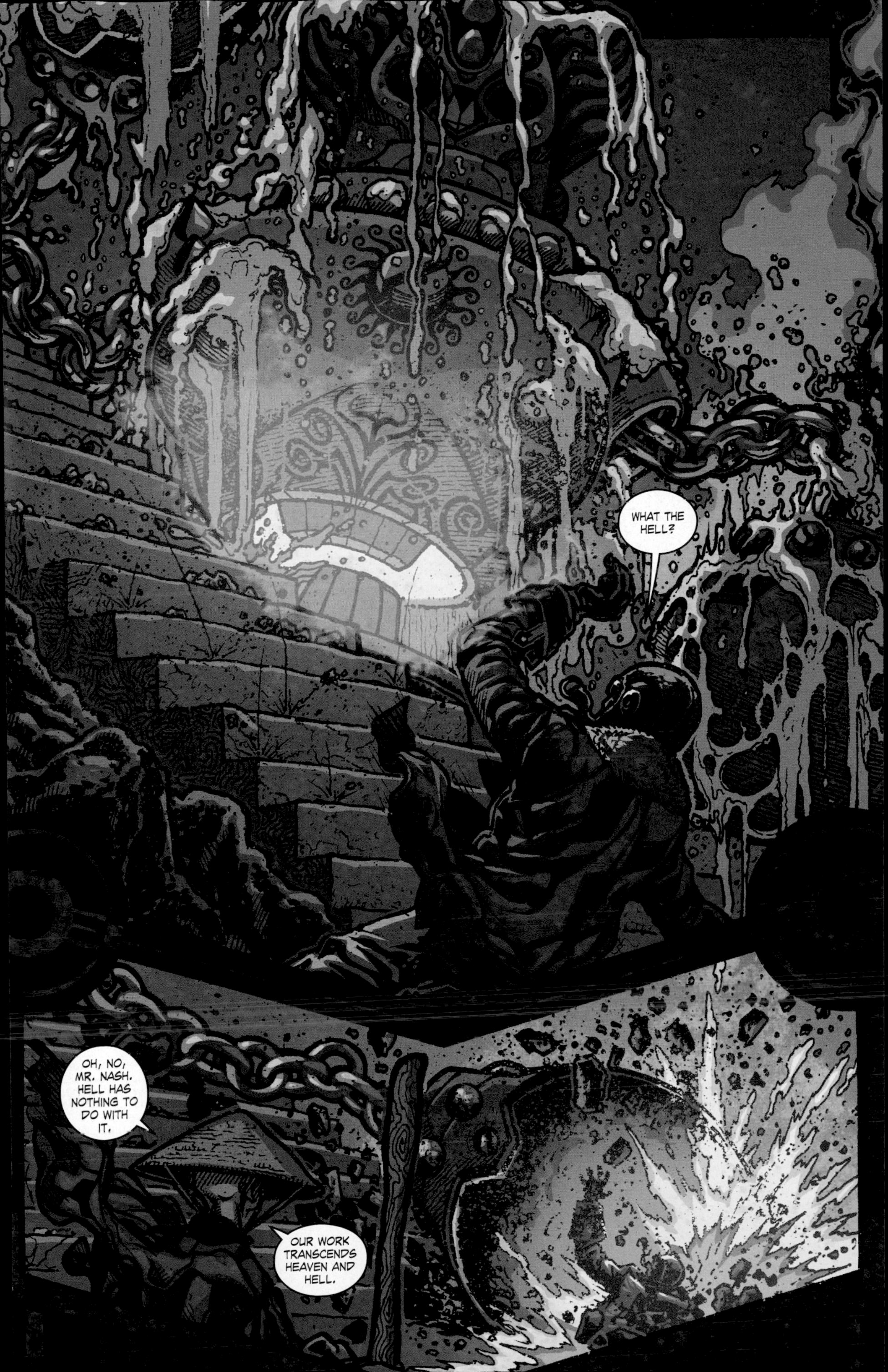
WHAT THE HELL?
OH, NO, MR. NASH. HELL HAS NOTHING TO DO WITH IT.
OUR WORK TRANSCENDS HEAVEN AND HELL.

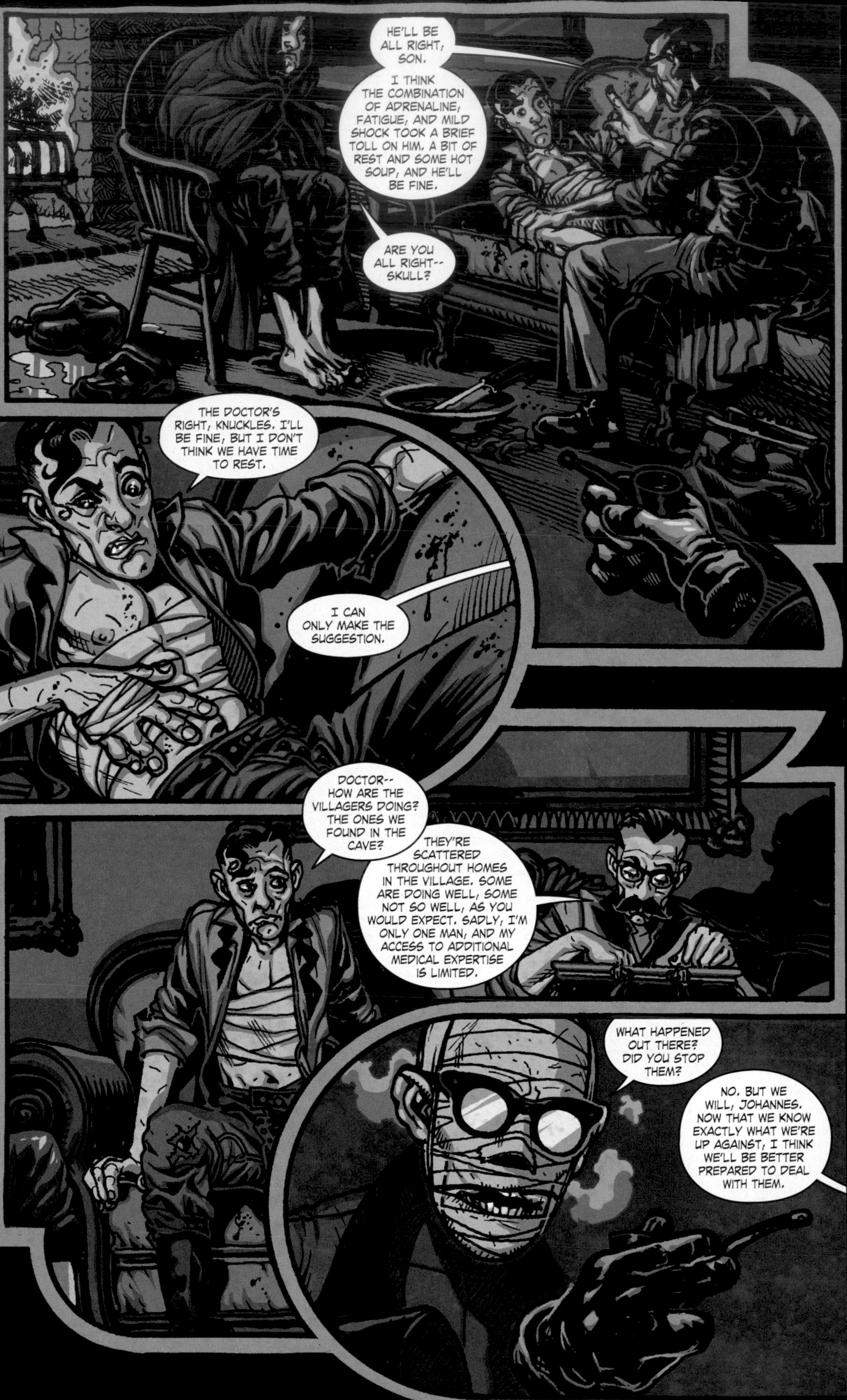
HE'LL BE ALL RIGHT, SON.
I THINK THE COMBINATION OF ADRENALINE, FATIGUE, AND MILD SHOCK TOOK A BRIEF TOLL ON HIM. A BIT OF REST AND SOME HOT SOUP, AND HE'LL BE FINE.
ARE YOU ALL RIGHT--SKULL?
THE DOCTOR'S RIGHT, KNUCKLES. I'LL BE FINE, BUT I DON'T THINK WE HAVE TIME TO REST.
I CAN ONLY MAKE THE SUGGESTION.
DOCTOR--HOW ARE THE VILLAGERS DOING? THE ONES WE FOUND IN THE CAVE?
THEY'RE SCATTERED THROUGHOUT HOMES IN THE VILLAGE. SOME ARE DOING WELL, SOME NOT SO WELL, AS YOU WOULD EXPECT. SADLY, I'M ONLY ONE MAN, AND MY ACCESS TO ADDITIONAL MEDICAL EXPERTISE IS LIMITED.
WHAT HAPPENED OUT THERE? DID YOU STOP THEM?
NO. BUT WE WILL, JOHANNES. NOW THAT WE KNOW EXACTLY WHAT WE'RE UP AGAINST, I THINK WE'LL BE BETTER PREPARED TO DEAL WITH THEM.

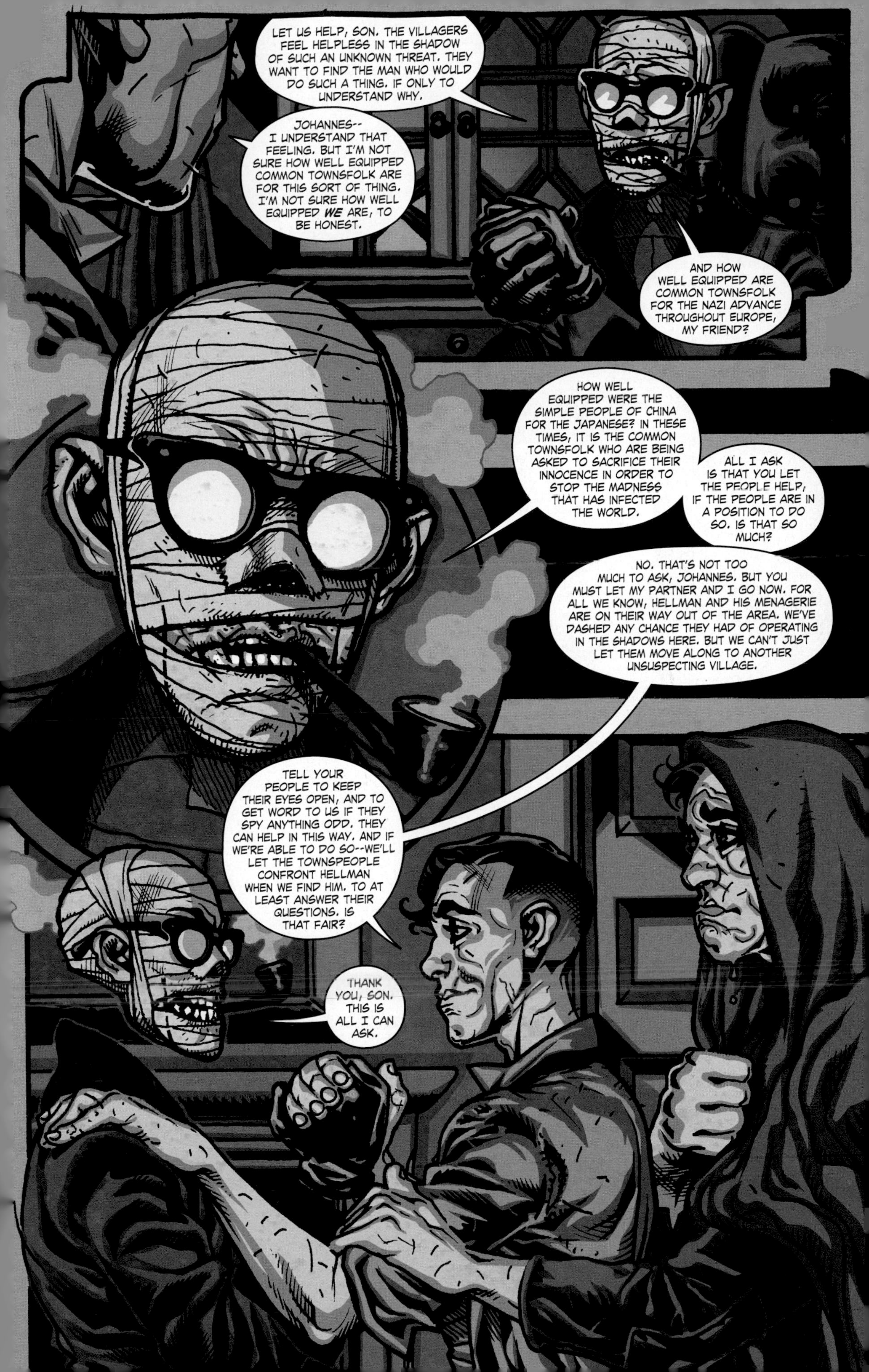
LET US HELP, SON. THE VILLAGERS FEEL HELPLESS IN THE SHADOW OF SUCH AN UNKNOWN THREAT. THEY WANT TO FIND THE MAN WHO WOULD DO SUCH A THING. IF ONLY TO UNDERSTAND WHY.
JOHANNES-- I UNDERSTAND THAT FEELING. BUT I'M NOT SURE HOW WELL EQUIPPED COMMON TOWNSFOLK ARE FOR THIS SORT OF THING. I'M NOT SURE HOW WELL EQUIPPED *WE* ARE, TO BE HONEST.
AND HOW WELL EQUIPPED ARE COMMON TOWNSFOLK FOR THE NAZI ADVANCE THROUGHOUT EUROPE, MY FRIEND?
HOW WELL EQUIPPED WERE THE SIMPLE PEOPLE OF CHINA FOR THE JAPANESE? IN THESE TIMES, IT IS THE COMMON TOWNSFOLK WHO ARE BEING ASKED TO SACRIFICE THEIR INNOCENCE IN ORDER TO STOP THE MADNESS THAT HAS INFECTED THE WORLD.
ALL I ASK IS THAT YOU LET THE PEOPLE HELP, IF THE PEOPLE ARE IN A POSITION TO DO SO. IS THAT SO MUCH?
NO. THAT'S NOT TOO MUCH TO ASK, JOHANNES. BUT YOU MUST LET MY PARTNER AND I GO NOW. FOR ALL WE KNOW, HELLMAN AND HIS MENAGERIE ARE ON THEIR WAY OUT OF THE AREA. WE'VE DASHED ANY CHANCE THEY HAD OF OPERATING IN THE SHADOWS HERE. BUT WE CAN'T JUST LET THEM MOVE ALONG TO ANOTHER UNSUSPECTING VILLAGE.
TELL YOUR PEOPLE TO KEEP THEIR EYES OPEN, AND TO GET WORD TO US IF THEY SPY ANYTHING ODD. THEY CAN HELP IN THIS WAY. AND IF WE'RE ABLE TO DO SO--WE'LL LET THE TOWNSPEOPLE CONFRONT HELLMAN WHEN WE FIND HIM. TO AT LEAST ANSWER THEIR QUESTIONS. IS THAT FAIR?
THANK YOU, SON. THIS IS ALL I CAN ASK.

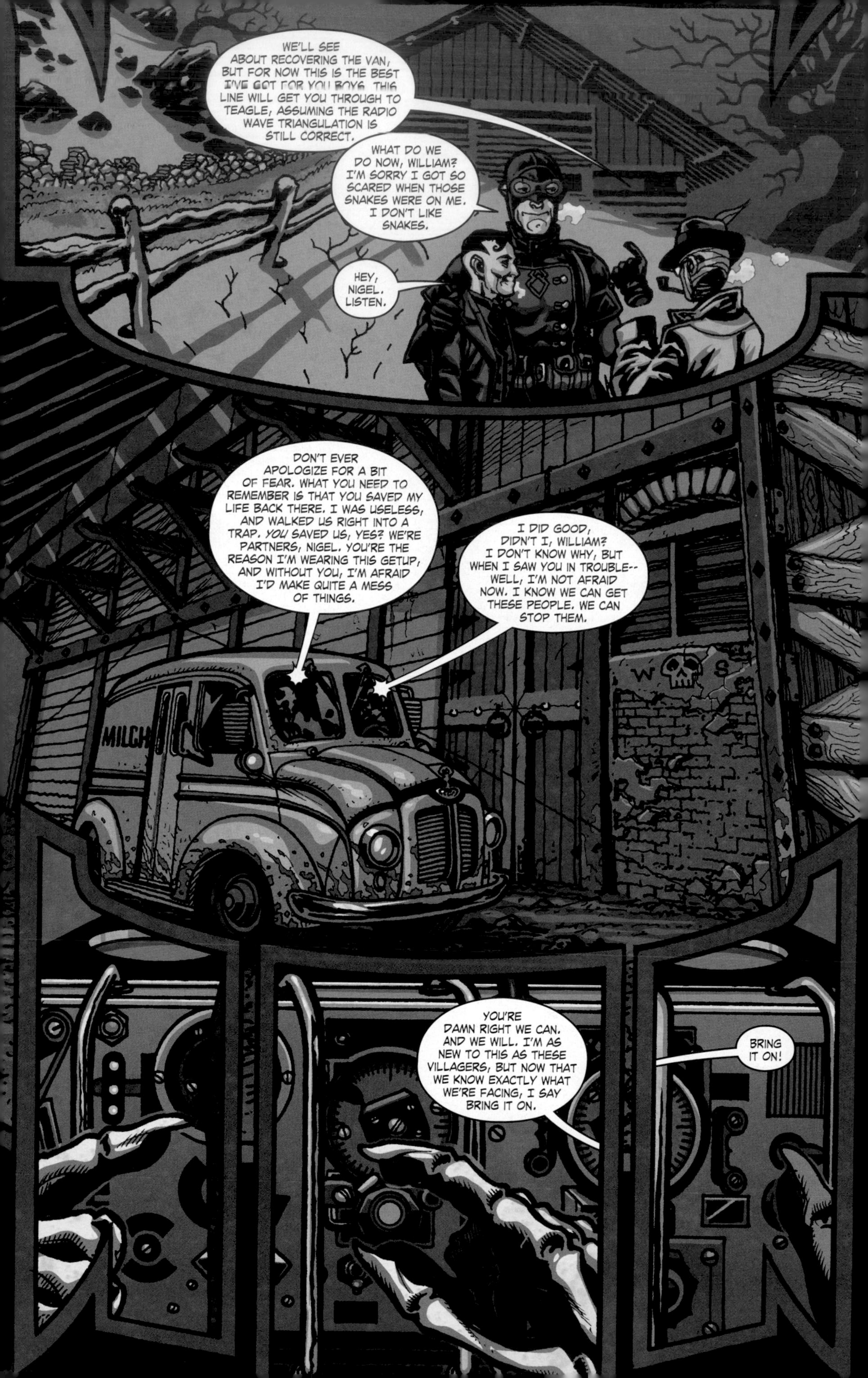
WE'LL SEE ABOUT RECOVERING THE VAN, BUT FOR NOW THIS IS THE BEST I'VE GOT FOR YOU BOYS. THIS LINE WILL GET YOU THROUGH TO TEAGLE, ASSUMING THE RADIO WAVE TRIANGULATION IS STILL CORRECT.
WHAT DO WE DO NOW, WILLIAM? I'M SORRY I GOT SO SCARED WHEN THOSE SNAKES WERE ON ME. I DON'T LIKE SNAKES.
HEY, NIGEL. LISTEN.
DON'T EVER APOLOGIZE FOR A BIT OF FEAR. WHAT YOU NEED TO REMEMBER IS THAT YOU SAVED MY LIFE BACK THERE. I WAS USELESS, AND WALKED US RIGHT INTO A TRAP. *YOU* SAVED US, YES? WE'RE PARTNERS, NIGEL. YOU'RE THE REASON I'M WEARING THIS GETUP, AND WITHOUT YOU, I'M AFRAID I'D MAKE QUITE A MESS OF THINGS.
I DID GOOD, DIDN'T I, WILLIAM? I DON'T KNOW WHY, BUT WHEN I SAW YOU IN TROUBLE-- WELL, I'M NOT AFRAID NOW. I KNOW WE CAN GET THESE PEOPLE. WE CAN STOP THEM.
MILCH
YOU'RE DAMN RIGHT WE CAN. AND WE WILL. I'M AS NEW TO THIS AS THESE VILLAGERS, BUT NOW THAT WE KNOW EXACTLY WHAT WE'RE FACING, I SAY BRING IT ON.
BRING IT ON!

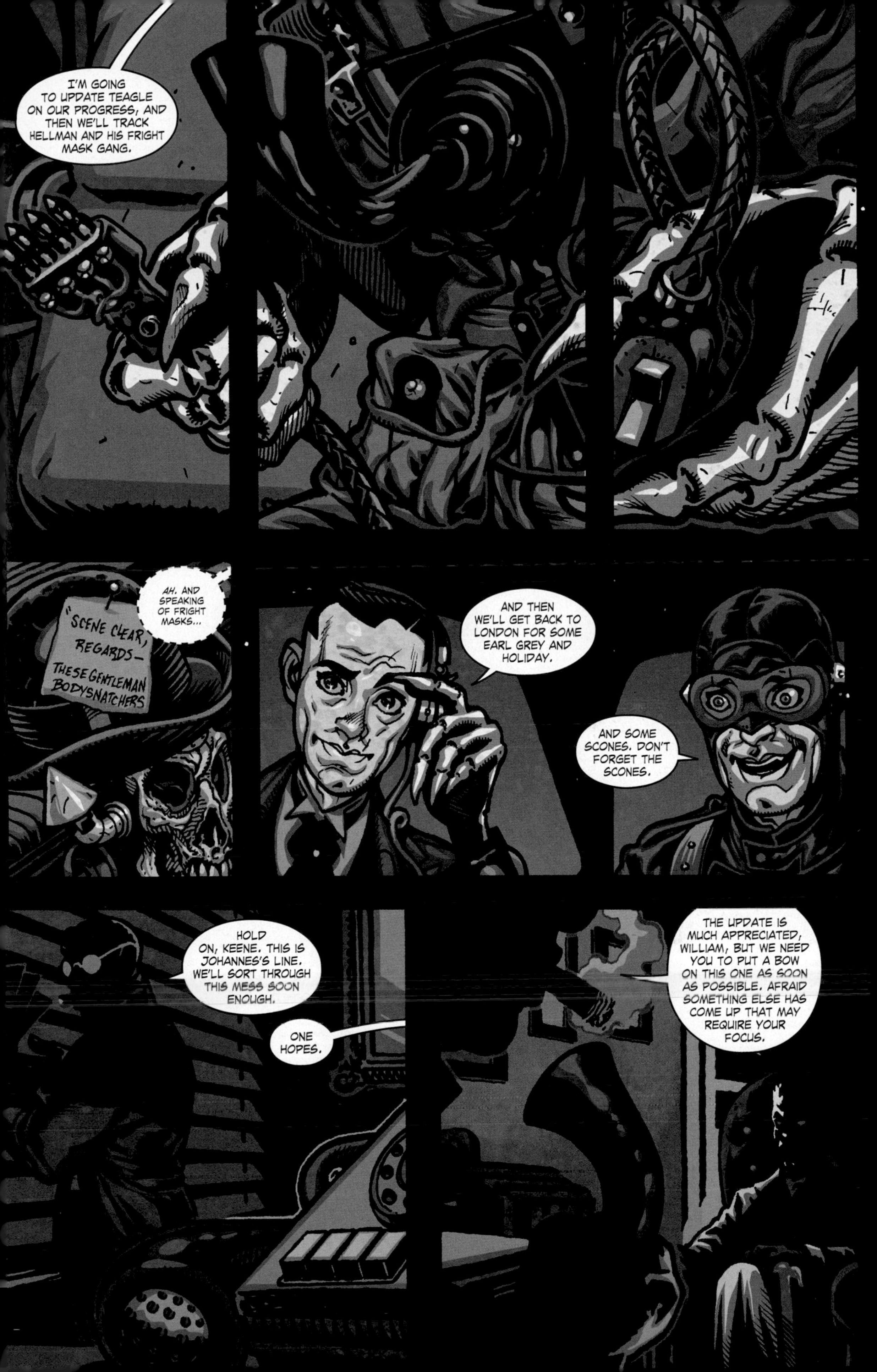
I'M GOING TO UPDATE TEAGLE ON OUR PROGRESS, AND THEN WE'LL TRACK HELLMAN AND HIS FRIGHT MASK GANG.
"SCENE CLEAR, REGARDS— THESE GENTLEMAN BODYSNATCHERS
AH. AND SPEAKING OF FRIGHT MASKS...
AND THEN WE'LL GET BACK TO LONDON FOR SOME EARL GREY AND HOLIDAY.
AND SOME SCONES. DON'T FORGET THE SCONES.
HOLD ON, KEENE. THIS IS JOHANNES'S LINE. WE'LL SORT THROUGH THIS MESS SOON ENOUGH.
ONE HOPES.
THE UPDATE IS MUCH APPRECIATED, WILLIAM, BUT WE NEED YOU TO PUT A BOW ON THIS ONE AS SOON AS POSSIBLE. AFRAID SOMETHING ELSE HAS COME UP THAT MAY REQUIRE YOUR FOCUS.

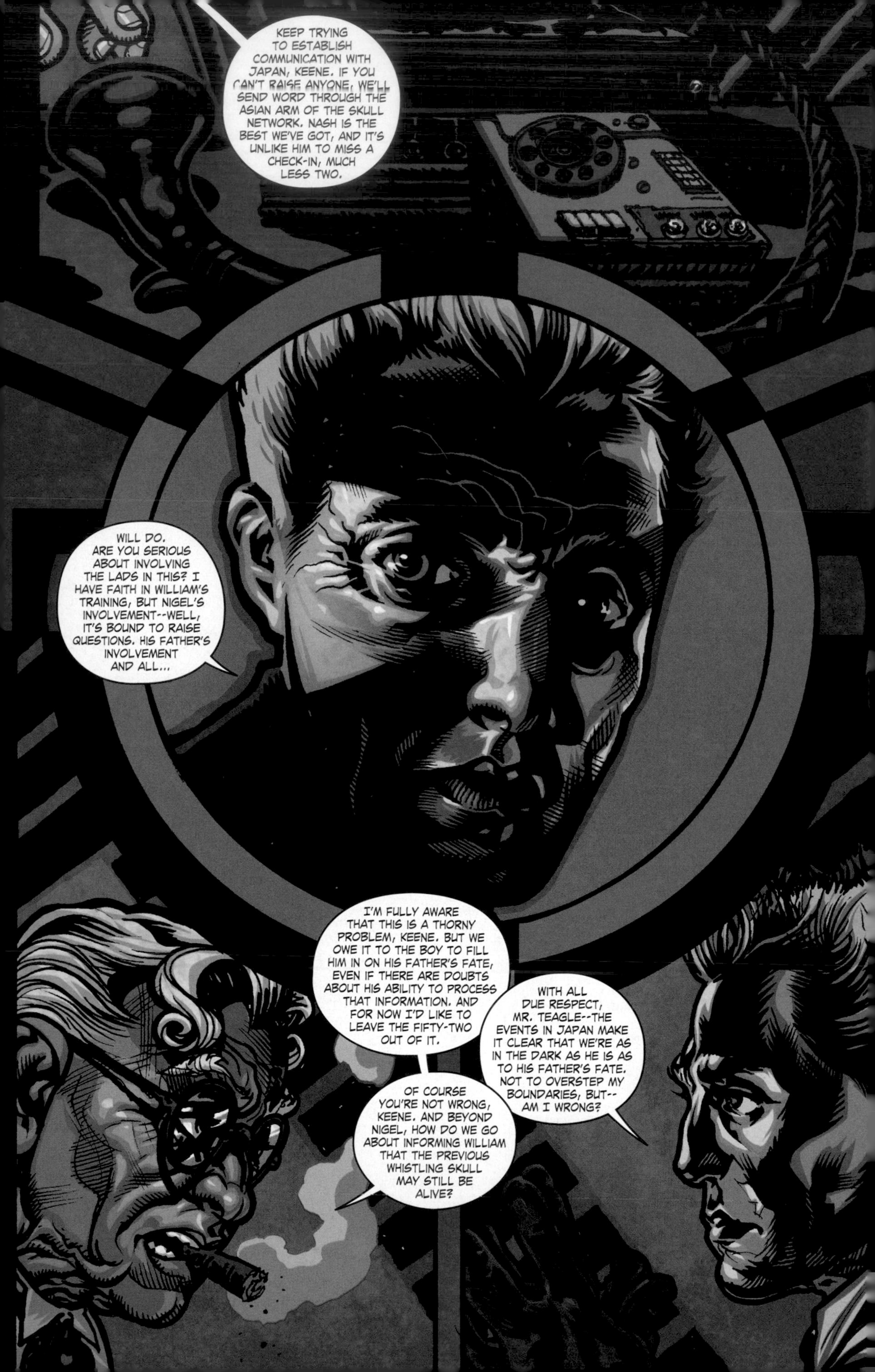
KEEP TRYING TO ESTABLISH COMMUNICATION WITH JAPAN, KEENE. IF YOU CAN'T RAISE ANYONE, WE'LL SEND WORD THROUGH THE ASIAN ARM OF THE SKULL NETWORK. NASH IS THE BEST WE'VE GOT, AND IT'S UNLIKE HIM TO MISS A CHECK-IN, MUCH LESS TWO.
WILL DO. ARE YOU SERIOUS ABOUT INVOLVING THE LADS IN THIS? I HAVE FAITH IN WILLIAM'S TRAINING, BUT NIGEL'S INVOLVEMENT--WELL, IT'S BOUND TO RAISE QUESTIONS. HIS FATHER'S INVOLVEMENT AND ALL...
I'M FULLY AWARE THAT THIS IS A THORNY PROBLEM, KEENE. BUT WE OWE IT TO THE BOY TO FILL HIM IN ON HIS FATHER'S FATE, EVEN IF THERE ARE DOUBTS ABOUT HIS ABILITY TO PROCESS THAT INFORMATION. AND FOR NOW I'D LIKE TO LEAVE THE FIFTY-TWO OUT OF IT.
WITH ALL DUE RESPECT, MR. TEAGLE--THE EVENTS IN JAPAN MAKE IT CLEAR THAT WE'RE AS IN THE DARK AS HE IS AS TO HIS FATHER'S FATE. NOT TO OVERSTEP MY BOUNDARIES, BUT-- AM I WRONG?
OF COURSE YOU'RE NOT WRONG, KEENE. AND BEYOND NIGEL, HOW DO WE GO ABOUT INFORMING WILLIAM THAT THE PREVIOUS WHISTLING SKULL MAY STILL BE ALIVE?

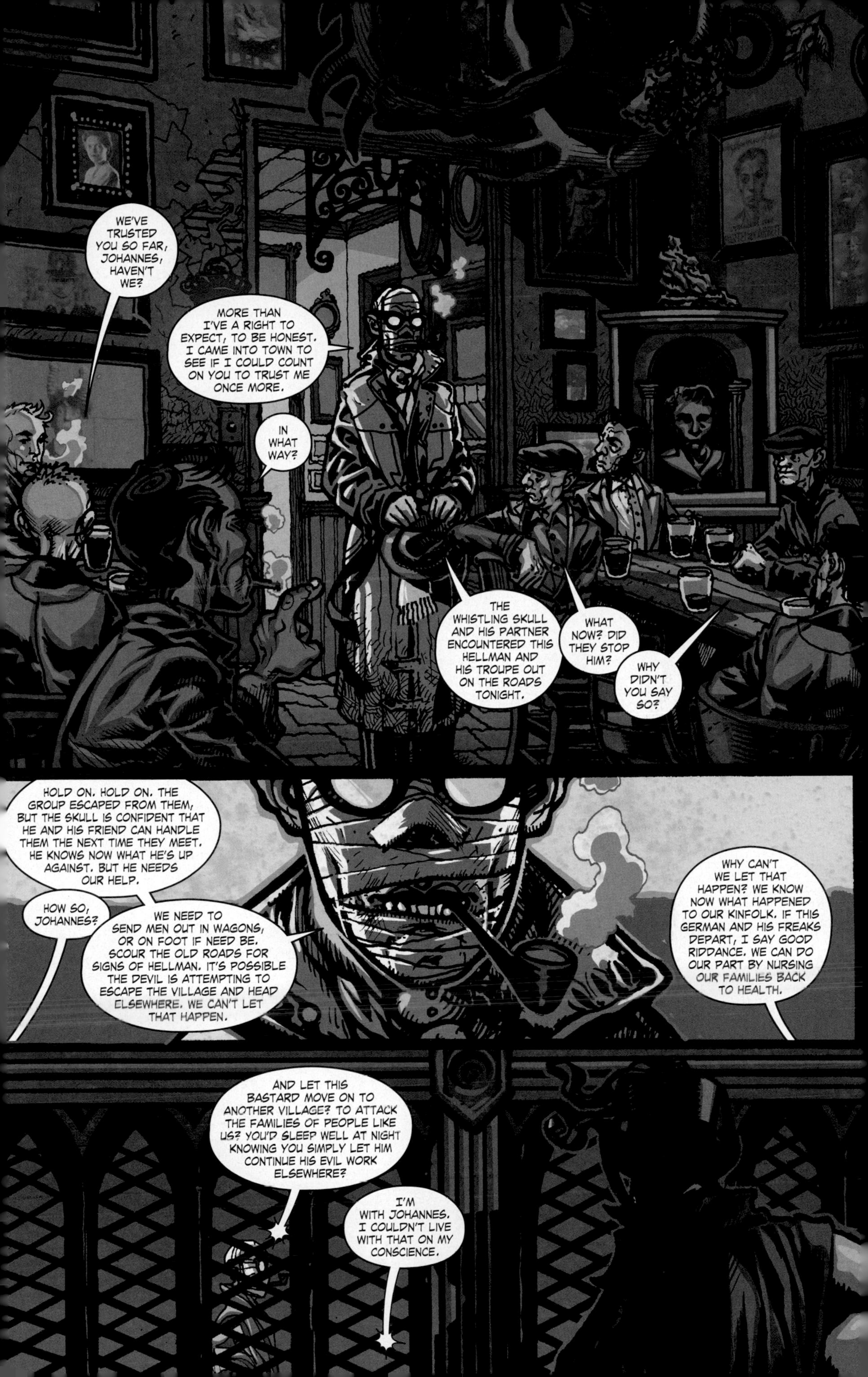
WE'VE TRUSTED YOU SO FAR, JOHANNES, HAVEN'T WE?
MORE THAN I'VE A RIGHT TO EXPECT, TO BE HONEST. I CAME INTO TOWN TO SEE IF I COULD COUNT ON YOU TO TRUST ME ONCE MORE.
IN WHAT WAY?
THE WHISTLING SKULL AND HIS PARTNER ENCOUNTERED THIS HELLMAN AND HIS TROUPE OUT ON THE ROADS TONIGHT.
WHAT NOW? DID THEY STOP HIM?
WHY DIDN'T YOU SAY SO?
HOLD ON. HOLD ON. THE GROUP ESCAPED FROM THEM, BUT THE SKULL IS CONFIDENT THAT HE AND HIS FRIEND CAN HANDLE THEM THE NEXT TIME THEY MEET. HE KNOWS NOW WHAT HE'S UP AGAINST. BUT HE NEEDS OUR HELP.
HOW SO, JOHANNES?
WE NEED TO SEND MEN OUT IN WAGONS, OR ON FOOT IF NEED BE. SCOUR THE OLD ROADS FOR SIGNS OF HELLMAN. IT'S POSSIBLE THE DEVIL IS ATTEMPTING TO ESCAPE THE VILLAGE AND HEAD ELSEWHERE. WE CAN'T LET THAT HAPPEN.
WHY CAN'T WE LET THAT HAPPEN? WE KNOW NOW WHAT HAPPENED TO OUR KINFOLK. IF THIS GERMAN AND HIS FREAKS DEPART, I SAY GOOD RIDDANCE. WE CAN DO OUR PART BY NURSING OUR FAMILIES BACK TO HEALTH.
AND LET THIS BASTARD MOVE ON TO ANOTHER VILLAGE? TO ATTACK THE FAMILIES OF PEOPLE LIKE US? YOU'D SLEEP WELL AT NIGHT KNOWING YOU SIMPLY LET HIM CONTINUE HIS EVIL WORK ELSEWHERE?
I'M WITH JOHANNES. I COULDN'T LIVE WITH THAT ON MY CONSCIENCE.

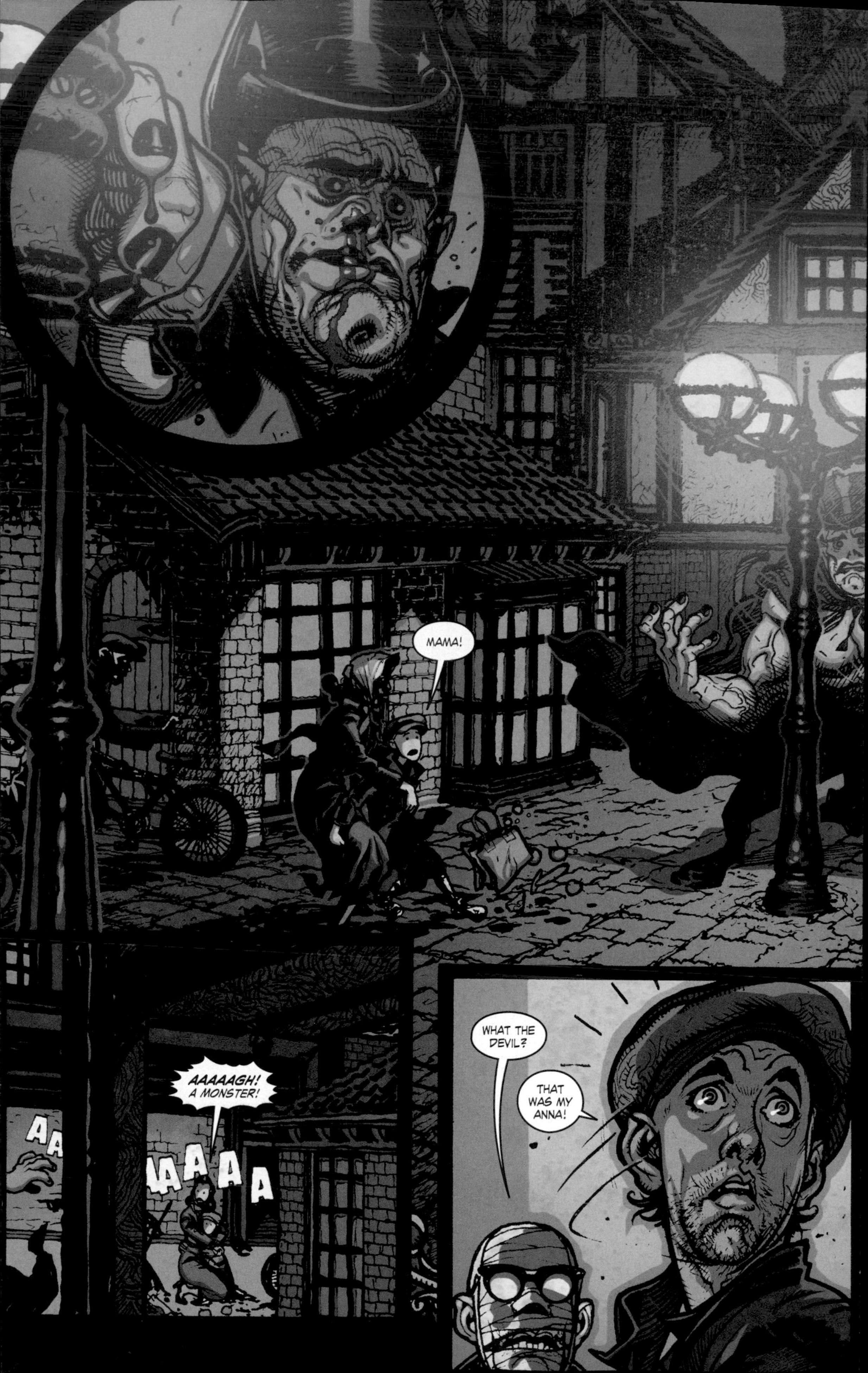
MAMA!
AAAAAGH! A MONSTER!
AAAAAAA
WHAT THE DEVIL?
THAT WAS MY ANNA!

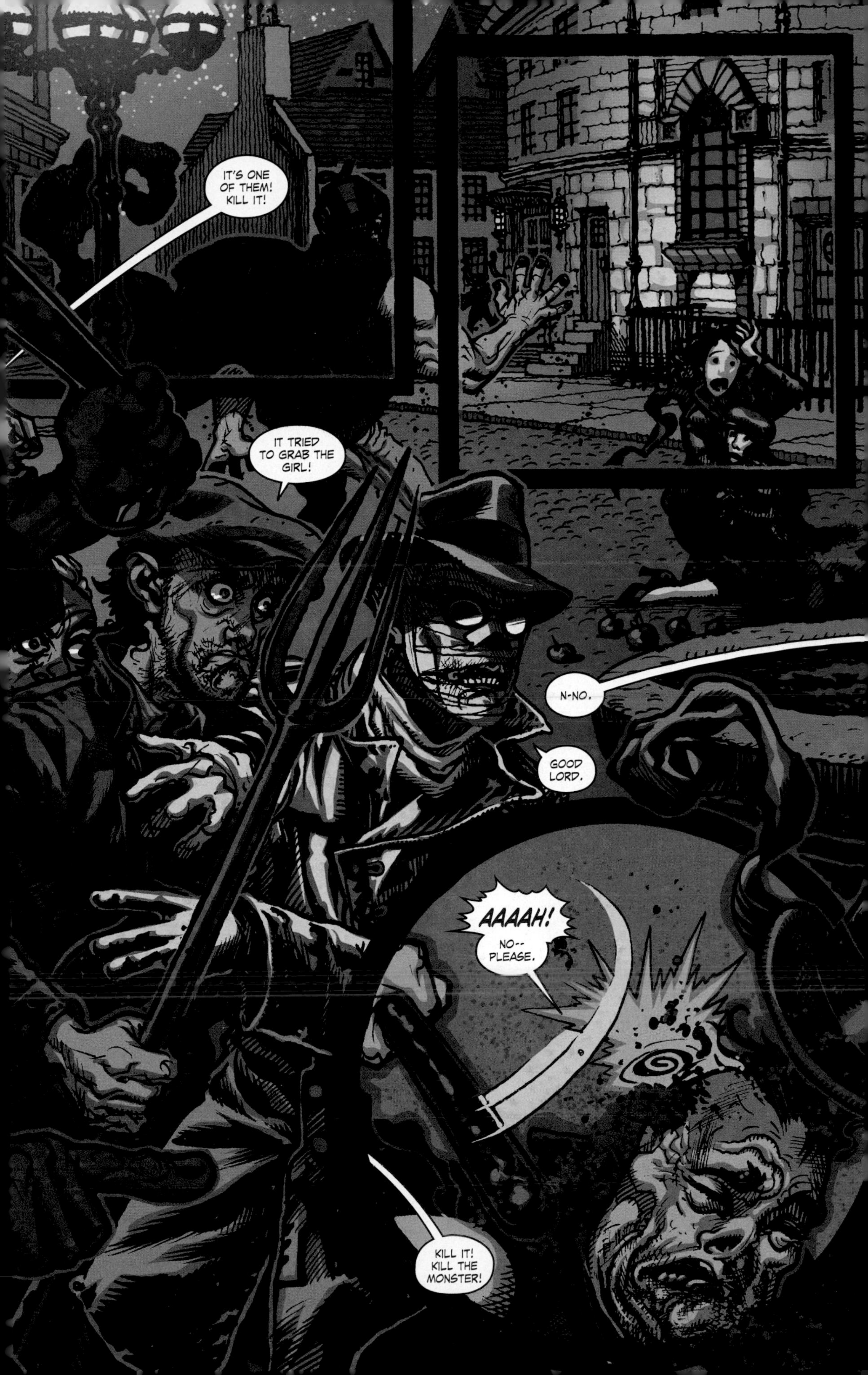
IT'S ONE OF THEM! KILL IT!
IT TRIED TO GRAB THE GIRL!
N-NO.
GOOD LORD.
AAAAH!
NO-- PLEASE.
KILL IT! KILL THE MONSTER!

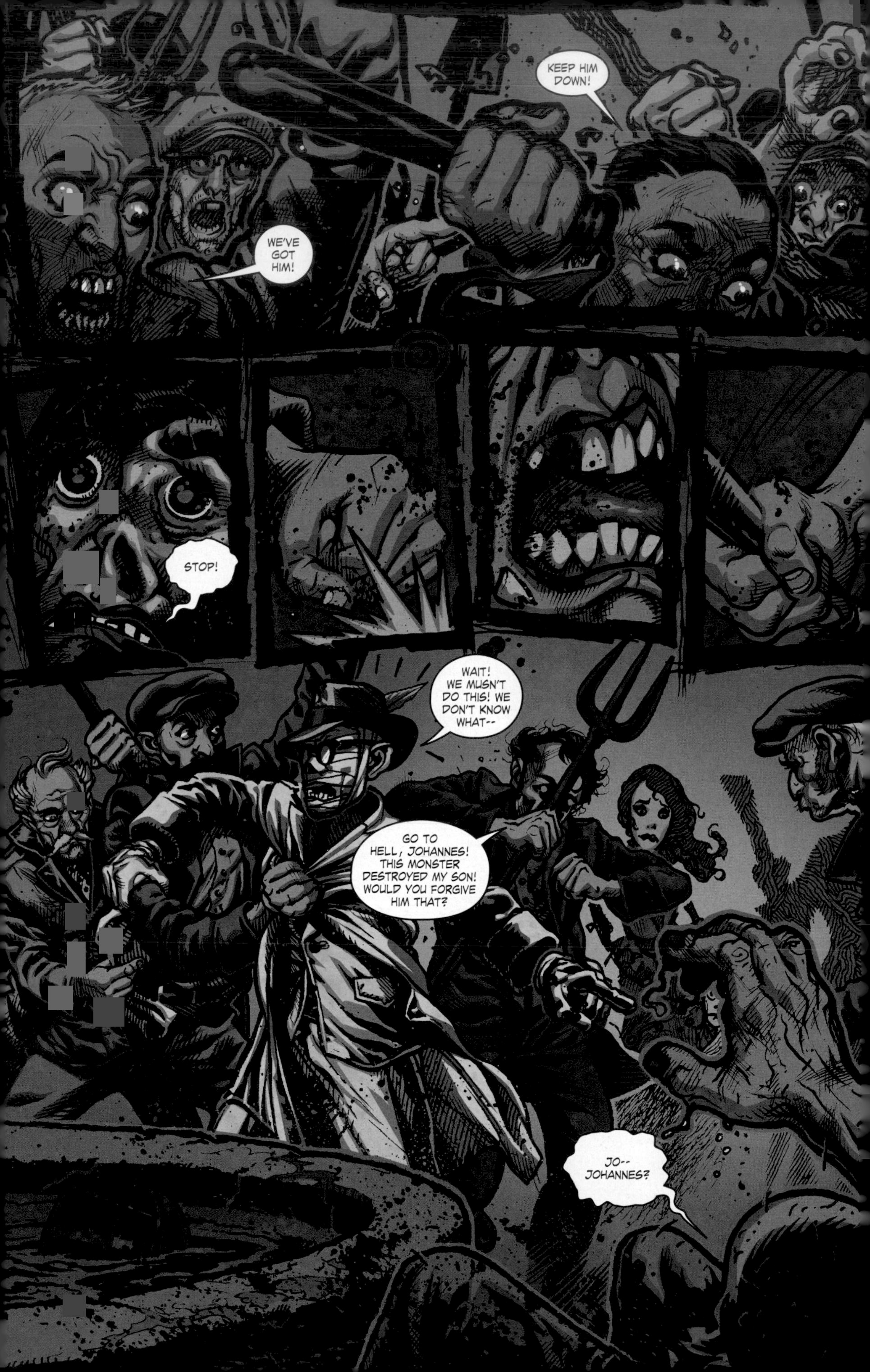
KEEP HIM DOWN!
WE'VE GOT HIM!
STOP!
WAIT! WE MUSN'T DO THIS! WE DON'T KNOW WHAT--
GO TO HELL, JOHANNES! THIS MONSTER DESTROYED MY SON! WOULD YOU FORGIVE HIM THAT?
JO-- JOHANNES?

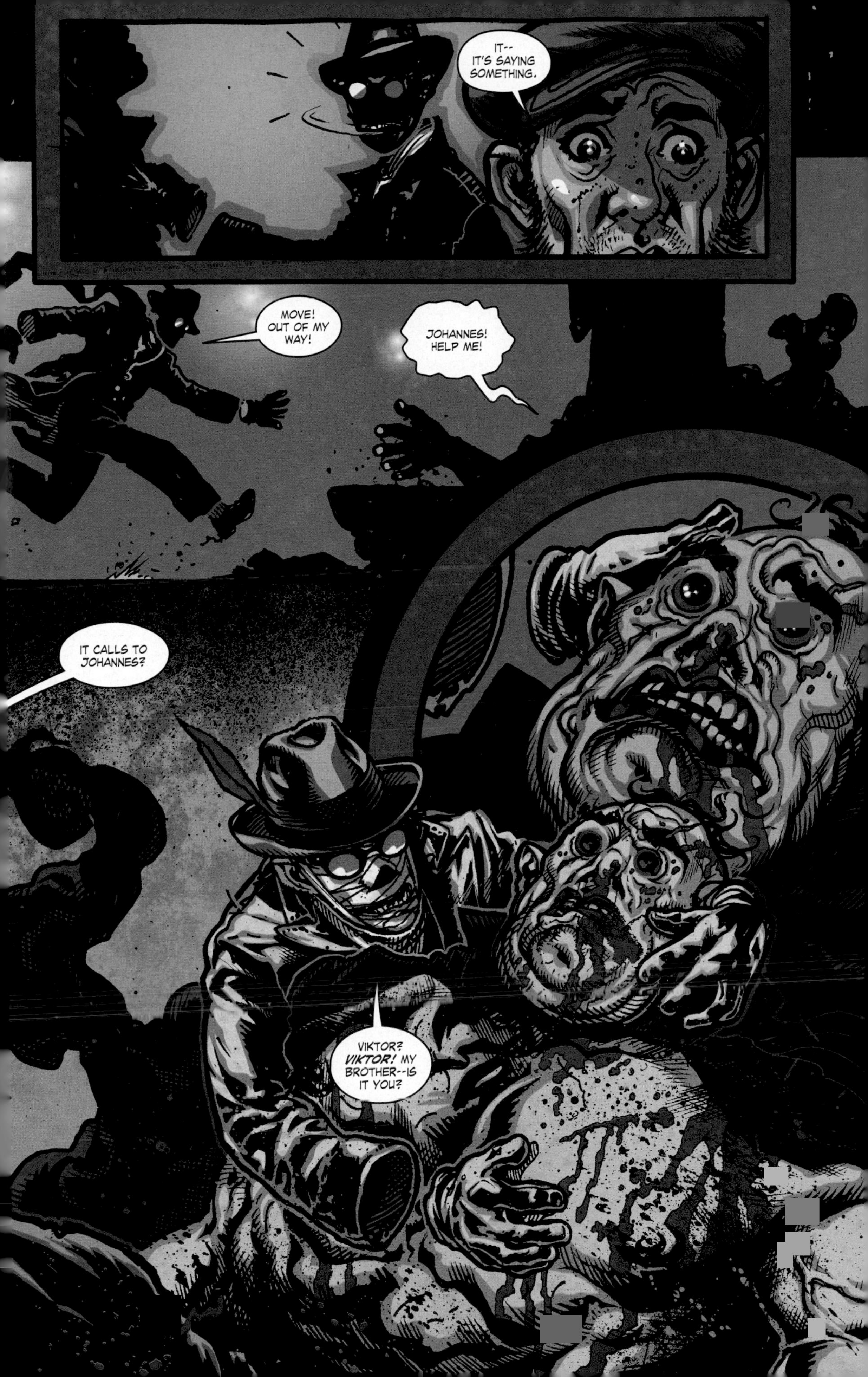
IT--
IT'S SAYING SOMETHING.
MOVE! OUT OF MY WAY!
JOHANNES! HELP ME!
IT CALLS TO JOHANNES?
VIKTOR? *VIKTOR!* MY BROTHER--IS IT YOU?

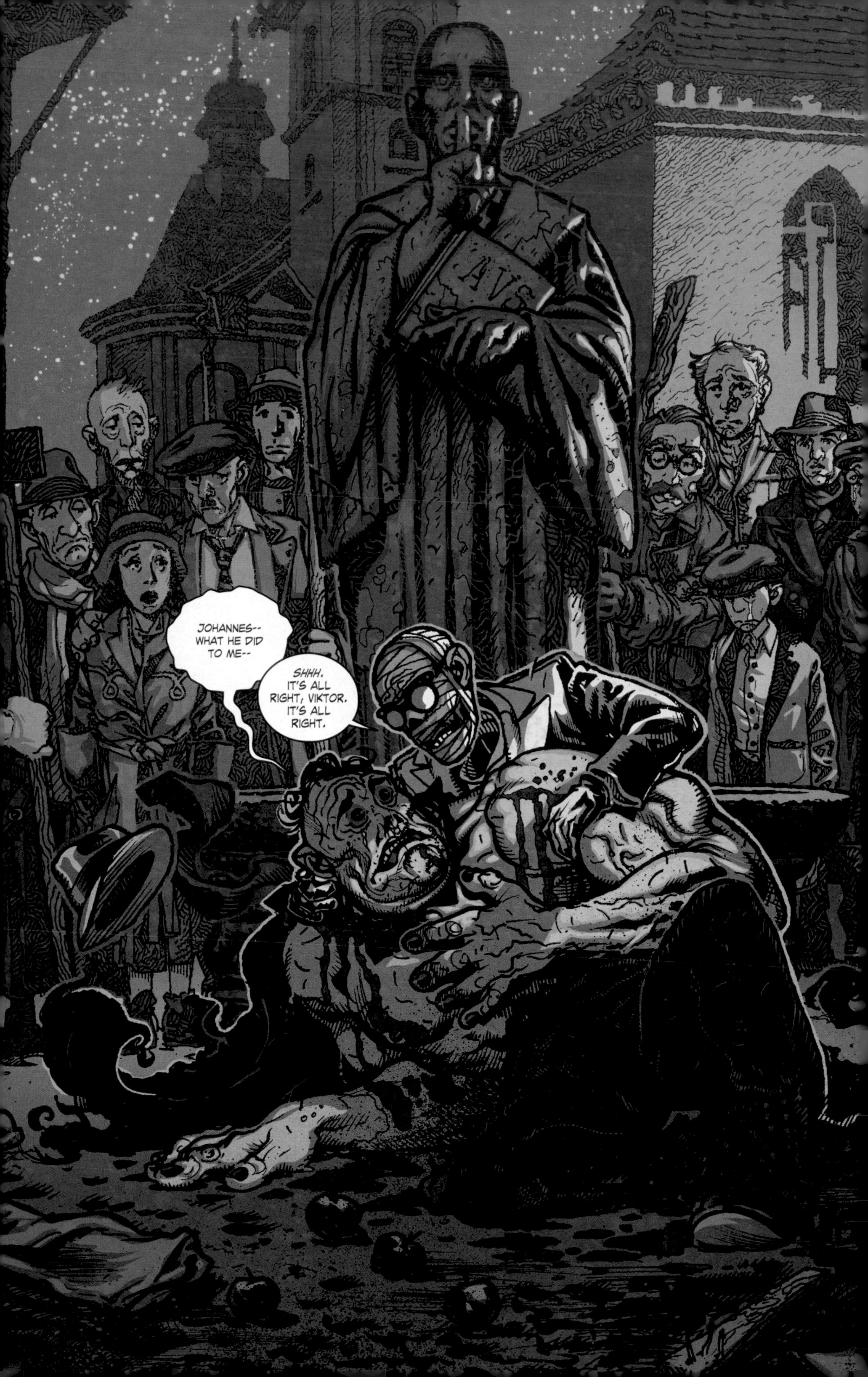
JOHANNES--
WHAT HE DID
TO ME--
SHHH.
IT'S ALL
RIGHT, VIKTOR.
IT'S ALL
RIGHT.

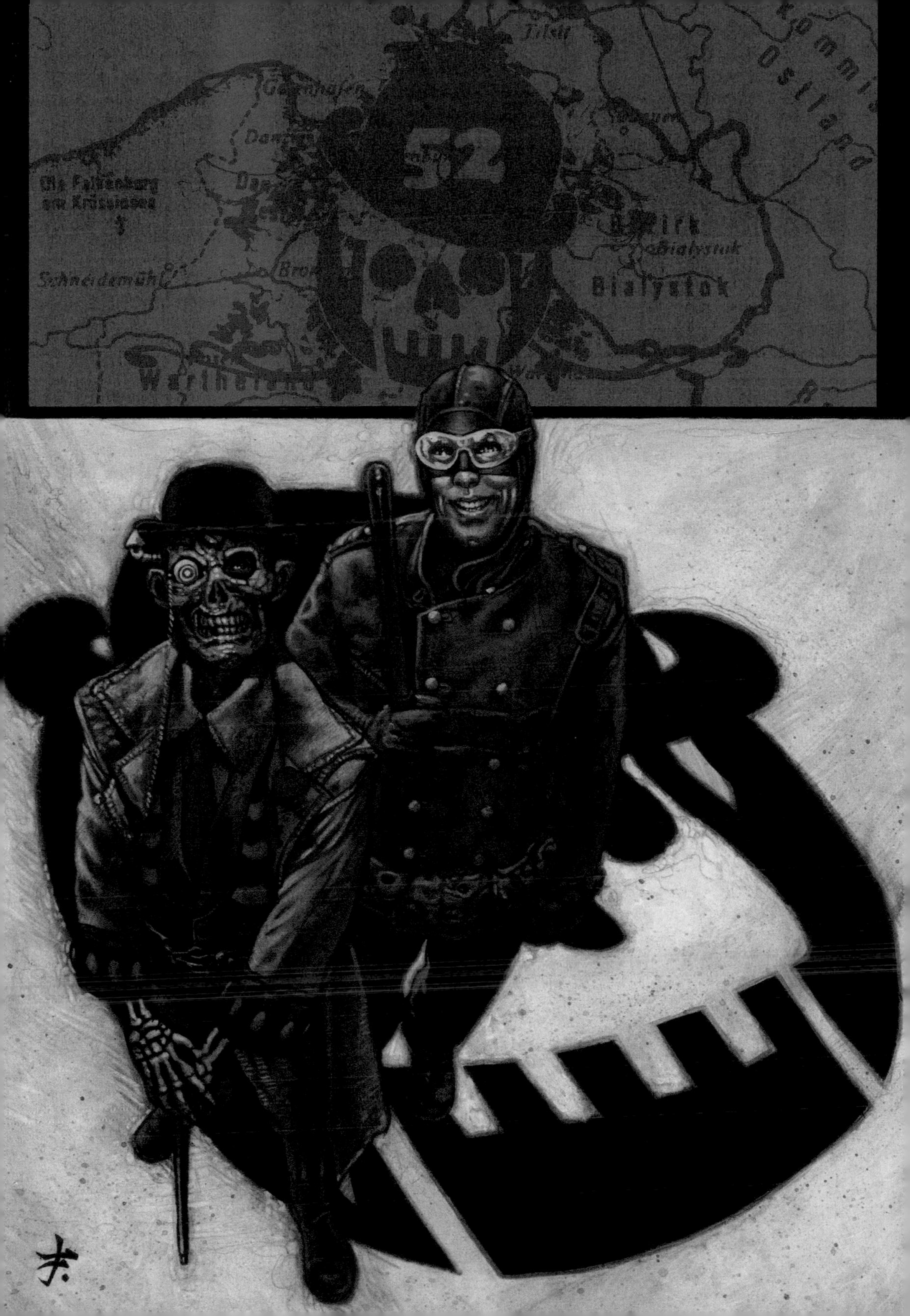

52
Tilsit
Schneidemühl
Bialystok

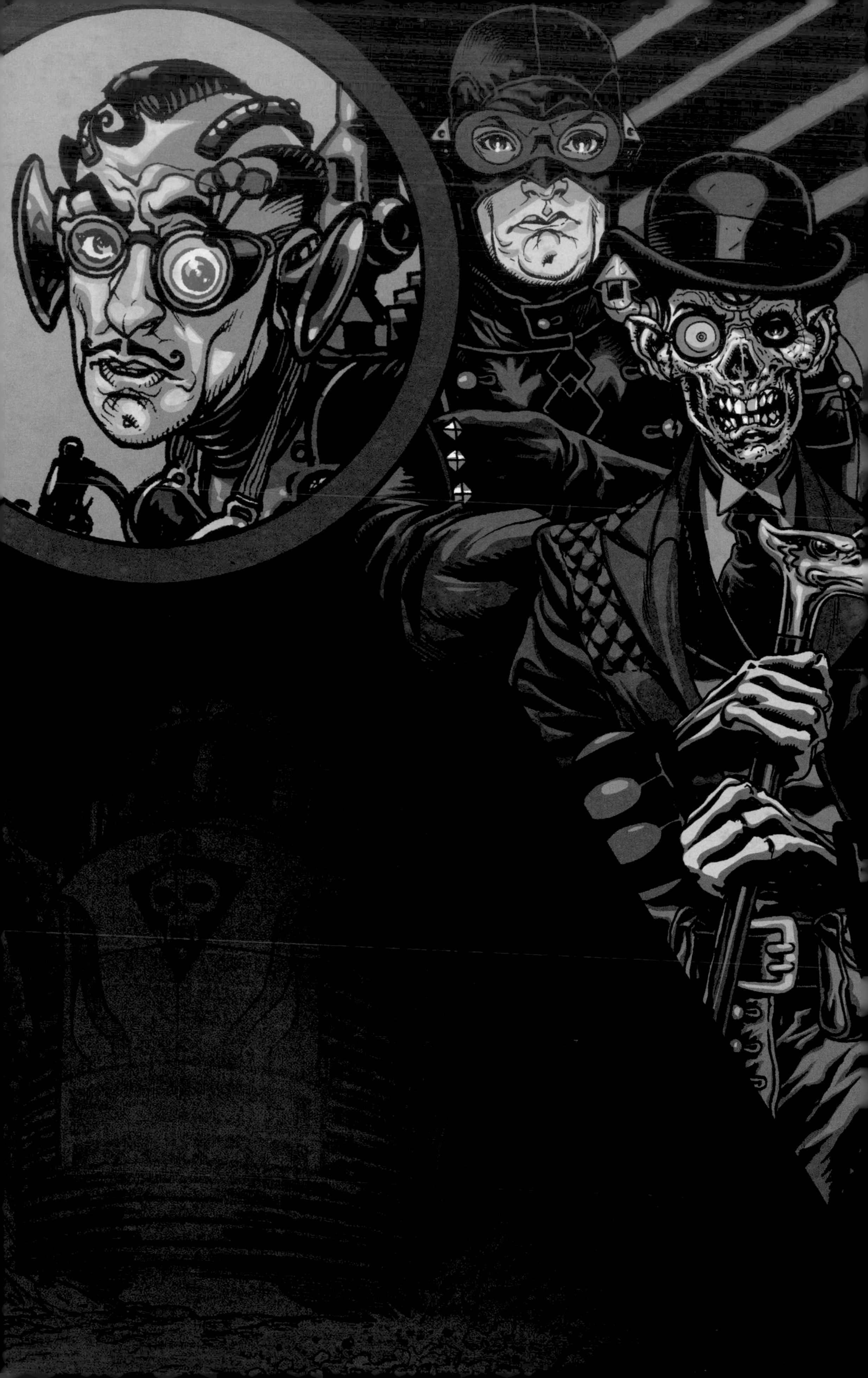

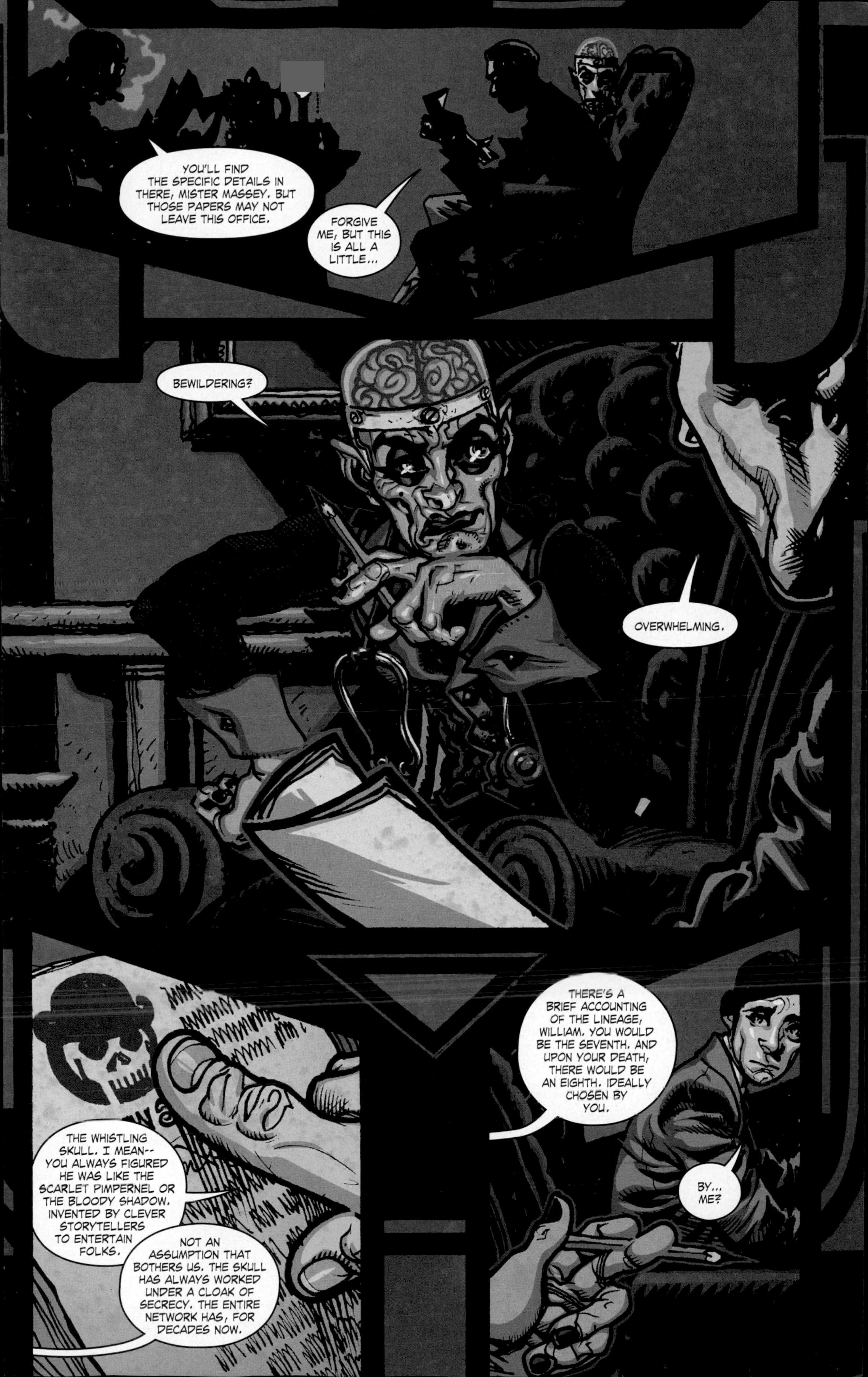
YOU'LL FIND THE SPECIFIC DETAILS IN THERE, MISTER MASSEY. BUT THOSE PAPERS MAY NOT LEAVE THIS OFFICE.
FORGIVE ME, BUT THIS IS ALL A LITTLE...
BEWILDERING?
OVERWHELMING.
THE WHISTLING SKULL. I MEAN-- YOU ALWAYS FIGURED HE WAS LIKE THE SCARLET PIMPERNEL OR THE BLOODY SHADOW. INVENTED BY CLEVER STORYTELLERS TO ENTERTAIN FOLKS.
NOT AN ASSUMPTION THAT BOTHERS US. THE SKULL HAS ALWAYS WORKED UNDER A CLOAK OF SECRECY. THE ENTIRE NETWORK HAS, FOR DECADES NOW.
THERE'S A BRIEF ACCOUNTING OF THE LINEAGE, WILLIAM. YOU WOULD BE THE SEVENTH. AND UPON YOUR DEATH, THERE WOULD BE AN EIGHTH. IDEALLY CHOSEN BY YOU.
BY... ME?

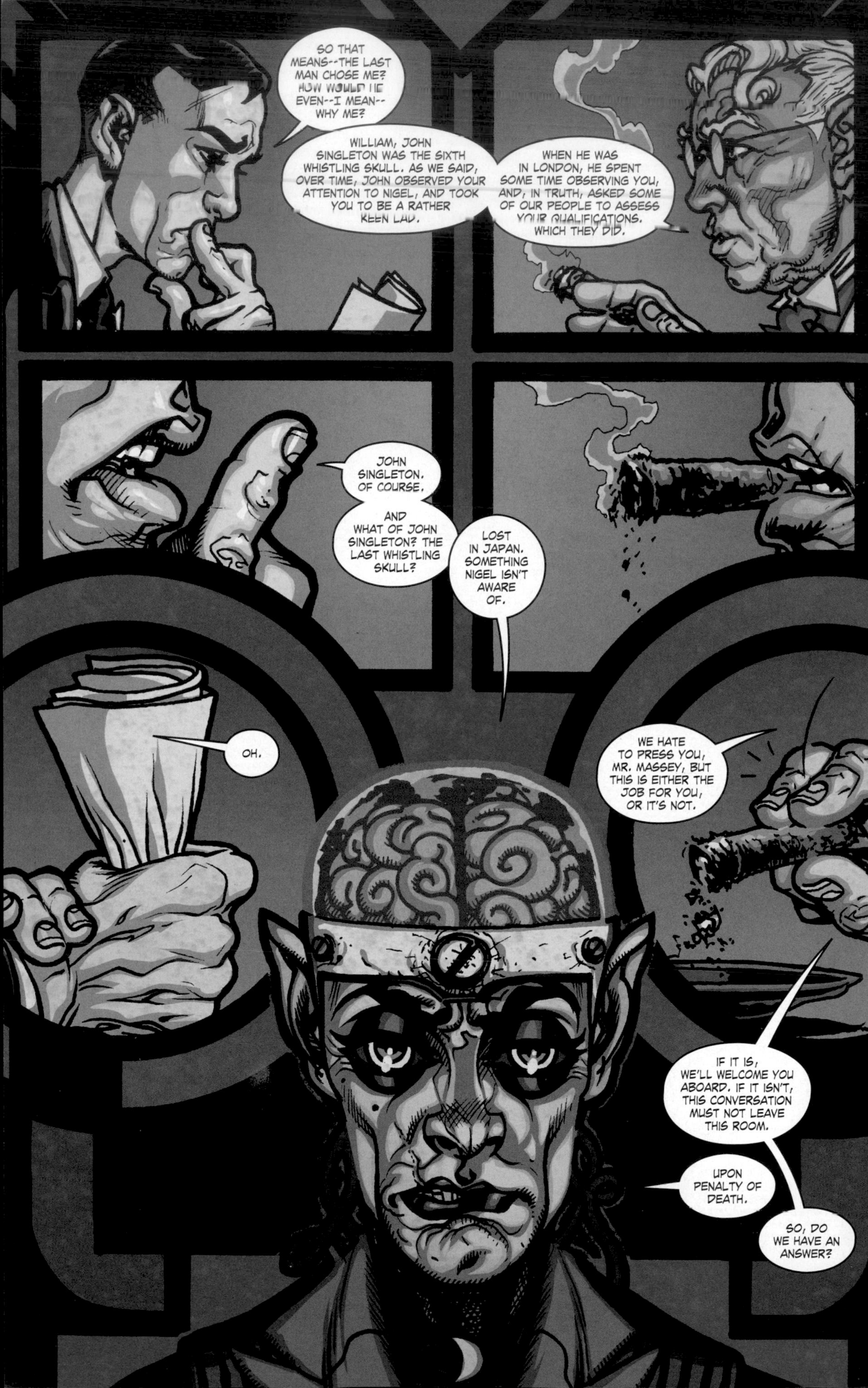
SO THAT MEANS--THE LAST MAN CHOSE ME? HOW WOULD HE EVEN--I MEAN--WHY ME?
WILLIAM, JOHN SINGLETON WAS THE SIXTH WHISTLING SKULL. AS WE SAID, OVER TIME, JOHN OBSERVED YOUR ATTENTION TO NIGEL, AND TOOK YOU TO BE A RATHER KEEN LAD.
WHEN HE WAS IN LONDON, HE SPENT SOME TIME OBSERVING YOU, AND, IN TRUTH, ASKED SOME OF OUR PEOPLE TO ASSESS YOUR QUALIFICATIONS. WHICH THEY DID.
JOHN SINGLETON. OF COURSE.
AND WHAT OF JOHN SINGLETON? THE LAST WHISTLING SKULL?
LOST IN JAPAN. SOMETHING NIGEL ISN'T AWARE OF.
OH.
WE HATE TO PRESS YOU, MR. MASSEY, BUT THIS IS EITHER THE JOB FOR YOU, OR IT'S NOT.
IF IT IS, WE'LL WELCOME YOU ABOARD. IF IT ISN'T, THIS CONVERSATION MUST NOT LEAVE THIS ROOM.
UPON PENALTY OF DEATH.
SO, DO WE HAVE AN ANSWER?

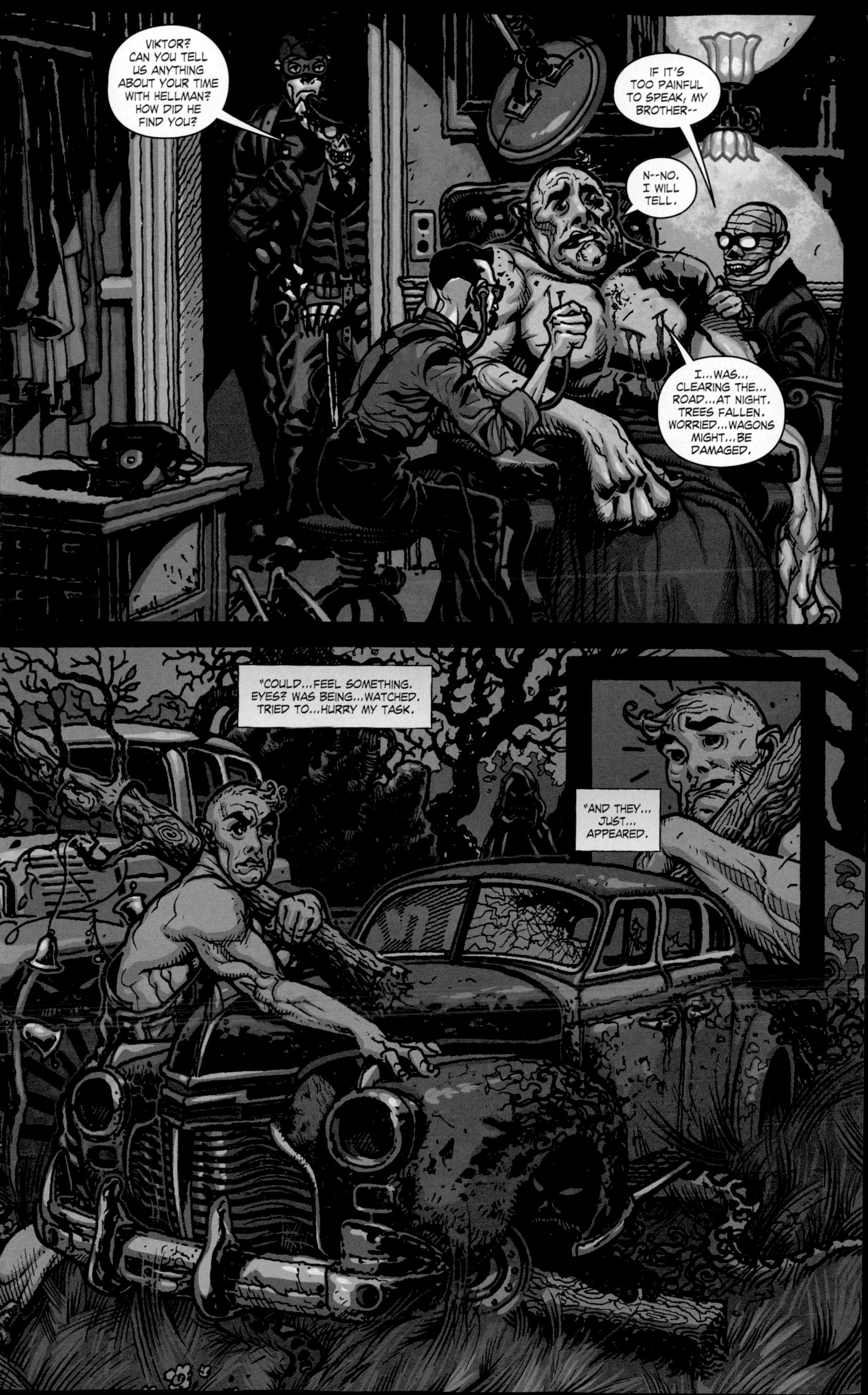
VIKTOR? CAN YOU TELL US ANYTHING ABOUT YOUR TIME WITH HELLMAN? HOW DID HE FIND YOU?
IF IT'S TOO PAINFUL TO SPEAK, MY BROTHER--
N--NO. I WILL TELL.
I...WAS... CLEARING THE... ROAD...AT NIGHT. TREES FALLEN. WORRIED...WAGONS MIGHT...BE DAMAGED.
"COULD...FEEL SOMETHING. EYES? WAS BEING...WATCHED. TRIED TO...HURRY MY TASK.
"AND THEY... JUST... APPEARED.

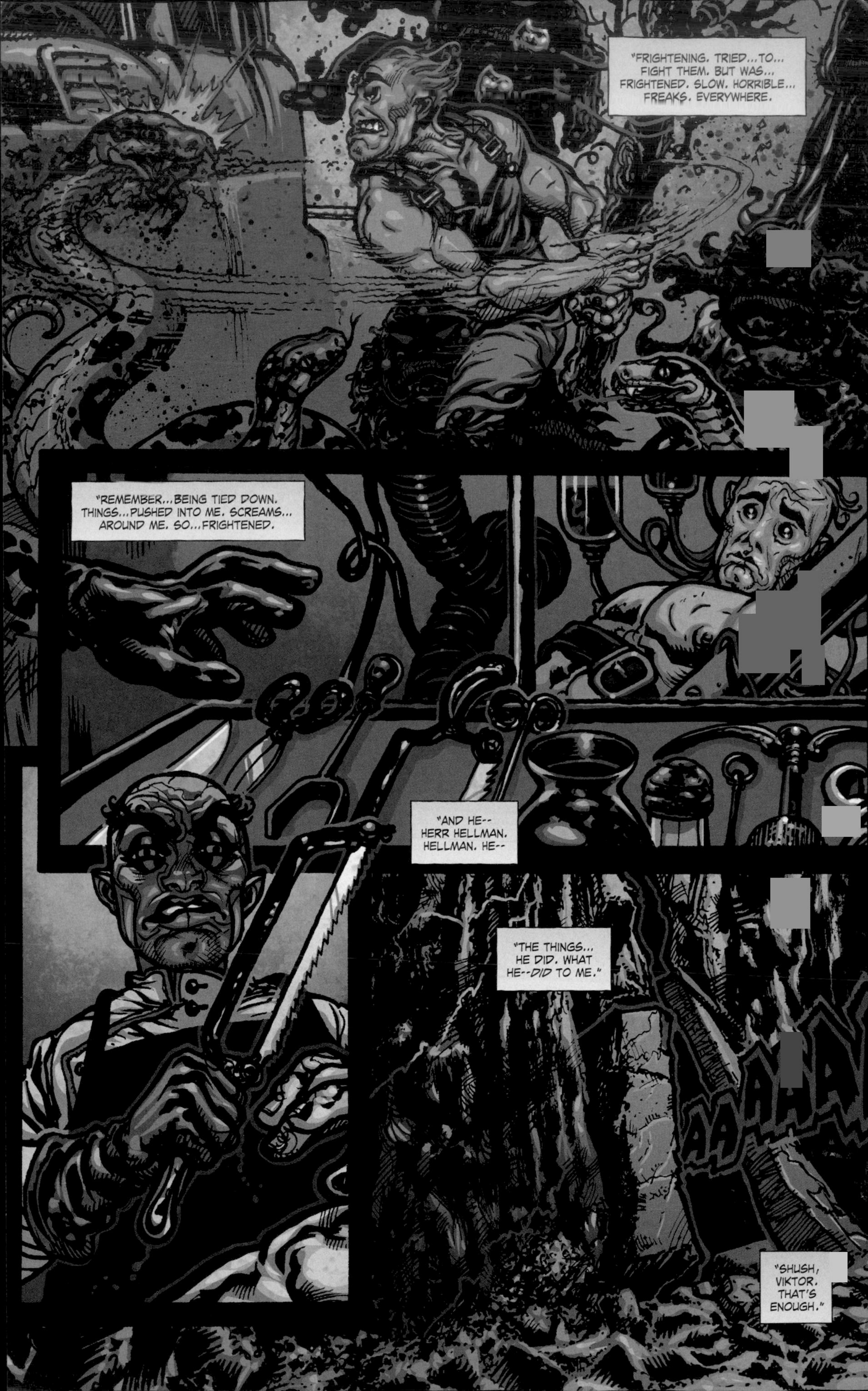
"FRIGHTENING. TRIED...TO... FIGHT THEM. BUT WAS... FRIGHTENED. SLOW. HORRIBLE... FREAKS. EVERYWHERE.
"REMEMBER...BEING TIED DOWN. THINGS...PUSHED INTO ME. SCREAMS... AROUND ME. SO...FRIGHTENED.
"AND HE-- HERR HELLMAN. HELLMAN. HE--
"THE THINGS... HE DID. WHAT HE--*DID* TO ME."
"SHUSH, VIKTOR. THAT'S ENOUGH."

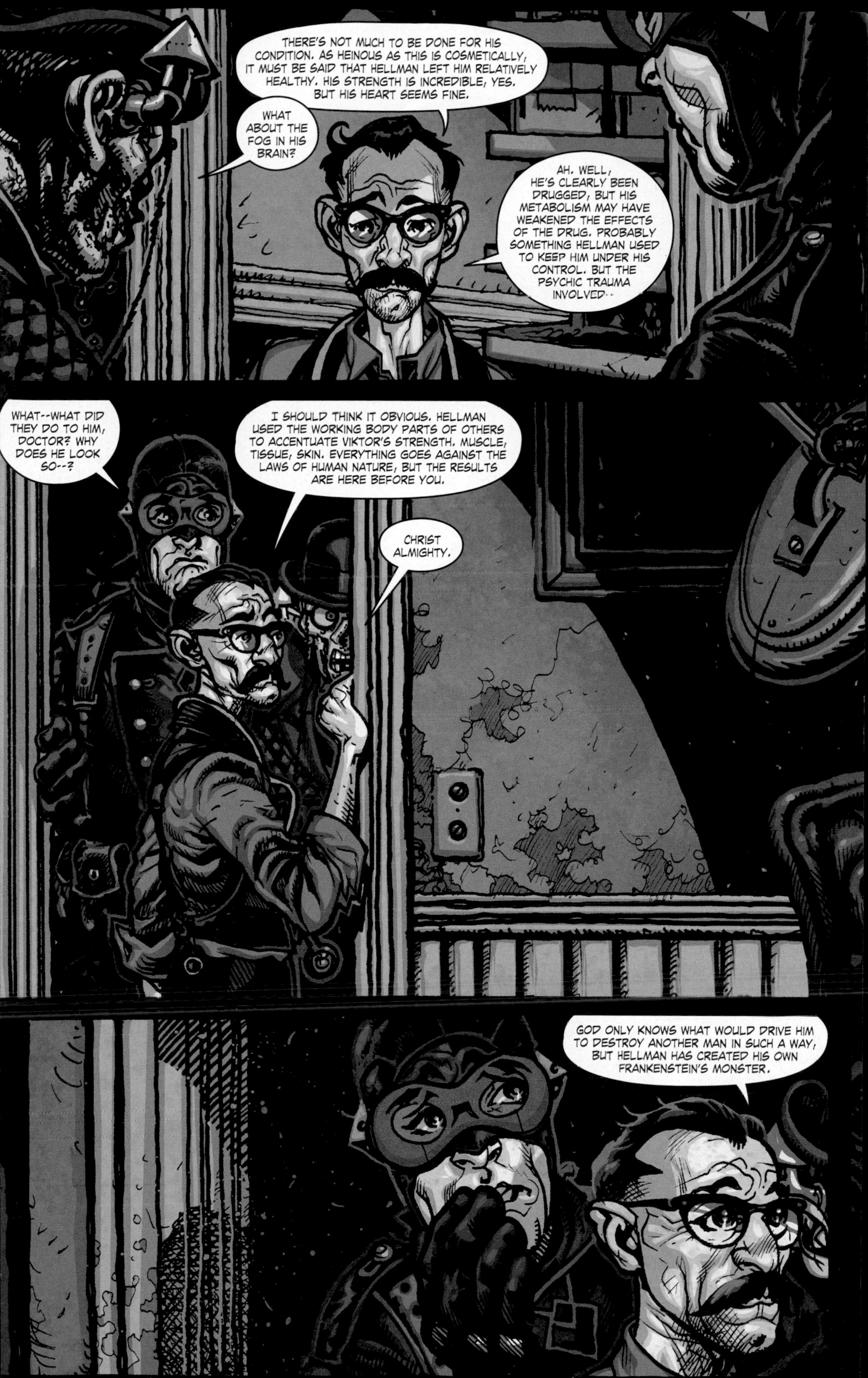
THERE'S NOT MUCH TO BE DONE FOR HIS CONDITION. AS HEINOUS AS THIS IS COSMETICALLY, IT MUST BE SAID THAT HELLMAN LEFT HIM RELATIVELY HEALTHY. HIS STRENGTH IS INCREDIBLE, YES. BUT HIS HEART SEEMS FINE.
WHAT ABOUT THE FOG IN HIS BRAIN?
AH. WELL, HE'S CLEARLY BEEN DRUGGED, BUT HIS METABOLISM MAY HAVE WEAKENED THE EFFECTS OF THE DRUG. PROBABLY SOMETHING HELLMAN USED TO KEEP HIM UNDER HIS CONTROL. BUT THE PSYCHIC TRAUMA INVOLVED--
WHAT--WHAT DID THEY DO TO HIM, DOCTOR? WHY DOES HE LOOK SO--?
I SHOULD THINK IT OBVIOUS. HELLMAN USED THE WORKING BODY PARTS OF OTHERS TO ACCENTUATE VIKTOR'S STRENGTH. MUSCLE, TISSUE, SKIN. EVERYTHING GOES AGAINST THE LAWS OF HUMAN NATURE, BUT THE RESULTS ARE HERE BEFORE YOU.
CHRIST ALMIGHTY.
GOD ONLY KNOWS WHAT WOULD DRIVE HIM TO DESTROY ANOTHER MAN IN SUCH A WAY, BUT HELLMAN HAS CREATED HIS OWN FRANKENSTEIN'S MONSTER.

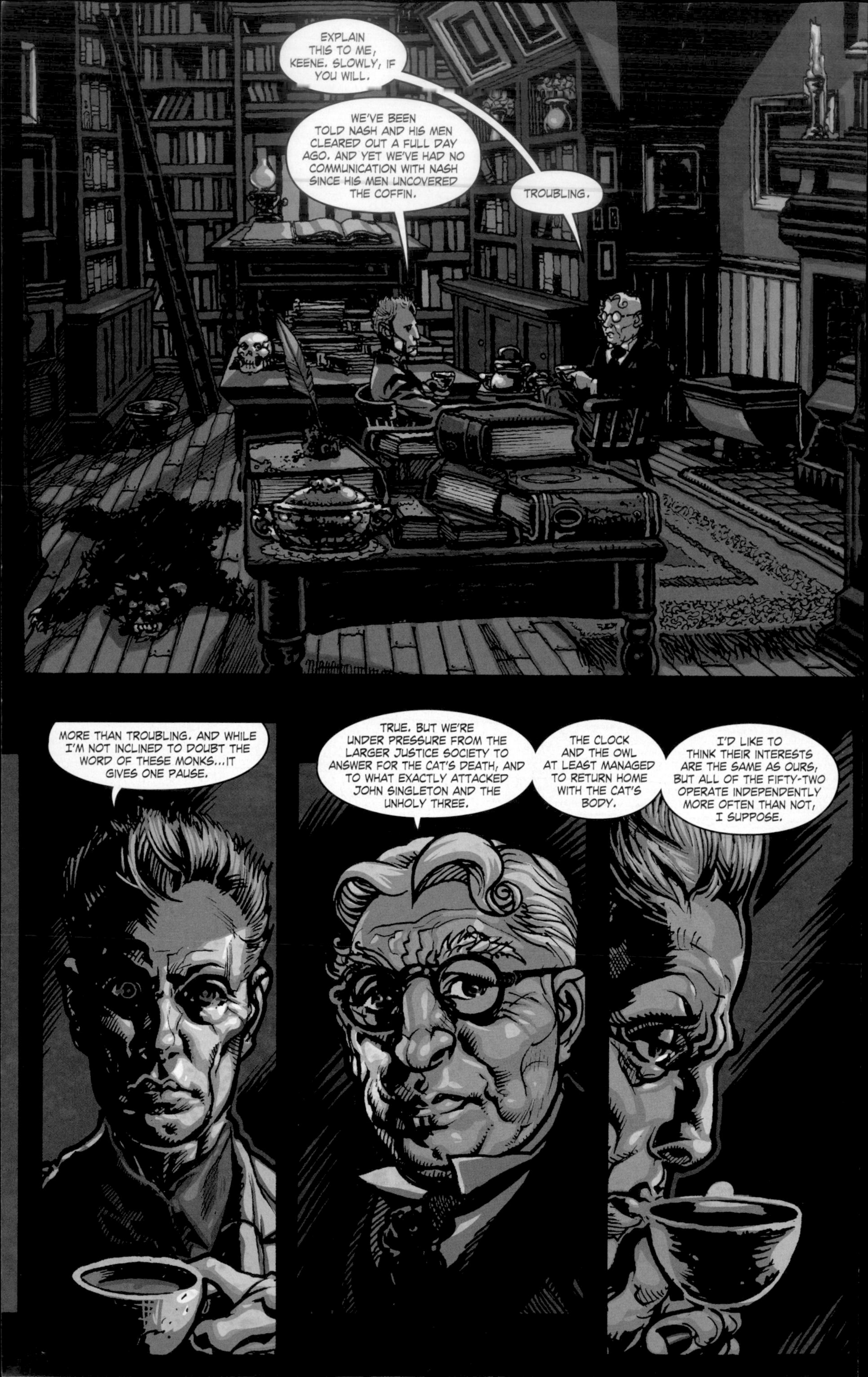
EXPLAIN THIS TO ME, KEENE. SLOWLY, IF YOU WILL.
WE'VE BEEN TOLD NASH AND HIS MEN CLEARED OUT A FULL DAY AGO. AND YET WE'VE HAD NO COMMUNICATION WITH NASH SINCE HIS MEN UNCOVERED THE COFFIN.
TROUBLING.
MORE THAN TROUBLING. AND WHILE I'M NOT INCLINED TO DOUBT THE WORD OF THESE MONKS...IT GIVES ONE PAUSE.
TRUE. BUT WE'RE UNDER PRESSURE FROM THE LARGER JUSTICE SOCIETY TO ANSWER FOR THE CAT'S DEATH, AND TO WHAT EXACTLY ATTACKED JOHN SINGLETON AND THE UNHOLY THREE.
THE CLOCK AND THE OWL AT LEAST MANAGED TO RETURN HOME WITH THE CAT'S BODY.
I'D LIKE TO THINK THEIR INTERESTS ARE THE SAME AS OURS, BUT ALL OF THE FIFTY-TWO OPERATE INDEPENDENTLY MORE OFTEN THAN NOT, I SUPPOSE.

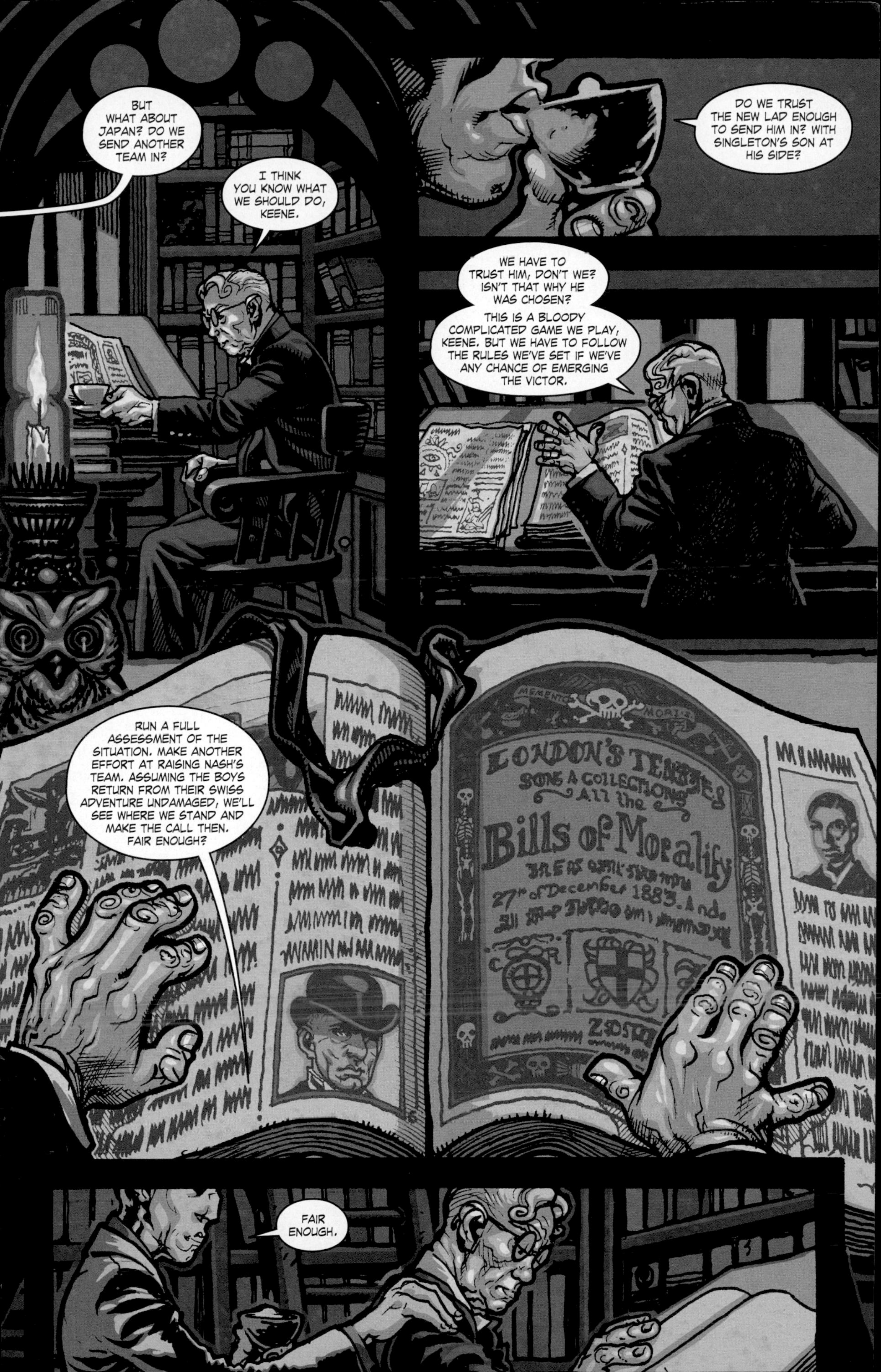
BUT WHAT ABOUT JAPAN? DO WE SEND ANOTHER TEAM IN?
I THINK YOU KNOW WHAT WE SHOULD DO, KEENE.
DO WE TRUST THE NEW LAD ENOUGH TO SEND HIM IN? WITH SINGLETON'S SON AT HIS SIDE?
WE HAVE TO TRUST HIM, DON'T WE? ISN'T THAT WHY HE WAS CHOSEN?
THIS IS A BLOODY COMPLICATED GAME WE PLAY, KEENE. BUT WE HAVE TO FOLLOW THE RULES WE'VE SET IF WE'VE ANY CHANCE OF EMERGING THE VICTOR.
RUN A FULL ASSESSMENT OF THE SITUATION. MAKE ANOTHER EFFORT AT RAISING NASH'S TEAM. ASSUMING THE BOYS RETURN FROM THEIR SWISS ADVENTURE UNDAMAGED, WE'LL SEE WHERE WE STAND AND MAKE THE CALL THEN. FAIR ENOUGH?
Bills of Moralify
27th of December 1883
FAIR ENOUGH.

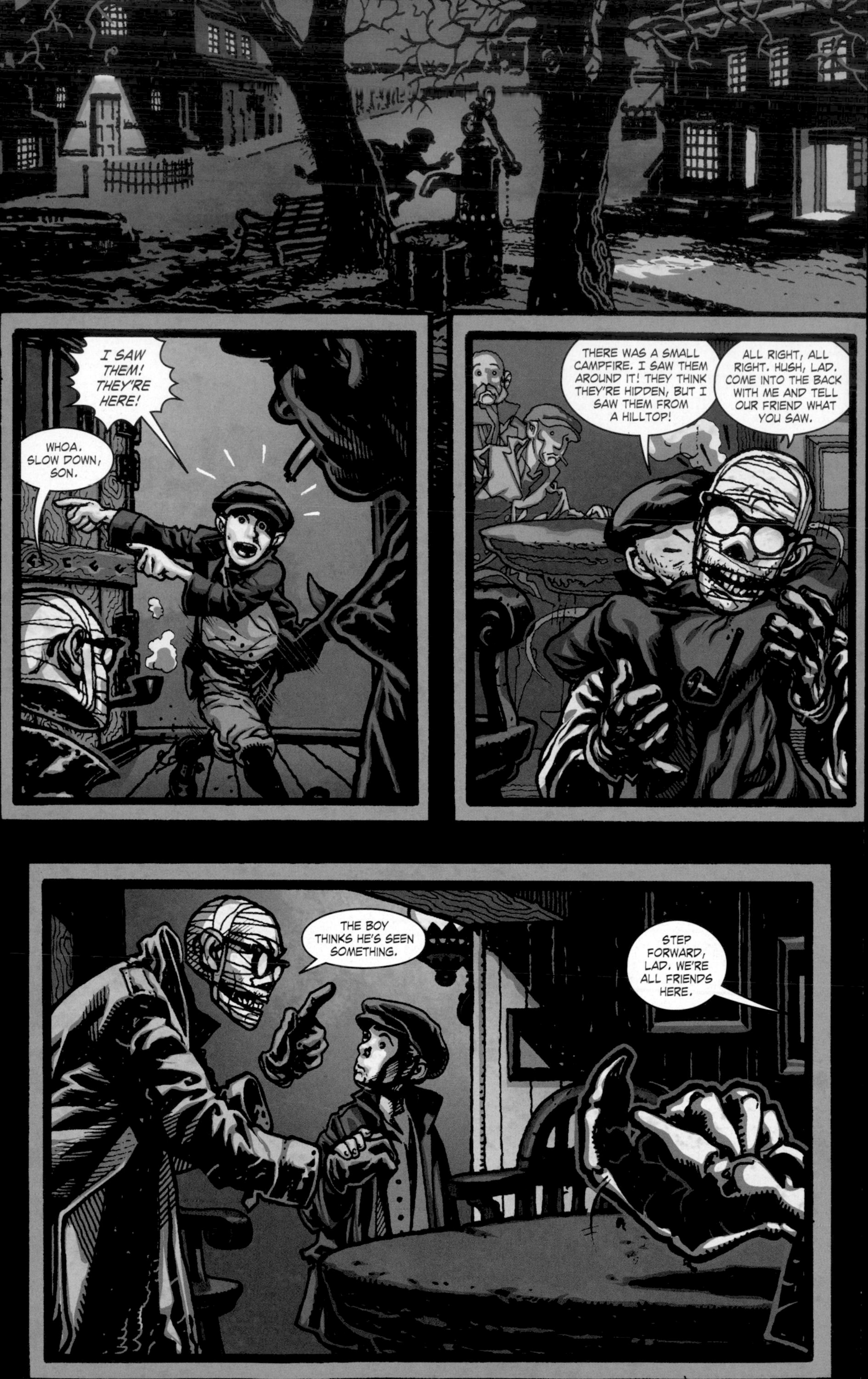
I SAW THEM! THEY'RE HERE!
WHOA. SLOW DOWN, SON.
THERE WAS A SMALL CAMPFIRE. I SAW THEM AROUND IT! THEY THINK THEY'RE HIDDEN, BUT I SAW THEM FROM A HILLTOP!
ALL RIGHT, ALL RIGHT. HUSH, LAD. COME INTO THE BACK WITH ME AND TELL OUR FRIEND WHAT YOU SAW.
THE BOY THINKS HE'S SEEN SOMETHING.
STEP FORWARD, LAD. WE'RE ALL FRIENDS HERE.

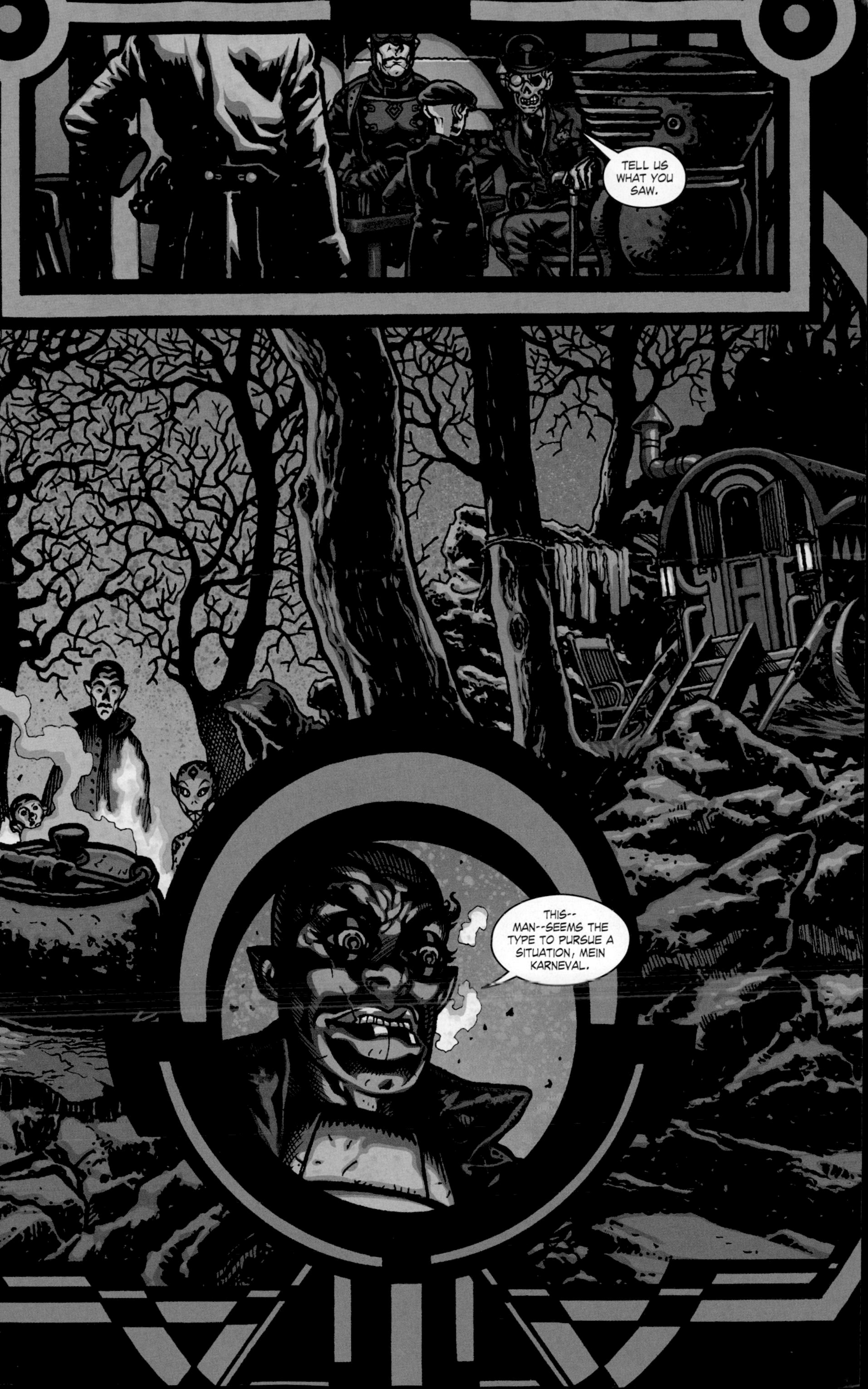
TELL US WHAT YOU SAW.
THIS-- MAN--SEEMS THE TYPE TO PURSUE A SITUATION, MEIN KARNEVAL.

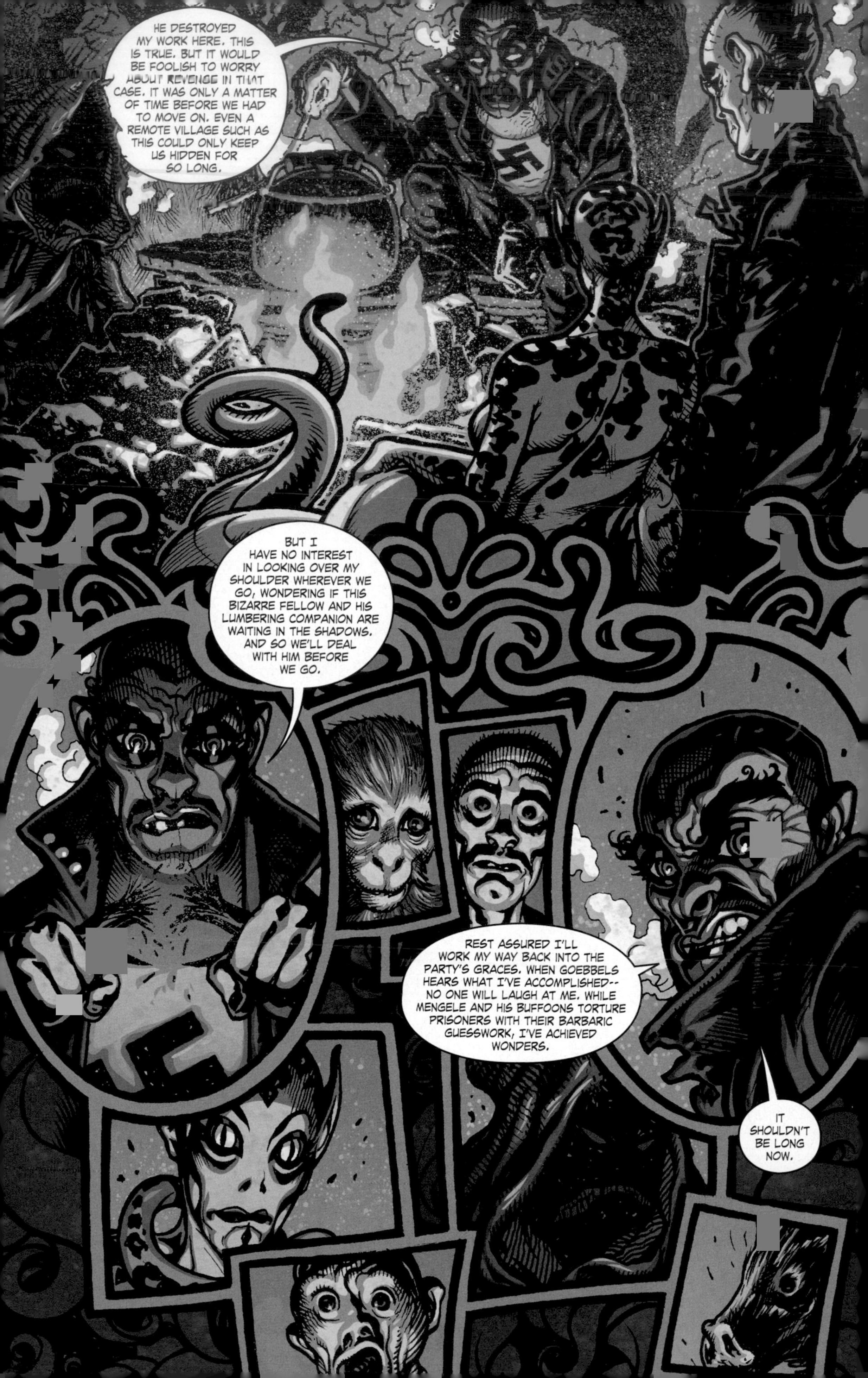
HE DESTROYED MY WORK HERE. THIS IS TRUE. BUT IT WOULD BE FOOLISH TO WORRY ABOUT REVENGE IN THAT CASE. IT WAS ONLY A MATTER OF TIME BEFORE WE HAD TO MOVE ON. EVEN A REMOTE VILLAGE SUCH AS THIS COULD ONLY KEEP US HIDDEN FOR SO LONG.
BUT I HAVE NO INTEREST IN LOOKING OVER MY SHOULDER WHEREVER WE GO, WONDERING IF THIS BIZARRE FELLOW AND HIS LUMBERING COMPANION ARE WAITING IN THE SHADOWS. AND SO WE'LL DEAL WITH HIM BEFORE WE GO.
REST ASSURED I'LL WORK MY WAY BACK INTO THE PARTY'S GRACES. WHEN GOEBBELS HEARS WHAT I'VE ACCOMPLISHED-- NO ONE WILL LAUGH AT ME. WHILE MENGELE AND HIS BUFFOONS TORTURE PRISONERS WITH THEIR BARBARIC GUESSWORK, I'VE ACHIEVED WONDERS.
IT SHOULDN'T BE LONG NOW.

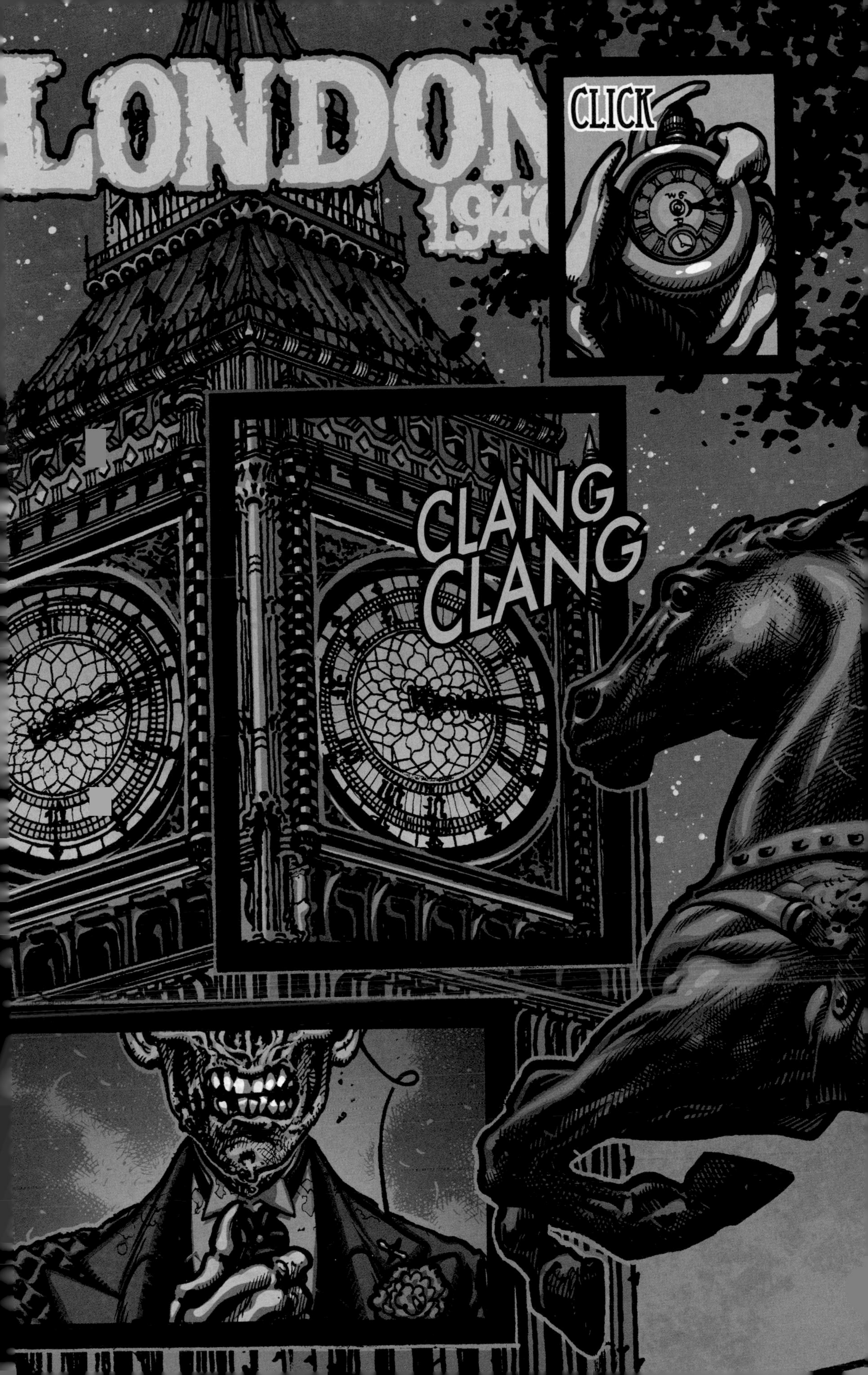
LONDON
1940
CLICK
CLANG
CLANG

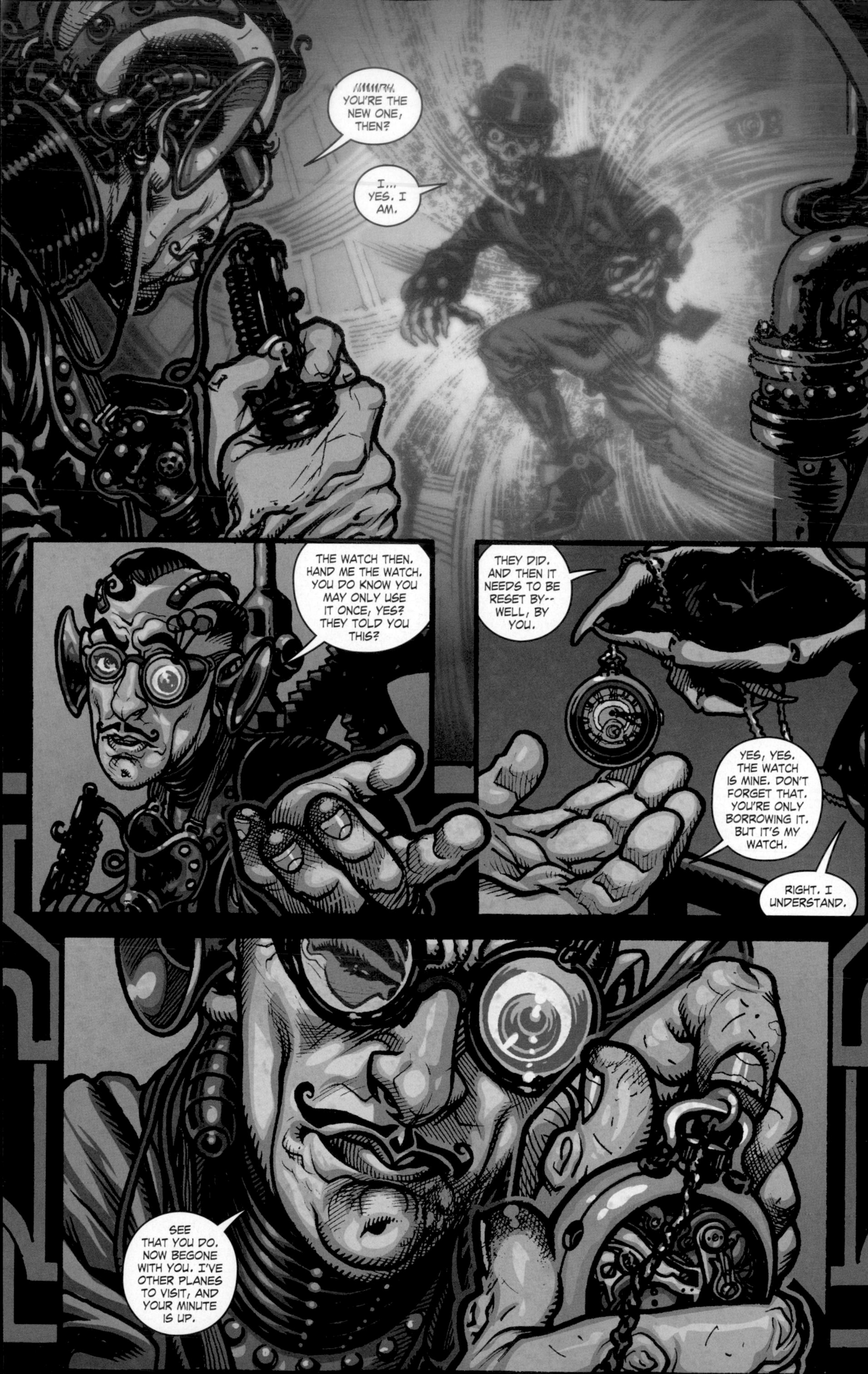
MMMRH. YOU'RE THE NEW ONE, THEN?
I... YES. I AM.
THE WATCH THEN. HAND ME THE WATCH. YOU DO KNOW YOU MAY ONLY USE IT ONCE, YES? THEY TOLD YOU THIS?
THEY DID. AND THEN IT NEEDS TO BE RESET BY-- WELL, BY YOU.
YES, YES. THE WATCH IS MINE. DON'T FORGET THAT. YOU'RE ONLY BORROWING IT. BUT IT'S MY WATCH.
RIGHT. I UNDERSTAND.
SEE THAT YOU DO. NOW BEGONE WITH YOU. I'VE OTHER PLANES TO VISIT, AND YOUR MINUTE IS UP.

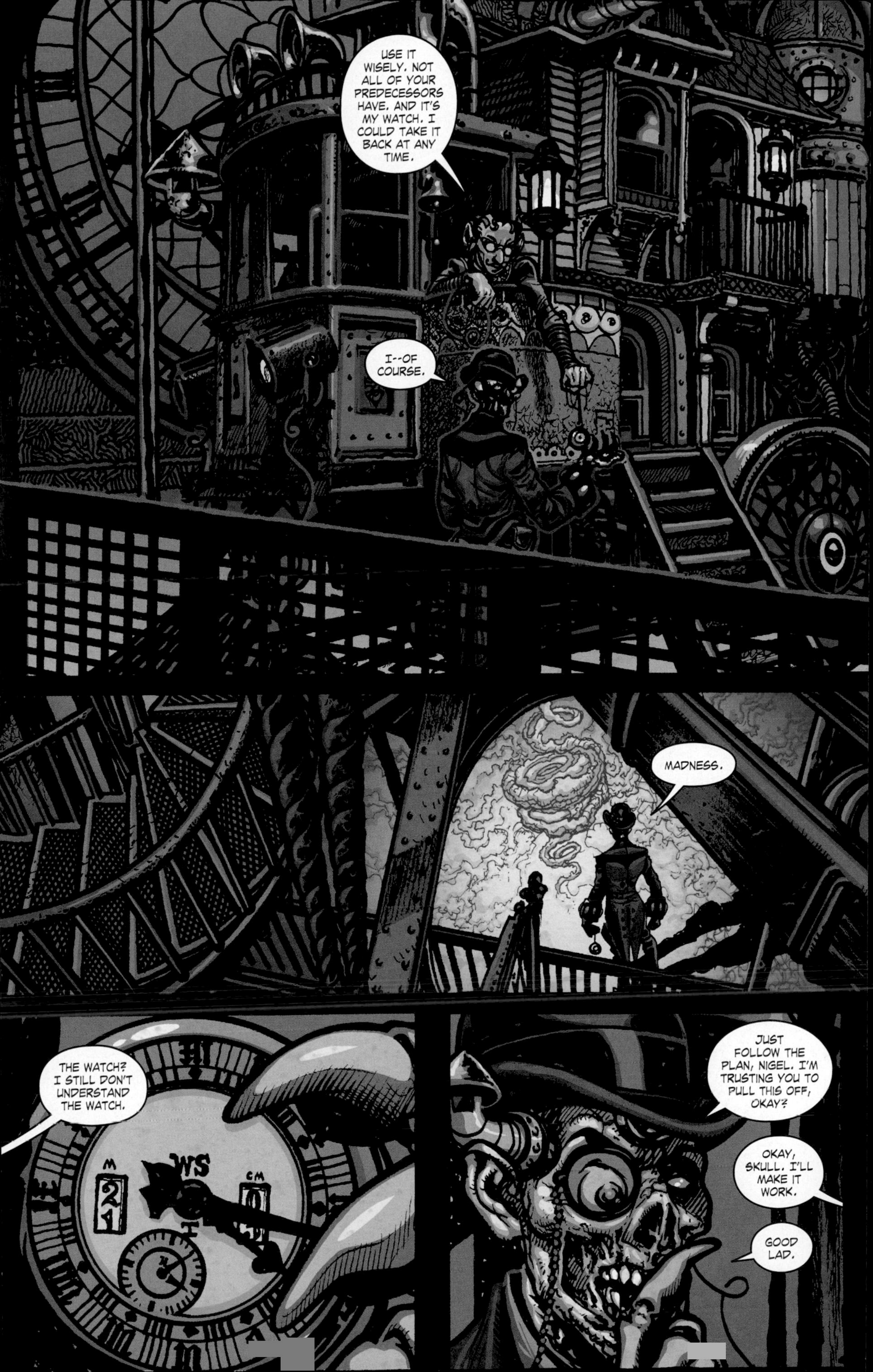
USE IT WISELY. NOT ALL OF YOUR PREDECESSORS HAVE. AND IT'S MY WATCH. I COULD TAKE IT BACK AT ANY TIME.
I--OF COURSE.
MADNESS.
THE WATCH? I STILL DON'T UNDERSTAND THE WATCH.
JUST FOLLOW THE PLAN, NIGEL. I'M TRUSTING YOU TO PULL THIS OFF, OKAY?
OKAY, SKULL. I'LL MAKE IT WORK.
GOOD LAD.

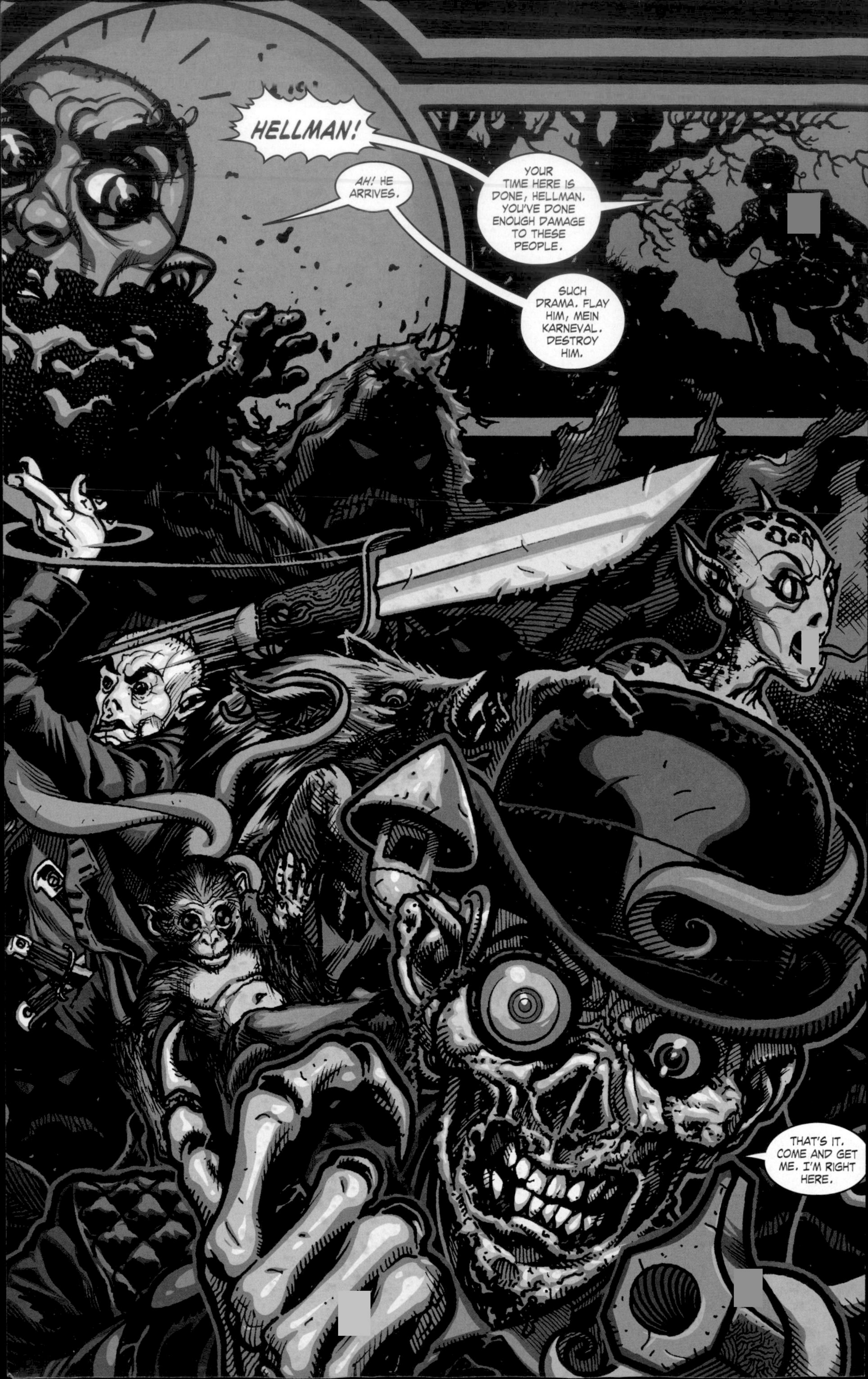
HELLMAN!
AH! HE ARRIVES.
YOUR TIME HERE IS DONE, HELLMAN. YOU'VE DONE ENOUGH DAMAGE TO THESE PEOPLE.
SUCH DRAMA. FLAY HIM, MEIN KARNEVAL. DESTROY HIM.
THAT'S IT. COME AND GET ME. I'M RIGHT HERE.

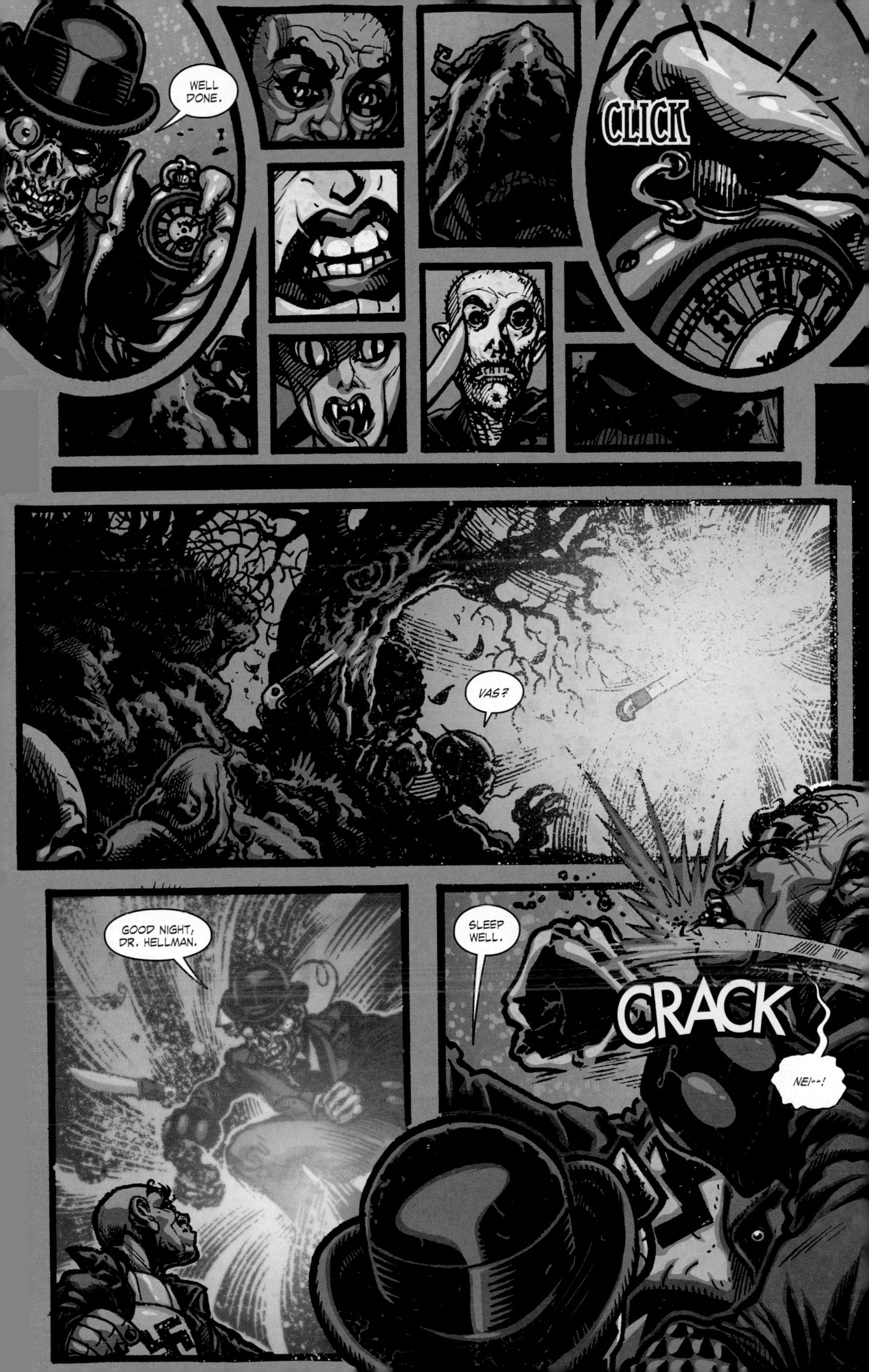
WELL DONE.
CLICK
VAS?
GOOD NIGHT, DR. HELLMAN.
SLEEP WELL.
CRACK
NEI--!

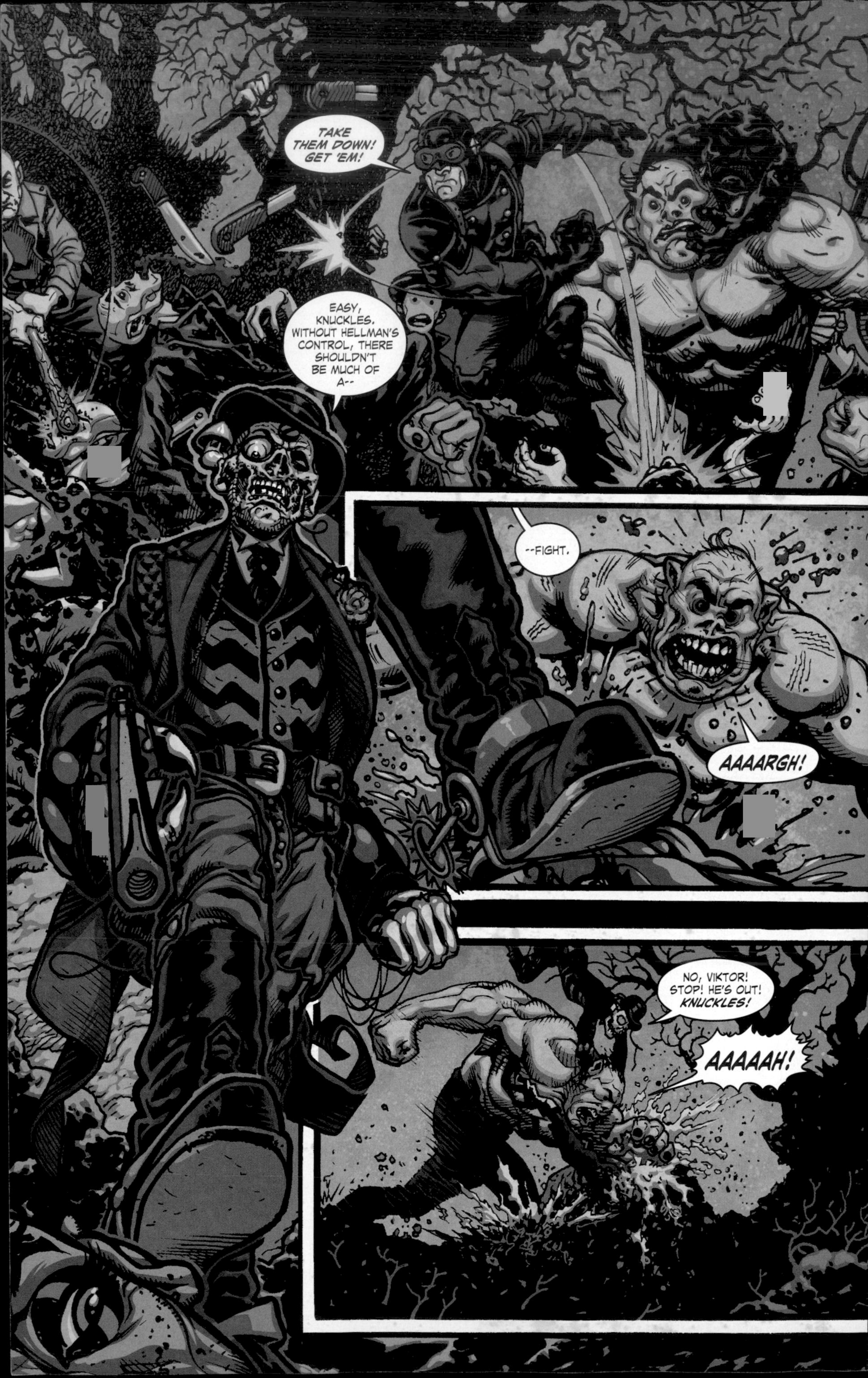
TAKE THEM DOWN! GET 'EM!
EASY, KNUCKLES. WITHOUT HELLMAN'S CONTROL, THERE SHOULDN'T BE MUCH OF A--
--FIGHT.
AAAARGH!
NO, VIKTOR! STOP! HE'S OUT! KNUCKLES!
AAAAAH!

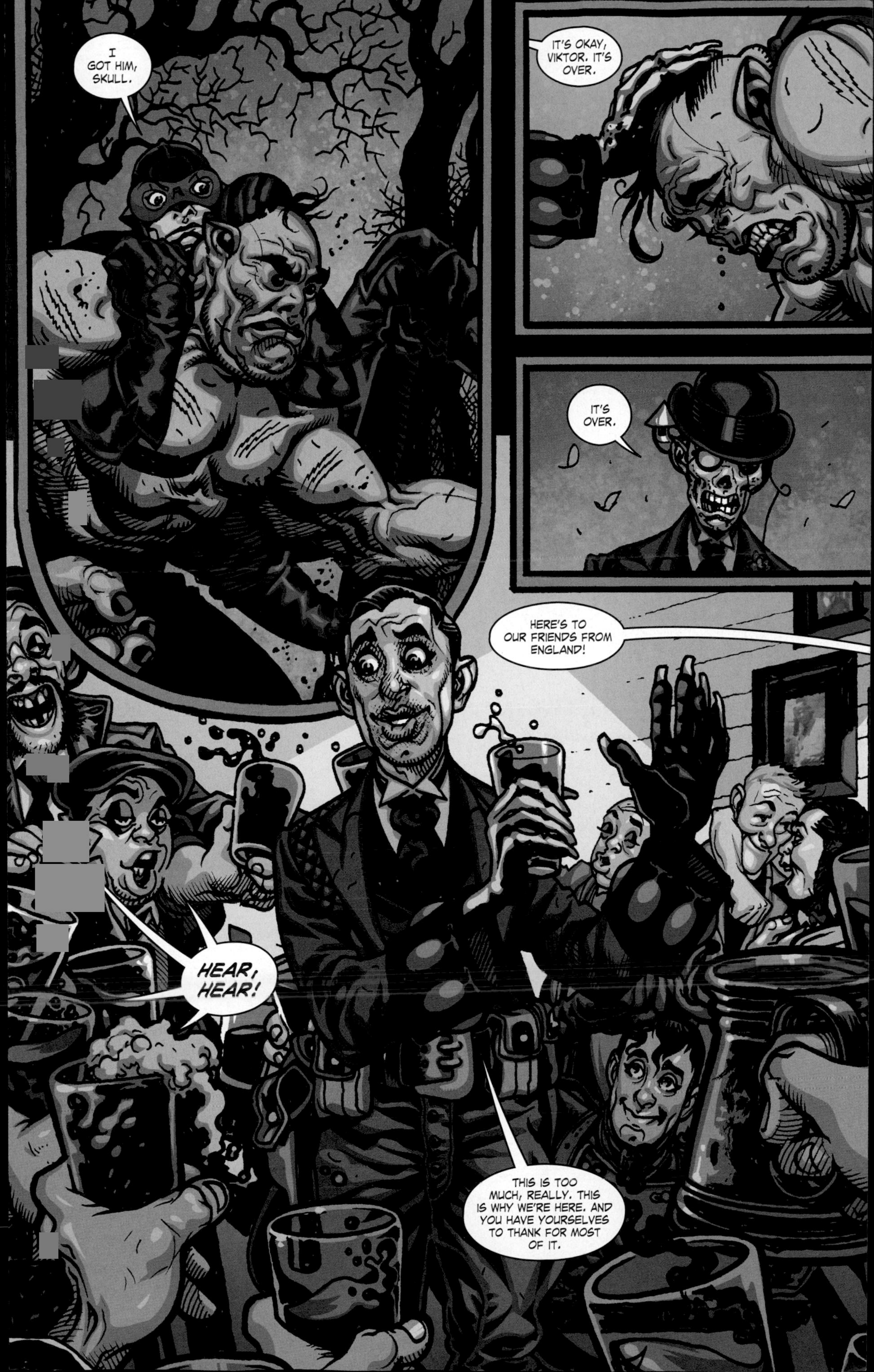
I GOT HIM, SKULL.
IT'S OKAY, VIKTOR. IT'S OVER.
IT'S OVER.
HERE'S TO OUR FRIENDS FROM ENGLAND!
HEAR, HEAR!
THIS IS TOO MUCH, REALLY. THIS IS WHY WE'RE HERE. AND YOU HAVE YOURSELVES TO THANK FOR MOST OF IT.

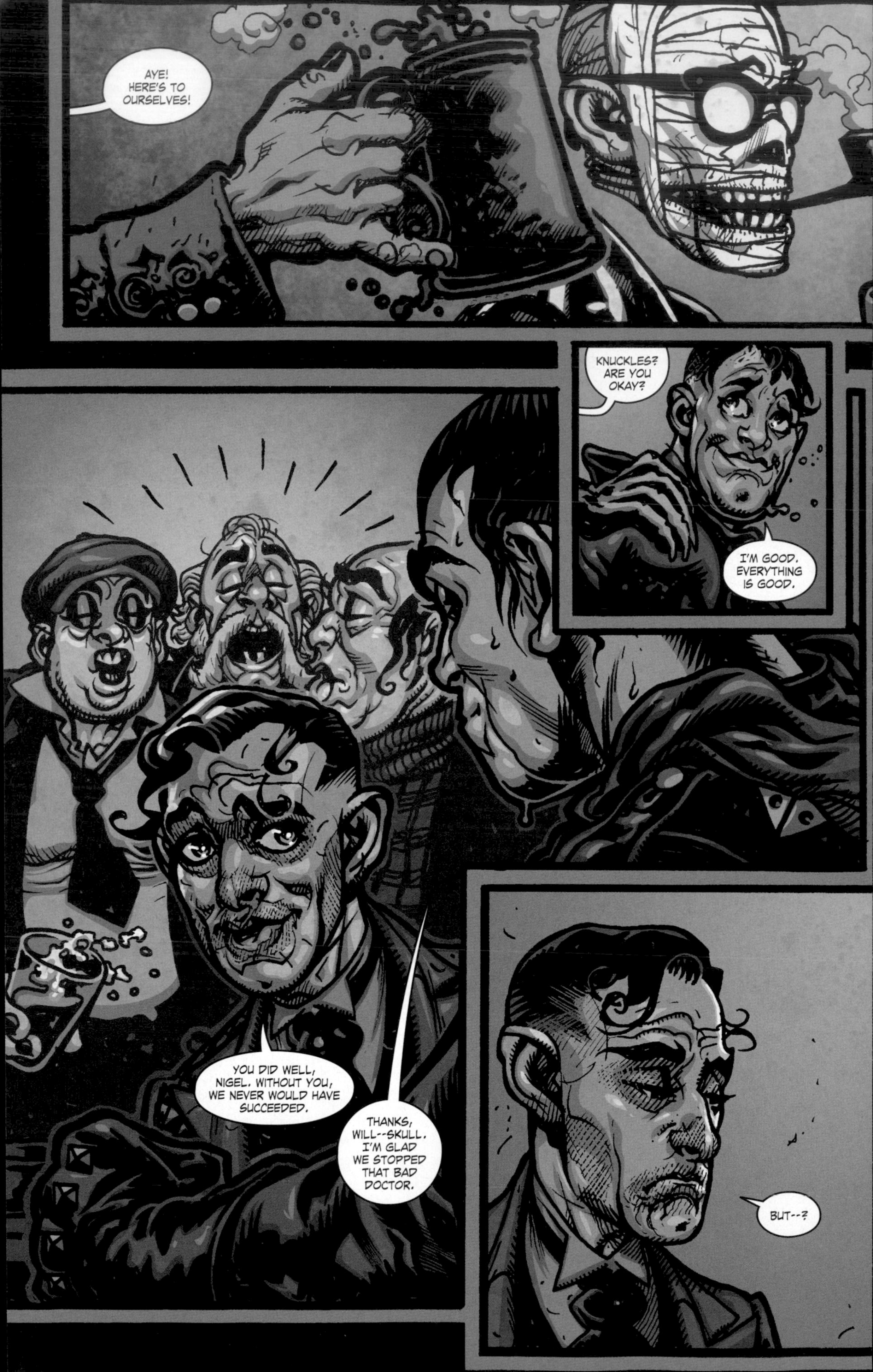
AYE! HERE'S TO OURSELVES!
KNUCKLES? ARE YOU OKAY?
I'M GOOD. EVERYTHING IS GOOD.
YOU DID WELL, NIGEL. WITHOUT YOU, WE NEVER WOULD HAVE SUCCEEDED.
THANKS, WILL--SKULL. I'M GLAD WE STOPPED THAT BAD DOCTOR.
BUT--?

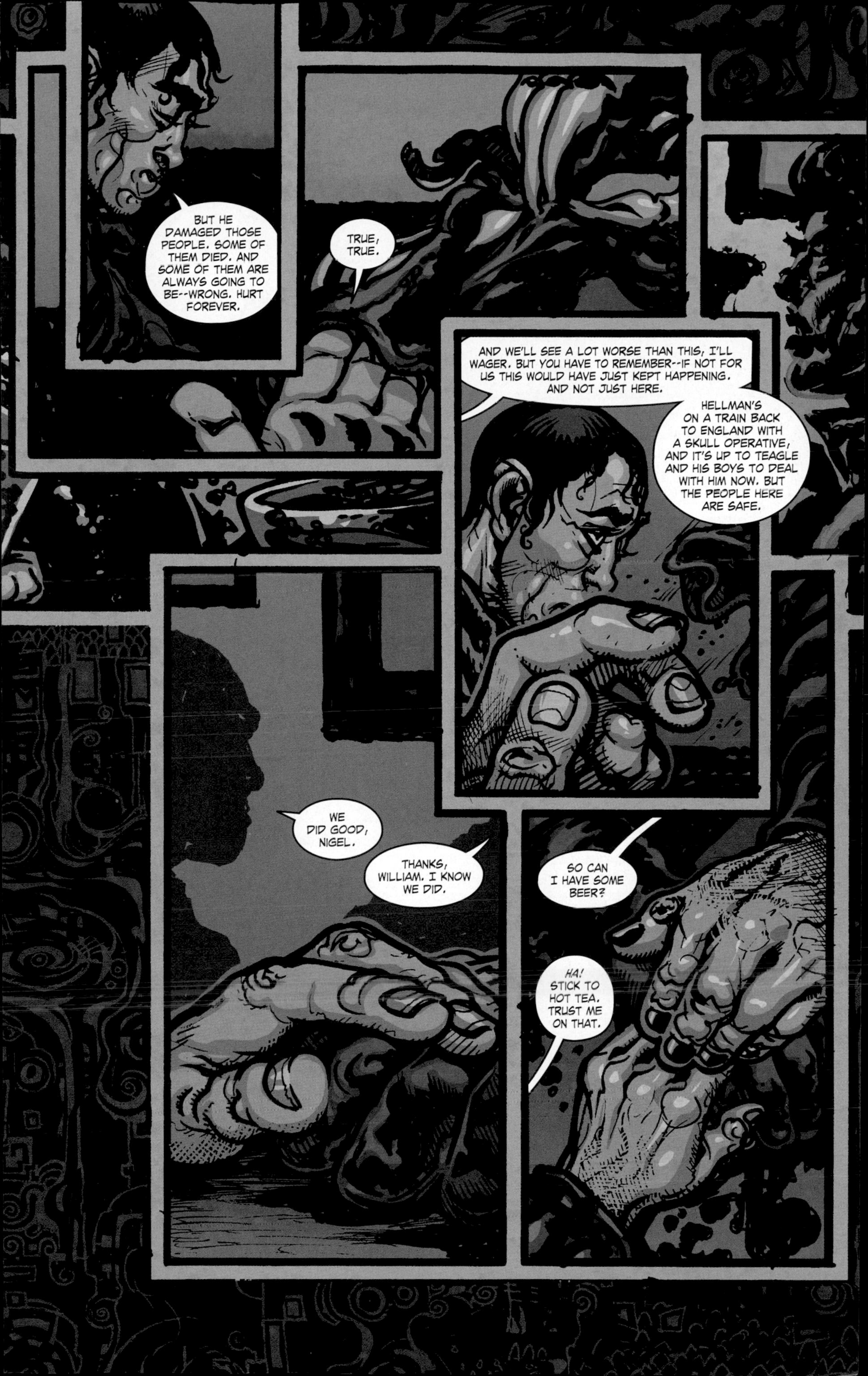
BUT HE DAMAGED THOSE PEOPLE. SOME OF THEM DIED. AND SOME OF THEM ARE ALWAYS GOING TO BE--WRONG. HURT FOREVER.
TRUE, TRUE.
AND WE'LL SEE A LOT WORSE THAN THIS, I'LL WAGER. BUT YOU HAVE TO REMEMBER--IF NOT FOR US THIS WOULD HAVE JUST KEPT HAPPENING. AND NOT JUST HERE.
HELLMAN'S ON A TRAIN BACK TO ENGLAND WITH A SKULL OPERATIVE, AND IT'S UP TO TEAGLE AND HIS BOYS TO DEAL WITH HIM NOW. BUT THE PEOPLE HERE ARE SAFE.
WE DID GOOD, NIGEL.
THANKS, WILLIAM. I KNOW WE DID.
SO CAN I HAVE SOME BEER?
HA! STICK TO HOT TEA. TRUST ME ON THAT.

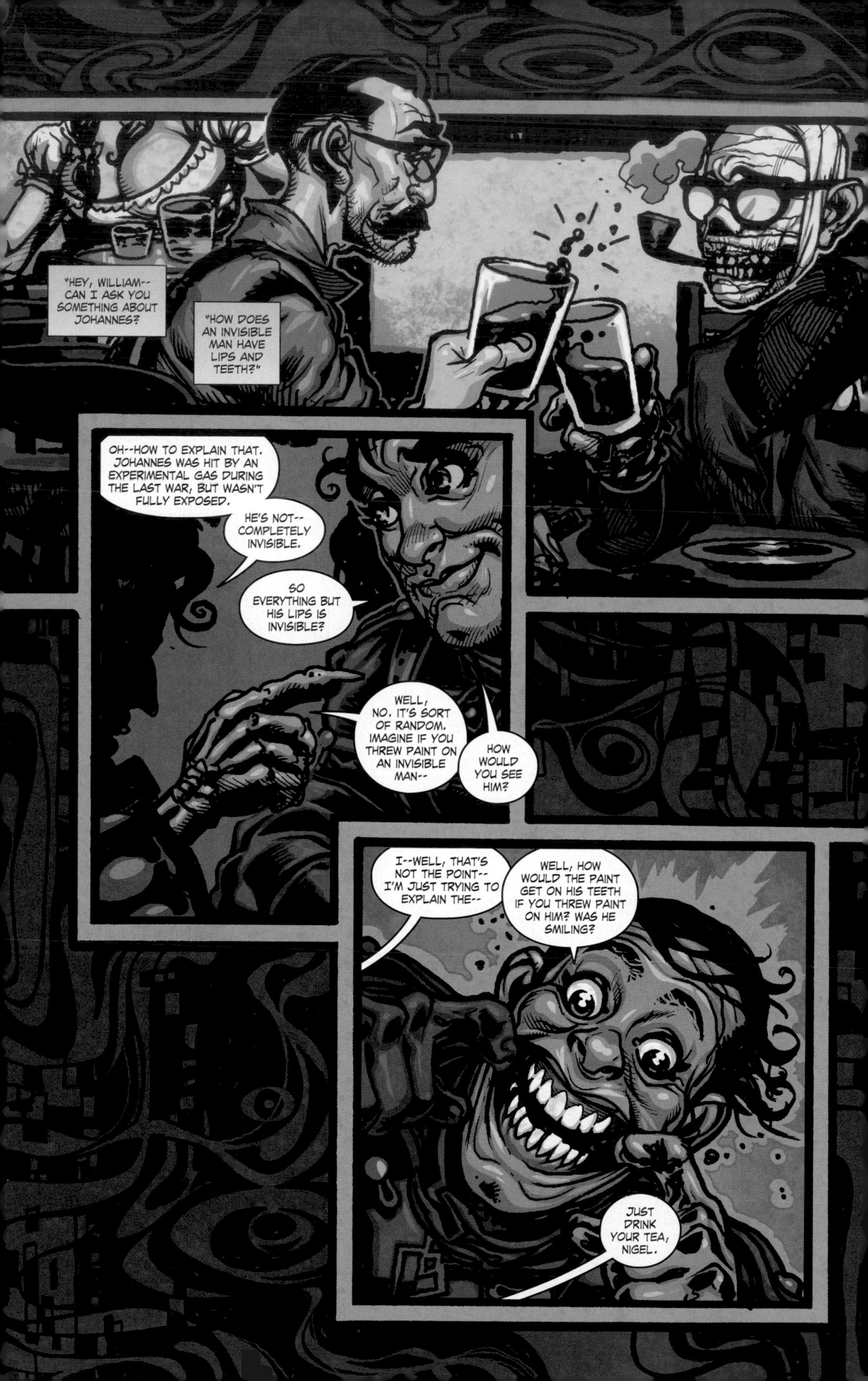
"HEY, WILLIAM--CAN I ASK YOU SOMETHING ABOUT JOHANNES?
"HOW DOES AN INVISIBLE MAN HAVE LIPS AND TEETH?"
OH--HOW TO EXPLAIN THAT. JOHANNES WAS HIT BY AN EXPERIMENTAL GAS DURING THE LAST WAR, BUT WASN'T FULLY EXPOSED.
HE'S NOT--COMPLETELY INVISIBLE.
SO EVERYTHING BUT HIS LIPS IS INVISIBLE?
WELL, NO. IT'S SORT OF RANDOM. IMAGINE IF YOU THREW PAINT ON AN INVISIBLE MAN--
HOW WOULD YOU SEE HIM?
I--WELL, THAT'S NOT THE POINT--I'M JUST TRYING TO EXPLAIN THE--
WELL, HOW WOULD THE PAINT GET ON HIS TEETH IF YOU THREW PAINT ON HIM? WAS HE SMILING?
JUST DRINK YOUR TEA, NIGEL.

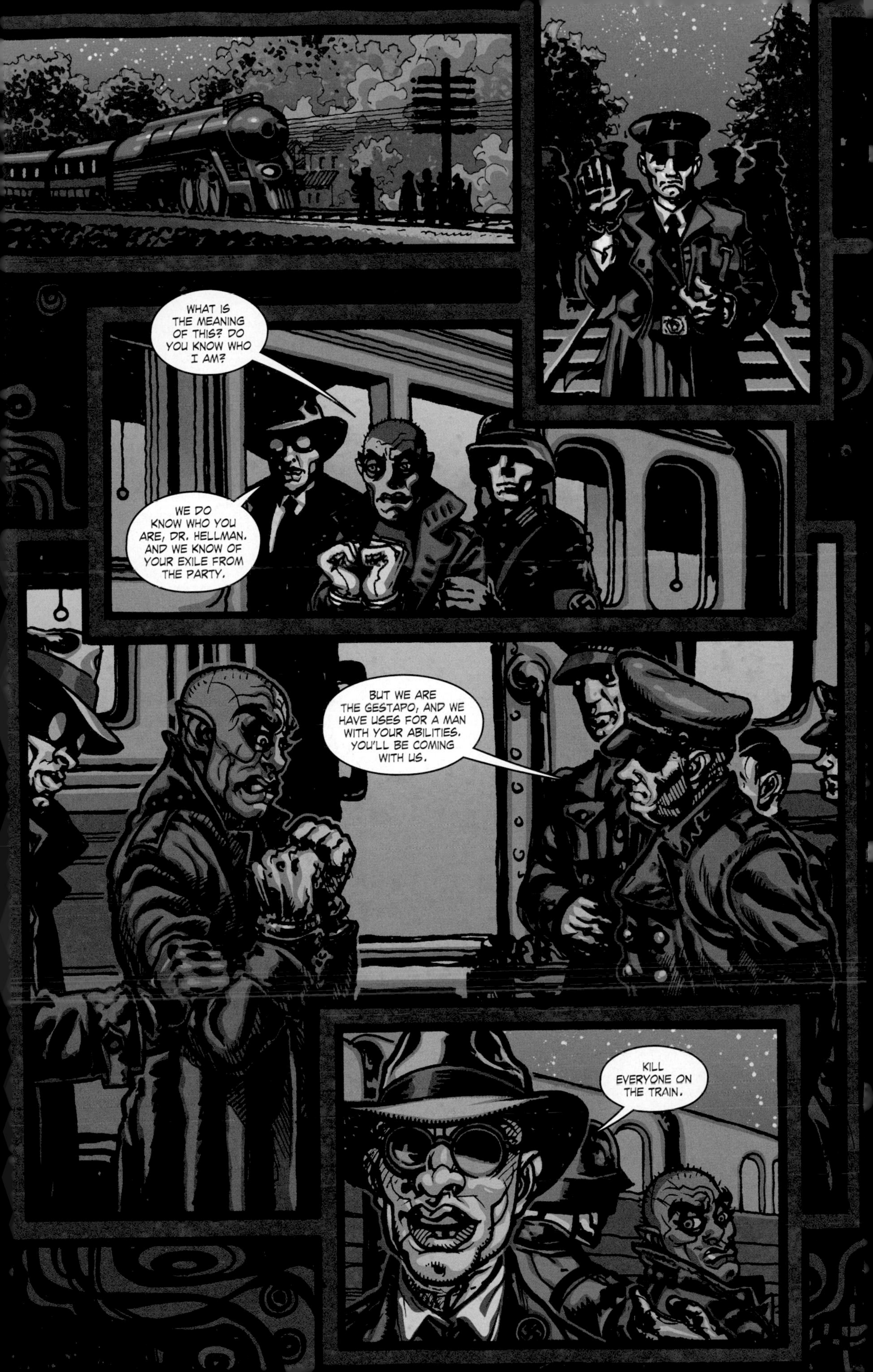
WHAT IS THE MEANING OF THIS? DO YOU KNOW WHO I AM?
WE DO KNOW WHO YOU ARE, DR. HELLMAN. AND WE KNOW OF YOUR EXILE FROM THE PARTY.
BUT WE ARE THE GESTAPO, AND WE HAVE USES FOR A MAN WITH YOUR ABILITIES. YOU'LL BE COMING WITH US.
KILL EVERYONE ON THE TRAIN.

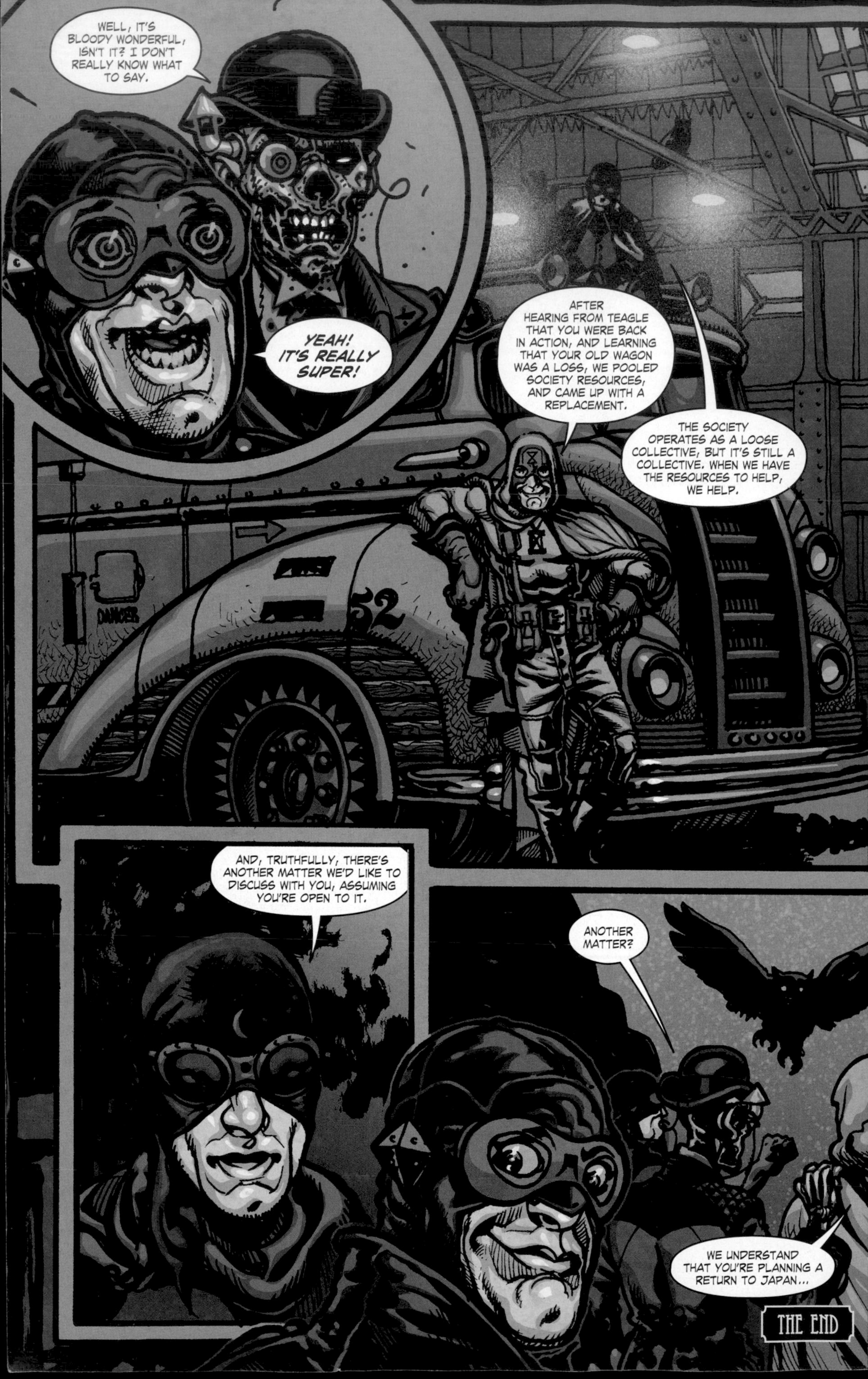
WELL, IT'S BLOODY WONDERFUL, ISN'T IT? I DON'T REALLY KNOW WHAT TO SAY.
YEAH! IT'S REALLY SUPER!
AFTER HEARING FROM TEAGLE THAT YOU WERE BACK IN ACTION, AND LEARNING THAT YOUR OLD WAGON WAS A LOSS, WE POOLED SOCIETY RESOURCES, AND CAME UP WITH A REPLACEMENT.
THE SOCIETY OPERATES AS A LOOSE COLLECTIVE, BUT IT'S STILL A COLLECTIVE. WHEN WE HAVE THE RESOURCES TO HELP, WE HELP.
52
DANGER
AND, TRUTHFULLY, THERE'S ANOTHER MATTER WE'D LIKE TO DISCUSS WITH YOU, ASSUMING YOU'RE OPEN TO IT.
ANOTHER MATTER?
WE UNDERSTAND THAT YOU'RE PLANNING A RETURN TO JAPAN...
THE END

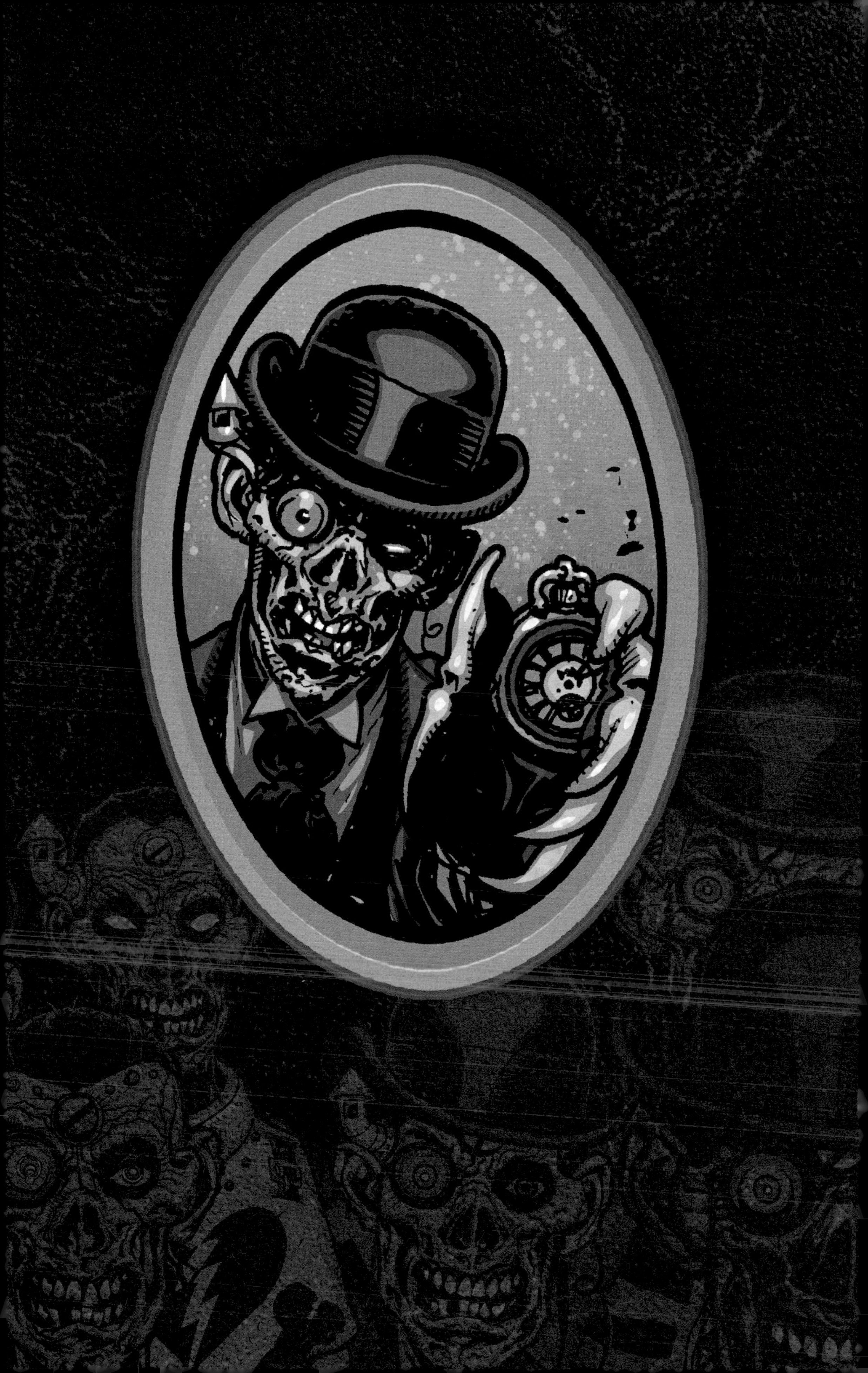

JSA LIBERTY FILES

THE WHISTLING SKULL

Character and Story Development Dossier by
B. CLAY MOORE

FROM THE DESK OF AGENT JOHN THUNDER;
FEDERAL LIAISON, THE 52

TOP SECRET

COMMUNIQUE 91A73
PRIORITY: High

ATTN: Sec'y Hull; State Dept.
CC: Gen. GC Marshall; Dept. of the Army

SUBJECT: The Whistling Skull, the Skeleton Cell, et al.

NOTE: This communique is a response to directive C67.

At present, few details are available re: "The Whistling Skull" and his true identity, although close observation from multiple agents indicates at least two men have operated under that identity in recent years. London operatives have identified a number of members of the Whistling Skull's cell, known colloquially as "the Skeleton." Unfortunately, many of the Skeleton associates operate under code names, and have successfully hidden their true identities from authorities. Of special note: "the Paperboy," a forger of considerable skill, whose documents have routinely passed inspection from expert examiners; "Dr. Moon," a possibly unlicensed doctor of psychiatry(?) whose methods reportedly violate any number of ethical and legal standards. The Skeleton also seems to employ a variety of odd operatives throughout Europe, and possibly stretching into Asia. Reports of individuals with unusual abilities assisting the Whistling Skull (and his current partner, referred to as "Knuckles" in earlier reports) have been verified (via reliable eyewitness accounts) in Switzerland, Ireland and Albania.

The Whistling Skull recently accepted membership in the 52 (following the official Army Air Corps induction of Captain Hop Harrigan, and the reclassification of his 52 operatives as enlisted servicemen) allowing for closer observation and accountability, although at present there is no evidence for concern re: Axis affiliation. The bulk of the Whistling Skull's activities seem to be removed from the war effort, or as removed as possible considering the situation in Europe. The London law firm of Teagle & Sons is our point of contact with the Skeleton cell, although to this point no extra surveillance measures have been deemed necessary.

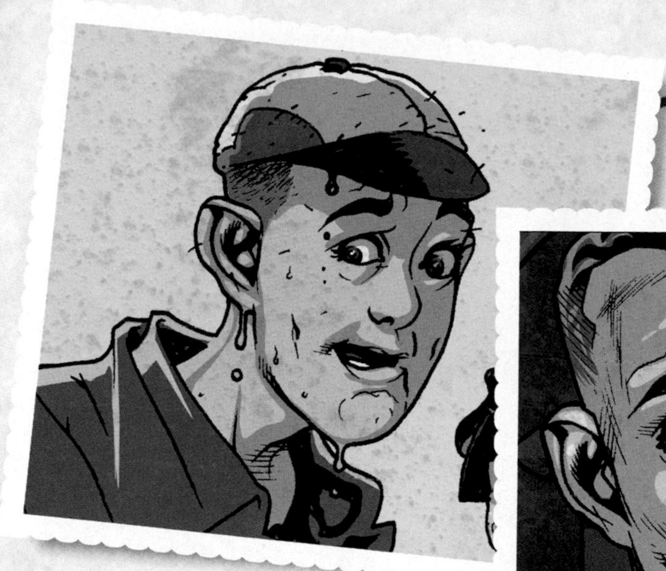

TOP SECRET

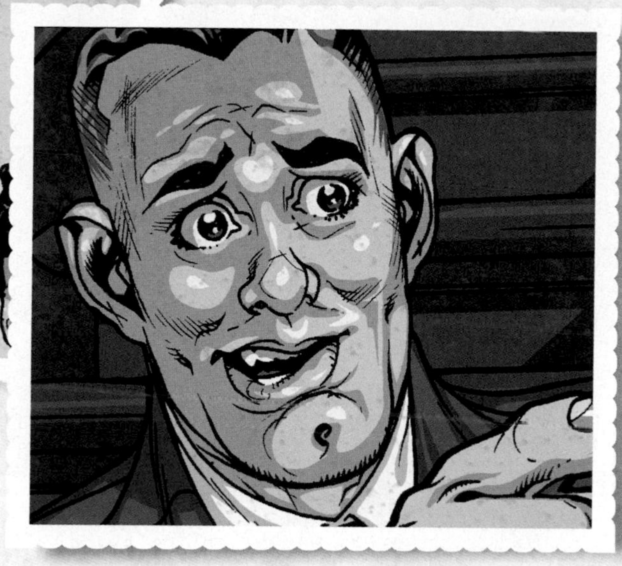

NIGEL SINGLETON:

In a more enlightened era, Nigel would perhaps be described as mentally challenged. The hulking young man possesses the intellect of a child, but his innate sense of fair play and his devotion to his companion and friend, William Massey, have helped him become a valuable asset in the Whistling Skull's war on those who would prey on the innocent. Although he doesn't realize it, Nigel's father, John, wore the mask of the Skull before William Massey. In an effort to help Nigel deal better with the taunts and physical assaults of fellow children, his father provided young Nigel with a skin-hardening salve developed by a group of fighting monks known as the Fighting Brotherhood of Divine Providence. Daily applications of this salve have left Nigel with fists that are as hard as tempered British steel. It was only natural that Nigel would choose the name "Knuckles" when he was asked to join the Whistling Skull's crusade.

TOP SECRET.

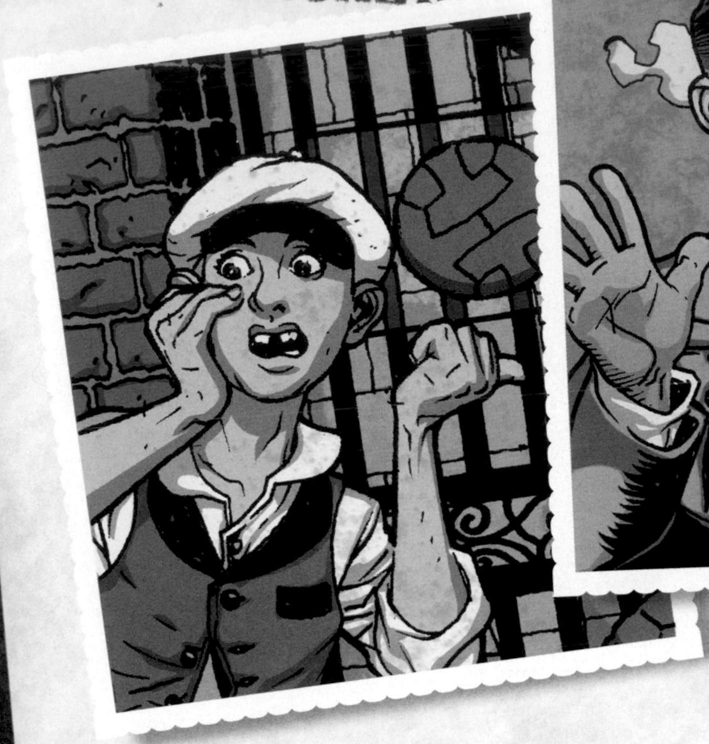

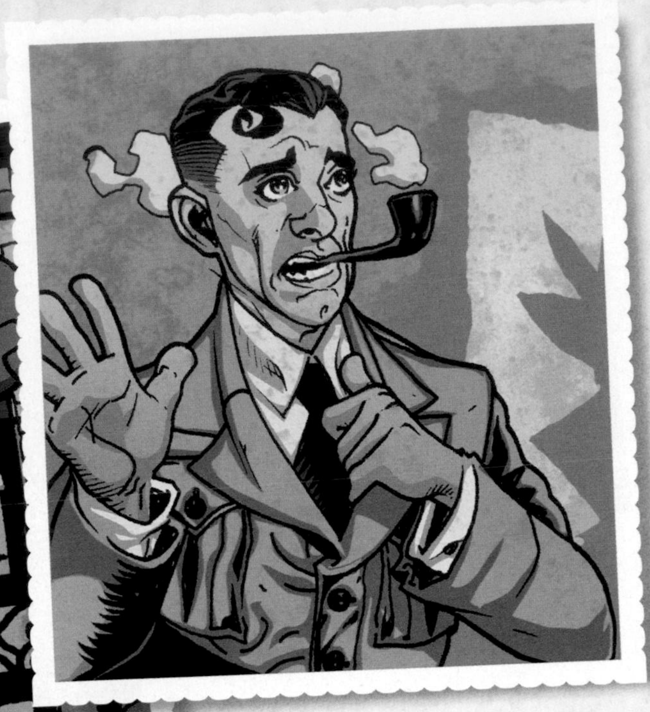

WILLIAM MASSEY:

A former London paperboy and childhood protector of Nigel Singleton, William Massey (quite to his surprise) was handpicked by his predecessor, John Singleton, to succeed Singleton as the shadowy enemy of injustice, the Whistling Skull. The seventh man to take up the mantle of the Skull, William's natural athletic grace and quick wit have been augmented through specialized training provided by the caretakers of the Whistling Skull legacy. Engaged to Miss Judith Lightwood, William finds himself learning on the go, attempting not to be distracted by thoughts of home as he and John Singleton's son, Nigel, pursue perpetrators of evil across the globe.

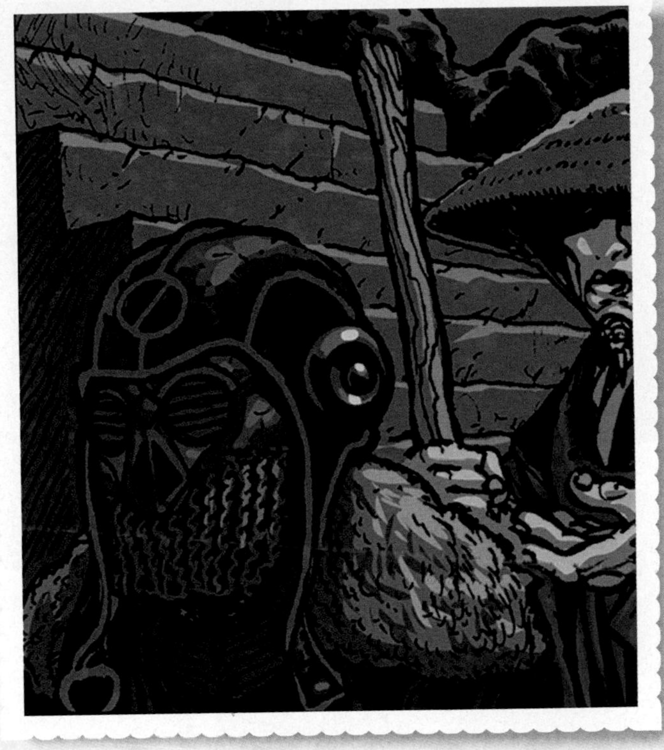

TOP SECRET

THESE GENTLEMEN BODYSNATCHERS:

Like many aspects of the Skeleton, the origins of These Gentlemen Bodysnatchers, sons of Teagle & Sons not suited to life behind a desk, are shrouded in mystery. What is known is that once the death of a Skull is confirmed, the Bodysnatchers are dispatched to recover the remains and eliminate signs of activity. Traditionally, the Bodysnatchers retrieve the remains and return them to London, where they are interred in the vault that contains the remains of every former Skull. The Bodysnatchers also serve to clean up crime scenes and generally handle evidence of the Skull's handiwork. And not always gently.

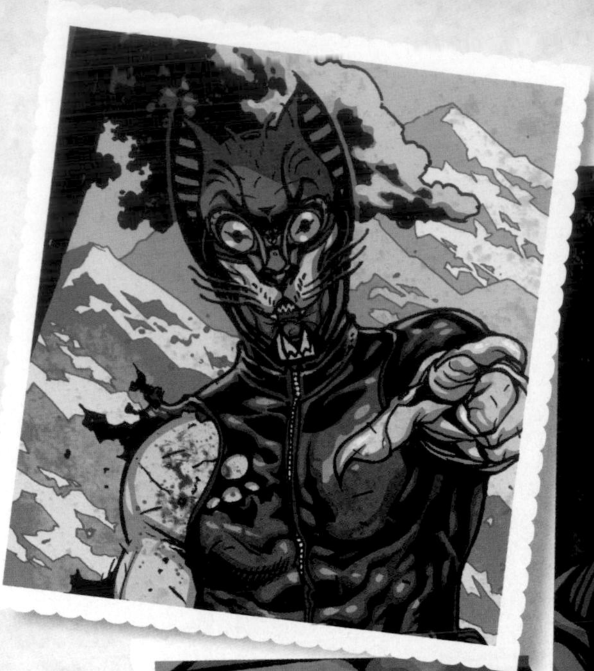

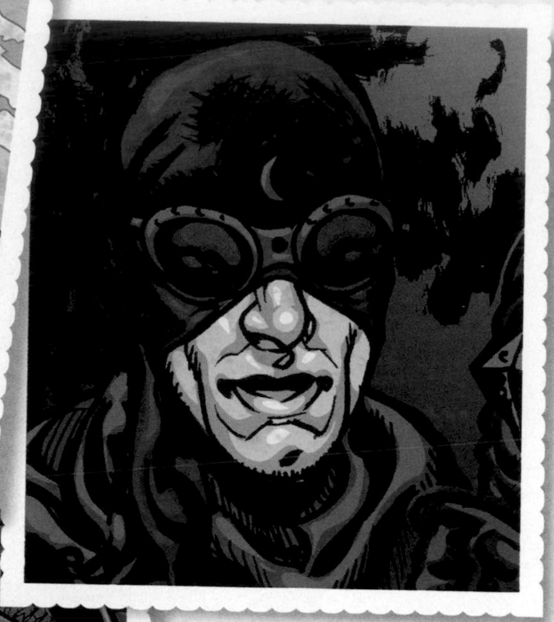

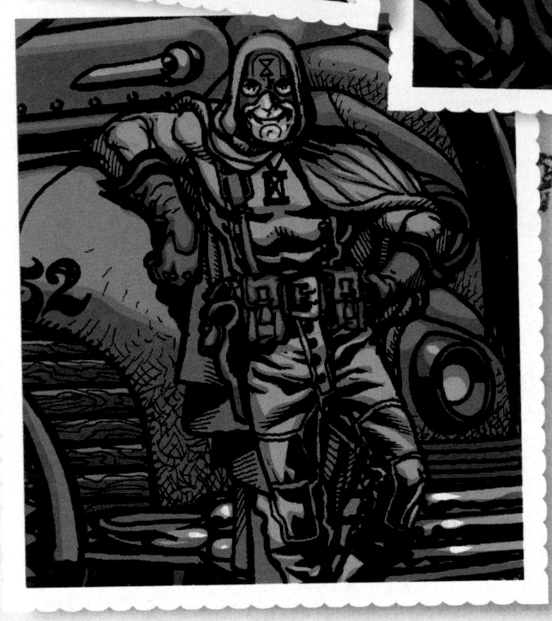

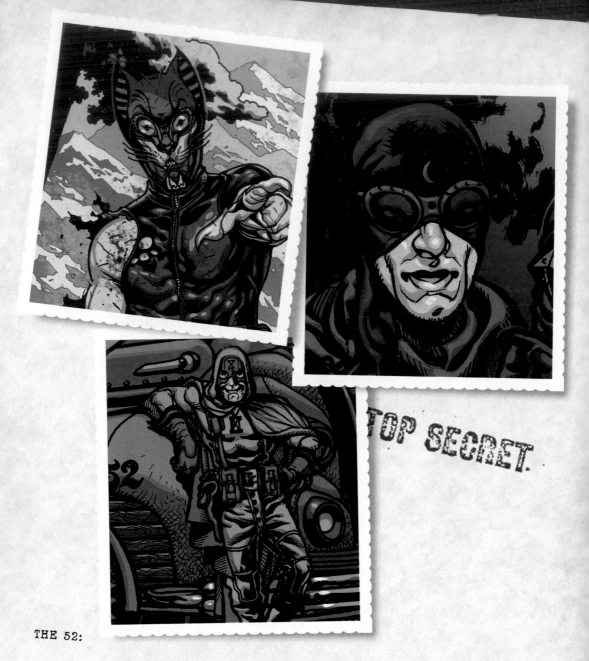

TOP SECRET.

THE 52:

The Whistling Skull and his Skeleton network are just one of fifty-two separate groups of adventurers that, combined, make up a veritable Justice Society dedicated to battling evil and injustice in a world fractured by war. Members of the 52 include the Unholy Three, currently comprising the Cat, the Owl and the Clock, and a small group of young guerrilla fighters known as the Boy Commandos. Each of the loosely affiliated groups battles with their own agenda in mind, but each is expected to lend support to one another when paths cross.

TOP SECRET

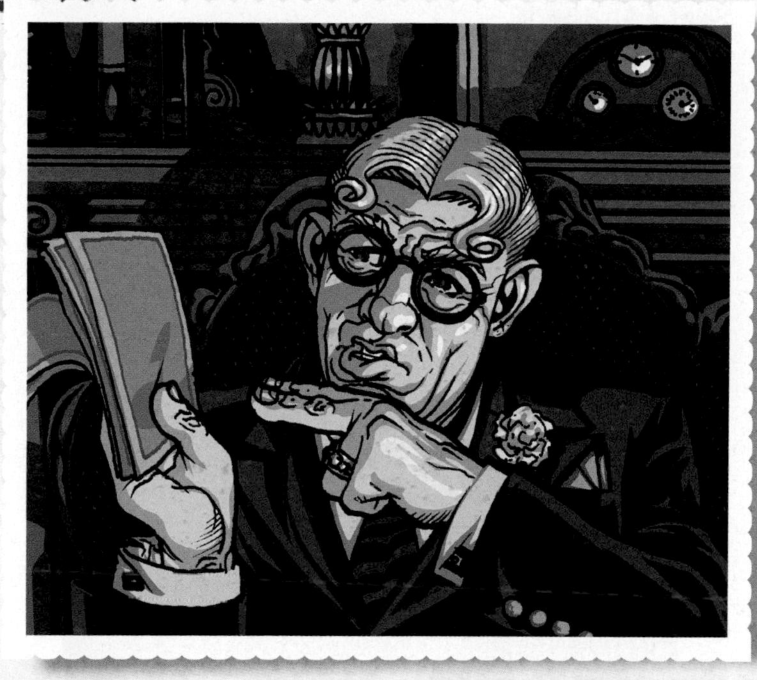

TEAGLE & SONS:

Teagle & Sons is one of the oldest law firms in London, with roots that predate the American Revolution. The firm is currently operating under the guidance of Phineas Teagle. Once entrusted with screening and selecting special agents for Buckingham Palace, the firm has spent over sixty years as the caretaker to the legacy of the Whistling Skull. Each Skull is chosen in secret by his predecessor, and the information is sealed away in an official Last Will & Testament. Upon confirmation of a Skull's death, the successor is called to the offices of the firm (travel provisions are made when necessary), and read the will in private. Without leaving the office, the appointed beneficiary is then asked to make his choice. The option to decline is always there, and if chosen, the beneficiary would simply be asked to sign a contract guaranteeing their silence, upon penalty of death.

No one has ever declined.

TOP SECRET

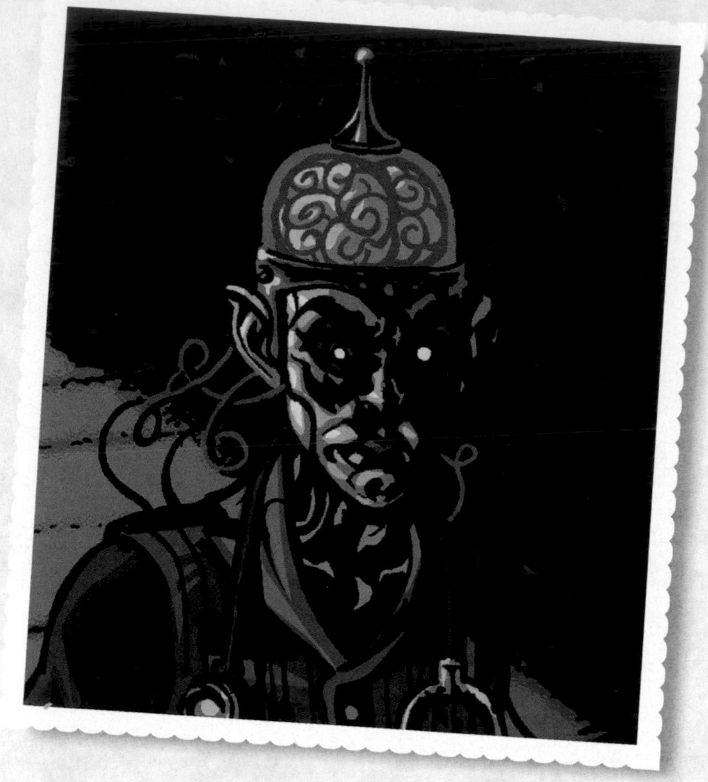

DR. MOON:

Dr. Archibald Moon is a mysterious mentalist and hypnotist operating under the auspices of Teagle & Sons, overseeing the mental and psychological conditioning of its agents, including the current Whistling Skull. One of Moon's most valuable innovations is a method of memory implantation, allowing the Whistling Skull to "grab" the memories of past Skulls, and apply their experiences in past lives to current situations. After each adventure, the Skull meets with Moon, is sent into a deep trance, and every nuance of his most recent outing is uncovered and duly recorded.

Moon's freakish appearance is evidently the result of personal experimentation on his physiology.

TOP SECRET

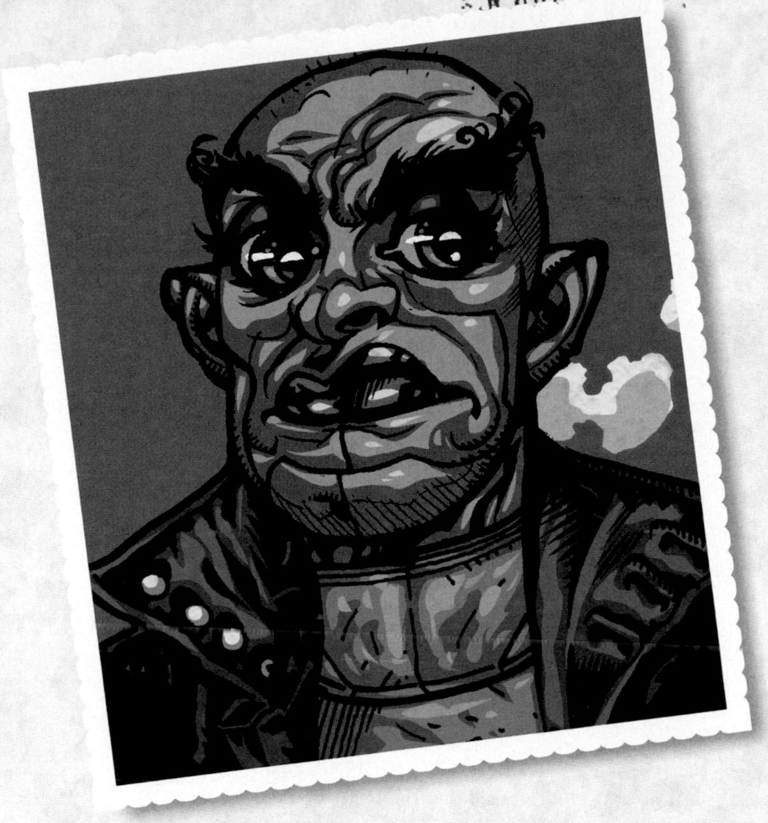

HAUPTMAN KLAUS HELLMAN:

Klaus Hellman's primary role as a member of the Third Reich was to oversee experimentations involving physical and behavioral modification of prisoners unfit for physical labor (for whatever reason). At some point, Hellman's renegade approach saw him fall out of favor with Adolf Hitler, who stripped Hellman of his rank and dismissed him from the Nazi party. Since then, Hellman has evidently traveled Europe with his "Karneval," a travelling freak show with a collection of hideously deformed human oddities, each one possessing a strange and unusual skill.

GATHER ROUND THE FIRE BRIGHT

A Folk Ballad
by B. Clay Moore

Gather round the fire bright
and hear a tale of woe
the story of young Billy White
and how he lost his life
and how the winds whipped him clean
and the rats dined on his bones

The lad he tried to force his will
upon his uncle's daughter
she of hair spun ebon black
and skin as clear as water
she ran from Billy far as she could
but he tracked her from behind
and snapped her neck that lonely night
deep in snow-covered wood.

Billy stared in horror then
at the deed that he had done
without a thought for burial
the lad he took to run

And as the tree limbs lashed his clothes
and snow crunched underfoot
a frightening sound came to his ears
and it foretold Billy's death
for the sound that Billy heard that night
was the whistling devil's breath

A flash of skull through broken limbs
a stumble in the snow
the looming shadow over him
then came the fatal blow

Billy White could run from sin
and whimper for reprieve
but he couldn't stop those barking guns
when cold iron burned with flame
and cries for penance have no pull
with a vengeful Whistling Skull

JSA LIBERTY FILES: THE WHISTLING SKULL #1
Variant Cover by Tony Harris

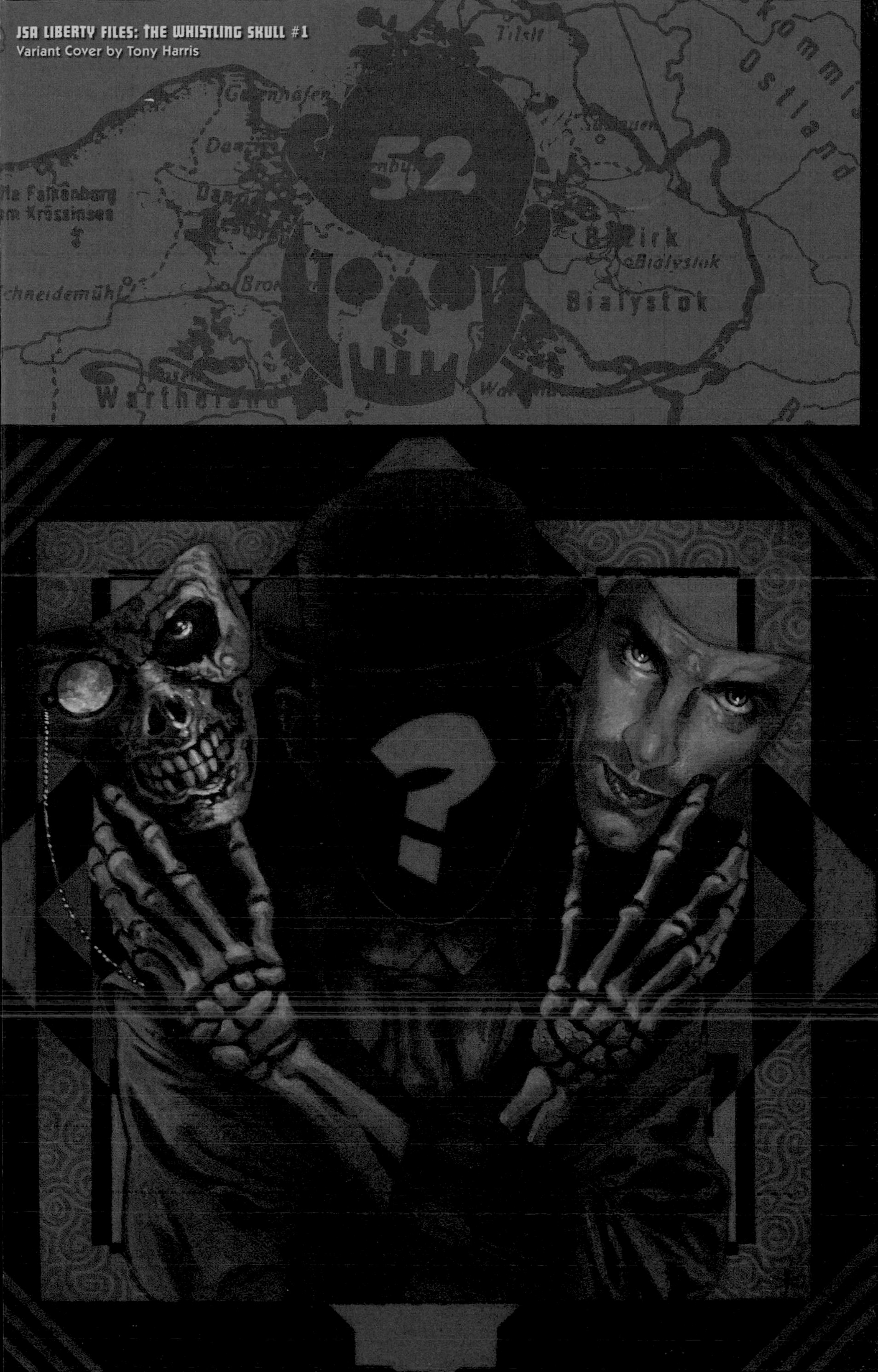
52
Danzig
Bialystok
Bialystok
Schneidemühl
Wartheland
Ostland

DC COMICS™

"The best-written superhero in comics."
—ENTERTAINMENT WEEKLY

"The quintessential superhero comic book of the 1990s."
—COMIC BOOK RESOURCES

FROM THE WRITER OF *SUPERMAN* & *EARTH 2*
JAMES ROBINSON
with TONY HARRIS

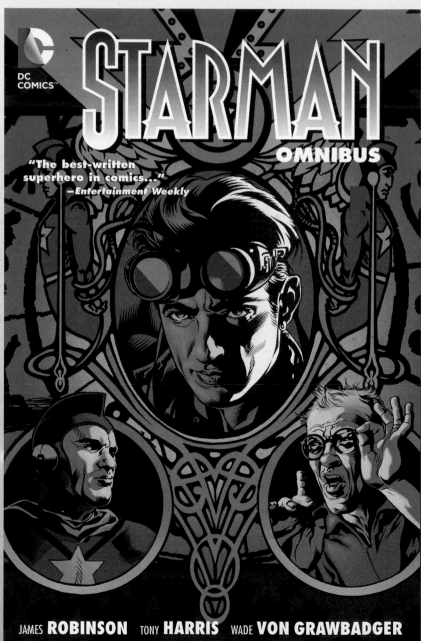

STARMAN OMNIBUS
VOL. 2

with TONY HARRIS
and others

STARMAN OMNIBUS
VOL. 6

with PETER SNEJBJERG
and others

READ THE ENTIRE
SERIES!

STARMAN OMNIBUS
VOL. 1
STARMAN OMNIBUS
VOL. 2
STARMAN OMNIBUS
VOL. 3
STARMAN OMNIBUS
VOL. 4
STARMAN OMNIBUS
VOL. 5
STARMAN OMNIBUS
VOL. 6